The Political Economy of Canada

The Political Economy of Canada:

An Introduction

Michael Howlett and M. Ramesh

Canadian Cataloguing in Publication Data

Howlett, Michael Patrick, 1955–
 The political economy of Canada

Includes bibliographical references and index.
ISBN 0–7710–4233–7

1. Economics – Canada.   I. Ramesh, M.   II. Title.

HB121.A2H68 1992   330.971   C91–094730–9

Typesetting by Colborne, Cox & Burns Inc.

Index prepared by Mark Hiltz

McClelland & Stewart Inc.
The Canadian Publishers
481 University Avenue
Toronto, Ontario
M5G 2E9

Printed and bound in Canada

Table of Contents

List of Tables

Acknowledgements

Canadian political economy is a daunting and challenging subject area, both for students and teachers. Although the rewards of grappling with the nature and history of Canadian political and economic life are plenty, it is difficult for students to come to terms with the material without some kind of a text; just as it is difficult for teachers to put together disparate readings into respectable text surrogates.

This pedagogical challenge is especially daunting given the time constraints that often prevail – when a huge subject matter must not only be broached but also completed within a relatively short space of time.

This book grew out of that challenge. It owes its origins to Rowland Lorimer, then director of the Centre for Canadian Studies at Simon Fraser University, who encouraged us to write it and first interested publishers in publishing it.

The book first saw the light of day as a course manual for Simon Fraser's Centre for Distance Education and benefited from the talents of members of the Centre's publication staff, including June Sturrock, Jane Fredeman, and Carol Lane. Centre Director Colin Yerbury and Dean of Arts Robert Brown provided financial support, as did the Publications Committee of Simon Fraser University under Vice-President William Leiss.

In the many drafts and revisions carried out on the text we had the benefit of comments, reviews, suggestions, and support from many colleagues at Simon Fraser University and the National University of Singapore and elsewhere, including Patrick Smith, Maureen Covell, David Brown, Gary Teeple, Allan Seager, Rebecca Raglon, Leena Tan, Alex Netherton, David Laycock, and reviewers at McClelland & Stewart. Wayne McIlroy, Ed Rouse, and Linda Young contributed invaluable research skills, while Natalie Minunzie, Jacqui Kenney, Brad Hornick, Mary Sibierski, and Ross Mackenzie ably field-tested the book.

At McClelland & Stewart, Michael Harrison stuck with us when the going got tough, Peter Buck saw the book to completion, Robert Clarke did a masterful job of copy-editing the text, and Mark Hiltz prepared the index at short notice.

We thank you all.

Michael Howlett, Vancouver
M. Ramesh, Singapore

CHAPTER 1

Introduction

Over the next ten to twenty years Canada and Canadians will face a number of serious challenges and crises, unlike any the country has met and overcome during the past century and a quarter. The failure of the Meech Lake Accord ensures that issues such as regional disparities and provincial and aboriginal rights will remain front and centre. But the Accord's failure and the resultant constitutional crisis also call into question the ability of Canadian governments to deal with a range of other problems – everything from the depletion of key natural resources and the need for environmental protection to the stresses of further economic integration with the United States. In addition, the country will have to adjust its economy not only to the continentalist pressures set in place by the Canada-U.S. Free Trade Agreement but also to the international pressures created by the globalization of business and commerce.

How will the governments at various levels react to these pressures, and how will they cope with the changes? Can the political and economic system deal with the challenges in its present form? These are two of the most important questions facing Canadians, but there are others. If changes are required, what will they look like? Will governments allow private actors to determine what goods will be produced and how – and simply turn a blind eye to the negative consequences of such a policy? Or will governments take on greater and greater roles in the economic life of the country, regulating and monitoring or even supplanting the market through the use of public agencies and enterprises?

The study of political economy sets out to address questions like these and to formulate answers. Its subject matter is the production and distribution of societal resources.[1] Every society has some mechanism for determining the use of its various resources: what is produced in what quantity, and how and in what manner the resources are distributed. All modern societies depend on two institutions for making such decisions: the state and the market. Because the state belongs to the realm of politics and the market belongs to the realm of the economy, the study of both institutions is an integral part of political economy.

Societies, however, differ significantly in the areas that are organized by these institutions. Some societies rely extensively on state production and allocation of goods and services, while others rely on the market. Even countries with a similar mix of state and market activities, moreover, can differ significantly in how they use state or market institutions to organize production and allocation activities. The specific mix of state and market institutions found within a nation-state constitutes that nation's political economy. Similarly, the specific mix of state and market institutions found in the relations that exist between nation-states constitutes the international political economy.

The study of political economy reveals a great deal about how a particular society or an international regime operates, because different groups of people benefit in different ways from the use of state and market institutions to regulate or control the production and allocation of goods. Political economy focuses on biases in the structure and processes of state and market – biases that systematically favour some members of society over others. For instance, in their normal course of operation markets invariably favour the owners of firms more than workers. Similarly, democracy, insofar as it is based on secret ballot and majority rule, favours large groups in society; providing, at least theoretically, workers with some numerical superiority vis-à-vis owners of enterprises.

Political economy therefore examines how the state and its associated political structures and processes affect the production and distribution of wealth. A state dominated by trade unions would have a different impact on the market than a state with weak unions and strong company owners. Conversely, political economy also examines how the market generates political conflicts and influences the organization and operation of the state. Markets inevitably lead to the unequal distribution of wealth, which manifests itself in unequal relationships between individuals and groups of individuals; this inequality forms a basis for political conflict in modern societies. The objective of political economy is to discover how the particular mix of state and market activities came about and who benefits; to assess the capability of both state and economic actors to alter this mix; and to explore how such changes might occur. It is a study with a broad scope: investigating, describing, and explaining the mixtures of state and market activities in different countries. Thus, the term "political economy," as William Carroll (1988) points out, is used to refer simultaneously to *an existing empirical subject*, to *a method of study* of that reality, and to *a body of theory* concerning that reality. The basis for all three facets, however, remains the particular relationship between states and markets found within and among nation-states.

Political-Economic Method: The Study of States and Markets

State

The concept of the state is ambiguous and contentious enough to yield, according to one observer, as many as 145 separate definitions (Rosenau, 1988, p.24). So instead of trying to define the term comprehensively, we will highlight a feature of state activity that is fundamental to the understanding of political economy: authority. As Max Weber ([1915] 1978) pointed out, the state possesses a monopoly on the use of legitimate coercion. The state is the only institution in society that has the legal authority, or the right, to command obedience from its citizens. In the case of recalcitrance or a refusal to obey, it can maintain its decisions through force if necessary. While gangsters, for example, sometimes back up their decisions through force, they do not have the legal authority to do so. Indeed, the state usually attempts to prevent gangsters from using force against others by putting them in jail or even executing them. The state is, in a legal sense, the most powerful social institution.

In this capacity the state, in theory, can determine how societal resources are allocated and distributed. It can choose to decide what can be produced and under what circumstances; how and under what circumstances goods, services, and the various inputs (land, labour, capital) can be bought and sold; and how the resulting income is to be distributed. In theory, all that it has to do is implement laws and regulations commanding a particular action; for example, antipollution and minimum wage laws or progressive taxation of income.

In practice, however, the state's ability to control societal actors is severely constrained. The availability of narcotics or sex on the market despite state prohibitions against their sale testifies to the limits of the state's regulatory capacity. The modern state is also severely restricted in its ability to control the production and distribution of societal resources and wealth, except in cases of national emergency or wartime. In the normal course of events the state is constrained from exercising its full powers by societal resistance contesting the legitimacy of its authority to act, as well as by the existence of other nation-states that can contest the effects of a particular state's actions on international relations.

Domestic resistance can have numerous sources. Certain groups with independent sources of wealth and power may object to state regulation of their activities; certain people may be ideologically or culturally predisposed to oppose state activity. An important source of domestic resistance arises from the fact that as a political institution the state makes decisions that confer benefits on certain groups in society and costs onto others. When this pattern of selective costs and benefits is repeated, the groups bearing the burden of costs may begin to question the legitimacy of the state's authority. States are subject to similar constraints at the international level. Some of the constraints are imposed by international laws; some of them arise because certain states are militarily and economically stronger; others derive from more subtle factors, such as dependence on foreign states for trade and investment.

In addition, a state's internal structure and processes can place limits on the available options. For example, the Canadian state may find it difficult to develop and implement coherent national policies because of the federal-provincial division of jurisdictions, which makes it difficult to co-ordinate governmental actions in many policy areas. The state's position as the most powerful institution in the society is also at the root of a dilemma. The state can issue authoritative commands and is quite capable of resolving issues that can be addressed through a command-penalty system. But issues requiring more subtle measures are its failing. In Charles Lindblom's (1977) colourful metaphor, the state has "strong thumbs, no fingers."

To be able to manage the economy efficiently, without the support of the market, the state must be able to somehow rank consumer priorities. Given that economic resources are finite, it is not possible to produce and distribute everything, everywhere, at the same time: there has to be a mechanism for deciding how much cheesecake, hospital care, and housing should be produced and in what order. While the state can attempt to control production and distribution by command-penalty measures, it cannot do the same with consumer demand. Despite its authority to produce whatever it wishes, the state cannot ensure that those goods and services will actually be consumed. State officials have little incentive to respond to consumer demand if their salaries and benefits are tied to production and not to consumption – as in many societies with extensive state apparatuses attempting to control production. In fact, these officials tend to face insurmountable problems in forecasting consumer demands even when they have been given some incentive to do so. One has only to visit a department store in Moscow and see the piles of unsold clothing that presumably no one wants to buy to appreciate how difficult it is for the state to produce goods in a manner that satisfies consumer demands. The list of organizational problems the state faces in its planning of production and distribution is extensive. (See Lindblom, 1977, pp.66-75, for more examples.)

Hence, there is a distinction to be made between what the state can theoretically accomplish and what it is able to accomplish in practice. Yet the state's ability to organize production and distribution must not be underestimated. Despite all the limitations, various states at various points in history have successfully organized and implemented monumental projects. The construction of the Egyptian pyramids and the Great

Wall of China is an example of ancient state-directed projects and has a modern counterpart in the contemporary Russian and U.S. space programs.

Market

The market carries out production and distribution of societal resources in a vastly different way than the state. Rather than relying on authority, markets work through exchange. A market is an arena in which people exchange land, labour, capital goods, and services. Unlike the state's authority, which is backed by coercion, the market's exchange is predicated upon voluntary action by individuals. If a person wants to exchange something, that person must, at least theoretically, voluntarily want to part with the property. The other party to the exchange must want to do the same. The market, therefore, is in theory an efficient mechanism for allowing consumer wants and desires to be expressed in a way that directs subsequent decisions on production and allocation.

Exchange in a market can take various forms. People can exchange things they don't want for other commodities they do want; this is known as barter exchange. In modern markets some barter transactions take place, but the usual mode of exchange is through the medium of money. When people want something, they must sell something else – their labour or their goods or property – for money. Then they use that money to buy what they want. They don't directly exchange one thing for another; they use money as an intermediary to make the exchange. But when something is exchanged for money, there has to be a way to determine its value – which means establishing a price. The determination of price, which is a complex subject, essentially depends on how much of a particular good is demanded by consumers and how much is supplied by producers at any given point in time. The producers' search for profits and the consumers' preference for certain goods – constrained by ability to pay – form the basis of price activity and, therefore, market exchange.

Unlike production by the state, then, production by the market does not require centralized information or co-ordination. Production decisions are taken by individual producers responding to the demands of individual consumers. There is no need for a central authority to draw up a list of priorities indicating which types and quantities of goods and services will be produced. Theoretically, consumers buy what they want and can afford. They make their decisions as carefully as possible ("rationally") because they know that the purchase of one item leaves less money for buying something else. On the other side, producers produce those items, and in such a manner, that will secure the highest profit. If the consumers or producers make a wrong choice, they absorb the cost and do their best to avoid repeating the mistake in future. This relatively simple mechanism has done wonders in organizing production in the modern world. It has led to technological innovations and a substantial improvement in the quality of material life for many people.

The voluntary nature of the market process and its ability to confer benefits on the populace, however, are open to question. Exchange presumes ownership, since one must own property (including cash) before it can be exchanged. This means that an initial endowment of property helps determine who is able to exchange what, at what times, and in what quantities; and therefore who is able to benefit the most from market exchange. This initial distribution of property is crucial to subsequent market activities and is never voluntary or conflict-free. Different groups and individuals in society possess different amounts of various items to exchange, and those with the most desirable forms of property can command higher prices and larger rewards from the market than can those who only possess less desirable forms of property.

This initial inequality greatly influences the sale of many items through the market, not least the sale of labour. For a starving person, the act of selling labour for wages does not represent a voluntary exchange between employee and employer. Similarly, the distribution of land ownership in Canada derives from the forceful occupation of aboriginal lands by European immigrants, which now gives European descendants a disproportional ability to engage in "voluntary" exchange with aboriginal peoples. Market exchange can be considered voluntary and mutually beneficial only if the existing distribution of property is taken for granted. Severe inequalities in initial distributions of wealth and property can greatly distort market exchange, and if those inequalities hinder intergenerational mobility and opportunity they can lead to severe resistance on the part of societal groups failing to benefit from the transactions.

In addition to these societal constraints, markets, like states, face organizational constraints on their ability to determine allocation and production decisions. There are certain instances in which markets, regardless of the initial distribution of property, will consistently fail to allocate goods and services efficiently. These situations, which are innate to markets, are known as *market failures*. They are innate in the sense that they are inevitable results of the market process.

The most common market failures relate to *public goods* (like street lighting and police protection, which the market does not produce because they are not profitable), *externalities* (for instance, when a factory dumps its waste in the river to maximize its profits and thus imposes costs on others who use the river), *inadequate information* (when consumers and investors lack the information necessary to make rational decisions, as in the case of purchasing medicines or buying stocks), and increasing returns to scale in certain industries, which leads to natural *monopolies* (such as electricity or telephone services in which large initial investments in infrastructure made by one firm prevent other competing firms from entering the market) (Wolf, Jr., 1988, pp.17-34). There are numerous instances of such failures.

States and Markets

Although, for the sake of clarity, we have referred to state and market forms of organization as separate entities, political economy presumes not the independence of states and markets but their mutual dependence and inter-twining. States and markets cannot be studied in isolation. Indeed, the inseparable nature of their relationships forms the very rationale for political economy. Otherwise, the state would be studied under political science and the market under economics and the rationale for the study of political economy would disappear.

States and markets are interdependent primarily because they need each other: they must overcome the societal and organizational constraints that each of them is incapable of facing alone. The state needs the market because of the market's efficiency in responding to consumer demands and co-ordinating an extensive production apparatus. Allocation of all resources by the state alone requires a machinery so complex that it con-sumes many of those same resources without significantly increasing either the quality or quantity of goods and services produced. Even in centrally planned economies (such as in the former Soviet Union or China), a good part of the routine allocation of goods and services has been carried out through legally sanctioned markets, not to mention illegal or "black" markets.

Markets need the state because, to function at all, they need a body that enforces property rights and private contracts. Otherwise, people could sell things they do not own or refuse to honour their commitments – actions that the market has no capacity to prevent. The state can perform these functions effectively because of its authority to enforce rights and con-tracts. In modern times, the state has gone beyond these basic functions and has established laws and built economic infrastructures to promote the orderly functioning of the market and to overcome market failures.

Both state and market forms of organizing production and allocation activities exist in all modern nation-states, although no two countries share exactly the same mix of state and market activities. The studies and theories of political economy explore the reasons for these different mixes.

The Subject of Political Economy: Capitalism and Democracy

The modern theories of political economy have a history of no more than two hundred years. During that period, capitalism has been the dominant economic system in Western nations. Similarly, democracy has formed the basis for political organization, first as an aspiration in the nineteenth century and then as a reality in the twentieth. Capitalism and democracy have been powerful forces in moulding the relationship between state and market and, correspondingly, in moulding the political-economic theories that explain this relationship.

Capitalism

Capitalism refers to a market-oriented type of political economy. More than this, it refers to a society in which control over the property required for production (capital) is concentrated in the hands of a small section of the populace, the capitalists. Capitalism as a socioeconomic system originated as a corollary to the breakdown of agriculturally based societies and their subsequent industrialization in Europe towards the end of the eighteenth century. It spread rapidly to North America and most of the rest of the world in the nineteenth century. In the twentieth century many nations rejected capitalism and adopted socialism – a state-oriented political economy in which "capital" is publicly owned and allocated – with the expressed intention of working towards the establishment of a communist political economy, in which "capital" is communally owned.

Canada has always had a capitalist political economy based on a somewhat particular mix of state and market institutions, and the two general theories of political economy that have been most prominent in Canada – liberalism and socialism – have both attempted to explain this mix of state and market activities.[2] Liberal political-economic theory is very much oriented towards the "perfection" or improvement of an actually existing capitalist political economy. Even the socialist theory – with the avowed purpose of working towards the replacement of capitalism – is a theory of capitalism in that it explains how capitalism originated and operates and how and why it will be replaced by socialism.

In capitalism, production is undertaken not for direct consumption by the producer but for purposes of sale, so the producer can use the money thus derived to purchase goods for consumption. This differs from precapitalist societies in which producers directly consumed much of what they produced, except for a small portion exchanged through barter. In capitalism, exchange takes place through markets among individuals usually unknown to each other.

Moreover, ownership of the production inputs – such as raw materials, machinery, and factory buildings – is in private hands, that is, in the hands of the capitalists. This implies that the owners of the means of production have the exclusive right to decide on the use of those means of production, a right guaranteed by the state. This feature of capitalism entitles the owners to decide what will be produced, in what manner, which also establishes the capitalists as the dominant social class. The corollary of this feature is that to earn a livelihood those who do not own the means of production must work for those who do. In capitalist societies, labour is the only productive input workers own. Consequently workers must sell their labour to the capitalists for wages.

Another critical feature of capitalism is the need for firms to make profits, or accumulate capital, in order for the economy as a whole to survive. Profit is to capitalism what motion is to bicycles: capitalism, like bicycles, cannot properly function by standing still. If an adequate return on investment is not forthcoming, capitalists will withhold their investment or invest it somewhere else. The result can be a decline in economic activity in the society and a general lowering of the society's living standards. This imposes an enormous pressure on the democratic state to ensure hospitable conditions for investment.

Democracy

Democracy is one of the most contentious concepts in the study of politics: one survey found 311 definitions of the concept (Cunningham, 1987, p.25). It is not our objective to resolve the debate. For our purposes, it is sufficient to regard democracy as a plan of political organization, a political decision-making system (Bealey, 1988, p.1). Göran Therborn succinctly defines democracy as "(1) a representative government elected by (2) an electorate consisting of the entire adult population, (3) whose votes carry equal weight, and (4) who are allowed to vote for any opinion without intimidation by the state apparatus" (Therborn, 1983, p.262).

Democracy confers entitlements upon citizens to choose who they want to have represent them in government. The method of election varies among nations, but the primary purpose is always to declare the candidate with the largest number of votes as the winner in periodic competitions to staff legislative and executive institutions of governments. What this condition does is establish that the government be formed by the representatives of the largest number of citizens and, depending on the type of system used, that through those representatives it be directly or indirectly accountable to the citizens. Elections as a means of removing a government, and of replacing it with another, were virtually unheard of until the nineteenth century and even today there are governments that find ingenious excuses to avoid submitting themselves to the judgement of the electorate.

It was only towards the end of the nineteenth century that Western nations began to establish democratic institutions, a process not completed until well after World War II when the franchise, or right to vote, was made universal for most adults in most Western nation-states (Therborn, 1983, p.264.) The intent of the restrictions was to limit the privilege of voting to social and economic elites. The removal of these barriers represented a major milestone in promoting social equality. From a political-economic perspective, insofar as democracy is based on the principle of secret ballot and majority rule, the non-owners of the means of production could at least theoretically use their numerical superiority to pressure governments to use state authority to offset the adverse effects of capitalist ownership of the means of production (Przeworski, 1985). As Adam Przeworski points out: "Political democracy constitutes the opportunity for workers to pursue some of their interests. Electoral politics constitutes the mechanism through which anyone can as a citizen express claims to goods and services. . . . Moreover . . . they can intervene in the very organization of production and allocation of profit" (1985, p.11).

Democracy, by requiring that governments be elected, permits the subordinate classes some degree of control over the state and thus shapes not only the internal functioning of the state but also, through the use of state authority, of the market. Democracy allows these classes to pressure the state to take actions that further their interests, including the removal of some of the most blatant and adverse effects of the market. Under the influence of the democratic process, in most countries the state has introduced income redistribution measures, in defiance of one of the basic tenets of capitalism that the market alone ought to determine distribution of income (Przeworski, 1991). Similarly, in many countries states have replaced private ownership of some means of production with public, or state, ownership.

Political-Economic Theory: Old and New Debates

In eighteenth-century Europe, political economy was an established area of study. It looked at how wealth was created and distributed and at the role of the government in the process, thus displaying acute sensitivity towards the interdependence of state and market. In fact, this idea of interdependence had been the general understanding of the relationship between economy and polity since ancient times (Staniland, 1985), and this understanding informed the early development of the two general theories of political economy: liberalism and socialism.

It was only in the twentieth century that economics and political science became separate disciplines. Both, especially economics, developed their own orthodoxy and spawned their own vocabulary to the extent that communication between scholars working in the two disciplines became nearly impossible. The separation became even more pronounced in the post-World War II period. Economics became increasingly mathematical and leaned towards a micro-economic analysis of the behaviour of individual producers and consumers in the market, with little direct reference to the state and its role in the market.

The lack of interest in political economy was partly a result of the aplomb that derived from the robust economic performance of most Western nations in the postwar period. In fact, so comfortable was the era that a U.S. scholar, Daniel Bell, had pronounced "the end of ideology" in politics and economy (Bell, 1960). While the economy was humming along there was little need for anything more than fine-tuning, for which the principles of economics were eminently suited.

All this changed with the international economic dislocations following from the drastic oil-price hike by the major oil-exporting nations in 1973. The economic problems of the 1970s and early 1980s – simultaneous high unemployment and high inflation (which in the then-prevailing economic theory were supposed to be inversely related) and the declining growth in productivity – refused to respond to the government measures that had worked so well in the previous two decades. It became increasingly apparent that the problems had their roots in the economy as well as politics and that any cure must simultaneously address both sectors. For example, the economists' solution to the problem of high inflation was reduction in government expenditures and/or money supply. What this solution disregarded was that such reductions would be extremely difficult for states to implement because of opposition from those who would be hurt. Similarly, the purely political solution of wage and price control, even if it was possible for a government to impose, created bottlenecks in the economy and aggravated economic problems. Efforts to cope with problems such as inflation made it abundantly clear that analysts must have a broad understanding of both economy and politics and especially of the relationship between the two.

Other factors also fuelled the resurgence of political economy in the 1970s. The increasing prominence of foreign investments after World War II came under severe scrutiny from scholars, who stirred fears concerning the economic dominance of the major capitalist nations by multinational corporations and asked whether this might be a prelude to political dominance. This debate inadvertently led to a consideration of the interdependence of politics and economies. The knowledge thus gained fostered the growth of a nationalist orientation among a number of scholars who became prominent in the field of political economy.

Yet another factor contributing to the resurgence of interest in political economy was the realization in the 1970s that there were systematic differences in the performances of industrialized nations along various criteria such as economic growth, unemployment, inflation, and productivity (Goldthorpe, 1984, p.3). If, after all, economic management is a simple task of applying basic economic principles, then all nations should be able to manage their economies more or less equally successfully. But in practice it turned out that nations consistently differed in their ability to choose and implement policies. For example, during the 1970s the Scandinavian countries were successful in keeping unemployment low and inflation only moderately high, whereas the United Kingdom and United States could do neither. The anomaly was eventually accounted for by differences in the political structures of these nations. It became clear that to understand economic performance it was also necessary to study politics. In a way, developments since the last century have come full circle, and political economy is fashionable once again.

Canadian Studies in Political Economy

Considering the short history of Canada as a nation, political economy has had a distinguished place in the development of the country's social sciences. In the early decades of this century Canadian scholars produced insightful and original works in the political-economic tradition. The main reason for this development, C.B. Macpherson has surmised, was the small size of the country's academic community, which meant that university teachers had to be generalists and teach courses in several related disciplines – an arrangement highly conducive to the emergence of political economy because of its general, cross-disciplinary nature. But as universities became larger in the 1960s, with the resulting tendency towards specialization, political economy was gradually eclipsed. The arrival of U.S. academics and the analytical tools they brought (Wood and Wood, 1970) reinforced the departure from the political economy tradition. Only in the late 1960s and early 1970s did Canadian political economy begin to re-emerge from the shadows.

Given the international economic trends, it is more than a coincidence that the discipline was experiencing a revival in other Western nations at the same time. But an additional factor that fuelled interest in Canadian political economy was the concern voiced about the increasingly high level of U.S. ownership of Canadian industries, a concern spurred by the publication of the Watkins Report (1968) and the Gray Report (1972) (Marchak, 1985, p.673). Nationalist concerns inspired interesting studies in Canadian political economy (Levitt, 1970; Lumsden, 1970; Teeple, 1972). The greater awareness of regional economic inequalities in Canada also spawned numerous remarkable studies in political economy. The discipline's growing popularity was manifested in the establishment of a political economy section under the Canadian Political Science Association at the Learned Society Meetings in 1976. That was followed by the establishment of *Studies in Political Economy*, a journal with socialist leanings, in 1979. Other academic journals in political science and sociology began to publish articles on the subject with greater frequency. As a result, the discipline became diversified and robust.

For most of this century there have been three broad traditions in Canadian political economy: liberalism, socialism, and the staples theory. Liberal political economists have been active since the eighteenth century, but recently they have become especially vocal with the acquisition of a formal (economic) model of politics afforded by *public choice theory*. This theory, developed in the United States in the 1960s, became immensely popular in the 1980s, securing its chief U.S. proponent, Prof. James Buchanan, a

Nobel Prize in 1986. Public choice theory marked a turning point in economics because of its avowed interest in both economy and politics. Public choice treats governments and voters in democratic societies as producers and consumers respectively and explains political outcomes as the result of the bargaining between the two. The political actors (politicians, bureaucrats, and voters) are guided by self-interest and rationality, just like their economic counterparts (producers and consumers).

Despite excellent studies by C.B. Macpherson (1953) and Stanley Ryerson (1963, 1968), it was only in the early 1970s that the application of Marxist analytical tools to questions of political economy became popular in Canada. However, socialist analyses of the Canadian political economy had been developed along Leninist lines after World War I by the Communist Party of Canada (CPC) and, after 1933, along social democratic lines by the Co-operative Commonwealth Federation (CCF) – the forerunner of today's New Democratic Party (NDP).

The staples school was influential in Canadian political economy between the 1920s and 1950s and thereafter almost disappeared, to be revived again as the Canadian "new political economy" in the late 1960s.[3] It has also generated several interpretations of the Canadian political economy, although these draw heavily on the general liberal and socialist theories.

Despite its recent revival in Canada, political economy is still at an early stage as an academic "discipline." It has not produced a textbook that could be used in university or college courses in the area. As a result, students have to rely on books and articles of varying quality published in widely divergent fields of political science, economics, history, and sociology. There is no consensus among Canadian political economists on subject matter, much less an agreement on research methods. Much of the scholarship in the area is polemical, with little grounding in theory or at times even in facts.

In the meantime, students continue to graduate in political science or economics without being exposed to the interrelationships that exist between Canadian politics and the economy. Textbooks on Canadian politics rarely mention the effect of the economy on their subject matter (see, for instance, Van Loon and Whittington, 1987). Similarly, textbooks on the Canadian economy impart no broad understanding of the role of politics in the country, apart from acknowledging that the state has played a major role in the nation's economic development (see Lipsey, Steiner and Purvis, 1987). A more systematic analysis of the relationship between the two disciplines is clearly required, and that is what this book sets out to do.

Plan of the Book

The purpose of this study is to conceptualize the structure and functioning of the Canadian political economy. It focuses on the state and market in

Canada, and on their broader context. But before embarking on the main study, we also discuss the existing theoretical interpretations of the subject, to show that the analyses of, and prescriptions for, the Canadian political economy derive from the theoretical assumptions of the analysts. Chapters 2, 3, and 4 examine the liberal, socialist, and staples theories respectively.

Chapter 5 studies the structure of the Canadian political economy with a view to ascertaining the constraints it imposes on state and market actors. Chapter 6 assesses Canada's place in the international political economy and shows how the destination/source of its trade and the international agreements to which it is a party constrain its policy choices. Chapters 7, 8, and 9 examine the organization of the three main actors in the Canadian political economy – the state, labour, and capital – and their capacity to affect each other and the nature of the domestic and international political economies.

Chapters 10 and 11 present two case studies of the nature of state activity in two important areas of the economy: fiscal and monetary management at the macro-level, and industrial development at the micro-level. These cases illustrate the difficulties Canadian governments face in attempting to overcome existing domestic and international constraints on effective state action in those and other policy areas. Chapter 12 summarizes and discusses the implications of our findings in relation to the questions the book set out to address.

Each study has, or should have, a methodological and theoretical framework of inquiry. This book follows an approach based on the premise that the organization of the state and society and the particular network of relationships between the two shape the political economy of a nation (Hall, 1986; Hall and Ikenberry, 1989). This modern institutionalist, or *neoinstitutionalist*, perspective attributes explanatory significance to social institutions (Albo and Jenson, 1989, p.200).

These political-economic institutions, in the words of Leon Lindberg, "constitute a historically specific constraint and opportunity structure that implies an enduring division of labour and rules of play that establishes distinctive capacities and incapacities, and that constrains the strategies any individual, economic agent, or political authority can adopt to achieve its aims" (Lindberg, 1982, p.24). In other words, a given set of institutions facilitates some interests and impedes others, in turn determining which interests are likely to be realized (Freeman, 1989; Ikenberry, 1988; Katzenstein, 1985). Using this approach we will show that the structure of the domestic and international political economies and the manner in which state, labour, and capital have been organized in Canada have shaped the country's particular mix of market and state. Ultimately we will argue that this mix is resistant to change and leaves Canada in a poor position to adapt its political economy to deal with difficulties arising from resource depletion and the globalization of manufacturing production.

Notes

1 Production in this context means the amount of various goods and services produced from available societal resources. Distribution refers to, first, the apportioning of income among those involved in production and, second, the apportioning of those goods and services produced among the populace for consumption.
2 The staples theory, discussed in Chapter 4, is not a general theory but applies only to Canada and other similar economies in the "New World."
3 The term "new" political economy as used in Canada refers to a school different from its counterpart in Europe and the United States. In the United States the term is also used for the public choice school. See Staniland (1985).

CHAPTER 2

Liberal Political Economy

Liberalism has been the dominant tradition in Canada in both the study and practice of political economy. What is called economics and much of what is called political science in capitalist industrialized nations is really liberal political economy. It is therefore important to understand the concept and its implications. Like any broad theory in the social sciences, liberalism has analytical as well as prescriptive components. Its analytical tools have been used by most mainstream economists in this century. More importantly, its prescriptions concerning the proper role of the state in capitalist market society have been adhered to by all Canadian governments, including the provincial governments led by the social democratic New Democratic Party.

Given their particular view of the state and market, liberal analysts and practitioners in government tend to recommend the adoption of certain measures and the avoidance of others. Their analyses and prescriptions lead broadly in the same direction: to steer clear of state activity in the marketplace as far as possible. The liberals' support for free trade and reductions in social welfare or regional development payments, for example, derives not so much from the results of empirical studies – since the evidence of such studies tends to be mixed – but from their theoretical premise favouring market over state forms for the organization of a nation's production and distribution systems. Therefore it is essential that we know what these fundamental assumptions are and how they fit into the liberal scheme of things.

Disregarding the flippant, and incorrect, sense in which the term liberalism is often used in the United States to describe an anticapitalist ideology, we will use it here to refer to *a composite system of institutions, beliefs, and practices that maintain and promote capitalism.* Liberalism "emerged in the seventeenth, eighteenth, and nineteenth centuries to justify the increasingly important capitalist mode of production. The opposite of liberal, then, is not a conservative but a defender of pre-capitalist social relations, on the one hand, and post-capitalist ones [communism and anarchism, for example], on the other" (Wolfe, 1977, p.4). Liberalism emerged in Europe as a political-economic theory partly to legitimize and partly to facilitate the development of capitalism. As capitalism matured and spread to North America and the Third World, encountering new problems in the process, liberal political economy itself adapted to reflect the changes.

In this chapter we will discuss liberalism from a historical perspective, tracing the development of the theory of market and considering its political implications, especially with regard to the role of the state in the market. This has proved to be a highly flexible and adaptive theory, which perhaps accounts for its popularity and longevity. Indeed, it has proved flexible enough to permit an increasing role for the state in the economy in response to changing political and economic circumstances, without ever having to depart too far from its fundamental assumptions concerning the superiority of the market form of organization. However, liberal political economy also suffers from a muddled conception of the state, which leads adherents of this view to analytical inaccuracies and unrealistic policy recommendations.

Fundamental Tenets

The basic precepts of liberal political economy are a mixture of factual observations, hypothetical assumptions, and normative (ideological) prescriptions; and these precepts and their flexibility explain the theory's resilience in the face of changing circumstances.

Liberal political economy begins with the assumption of the *primacy of the individual* in society or *methodological individualism*. While all social theories recognize the individual as a distinct entity, liberalism uniquely emphasizes a person's importance and reduces all social activity to individual behaviour. Liberalism views individuals as having inalienable natural rights, including the right to own property and to enter into contracts with other individuals concerning the disposition of that property (Macpherson, 1962). These rights have to be protected from intrusion by collective social organizations such as the state, churches, or trade unions. Consequently, a good society in liberal philosophy is one that guarantees individuals' freedom to pursue their interests and realize their potentials. This freedom should be restricted only when one person's freedom erodes that of another.

In contrast to the emphasis on freedom of individuals, liberalism says little about the equality of individuals. Indeed, it treats equality as an adjunct of liberty. Equality merely means *equality of opportunity*: that all people should be free to pursue their own goals, constrained only by their own physical and mental endowments; only such a limited form of equality is consistent with individual liberty. Liberalism rules out any measure designed to promote *equality of outcome* – that is, political measures designed to ensure that economic processes equally benefit all individuals – because this would involve imposing restrictions on some so others can benefit. Thus, liberalism disapproves of income redistribution measures (progressive taxation, for example) to advance the lot of the poor because these measures involve forcible confiscation of wealth that belongs to the rich. In the twentieth century, however, the theory has been more favourably disposed towards accepting a minimum standard of wealth distribution.

Despite its emphasis on individuals and their freedom, liberal theory does not ignore the state. In fact the state has to be strong, to ensure that some people do not deprive others of their freedom. Beyond protecting freedom, however, in the liberal view the state has only a few other functions; it undertakes aspects of social life that individuals operating in the marketplace will not undertake, such as providing public goods, maintaining internal peace, and protecting society from external aggression. But this strong state itself must be restricted, lest it encroach upon the private realm of individuals. Liberalism therefore provides for a complex mechanism to keep the state in check. Representative government, whereby the government is chosen by the people, is one such control mechanism, as is the notion of the division of powers between different branches of the state whereby one branch "checks and balances" the activities of the others.

The primacy of individuals is reflected in the liberals' view of the economy as well. Freedom to pursue the livelihood of one's choice and to accumulate wealth is sacrosanct. The mechanism through which individuals can pursue their interests in an unencumbered fashion is, of course, the market. Here all individuals selfishly pursue their own interests according to their own abilities and preferences. Unlike other social philosophies that frown upon selfish behaviour, liberalism celebrates it. Liberals see exchange in the marketplace as benefiting everyone who engages in it, and the net result of this activity is the enhancement of society's welfare as a whole.

A related economic assumption is that individuals are rational or calculating actors. They decide rationally what they want and choose the least costly way of achieving it. This is not to say that the end result of their choice is rational, rather simply that they arrive at their choice through reasoning. People can rationally decide what they want to produce or consume, and hence they should be allowed to do so. Restrictions on individual preferences and actions are viewed as harmful to the individual as well as to society, because such restrictions prevent the realization of the benefits of free exchange. For this reason, liberal political economy is sometimes referred to as a "laissez faire" ("leave it alone," referring to the economy) theory.

The Market From Classical to Post-Keynesian Theory

Liberal economic theory was formulated in the late eighteenth century. Until then there were two approaches, too crude to be called theories, that enjoyed a substantial following in Europe: *mercantilism* and *physiocracy*. The mercantilists saw the primary economic objective of any nation as maximizing its international balance of trade. They recommended government efforts to assist exporting industries and protect home industries from imports. The physiocrats believed that agriculture was the only economic activity that generated an economic surplus (return over cost) that could be used to pay for other amenities of civilization. This line of reasoning led them to recommend policies to support agriculture and the activities of landowning classes.

Historical Foundations

Classical Political Economy

The origin of classical political economy coincided with, and indeed aided, the emergence of capitalism as a decisive force in Europe, especially England (Wolfe, 1981). The main theorists associated with the classical school – Adam Smith (1723-90), David Ricardo (1772-1823), Thomas Malthus (1766-1834), James Mill (1773-1836), and Mill's son John Stuart Mill (1806-73) – laid down the framework that still forms the cornerstone of liberal political economy.

Adam Smith's *Wealth of Nations* (1776) was the first book in political economy to lay out a complete, abstract model of the nature, structure, and workings of the capitalist system. According to Smith, the self-serving behaviour of individuals – deriving from the natural and universal human instinct for self-preservation and self-advancement – benefits not only those concerned but also the whole society. In his most famous passage Smith states: "It is not from the benevolence of the butcher, the brewer, or the baker, that we expect our dinner, but from their regard to their own interest. We address ourselves, not to their humanity but to their self-love" ([1776] 1979, Book 1, Chapter 2). According to Smith, each individual pursuing his own selfish interest is "led by an invisible hand to promote an end which was no part of his intention" (ibid., Book 4, Chapter 2). The underlying reason is that if all individuals were better off as a result of advancing their own separate interests, the society they formed would also be better off. Smith argues that this process should take place without outside intervention, which would only discourage individual enterprise and thus diminish economic well-being. As such, Smith advocated policies designed to minimize interference by authority – church or state – with individual freedom. In its two hundred years of subsequent development, liberal theory still retains the essence of these teachings.

Classical liberal political economy sees the *accumulation of capital* (profits) and the resulting investments as the growth-propelling force in the economy. What is actually accumulated is the "surplus" left after paying for the costs of production. Liberal political economy postulates that the accumulation of capital is helped most by the establishment of conditions for making profits, which can be reinvested continuously to make even more profit, with the process leading to the increased material well-being of the entire society. The liberal theory thus originally focused on suppliers and the supply side of economics, unlike later developments in the theory, which would attribute equal importance to both demand and supply.

Another important feature of classical political economy is its authors' varying degree of adherence to the *labour theory of value*, an idea developed formally by David Ricardo, though Smith had pursued it as well. This theory states that the prices of goods are strictly proportional to the value of labour embodied in them; a natural object has no value until human labour is applied to it, transforming it into a usable good or commodity. While capital goods (such as machinery) also contribute to value, they are themselves, like other consumer goods, embodiments of labour. In developing the labour theory, the classical economists created the noose on which Karl Marx would try to hang the political-economic system they so assiduously nurtured. Not surprisingly, the labour theory was abandoned by later liberal economists.

The theory of *income distribution* in classical political economy states that income is a function of whether an individual owns labour, land, or capital. Labour is paid wages according to what is required for its "subsistence," defined as those commodities needed for the physical survival and reproduction of the workforce. Landowners receive rent, defined as the produce over and above the production costs of cultivating the least productive land (marginally productive land, in later parlance). The classicals were, however, confused about profit. They could understand rent for the landlord, and they could explain wages, but what they could not explain was that if labour created value, then for what reason did profit accrue to the capitalists? The implication was clear that profit was theft by another name.[1] While the classical economists recognized the unfairness of income distribution in capitalism, they did not oppose it because of their belief that the accumulation of profits was essential for expanding production, and that the benefits of this accumulation were spread by the market right across society, even though profits benefited the capitalists more than others.

The *theory of comparative advantage* developed by classical political economists still forms the basis of modern international trade theory. While Smith referred to it, again it was Ricardo who developed the theory in its most sophisticated form. Extending the principle of free exchange to the international arena, the theory states that free international trade benefits both countries involved in a trade relationship. Competition resulting from free international trade confers benefits similar to its counterpart in the domestic economy because of the greater efficiency that competition engenders. So even if a country were more efficient than its trading partners in every type of economic activity, it would still be beneficial to concentrate on those goods in which its efficiency was the greatest and import the rest. The theory as developed by the classical economists has been refined over the years – and is known as the Heckscher-Ohlin-Samuelson model in its present incarnation – but the underlying reasoning remains the same. It is on this ground that liberal economists support Canada's free trade agreement with the United States.

Marginalism and Neoclassical Economics

The publication of separate books with similar implications by Stanley Jevons (1965) and Carl Menger (1950) in 1871 and Leon Walras (1965) in 1874 marked the beginning of *marginalism*. While little in their works was entirely new, these authors offered a new approach to the kind of liberal economic theory developed by the classicals. They theorized about the determination of prices, a question that had vexed their predecessors, and after stating the answer they explained the entire economy based on their postulates.

Marginalism argues that people receive utility (that is, pleasure or satisfaction) from consuming commodities (or services). However, the consumption of each additional unit gives increasingly less utility, until a point of "marginal utility" is reached at which further consumption yields no additional utility. So it is important to find out the marginal point at which consumption stops. Thus, a cup of water that normally has no value becomes exceedingly valuable when the stock of water has been depleted – during a drought, for instance – and only a cup remains. It is the value of the last unit of a product still sought by consumers that determines its price. Thus, the utility of any good or service diminishes with increasing availability, and, as such, it is the utility of the least wanted, the point of marginal utility, that sets the value for all units. The marginal value is the price of the product or service in question.

This apparently simple concept applies not only to consumers but also to producers. Producers continue to hire (demand) factors of production (that is to say, land, labour, and capital) until they reach the point when the hiring of an additional unit will provide no additional utility, and it is this point of marginal utility that determines rents, wages, and interest. These simple hypotheses about consumers' and suppliers' behaviour are meant to explain what is consumed and what is produced and how income is distributed in society.

The implications of this formulation are more serious than they might appear. Unlike the classical economists, who were searching for an answer to what "created" value, the marginalists avoided the question altogether by simply assuming that value was the same as price, which was determined by the subjective preferences of producers and consumers. Using this theory meant that mainstream economics no longer had to wrestle with the revolutionary implications of the idea that labour was the source of value (Dasgupta, 1985, p.15).

After the publication of *Principles of Economics* by Alfred Marshall in 1890, *neoclassical economics* quickly became the dominant mode of economic thinking and continues to form the essence of what we know as economics today. Neoclassical economics was nothing more than a formalized and technically refined statement of the marginalists' ideas, which themselves were for the most part an extension of what had been said by the classical political economists. In neoclassical economics, economic decisions are viewed as representing the point at which demand and supply intersect, just as a cloth is cut at the point – in Marshall's graphic analogy – where the blades of scissors meet. The understanding of how the prices of commodities and factors of production are determined answers all questions concerning what is produced and consumed and how income is distributed. The theory is indeed remarkable in its brevity, simplicity, and elegance; a few simple assumptions explain the operation of the entire economy.

In the simplified model of the economy found in neoclassical economics, the resources available to households and firms are assumed as given. The market is assumed to be perfectly competitive: that is, neither the producers nor consumers can directly manipulate prices. Consumers buy more when the prices are low, and firms supply more when the prices are high. The utility-maximizing consumers and the profit-maximizing producers are rational agents constantly juggling what they want to buy or sell in response to changes in price signals.

Prices are determined at the point at which demand equals supply; there will be a mismatch between the two at any other price. If the price is higher, supply will increase but the demand will be lower, resulting in a surplus. If the price is lower, demand will be higher but the suppliers will reduce supply, thus causing a shortage. Hence the perennially downward-sloping demand curve and the upward-sloping supply curve. In the case of changes in the level of demand or supply, the change is reflected in the price, which will adjust to a new equilibrium. When the demand and supply are at equilibrium, both consumers and firms are satisfied and there is no pressure for change. When the price of everything in the economy has been individually arrived at in this manner, the whole economy is said to be in equilibrium, and as a result neoclassical economics is sometimes referred to as *general equilibrium theory*. To reiterate, the mechanism applies not only to goods and services but also to the prices of labour (wages), capital (interest), and land (rent).

If the forces of demand and supply working through price signals in the market determine everything in the economy, there is very little role for outside intervention in the marketplace, such as by the state. This description, however, is a deliberate abstraction of a perfectly competitive market. When one or more conditions of a competitive market are not met, there is a role for outside intervention to correct the failure. As a result, liberal political economy has developed a theory of the state and requisite state activities to deal with these circumstances of imperfect competition and market failures at the micro-level of economic activity.

Neoclassical economics also has a specific vision of how the macro-economy operates. Macro-economy deals with the economy as a whole, especially economy-wide aggregates such as the level of employment, prices, and national income, and the economic growth rate (Grant and Nath, 1984, p.77). In the neoclassical conception of the macro-economy, money flows from firms to the public in the form of wages, profits, interest, and rent. In turn, the public spends most of its earnings on consuming goods and services, thus transferring the money back to firms. What is not spent on consumption is saved. Savings in turn are invested in productive activity, and investment is the growth-propelling element in the economy. The rate of savings and the corresponding level of investment are determined by interest rates.

In orthodox neoclassical economics, the macro-economy, like the micro-economy, exists as an efficient system in which the different economic components of the system rest in perfect balance. There might be some maladjustments, but those problems are purely temporary because the market will eventually clear in the long run. According to this view, for example, in a competitive market the unemployment of capital or labour is not possible in the long run. If unemployment exists it is because workers are refusing to work unless they are paid more than the value of their marginal productivity. In other words, unemployment is voluntary. As such, there is no role for government intervention in the macro-economy. The British economist John Maynard Keynes disagreed with this neoclassical conception of the macro-economy and developed a new theory and new instruments to deal with macro-economic market failures. Many liberal economists, however, continue to stick to the orthodox position, and the battle between Keynesians and neoclassical economists continues to represent a major division within the liberal camp.

In a matter of just a few decades neoclassical economics assumed a complete dominance over liberal political-economic thinking. Several factors nurtured its popularity. Primarily, it conveniently circumvented the question of what creates value, a question that had bedevilled the classical economists and dangerously suggested the importance of labour over all else in production. Its avoidance of this difficult question and its alternative focus on the question of price determination made it readily acceptable to most liberal economists. The theory also offered quantitative precision, which appealed to those searching for a "science" of economics. The essential simplicity of the theory combined with its ability to explain the complex interdependence of economic phenomena made it almost irresistible. But perhaps its greatest charm was that it did not pose a threat to the status quo, as did its main alternative, socialist theory, itself an outgrowth of classical political economy but with a focus on the politics of production rather than the economics of exchange.

Welfare Economics

The interwar period (1919-39) saw the development of a new branch of economics known as *welfare economics*, inspired by *The Economics of Welfare*, an influential text written by A.C. Pigou during World War I. This version of liberal political economy emerged as a result of investigations into how extensive state activities undertaken in Britain during World War I had resulted in the improvement of the economic welfare of the society as a whole. The term has nothing to do with social welfare programs per se but refers rather to the welfare of the society as a whole, that is, to the welfare of the aggregate of individuals.

The mainstream welfare economics theory is based on the norms of *Pareto optimality* – named after the Italian economist Vilfredo Pareto – which state that a social situation is optimal when no one person's position can be improved without worsening the position of another person. Social improvement in this sense is defined as movement from a non-Pareto optimal towards a Pareto optimal position. This matter of economic position is an ethical standard defining what is best for society, although it is not often recognized as such by adherents to the neoclassical orthodoxy. The theory derives from the branch of social philosophy called *utilitarianism* and rests on the normative assumptions that: (1) societal welfare depends on individuals' subjective sense of satisfaction, and (2) satisfaction is best achieved by letting individuals' preferences determine the use of societal resources (Rhoads, 1985, p.62). Because people have different tastes there is no unique Pareto optimum, and infinite patterns of allocation are possible depending on the distribution of income and wealth in the society.

Theoretically, the prime example of a Pareto optimal situation is a perfectly competitive neoclassical market in which economic resources are allocated in the most efficient manner possible through the price mechanism. So long as the market is perfectly competitive, Pareto optimality obtains and there is no place for corrective measures, which would only upset the optimality. But when there is a market distortion that is deemed to be inhibiting the realization of optimal results, the state should intervene to correct the distortion. The purpose of the intervention is to promote the optimal level of *economic efficiency*.

Even Adam Smith had recognized that the market would not produce public goods such as street lighting or national defence. Because of this Smith had supported the provision of certain public goods by the state. But he saw such goods as exceptions to the general rule of production and allocation of societal resources through market mechanisms. It was only during the twentieth century that liberal economists began to discover the extent to which a market left on its own did not yield optimal results. With the passage of time, an increasingly large number of market failures had been detected, forming a justification among welfare economists for expanding the state's role in the economy.

One form of market failure is the emergence of *monopoly*, a condition that distorts competition and hence hampers the achievement of optimal results. In conditions of monopoly, the sellers or buyers are not price-takers – as they should be if competition is to prevail – but price-fixers. In fact, some industries such as electricity supply or telephone services (natural monopolies) are marked by increasing returns to scale, which means that a single firm can grow to dominate the industry. *Imperfect knowledge* among buyers and sellers also leads to market failure by yielding similarly non-optimal results. In such situations, the welfare theorists argue, the government has a role to play in regulating monopolies and providing market information to buyers and sellers to facilitate the working of a competitive market, which is then expected to lead to Pareto optimal results.

Another variety of market failure is the existence of *externalities*, or spillover effects. Producers and consumers make economic decisions on the basis of how the decisions benefit themselves, but when they do so these decisions can have an adverse effect on others. For instance, a company dealing with dangerous chemicals might consider it more profitable to dump its waste in the public water system. While this action would clearly be more efficient as far as the firm is concerned, it would be inefficient for the society as a whole. In such a situation, welfare economics suggests government intervention to contain industrial pollution. This is an example of negative externality, but there are also positive externalities, which the government is supposed to promote. Education, for instance, is regarded as an area in which the market fails to deliver the proper goods; but because the social benefits of a literate population are high, the government should intervene and support its provision. Later on, positive externalities requiring state intervention came to include support for infant industries and industrial adjustment.

Finally, markets cannot be expected to lead to an equitable distribution of income. People starting with more wealth will be able to secure a disproportionate amount of subsequent economic activity and economic benefits. If nothing else, the old and the infirm would find it rough going in a purely market-based society. This warrants state intervention to support some degree of income redistribution. However, this is a different form of state intervention, because it does not lead to Pareto optimality. In fact, it is a denial of the principle because it involves the improvement in conditions of the poor at the expense of the wealthy. Be that as it may, a limited degree of income redistribution is now an accepted part of welfare economics.

Keynesian Economics

The development of Keynesianism in the 1930s had an impact similar to welfare economics in detecting market deficiencies and extending the state's role in the economy. While the interventions inspired by welfare economics were of a *micro-economic nature* – that is to say, they dealt with particular market failures – Keynesian interventions were *macro-economic*, aimed at adjusting the operation of the whole economy. The theory first appeared in the context of the Great Depression and was proposed by John Maynard Keynes (1883-1946) in his book *The General Theory of Employment, Interest, and Money* (1936).

In the process of analyzing the Depression and proposing solutions to it, Keynes had to modify certain key assumptions of the neoclassical theory. The orthodox position that in a competitive market unemployment of capital or labour was not possible, except when workers refused to work for market-determined wages, sounded like a cruel joke in the 1930s. During that decade unemployment in Europe and North America had reached between one-quarter and one-third of the workforce, and many individuals could not find employment even if they were willing to work for less than subsistence wages. But neoclassical economists and most politicians remained unswayed from their belief that allowing the market to operate freely – which would reduce wages to the level of workers' marginal productivity – was the only solution to the crisis. Keynes disagreed, arguing that the market does not always adjust automatically to create full employment of factors. In cases when it does not, he said, the state must intervene to correct the situation.

Keynes said it was possible, as in the existing Depression, that aggregate demand and supply would equilibrate at a level less than optimal, leaving resources unemployed. This view, of course, contrasted with the orthodox neoclassical assumption that in the long run demand and supply were always at equilibrium at the optimal point. Keynes saw the problem as arising from inadequate aggregate demand for commodities, capital, and labour. Inadequate demand, in turn, had its origin in the existence of savings that were not being invested because of a lack of business confidence. If businesses expect the demand for their product to be low, they cut back on their investment (which leaves unused savings) and lay off workers. The resulting unemployment reduces the workers' income, so in turn workers have to reduce their consumption, which leads to further cutbacks by businesses, thus locking the economy in a downward spiral of decline.

Keynes's solution involved the calculated use of government revenues and expenditures, or *fiscal and monetary policies.* He theorized that to boost aggregate demand (for goods and services by consumers and for raw materials, labour, and capital by businesses), the government could increase the money supply, which would reduce interest rates, which in turn would cause firms to invest by borrowing from people's savings. The increase in demand caused by increased investment would put the economy in an upswing, and because of multiplier effects the economy would gain momentum as it grew.

But Keynes did not believe this solution would be enough. He added that the government would also have to step in, borrow the excess savings (which businesses were not using) directly, and invest the money thus raised in public projects. These projects would create employment, which would lead to increased consumer spending and thus higher aggregate demand, which in turn would lead to increased production and higher investment by firms. Once economic growth had reached a point where it employed all the available resources, the government could cut back on its spending. The budget deficit incurred in borrowing money to finance public projects would be paid back in the long run by the increase in tax revenues caused by increased economic activity.

Not surprisingly, orthodox neoclassical economists were suspicious of any theory that involved increased government intervention. But the out-break of World War II vindicated Keynes. The preparations for war entailed increased government expenditures on military personnel and hardware, and the inadvertent result of this spending was the complete elimination of unemployment and the operation of the Western economies at full capac-ity. The increased state expenditures were financed largely through borrow-ings from the public (such as Canada Victory Bonds).

After the end of the war, many Western governments attempted to adopt Keynesianism as a normal theory of economic management. Keynesian tools – adjusting the level of money supply and/or public spending – were sometimes used or urged as an attempt to boost or slow the economy: governments sometimes felt the need to slow the economy to check inflation or "overheating." The policies came to be called the strategy of "leaning against the wind" or "fine tuning," and the theory was eventually incorpo-rated into the mainstream of liberal political economics. Nevertheless, doubts remained among some neoclassical economists, who were uneasy with any theory calling for increased state intervention in the economy.

While Keynesianism represented a major breakthrough in liberal eco-nomics, it should not be construed as a radical departure from the princi-ples of neoclassical economics. Like its predecessors, it sees the government's role in the economy as no more than acting to correct the (macro-economic) shortcomings of the market. Keynes had no quarrel with the micro-economic assumptions of neoclassical theory that a free, competitive market leads to the most efficient (optimal) allocation of resources or that income is paid according to the factors' marginal productivity. He did, however, reject the fundamental assumption of neoclassical economics that in the long run the market adjusts automatically to create full employment of capital and labour (Hunt, 1979, p.395).

While the principles of Keynesian proposals were not radical, the implications for the relationship between state and market were revolutionary. The maintenance of full employment provided a rationale, if only unintentionally, for the state to engage continuously in income redistribution without eroding the foundations of capitalist economies. This suited the aims of socialist and labour parties, in or out of government, very well. As Przeworski argues:

> The fact is that social democrats everywhere soon discovered in Keynes' ideas, particularly after the appearance of his *General Theory*, something they urgently needed: a distinct policy for administering capitalist economies. The Keynesian revolution – and this is what it was – provided social democrats with a goal and hence the justification of their governmental role, and simultaneously transformed the ideological significance of distributive policies that favored the working class. . . .
>
> And this was not yet all: Keynesianism was not only a theory that justified socialist participation in government but, even more fortuitously from the social democratic point of view, it was a theory that suddenly granted a universalistic status to the interests of workers. Earlier, all demands for increased consumption were viewed as inimical to the national interest: higher wages meant lower profits and hence a reduced opportunity for investment and future development. (1985, pp.36-37)

Transferring more income to workers was no longer seen as inimical to capitalism because the transfer gave workers more money to buy things produced by capitalists, who made profits in the process. This was surely a no-lose situation. Or so it appeared until the 1970s, when sluggish economic growth made it difficult to pay for income-maintenance programs (Wolfe, 1977; Wolfe, 1981).

The enthusiasm of socialist governments in the West for Keynesianism is not without irony. As Anthony Arblaster comments: "Keynes was never a socialist, and did not see his policies as a strategy for socialism, but as the adaptation of capitalism that would enable it to survive crisis and retain the precious legacy of individualism. . . . Keynes [was] among many early twentieth-century radicals and liberals who did not consider themselves socialists because they were not, in the final analysis, anti-capitalist even if they were anti-*laissez-faire*" (1984, p.295).

Contemporary Debates

The contemporary debates in liberal political economy consist of three different yet overlapping strands: Keynesian-welfare, neoconservative, and post-Keynesian. The distinctions among them relate mainly to the extent to which they believe in self-regulating markets and the corresponding need or lack of a need for state action to correct market failures. The post-Keynesians propose the highest level of state intervention in the economy and the neoconservatives the least, and the Keynesian-welfare theorists fall somewhere in between. While the differences among them are significant in both theoretical and practical senses, they are still all liberals who believe in private property and the use of market mechanisms as the bases of political-economic organization.

Keynesian-Welfare Economics

The Keynesian-welfare economists are moderate liberals who may form the majority in the discipline. They acknowledge the shortcomings of the market and the role of the state in correcting those shortcomings, yet they would subject the state to efficiency tests before allowing it to intervene in the market process. The Keynesian-welfare analysts fully accept neoclassical assumptions regarding the operation of the market and its general superiority over the state as a mechanism for allocating and distributing economic resources. Yet they agree that there are specific circumstances in which the state might be more efficient than the market. They concede, following Keynes, that the operation of the market generates macro-economic instabilities, which the state can and should balance. They also generally accept the principles of welfare economics as a guide for correcting micro-economic market failures.

However, the Keynesian-welfare theorists would have the state correct market failures only as a last resort. Since liberal political economy begins with the assumption of the greater efficiency of the market, there is a limit to how far any analyst working in the tradition can go in approving the state's role in the economy. So while Keynesian-welfare economists theoretically recognize the ability of the state to overcome certain shortcomings of the market, they are hesitant to recommend state actions in practice.

Macro-economic stabilization meets with the Keynesian-welfare economists' approval; so does provision of essential public goods and regulating the level of competition and a certain degree of income redistribution. Beyond those basics, they evaluate government intervention in the area of externalities based on the criterion of efficiency; that is, the benefits to the society as a whole should be greater than the costs. Once the benefits have been determined, their choice of policy instrument leans towards the one that causes least distortion in the market. By these criteria, it would seem that a typical Keynesian-welfare economist in Canada would find the present form and level of state intervention in the economy to be inappropriate and excessive, a conclusion not very different from that of the neoconservatives.

Neoconservative Economics

The neoconservatives should more appropriately be called orthodox neoclassicals or ultraliberals, given their resemblance to the early neoclassical liberals, but neoconservative is the term generally used to describe them. They are conservative only to the extent that they reject most of the modifications introduced in liberal economics since the turn of the century. Otherwise, except for a small minority, they do not necessarily favour church supremacy, aristocracy, and traditional family values – the hallmarks of political conservatism. The neoconservatives form a minority among professional economists, but their consistent reasoning and impassioned debating style (and friendly governments in certain countries) more than compensate for their small number. Some of them have gone on to win the Nobel Prize in economics, most notably Friedrich von Hayek, Milton Friedman, George Stigler, and James Buchanan. Michael Walker of the Fraser Institute in Vancouver is the best known neoconservative economist in Canada, although the brand of neoconservatism favoured by the Fraser Institute is moderate compared to that espoused in the United States and elsewhere.

While there are some differences within the neoconservative school of thought – such as those among the monetarists, the supply-siders, and the new classicals – there are points on which they all agree. What distinguishes the neoconservative economists is the supreme importance they attribute to individuals and their freedom: they emphasize individual freedom even more than economic efficiency. They prefer the market to the state because the market is based on the principle of free choice among individuals whereas the authority of the state rests on coercion.

The neoconservative economists believe in all the principles of undiluted neoclassical economics, including the principle of a self-adjusting market at both the micro and macro levels. Although they now present those principles in a more sophisticated form, the implication remains the same: keep the state out of the market. They concede that there might be instances of market failure, but they do not see state intervention as a solution. They believe that the only kind of market failure that should be corrected by the state is the provision of pure public goods (Rowley, 1983, p.23), such as national defence, prison services, and tax collection. They believe that street lighting, police, fire services, and parks and pleasure grounds can be "partially" provided by the market (ibid., p.25).

As far as the other market failures mentioned in the welfare economics literature are concerned, the neoconservatives either disagree that they are failures or doubt that state intervention can correct them. In fact, they believe that the state is more likely to aggravate the situation because of the rigidities and inefficiencies of bureaucratic actions. Recently, the public choice theory has provided the neoconservatives with a formal method of demonstrating the inherent inefficiency of the state. Even if the state turned out to be more efficient than the market in certain instances, however, many neoconservatives would still reject state intervention in the market on grounds that the measure would erode individual freedom. Neoconservatives also object to the use of the norm of Pareto optimality as a guide for state intervention because it does not explicitly forbid the state from entering areas that belong to the private realm of individuals. In the words of one ardent neoconservative, Charles Rowley:

> Paretian welfare economics, by its concentration upon problems of market failure and by its explicit or implicit support for the notion of perfect government, has contributed not a little during the post-war period to the destruction of the liberal order in Western society. Yet further, the contributions of economists working in the field of social choice, masquerading in utilitarian guise, have encouraged the notion . . . of the "dictatorial social decision-maker" which is totalitarian in nature and which is ends- rather than process-oriented in the best traditions of Marxist and Fascist dogmas. (Rowley, 1983, p.28)

Neoconservative economics consists of various strands – such as monetarism, supply-side economics, and new classical economics – whose adherents disagree among themselves on points of emphasis. The implications of their analyses are the same, though, as they all seek to reduce the role of the state in the economy. In contrast to the Keynesian preoccupation with maintaining full employment, the neoconservatives strive towards price stability because of their belief that inflation is a greater economic evil than unemployment (Grant and Nath, 1984, p.92). They view inflation as purely a monetary phenomenon that originates in the growth in the money supply, which in turn results from governments' need to finance constantly expanding expenditures. They argue that because the increase in money supply is unmatched by the growth in the supply of goods and services (that is, an increasing amount of money begins to chase a fixed amount of goods), inflation is the inevitable result. They therefore propose restraint in the money supply as a solution to inflation. The general slowdown in economic activity and the ensuing unemployment caused by the monetary squeeze are regarded as unavoidable, indeed necessary, for checking inflation.

In addition, the neoconservative economists believe that economies are characterized by a "natural rate of unemployment." A market economy always consists of people who at a given time are in the process of changing jobs and hence unemployed. Other people are unemployed because of government measures such as minimum wage laws, unemployment insurance, welfare payments, and collective agreements negotiated by trade unions that inhibit job-seekers from accepting wages commensurate with their marginal productivity. Government measures to reduce unemployment, as proposed by Keynes, only serve to fuel inflation. The implication of this position is that the government is responsible for any unemployment above the "natural" level. As such the solution to unemployment lies in eliminating the factors that inhibit the operation of labour markets: trade union rights, minimum wages, and unemployment and other welfare payments made by governments.

Another strand in neoconservative economics is the focus on creating conditions conducive for expanding production. While the monetarist solution of reducing money supply works at the level of reducing aggregate demand, the supply-side measures work by expanding supply, that is, by increasing the total production of goods and services. Since it is the capitalists who organize production, the government should encourage them by reducing the taxes on their profits. This would lead them to expand production, which would generate not only additional profit for them but also more jobs and higher income for their workers.

The neoconservative economists often go to great lengths to proclaim that their theories are "value-free," "positive," and "non-ideological." Regardless of these claims, their theories are as ideological as those they criticize. Neoconservative theories are founded on an overwhelming faith in individualism and the universal benefits of the market and, as a corollary, on a doctrinaire opposition to state interference. Be that as it may, even the critics of neoconservative political economy usually concede that its proponents are highly consistent in their analyses. No doubt they oppose welfare payments to poor individuals, but they also oppose subsidies to firms. What the neoconservatives do not admit, however, is that implementation of their proposals would cause more hardship to the poor than to the owners of firms. Unlike the moderate mainstream Keynesian-welfare economists, whose theories often represent awkward efforts to reconcile market principles with extensive state intervention in the economy, the neoconservative economists do not have to live with such dilemmas.

Post-Keynesian Economics

In contrast to the neoconservatives, who call for a reduced state role in the economy, the post-Keynesians ask for its expansion. The origin of this line of thinking is said to lie in the works of, in addition to Keynes, Joan Robinson, Michael Kalecki, Nicholas Kaldor, and John Kenneth Galbraith (Gonick, 1987, p.145). While clearly in the minority among contemporary liberal economists, this group forms a substantial force. The economic success of Japan is often cited by post-Keynesians as proof that capitalist economies need state guidance.

Post-Keynesians argue that the problems of advanced capitalism require more and not less state intervention in the economy. They argue that neoclassical economic theory was designed to account for an economy consisting of small firms and unorganized workers, which enabled market forces to operate efficiently without state intervention. With the rise of large corporations and trade unions, a self-correcting market is no longer possible. Given the changed circumstances, post-Keynesians say it is the market power of producer and labour, and not the competitive forces of demand and supply, that determines prices and wages (Cornwall and Maclean, 1984, p.92).

Post-Keynesians view the manipulation of the market by huge corporations and trade unions as the source of economic problems. They say that inflation results from excessive wage increases secured by organized labour combined with the ability of firms to pass these costs on to consumers because of their monopolistic position in the market. To check this malady, post-Keynesians argue for a negotiated "incomes policy" that would restrain wage demands in return for lower unemployment. The arrangement would be sponsored by the state and would involve a commitment by business and labour to hold back prices and wages. The corporatist political institutions in Scandinavia and Austria, and to a lesser extent in West Germany and Netherlands, are cited as models to be emulated.

In addition, the post-Keynesians propose active industrial and labour market policies. These would consist of formal co-operation among state, business, and labour to identify industries of the future and direct investments towards those industries. This would be accompanied by enhanced public subsidies for corporate research and development and retraining of workers to equip them to work in growing industries. In the meantime, while the industrial restructuring is taking place, it might be necessary to protect domestic industries from imports. The purpose of these measures would not be to retard market forces, but to assist them. Capital and labour would not be shielded from changing market forces but supported in anticipating the changes and becoming prepared for them (Crane, 1981).

The post-Keynesian understanding of the market is not without its problems. It presumes that it is possible to predict market trends and plan accordingly. Markets, however, are notoriously unpredictable and formal co-operation among societal groups and the state must be highly flexible to respond efficiently to changing market conditions. Moreover, collaboration is not as costless a process as the post-Keynesians make it appear. Firms lose their autonomy to governments and labour, which constrains and restricts their management prerogatives, and they are unlikely to give up those prerogatives without resistance.

The State in Liberal Theory

The raison d'être of all liberal theories of political economy has been to maintain capitalism and rationalize the dominance of the market. But to be able to do so, liberal political economy has had to allow for the reality of an increasing state presence in the market. It is essentially a theory of the market that has had to include the state on grounds of contingency to perform functions that would not otherwise be performed. Liberal political economy contains two slightly different formulations concerning the state. The first is the idea of the *supplementary* or *residual state*: the notion contained in classical and neoconservative liberal political economy that the state should only undertake those activities – such as the provision of pure public goods – that markets cannot perform. The second is the notion of the *corrective state*: the idea found in welfare-Keynesian analyses that the state can act in a variety of other areas of market activity to correct micro- or macro-level market failures.

Significantly, both analyses undertheorize the state. They treat the state as an inert subject that ought to do whatever it is that the market cannot do. The state is not considered to be in any way constrained by the society in which it exists or by its organizational capacity (Schott, 1984, p.60). In fact, the capacity of the state to act and the forces that act upon the state are usually not considered at all. Instead it is simply assumed that the state can and will act either to provide goods and services or to correct market failures out of a concern for economic efficiency. The post-Keynesians are the only liberal political economists who avoid these overly simplistic conceptions of the state.

The State in Neoclassical and Neoconservative Economics

Liberalism's opposition to the state and preference for the market, which have been its most persistent features, must be understood in the context in which it was born. The feudal state was highly active in promoting the interests of landlords and mercantilists by keeping food prices high and providing special privileges to certain companies in the form of monopoly rights, protection from imports, and the backing of the armed forces. The Hudson's Bay Company and the East India Company are prime examples of such firms. Because these measures discriminated against the emerging capitalist class, a political-economic theory opposed to state intervention in the affairs of society was developed. Adam Smith proposed an economic system based on pursuit of self-interest by individuals rather than direction by state: "The ordinary revolutions of war and government easily dry up the sources of that wealth which arises from Commerce only" (Smith, [1776] 1987, p.520).

Smith argued that state interventions tend to misdirect resources and diminish their contribution to society's economic well-being; but he thought that the state's interest in expanding its control over society would prevail unless individuals in society prevented this behaviour from occurring by consciously restricting the size and activities of the state and promoting market exchange wherever possible.

The neoclassical economists continued this line of thinking. In both classical and neoclassical economics, the role of the state in the economy is to be residual and supplementary to the market. When the understanding of what the market cannot do itself expanded in the twentieth century, leading to the corresponding prescriptions of welfare economists and Keynesians for increases in state economic activity, the state was still assumed to be a cipher as well as omnipotent: an agency that takes orders from wise economists and then implements them faithfully, unencumbered by any societal or internal state forces. The state, for instance, should know that it is less efficient than the market in most instances and hence should defer to the market's superiority in organizing social relations. After all, what objectives other than the promotion of individual freedom and economic efficiency could the state pursue? But that is not all. The state should also be aware that there are selfish interests out there in the society, which would impose additional demands for goods and services on the state. Apparently, the state should also be able to resist such demands and consciously restrict its functions to providing public goods.

Curiously absent in this innocent conception is the recognition that the state itself might not be inert – a point argued forcefully by "statist" theorists such as Theda Skocpol (1985) and Eric Nordlinger (1981) – and that the state might initiate actions for which there are no societal pressures; or that the converse might also be true, that the state might not be able to resist societal demands placed upon it. More importantly, the state might not have the capacity to carry out its decisions. To simply assume that the state should do no more than provide public goods is not an adequate starting point for an analysis of the role the state plays in society. A more fruitful line of analysis would be to recognize that economic efficiency is only one among many objectives of a state.

The neoconservatives display a greater awareness of the reality of the state's existence in the market. The state, far from being "an exogenous force, trying to do good . . . is [regarded as] at least partially endogenous and the policies it institutes will reflect vested interests in society" (Colander, 1984, p.2). The neoconservatives recognize that the state has a monopoly over coercion and that democracy provides self-interested individuals with the ability to press demands on the state, which the state (through its equally self-interested politicians and bureaucrats) is forever eager to meet. Voters need material benefits, politicians need votes, and the state's coercive taxation system is required to pay for it all (Buchanan and Wagner, 1977; Brennan and Buchanan, 1980). The result, according to neoconservatives, is unmitigated economic inefficiency as states expand their activities into more and more areas of economic activity best left to market devices.

The neoconservatives would weed out the problem – excessive state intervention in the economy – from its roots; they would impose clear limits on what the state can do. They would replace the present constitution with a "Constitution of Liberty" (Hayek, 1960), which would provide for limitations on power to tax, balanced budgets, and a reduction in the public provision of goods (Rowley, 1983, pp.55-61). However, not much hope is held out for the adoption of such a constitution because (again) there are vested interests in society that benefit from profligate governments. As a result, many neoconservatives (Friedman, for example) would settle for a more limited program of reforms: public expenditures determined by benefit-cost considerations, tax rates that are kept fixed, and growth in the money supply fixed at a certain constant rate (Schott, 1984, p.60). These proposals imply that the Keynesian instruments of activist fiscal and monetary policies will be taken away from the government and what little money is left to spend will be used only after econometric evaluations show that projected benefits of the proposed action will exceed estimated costs. In the words of David Wolfe, the state will assume the role of "a disciplinarian, restraining individuals and enterprises for the sake of their mutual long-term interest" (1981, p.71).

While more realistic than many of their predecessors, neoconservatives continue to conceive of the state as an instrument whose only function is to promote economic efficiency and act as a supplement to the market. Their conception of political economy exaggerates the market's efficiency while continuing to undertheorize the question of state autonomy. More seriously, it suggests a vision of a thoroughly undemocratic state, since only a state detached from democratic electoral pressures would be able to go against the wishes of the people in the name of promoting economic efficiency through market mechanisms. Imposing restrictions on the government's ability to respond to democratically expressed demands would be a repudiation of many of the political advances made this century. There is also another ominous side to neoconservatism: it rationalizes the dominance of those who benefit disproportionately from uncontrolled markets – the business community – over those who do not – the workers and the unemployed poor.

The State in Keynesian-Welfare and Post-Keynesian Economics

Keynesians and post-Keynesians recognize that as capitalism matured it encountered new problems, which required new solutions, many of them involving state intervention in the economy to correct the shortcomings of the market (Nell, 1988; Wolfe, 1981). By the end of the nineteenth century, the logic of market competition had taken its toll on small producers, and the industrial landscape was dominated by large corporations enjoying near-monopoly positions in the market. Similarly, the new trade union movement had begun to erode the employers' superior bargaining capacity vis-à-vis the workers. The product or labour markets were not as competitive as they once used to be, which posed problems for a theory which was developed to explain early capitalist societies.

Although welfare, Keynesian, and post-Keynesian economics justify and permit a substantial degree of state intervention in the economy, the market is still the favoured mechanism for determining production and distribution, and the state is to be employed only at times when the market is found to be inadequate. Even the post-Keynesians argue only for measures, no matter how interventionist, that reinforce and do not replace the market.

Keynesians would have the state hold back on fiscal expenditures and money supply in times of economic expansion and do the opposite in conditions of economic slowdown. Without these countervailing measures, the state would be prolonging the adverse effects of both economic booms and recessions. In welfare economics, the state's role is similarly confined, to achieving Pareto optimality. Once a market failure has been identified, the government should intervene to correct it. The state should check any negative externalities through taxes, subsidies, or regulations. The state should either provide desirable public goods (merit goods) directly or subsidize their provision by the market. Monopoly behaviour by firms should be tackled through regulations.

The one feature common to all these recommendations is that they treat the state's objectives as given: the pursuit of economic efficiency. Why the state would pursue this goal and not others is unclear. After all, the state itself is embedded in the society that it manipulates and that manipulates it, in complex ways. For instance, the state might decide, either independently or because of societal pressures, to develop a particular industry by offering subsidies regardless of what welfare economists argue would constitute an economic optimum. Similarly, if business and organized labour unite and forcefully demand that interest rates be brought down, few states would have the capacity to resist the demand on the grounds that Keynesian economic theory demands the opposite. As Kerry Schott states: "There is little to be gained from advising a state what it ought to do about economic policy if the state in question is not equipped, either institutionally or in motive, to follow such advice" (Schott, 1984, p.69).

What the state does in the economy is determined by what it is capable of doing, and its capacity for autonomous activity is conditioned by its own internal organizational structure and the organization of the economy and society in which it exists. The character of the state – such as whether it is internally cohesive or fragmented – and the character of the main social classes – the level of unity or fragmentation within capital and labour – shape what states can and cannot do. A state that is internally cohesive and enjoys the society's support can follow a coherent policy, if it chooses to do so. If it doesn't it becomes subject to contradictory societal pressures, which are reflected in its role in the economy. In such circumstances it matters little in practical terms whether its actions promote economic efficiency in terms of welfare or Keynesian economics.

The post-Keynesians must be given credit for understanding the organizational constraints on the state's role in the economy. Their explanation of inflation and unemployment as being rooted in the lack of social consensus and their proposal for a greater degree of co-operation among state, business, and labour in managing the economy illustrate their sensitivity towards social institutions. Yet post-Keynesianism is not without its problems. References to the example provided by the political practices of corporatism in Sweden, for example, are ironic given the debate raging in that country regarding the future of its political economy, and those accounts say little about how Swedish institutions and processes are to be recreated in other countries. Any attempt to reform the state and societal institutions along corporatist lines will be constrained by the same fragmentations that are the source of the problems those institutions were expected to address in the first place. Weak and fragmented institutions cannot be expected to undertake the establishment of cohesive institutions. If emulating Sweden or Japan were easy we would have seen a lot of nations adopting political-economic institutions patterned after them. Thus, the post-Keynesians can be said to be more successful in explaining the success of the political economy of certain capitalist nations than in prescribing solutions for the others that are less successful.

Liberal Political Economy in Canada

The high level of state involvement in Canadian economic development does not negate Canadian political economy's primarily liberal character, nor does it prevent the liberal political economists from retaining a basic market-oriented approach in their analyses. This is because intervention in Canada has always been directed at supplementing rather than supplanting the operation of the market. The Macdonald Commission was correct in its observation that: "The 'positive state' tradition in our history, which has supported an influential role for governments in the economy, has nevertheless always assumed that most economic decision making will be in private hands" (Macdonald Commission, 1985, Vol.I, p.47).

The dominance of liberalism in Canadian political and economic discourse is reflected in academic research and scholarly works in the area. In terms of the sheer volume of studies on Canadian political economy undertaken by economists, the liberals have been in a clear majority. The fact that it is easier to get research funds for projects following conventional approaches only partly explains the large output. Another reason is that the theory is in tune with the ethos of the politico-economic system it describes, which makes its explanations sound more reasonable than those taken from outside the orthodoxy.

Nevertheless, liberal political economy is neither homogeneous nor monolithic in Canada or elsewhere. Instead, liberalism includes a range of widely divergent approaches allowing for different levels and types of state intervention in the economy. We can classify the contemporary studies on Canadian political economy following liberal precepts into two broad categories: Keynesian-welfare and neoclassical-neoconservative. While there are theoretical differences between the two, in practice these differences are superficial; they both arrive at conclusions, albeit through different routes, that permit only a minor role for the state in the economy.

Keynesian-Welfare Political Economy

The Keynesian-welfare school has been the most influential in Canada, and it has formed the mainstream among the analysts and practitioners of the liberal theory in this country. While there are significant differences among individual analysts, they are all middle-of-the-road liberals, willing to compromise and live with imperfect states and imperfect markets. The Economic Council of Canada, the Institute for Research on Public Policy, and the C.D. Howe Institute are the main research institutions following this approach to Canadian political economy. The report of the Macdonald Commission may also be classified in this category, although it borders on the neoconservative end of the spectrum.

A statement by Judith Maxwell, formerly the head of the C.D. Howe Research Institute and later of the Economic Council of Canada, illustrates the Keynesian-welfare "principles" for defining the government's role in the economy:

> First, government taxation, expenditure and regulation must nurture the incentives for individuals to be productive and for corporations to be efficient.
>
> Second, governments must respect resource constraint. . . . The spending must therefore be justified by an acceptable social rate of return.
>
> Third, governments must develop incentives for greater efficiency within their own organization, so that public servants are rewarded in some way for actions that improve the efficiency of existing programs and for applying more rigorous efficiency tests on new programs. (Maxwell, 1977, pp.12-13)

Maxwell is not opposed to government intervention in the economy as such, but would have state action bound by the efficiency criterion analogous to the market.

Although the Keynesian-welfare political economists, unlike the neoconservatives, are not averse to using monetary and fiscal tools to stabilize the macro-economy (Economic Council, 1983; Macdonald Commission, 1985), the high inflation of the 1970s did veer many of them towards favouring fiscal and monetary restraint, undermining the primacy of reducing unemployment as a policy objective and drawing their analysis closer to that of the monetarists. Even then, however, the Keynesian-welfare analysis did not advocate containing inflation exclusively through demand-restraint measures (squeezing money supply and sharply cutting back on government expenditures) that would adversely affect the weaker sections of the society by increasing unemployment (Economic Council, 1983, p.13). Instead, it was suggested that some form of income policy be adopted whereby the state, business, and labour work together to contain demands for increases in wages and prices to keep unemployment low without fuelling inflationary pressures (Economic Council, 1983, p.16; Macdonald Commission, 1985, Vol.II, p.360).

At the micro-economic level, the Keynesian-welfare analysts in Canada favour only isolated state interventions to augment market forces. They usually support state interventions to facilitate adjustment to changed market conditions – such as assistance to industries, communities, and workers faced with dislocations because of changes in demand or technology (Economic Council, 1983; C.D. Howe Institute, 1983; Macdonald Commission, 1985).

Since they favour micro-economic interventions that assist rather than suppress market forces, they are suspicious of industrial strategy proposals that seek to "engineer" comparative advantage through manipulation of market forces, as is arguably done in Japan, France, and South Korea. Expressing its cynicism towards the state playing an activist role in shaping the economy, the Economic Council has re-emphasized "the merits of letting competitive [market] forces sort out the 'winners' and 'losers' in the domestic economy" (1983). For the same reason, the Council is opposed to broad measures to promote manufacturing industries to reduce the natural-resource orientation of the Canadian economy. As the Economic Council argues, "Canada must be less preoccupied with the manufacturing sector and ensure that trade opportunities are pursued in all sectors" (1983).

The Economic Council acknowledges the need for government assistance for industrial research and development in Canada. But to ensure economic efficiency it has also emphasized the primacy of the market and the need for a cost-benefit analysis of government action (Economic Council, 1987). In keeping with the desire to adhere as closely to the market principle as possible, the Keynesian-welfare economists recommend that assistance for research and development should not be targeted to particular industries, but should be made generally available to all industries engaged in research and development. Similarly, they favour higher expenditures on labour training and education in science and technology because these activities do not directly distort the market, as would measures directed at promoting the technological capabilities of certain "winning" industries (ibid.). They also support co-operation between the state and social groups on efficiency grounds, although not as strongly as do the post-Keynesians.

The apparent contradiction in acknowledging the need for state intervention but yet not approving of it was nowhere more evident than in the Macdonald Commission's comments on industrial development:

A fundamental change is taking place in the world economy, a change that casts doubts on the wisdom of the hands-off approach. . . . At the same time, our analysis leads us to conclude that governments generally lack the capability to orchestrate, or even formulate, a comprehensive, detailed, industrial strategy of the kind advocated by the more ardent interventionists. Even if a detailed strategy were possible, it would not be desirable. The world is just too complex, and the need for flexibility and adaptability too great, to justify confining the private sector in such a strait-jacket. (Macdonald Commission, 1985, Vol. II, p.138)

The concern for efficiency also guides the Keynesian-welfare attitude towards regulations and public enterprises (Economic Council, 1981, 1986; Macdonald Commission, 1985). The analysts recommend the elimination of the measures that cause inefficiencies. However, they do not issue a wholesale condemnation of the use of such instruments, as in the case of neoconservative analyses.

The commitment to economic efficiency also leads Keynesian-welfare liberal political economists to accept the doctrine of the theory of comparative advantage. They argue that hurdles to international trade promote economic inefficiencies, increase prices, and allow domestic producers to misuse their monopoly position, without doing anything to promote the long-term competitiveness of the protected industries. In the words of the Macdonald Commission, "Our basic international stance complements our domestic stance. We must seek an end to those patterns of government involvement in the economy which may generate disincentives, retard flexibility, and work against the desired allocation of resources" (1985, Vol.I, p.50).

The fact that a nation's exports might consist entirely of semimanufactured or crude products does not concern these analysts because such exports generate national wealth just as much as manufactured products. In fact, they derisively describe those favouring manufacturing industries, usually the economic nationalists, as having a "manufacturing fetish."

Following from their belief in the theory of comparative advantage is their near obsession with free trade with the United States, an attitude they share with neoconservatives. The reciprocal reduction in trade barriers will, they argue, enable Canadian producers to produce for the continental economy and specialize in certain product lines; what is not produced domestically will be imported more cheaply from the South. Similarly, they do not oppose foreign investments, which (when inspired by reasons other than avoidance of tariffs) produce lasting employment and bring much needed capital and advanced technology. They do not attach much significance to the profits repatriated by parent firms or to balance of payment problems, which are deemed to be resolvable through adjustments in exchange rates.

The feature that most clearly distinguishes the Keynesian-welfare economists from their neoconservative counterparts is their concern for social equity, which co-exists with their concern for economic efficiency. The Economic Council asserts: "Social goals and programs are not residual to the economic system. They contribute fundamentally to the smooth functioning of our economy, and they reflect the basic values of Canadians. Our economic and social goals and programs are not separable; nor are social goals subordinate to economic goals" (1983, p.62).

But even in matters related to equity, concerns for economic efficiency are not forgotten. The Council also emphasizes the need for improving "the manner in which governments deliver goods and services."

> Productivity improvements in this area could release considerable resources for other components of economic growth and welfare gains. There is little doubt that our major social programs (health, education, old age pensions, and income maintenance) leave a great deal to be desired in terms of their design and management. . . . The recommendations of the Council, however, do not represent an attack on our social programs. On the contrary, the Council firmly believes that our social programs are not only affordable but a prerequisite to economic growth. (Ibid.)

Similarly, the Macdonald Commission states that equity is an important objective guiding its report:

> Commissioners have concluded that our social policies should serve four values:
> - Equity in the distribution of rewards based on social justice which leads us to prefer outcomes different from those that market mechanisms generate.
> - Security that provides a degree of protection against such risks as illness or the dislocations of a dynamic economy.
> - Opportunity to participate in the economy in order to improve our position and to sustain our self-identity which, in the modern world, is closely tied to work.
> - Sharing, the moral expression of our feelings of community, from which derive our sense of equity and our willingness to provide reasonable security for one another and to distribute employment opportunity fairly. (1985, Vol.I, pp.46-47)

These objectives were to be pursued without compromising efficiency. Indeed, the Commission is quite candid about the relationship between equity and efficiency, stating: "We properly, therefore, apply efficiency criteria to our social policy instruments and, other things being equal, prefer instruments which impose minimum constraints on market mechanisms and thus minimum constraints on efficiency."

The Economic Council supports unemployment insurance on equity grounds, yet recommends its re-examination: "The 'safety net' against the hardships of unemployment has a number of faults, not the least of which is the fact that it tends to encourage the unemployed to stay in slow-growth regions" (1983, p.68). Similarly, the Macdonald Commission recommends cutbacks in unemployment insurance benefits for all but those in the lowest-income bracket and replacement with another program, which it says "will offer adjustment assistance for Canadians, provided that they are willing to move or to undertake retraining to improve their employment prospects. Entitlement to use the [program] must be based on willingness to undertake adaptive behavior" (1985, Vol.I, p.54). As these examples show, the political economists of this school are not opposed to promoting social equity through state intervention, as long as efficiency is not sacrificed.

This virtually exclusive concentration on economic factors leads Keynesian-welfare economists to serious omissions. The fact that they do not include power in their analysis, for example, leads them to make sterile recommendations that are virtually impossible to implement in a democratic society. In such a society, of course, questions about who will demand what from the state and how these demands will be articulated, interpreted, and responded to are answered through the democratic process and associated state institutions. States are affected by these processes and cannot simply refuse proposals for action that enjoy societal support on the grounds that they are inefficient. The reverse is also true: states cannot adopt proposals for action, however efficient they may seem in theory, if they do not enjoy societal support for this action.

There is also an inherent tension between the Keynesian-welfare emphasis on efficiency and the compromise on measures to promote equity. No theoretical argument in their repertoire can indicate exactly how much efficiency can be sacrificed to promote equity. To suggest that the government ought to correct inequities up to the point beyond which the public finds the resulting inefficiencies unacceptable does not make theoretical sense. If that were to be the case, then why stop at income distribution? Why not allow the same level of state intervention in every area of society? Such inherent contradictions are reflected in their policy suggestions, which satisfy neither the neoconservatives nor those committed to greater social equality in distribution of wealth.

Neoconservative Political Economy

While the neoconservatives form only a fringe element in Canadian politics and academia, their vociferousness makes up for their small numbers. They argue for economic efficiency, stress freedom, and disparage any argument based on equality other than the equality of opportunity to engage in market exchange or cast votes. They see measures to promote equality in income distribution – such as minimum wage laws, progressive taxation, government-provided universal health care, and education – as curtailments of individual freedom. They view the extension of the welfare state as an extension of the concept of "social justice," which gained currency in the twentieth century.

As the Fraser Institute notes in its submission to the Macdonald Commission: "The basic and most destructive implication of this concept [social justice] was that long-held doctrines of individual justice could be, indeed had to be, set aside in favour of the 'higher goal' of justice for some collective" (Fraser Institute, 1983,p.3). The Institute blames efforts to emphasize social justice over individual freedom as the main source of problems in the modern political economy. Therefore, it encouraged the Commission to move towards "a renewed emphasis on individualism, a deep skepticism about the ability of government to do good and a growing awareness of government's ability to cause harm" (ibid., p.6). It suggested that instead of proposing new solutions for the government to follow, the Commission should recommend a cutback in the level of government intervention in the economy.

On the macro-economic front, the neoconservatives are unabashedly monetarist. The Fraser Institute blames the high unemployment of the 1970s and 1980s on high wages, not deficiency of aggregate demand (Grubel and Bonnici, 1986). The Institute has repeatedly attacked inflation as the main economic problem affecting Canada. Following its opposition to any government measure, it opposed wage and price controls during the mid-1970s because of their coercive nature (Walker et al., 1976).

The scholars associated with the Fraser Institute are similarly opposed to micro-economic interventions. They are vehemently opposed to industrial policies that would promote manufacturing industries (Watkins and Walker, 1981; Palda, 1979, 1984). Commenting on Alberta's industrial strategy, Michael Walker states: "The economic structure of the province is predominantly reflecting the effects of market forces and not a conjunction of factors the effects of which the actions of the provincial government can offset. The consequence is that intervention to foster diversification may be very expensive but in the end ineffectual" (1984, p.xiii). The Institute views the demand for greater spending on research and development as no more than a selfish ploy by the Canadian scientific community to improve its income and employment opportunities at public expense (Palda, 1979).

One of the chief targets of neoconservative attacks is the trade union movement, which is viewed as developing coercive organizations that prevent market forces from setting wages. In the neoconservative view, trade unions artificially bid up wages, which causes economic inefficiencies and fuels inflation. The neoconservatives are not, however, opposed to monopolies – which would also seem to bid the prices of outputs above market levels – because they believe that even a monopolistic firm is under competitive pressure. When competition is lacking, it is because of government policies inhibiting competition.

One of the more creative applications of neoconservative theory centres around government measures to promote non-discrimination in the workplace (Block and Walker, 1985). Neoconservatives argue that employers with the proclivity to discriminate have to pay more to hire workers of their preferred race, sex, or colour. This leads those employers to become uncompetitive with the companies that do not discriminate and hence do not have to bear the additional wage costs. Ultimately, the discriminators will stop indulging in their prejudices or be wiped out by competition. The analysis does not address how this process will occur in an economy that has more than enough unemployed workers from the employers' preferred group looking for jobs.

On international trade, the neoconservative position is similar to that of the Keynesian-welfare liberals. The Canada-U.S. Free Trade Agreement was supported equally fervently by both the schools; indeed, it was backed by virtually all liberal political economists.

Unlike the mainstream liberals who are constantly haunted by their conflicting adherence to economic efficiency through the market and their recognition of the need for state intervention, the neoconservatives have no such dilemmas. Nor do they need to cope with the difficulties of state planning, having ruled that out in the first place.

Post-Keynesian Political Economy

The post-Keynesian school emerged in Canada in the 1970s for the same reasons as it did in other industrialized nations: the simultaneous existence of high rates of inflation and unemployment at the macro-economic level and problems faced by many declining industries at the micro-economic level. These problems refused to respond to measures inspired by Keynesian and welfare economics – measures that, as we've seen, came under attack from neoconservatives as being at the root of the problem. The post-Keynesian solution of enhanced state intervention appealed to liberal analysts who found the neoconservative prescriptions unacceptable because of the hardships they imposed on the weaker sections of society. Post-Keynesianism also appealed to many social democrats and staples theorists because it offered solutions to reduce U.S. dominance of the Canadian economy and further the interests of the subordinate classes without overthrowing capitalism. Many of the scholars associated with the Canadian Institute for Economic Policy, Science Council of Canada, New Democratic Party, and Canadian Labour Congress can be classified as post-Keynesian in their approaches to political economy.

After identifying high levels of unemployment and slow economic growth rates as the main problems of the Canadian economy in the early

1980s, John Cornwall and Wendy Maclean, two prominent post-Keynesians in Canada, offer this "package" of solutions:

First, an incentive incomes policy, preferably with some measure of real wage insurance, must be designed that will receive widespread support from labour. Second, a stimulative aggregate demand policy is needed as evidence of a commitment to full employment, coupled with assurances that there will be no cutbacks in the welfare state. Third, there must be an industrial policy that incorporates as a long-term strategy the development of institutions and attitudes fostering cooperative industrial relations. Fourth, programs must also be included that greatly assist research and development, and encourage investment in the manufacture of goods with high income elasticities of demand, so that new products and processes will allow faster productivity growth and the development and expansion of international markets for Canadian manufactures. (1984, p.96)

They expect adoption of these recommendations to stimulate economic growth, thus reducing unemployment, without fuelling inflation. Post-Keynesians, however, are aware that adoption of these policies would require fundamental changes in attitudes among existing interests in society: "These changes involve a vastly different attitude by capital, labour and the general public towards the federal government and its role in ensuring the proper functioning of the Canadian economy, and a radical change in attitudes that employers and labour groups now hold towards each other" (ibid., p.97).

Post-Keynesians see the public opposition to expansion of the state's role in the economy as a problem that must be overcome. Similarly, capital and labour must give up their antagonistic attitudes towards each other. Exactly how this change in attitudes is going to come about remains a mystery.

The Canadian Institute for Economic Policy's submission to the Macdonald Commission contains this line of analysis and offers similar recommendations for improvement (Rotstein, 1984). It opposes monetarism and trade liberalization and, instead, proposes an incomes policy and some protection for domestic import-competing industries. It also calls for an interventionist industrial policy to channel investments away from declining industries towards growing industries and research and development. As a part of its industrial policy it recommends restrictions on foreign firms operating in Canada. It recognizes that its comprehensive battery of measures would require a broad "social consensus" lacking in Canada, but again it offers no concrete proposals for overcoming this problem.

Many former members of the New Democratic Party have also proposed post-Keynesian solutions to Canada's economic problems in opposition to the NDP's more orthodox Keynesian programs and policies. In his book *Rethinking the Economy* (1984) James Laxer argues the post-Keynesian position strongly. He locates the problems faced by the Canadian economy in the country's weak manufacturing sector and high levels of U.S. investment. To rebuild the economy he proposes a concerted effort to reduce the influence of U.S. capital, especially through the mobilization of domestic savings by the federal government to promote investment in "those sectors of the economy where domestic and export markets have great potential." This effort would be led by public enterprises and would involve restrictions placed on the activities of foreign corporations operating in Canada. Laxer, like other post-Keynesians, suggests that the labour movement will have to abandon its historical reliance on the adversarial system and learn to co-operate with government and business in accepting technological change. The union movement's emphasis should shift from preservation of working conditions and jobs to aiding labour adjustment through retraining.

Once again, however, this version of a post-Keynesian analysis has little to say about the resilience of political and social institutions and their capabilities for resisting change. The analysis ignores the fact that Canada does not have the institutional base required for the co-ordination and co-operation of the state, labour, and capital in establishing government policy directions – no matter how imperative it is for the growth and development of Canadian society that they do co-operate.

Note

1 The classical economists were surprisingly candid in admitting how people derived their income in capitalism and how the arrangement discriminated against labour. On various occasions Smith said that rent and profits were "deductions" from the produce of labour, that landlords "love to reap where they never sowed," and that their profits "bear no proportion to the quantity, the hardship, or the ingenuity of the capitalist's labour of inspection and direction." He observed that in a contest between capitalists and workers for higher income, the workers always lose because they do not have the savings to hold out for long against the capitalists. Although Ricardo was a much more detached scholar than Smith, even his theory showed the inverse relationship between profits and wages. Furthermore, he was aware that the introduction of machines in the production process reduced the wages fund available to pay labour while increasing the level of profit. John Stuart Mill went further than the others and saw private property as the result of conquest and violence. He was appalled by the "suffering and injustices" of capitalism but at the same time believed that it could be improved by limiting population growth and making education universally available.

CHAPTER 3

Socialist Political Economy

If liberal political economy is dominant among the capitalist nations at the level of both theory and practice, for many of the remaining nations of the world socialist political economy has served as the dominant model. Nearly a third of the world's population has been ruled by governments calling themselves socialist. Even in capitalist nations, especially in Europe, there are or have been governments that profess to be socialist. In Canada, the New Democratic Party – which at various times has ruled British Columbia, Saskatchewan, Manitoba, and Ontario – practises a form of socialism. In nations where there is no socialist party in government or forming a strong opposition party, a good number of intellectuals and workers are working towards overcoming this weakness.

Socialism is a critical theory: it developed out of the same roots in classical political economy as liberalism did, but it has always maintained a guarded distance from capitalism. Unlike liberal political economy, socialist political economy has never embraced capitalism as a model but has instead focused on the inequities of a market system of exchange and how that system operates to the benefit of some groups and individuals in society, at the expense of others.

This has been socialist political economy's greatest strength and its greatest weakness. It has been its greatest strength because from the very beginning it has pointed out the gaps between liberal theory and the actual practices of market societies. Unlike liberal political economy, socialist political economy has never endorsed the neoclassical model of a perfectly competitive economy and has not had to debate the validity of incorporating market failures into abstract models of market behaviour. For similar reasons, socialist political economy from the outset has recognized the importance of the state's extensive activities in the market. It did not require a major "revolution" in socialist thinking to incorporate state actions into its theory of political economy, as was the case with twentieth-century liberal political economy. Socialist political economy, then, fared much better than did liberal political economy in its description of the workings of a capitalist political economy. From the outset socialist political economy could deal fully with questions about monopolies, market failures, and state "interventions," questions that perplexed and continue to perplex liberal political economy.

That same critical stance proved also to be the theory's greatest weakness, because the general condemnation of capitalism led inevitably to the proposal that capitalism be replaced with an entirely different system of organizing production in society: a socialist or communist system based on extensive if not complete state control over productive activities.

Rather than propose reforms to capitalist economies or engage in extensive empirical investigations into how such economies have developed, most socialist political economists have chosen simply to criticize the existing system and to suggest that the problems can only be solved by capitalism's complete replacement. Exactly what this replacement would look like is unclear, and so is the method by which capitalism would be overthrown and socialism achieved. Much work in socialist political economy, therefore, has concentrated on these questions, [1] for the most part forfeiting the field for suggestions about moderate or piecemeal reforms to liberal political economy. Not surprisingly but somewhat incongruously, many moderate socialists have been heavily influenced by liberal political economy and have embraced many of the analyses and positions put forward by Keynesian-welfare liberals calling for limited increases in state-led economic development. In fact, in Canada and elsewhere, the positions and reforms advocated by the most moderate socialists – social democrats – are virtually indistinguishable from those of mainstream Keynesians.

As a theory, socialism is an alternative to the liberal theory, with its own comprehensive explanation of the interrelationships between politics and economy. Moreover, socialist theory does not rest on the study of the allocation and distribution of resources by an abstract market mechanism, as does the liberal theory, but also inquires into the historical, social, and political conditions under which markets operate, whom they benefit, and how they can be changed. While this approach provides a better understanding of political economy, it also presents problems for students trying to understand the theory itself. Problems of understanding are further increased by the substantial differences among the various socialist theorists themselves.

Nevertheless there is a core of interrelated concepts that inform all socialist political economy, a core formed on the basis of the works of Karl Marx (1818-83) and his long-time collaborator Friedrich Engels (1820-95) and, especially, on the basis of the critique of capitalism put forward by Marx in his work *Das Kapital*. Volume one of *Das Kapital* was published in 1871, at about the same time marginalist and neoclassical economics were being established. Volumes two and three were published posthumously by Engels.

Socialist political economy must be understood in the context of its beginnings in the mid-nineteenth century, when capitalism was already a dominant economic system in many European nations. While capitalism increased the nations' total wealth wherever it spread, earlier expectations that this would improve general living conditions began to appear increasingly illusory. Instead, capitalism created an ever-expanding working class dependent on the capitalists for meagre wages. The extreme disparities in wealth between the capitalists and the working class led many early socialist thinkers to develop ideas about improving the living conditions of the working poor. Their recognition that the individualism fostered by capitalism was at the root of the problem led them to propose social co-operation instead of market competition as a solution. They believed that once the unfairness of the system was pointed out, the capitalists would show compassion and curb their excesses. Marx, however, believed that it was not the attitude of the capitalists but the nature of capitalism itself that was at the root of the problem and that the only solution was its replacement by socialism. Thus, just as liberal political-economic theory can be understood as an attempt to maintain and promote capitalism, the socialist theory based on the works of Marx can be seen as an effort to demonstrate capitalism's weaknesses and accelerate its demise.

After Marx's death various efforts were made by socialist political economists to apply his methodology and conceptual analysis of the structure and dynamics of a capitalist economy to the investigation of the continuing development of such a political-economic system. Discussing the development of socialist political economy after Marx, however, is a daunting challenge; writings in this area have been many, and many of them are inconsistent. Our task is made somewhat simpler, however, by our focus on the institutions of states and markets and their effects on the production and distribution of societal resources. Many of the writings in the socialist tradition since Marx have been concerned with other elements of his writings, such as their methodological, philosophical, ontological, and epistemological bases, rather than with questions pertaining to the production and distribution of wealth in society (Jay, 1973; McLellan, 1979). Nor, since the Canadian political economy is a capitalist market economy, do we need to examine the plentiful works of those scholars working in socialist countries who have grappled with the complexities of applying Marxist principles to actually existing socialist economies (Berry, 1977; Nove, 1986; Brus, 1973; Horvat, 1982; Radice, 1975).

Two post-Marx socialist theories are, however, relevant here. The first concerns efforts made by socialists such as Vladimir Lenin and Rosa Luxemburg prior to World War I to expand Marx's insights to the global level in their evaluation of the workings of the then imperial-colonial international political economy. These writings and insights in turn have had a great influence on the development in Africa, Asia, and Latin America of theories of *dependency* or *underdevelopment*, which once again, following the demise of the old international system during World War II, attempted to link developments in peripheral countries with economic activities originating in the developed world.

The second strain of socialist political economy is a *social democratic* variant concerned with theorizing the transition of capitalist economies from a competitive to a "monopoly" stage. Such writings and theories focus attention not on the extension of capitalist relations from Europe throughout the world but on the implications for domestic politics of the increasing concentration of capital and the decline of the competitive capitalist economy that Marx had so thoroughly analyzed. These analyses of the development of *monopoly capital* have had a great influence on the development of contemporary European and North American socialist thought.

Fundamental Tenets

Socialist political economy is based on Marx's historical analysis of economic institutions and processes. Marx criticized liberal economists for lacking a historical perspective, which led them to view capitalism as a timeless, universal economic system. Had they studied history, Marx argued, they would have found that capitalism was preceded by other forms or *modes of production*, such as feudalism and slavery, each of which grew out of a previous form of political-economic organization. It follows that capitalism itself is subject to change and eventual replacement by another system, which Marx argued would be socialist or communist in nature – that is, in which property and production would be socially or communally owned and controlled.

For Marx, the specific details of the various modes of production vary across nations and time because of the particularities of each nation's history. Marx was also aware that in the period of transition from one mode of production to another, the economy and society will exhibit the features of several modes. Because different modes of production may co-exist for lengthy periods of time, the form of society existing at any particular point in time, or *conjuncture*, is sometimes referred to as a *social formation*.

Marx viewed history as humankind's struggle with nature to improve its living conditions. Unlike animals, human beings do not adapt to nature as they find it. Instead, they constantly seek to change it and improve their living conditions. According to Marx, the material or economic structure of production was the "base" of other aspects of the society – such as laws, politics, ideology – which formed a secondary "superstructure." These attributes of human society vary according to the particular nature of the social formation present in any given country. The fundamental "base-superstructure" relationship, however, always exists and is captured in Marx's reference to the superstructure as the *relations of production*. The relations of production have their roots in, and are determined by, the material conditions, or *means of production*. In Marx's own words, "The mode of production of material life conditions the social, political, and intellectual life process in general. It is not the consciousness of men that determines their being, but, on the contrary, their social being that determines their consciousness" (Marx, [1859] 1974a, p.182). This statement must not be understood in terms of economic causes and superstructural effects, which would amount to a crude form of economic determinism or "economism," which Marx himself rejected. Rather, Marx merely intended to indicate, without denying that the two are mutually interactive and interacting, that the economic structure is more fundamental than political and social institutions and ideas in the analysis of human history. Recognizing the common misunderstanding of Marx's position and its reduction to "economism," Engels explains it thus:

> According to the materialist conception of history, the *ultimately* determining element in history is the production and reproduction of real life. More than this neither Marx nor I have ever asserted. Hence if somebody twists this into saying that the economic element is the *only* determining one, he transforms that proposition into a meaningless, abstract, senseless phrase. The economic situation is the basis, but the various elements of the superstructure . . . also exercise their influence upon the course of the historical struggles, and in many cases preponderate in determining their form [though not the substance]. ([1890] 1972, p.640)

In fact, for Marx and Engels and all socialist thinkers influenced by their works, the motive force in history is essentially political – as suggested by Engels's reference to the importance of "historical struggles."

For Marx, the nature of social groups is intimately linked with the means and relations of production found in society. At least theoretically, each mode of production involves the differentiation of the populace into those who control economic surpluses and those who generate them. These two groups or *classes* are engaged in a constant struggle with each other over the division of surplus. The exact character of class stratification and the nature of class conflict in any given society, however, differ in the different modes of production, depending on the innate characteristics of each mode. Thus feudalism generates its own unique classes and class struggle, as does capitalism. The number of classes and their relationship to each other are made more complex by the fact that different modes of production can co-exist in different social formations, making the analysis of the class content of any society a complex and difficult matter.

Each mode of production has its own technology and social relations for organizing production, and these have a pervasive impact on every aspect of the society. Marx regards the history of humanity as a succession of different modes of production. Each of them were appropriate in their time but they gradually lost their usefulness and were eventually replaced as a result of *class struggles*. Thus, for example, feudalism was marked by a technology and landlord-serf/tenant relationship suitable for agricultural production, and the social, political, ideological, and religious ideas and institutions of the time were geared towards its maintenance. Over time, the feudal mode of production and especially the feudal relations of production became a barrier to increased production because they prevented the reorganization of production and the introduction of more productive technologies. Struggles between the peasantry, the aristocracy, and the emerging urban trading and manufacturing class led to the demise of the old system and its replacement with a new system, capitalism, in which the relations of production corresponded more closely with the ability of society to produce more goods. Production in the new system was based on, among other things, private property, labour mobility, economic and political dominance of the capitalists, and the extensive use of machines and a specialized division of labour. Again, these features of the capitalist mode of production were reflected in liberal theory, government policy, and an ideology that served to legitimize and "rationalize" the existing political-economic order.

In Marxist theory, then, class is understood somewhat differently from its meaning in everyday use. The term is often used to distinguish between the rich and the poor, the classes of "haves" and "have nots." It is also used to refer to those wielding power and those excluded from it, the classes of powerful and powerless. Marxist theory is only indirectly concerned with wealth or power. It refers directly to the "groups of people sharing a common relationship to the means of production." In every mode of production (except the "primitive" mode in ancient times and the postcapitalist "communist" mode) there are people who own the tools and facilities of production and those who work for them. The owners are in a unique position to exploit the workers. In feudalism, the landlords owned land, which serfs or tenants tilled, and a part of the resulting produce accrued to the owners. Capitalism, too, is marked by the existence of two broad classes, the capitalist class and the working class; the former owns the means of production, and the latter works for wages. Within the two broad classes, there are numerous subclasses or "class fractions" that occupy intermediate positions. These include managers, who do not own factories but act as the representatives of the capitalists at the factory. There are also small-time capitalists, such as corner-grocery-store owners, who own their own means of production but do not usually employ workers. Marx sometimes referred to this broad grouping of capitalists and those sharing similar economic interests as the *bourgeoisie*. Correspondingly, there are unemployed, poor, and self-employed artisans who neither work for anyone nor exploit others and generally have interests in common with the working class. Marx sometimes referred to this broad category of workers and those sharing similar economic circumstances as the *proletariat*.

The existence of classes at the polar ends of the production process (as well as at positions in between) breeds class conflicts. As Marx puts it in the *Communist Manifesto*: "The history of all heretofore existing societies is the history of class struggles." The existing distribution of the ownership of the means of production, and the wealth and power that go with it, are opposed by those who are denied its benefits and defended by those who gain from it. At times this precipitates into open revolts or revolutions. More often, the struggles manifest themselves in more subtle forms, such as political, ideological, and religious conflicts. Examples of such struggles include the support for liberalism by the bourgeoisie, and opposition to Sunday-shopping laws by small-store owners or to minimum wage laws by all employers. Similarly, the support for socialism, old age pensions, unemployment insurance, progressive taxation, and collective bargaining rights by the proletariat can also be seen as a manifestation of class struggle. Marx does not attribute the source of the conflicts to the heartlessness of the landlords or capitalists but to the intrinsic nature of a mode of production.

Marxist, Leninist, and Social Democratic Theory

Marx's Political Economy

Like the classical economists, Marx set about to inquire into the origin of value. When a commodity is produced, he asked, what gives it a value? This is an issue that liberal economists from the marginalists onward have side-stepped, assuming that value was the same as price, which is determined by the forces of demand and supply. But Marx, and Ricardo before him, faced the question head on and concluded that labour is the source of all value. Marx uses several hundred pages in *Das Kapital* to explain how he arrived at his *labour theory of value*, and here we will simply note the major strands in his reasoning.

Unlike Smith and, especially, Ricardo, Marx is not concerned about showing labour as the common element in all products, which would enable labour to be the key for determining the exchange ratio of goods. For example, two chairs exchange for one desk, or a chair sells for five dollars and a desk for ten dollars because it takes twice as much labour-time to produce a desk compared to a chair. Marx goes beyond this distinction and shows that the creation of value entails the creation of *surplus value*, which, under capitalism, accrues to capitalists as profit.

Marx argues that in the long run the value (or *true* price) of a commodity is equal to the amount of direct and indirect labour embodied in it; the surplus labour (which is what yields profit) is included as a part of direct labour. While the concept of direct labour (which Marx calls "variable capital") is the same as what we commonly understand by the word labour, indirect labour ("constant capital" in Marx's phraseology) is understood as the labour embodied in the various capital and intermediate goods involved in the production of a commodity; for example, machinery and raw materials. Marx regards capital as indirect labour because, as in Ricardo's theory, it embodies "frozen" labour or labour that was performed in the past. For Marx, surplus value, which is something akin to profit, is the result of the surplus labour employed in production. Thus, for Marx the value of a commodity (C) is equal to the sum of capital costs (c), labour costs (v), and surplus labour (s): all derivatives of labour. The formula for value is

$$C = c + v + s$$

The unit of labour that Marx uses in determining the value of each commodity is the "average," or "abstract," amount of labour required to produce all commodities in the economy. To determine the labour needed to produce a commodity he averages the different skill levels required in various industries to arrive at an abstract standard of measurement. In this computation, every instance of skilled labour is reduced to a simple multiple of unskilled labour.

Because value is understood as a sum of abstract labour embodied in a commodity, it is not exactly the same as price, which is determined in the market by the forces of demand and supply. Marx was well aware of the difference between value and price and clearly recognized that the prices of individual commodities could diverge from their value in the short run, due to oversupply or underproduction; and that even in the long run they could diverge systematically because of the differing levels of capital required to produce different commodities.

Marx recognized, as did the classical economists, that profit is the engine of economic growth in capitalism. He, therefore, made it the centrepiece of his analysis, although he rarely uses the word. Instead, he speaks of surplus value, because he regards the amount as a surplus over and above what capitalists pay for labour's contribution to production. In capitalism, the means of production (machines and raw materials, for example) are owned by the capitalists while the workers own labour power, or the capacity to work. Lacking ownership of the means of production, the workers cannot engage in production on their own and, hence, must sell their labour to the capitalists or starve. While the capitalists need labour just as much to carry out production, they are not faced with starvation if they interrupt it. The relative weakness of the workers allows capitalists to exploit them by denying them a full reward for their contribution to production. As Adam Smith notes in *The Wealth of Nations*, "In the long-run the workman may be as necessary to his master as his master is to him; but the necessity is not so immediate" (Smith, [1776] 1987, p.169).

Building upon these assumptions, Marx argues that capitalists pay the workers not an amount equivalent to their creation of value but an amount necessary for the worker's subsistence; and that capitalists appropriate the rest as profit. By *subsistence*, Marx means some socially defined consumption norm rather than physical subsistence, even though at times he appears to suggest the latter. Marx was aware that it was theoretically possible for workers to bid for wages above subsistence levels because of their indispensability to production, but he argues they were not usually able to do so over the long term because of the existence of a large pool of unemployed workers (the "reserve army of the unemployed," as he calls it) who are instrumental in driving wages down to a subsistence level.

To understand how surplus value is created and appropriated, imagine a worker who has to perform six hours of work to subsist. A capitalist who owns the means of production can compel that worker to work for ten hours while paying for only six. The value of what is produced during the extra four hours is a surplus over and above what the worker is paid and accrues to the capitalist as "surplus labour," or profit.

In Marx's theory, the employment of capital itself creates no additional value, and hence no surplus value, because the surplus value created in its production had already been appropriated by the original capitalists. He regards labour as the only source of value, including the part of it that accrues to the capitalists as profits. Thus, the only way a capitalist can increase surplus value is by increasing the productivity of labour or by forcing workers to work longer hours; that is, through the generation of *relative* and *absolute surplus value*, respectively.

Once the capitalist mode of production is established, it gradually spreads to every sphere of economic activity because of its efficiency in organizing production and generating surplus value. The capitalists do not, however, consume the entire income derived from appropriation of surplus value. The logic of capitalism is such that they must save a good part of the surplus to be able to invest in expanding production, in hiring more capital, more sophisticated technology, and more labour, so they can accumulate yet more surplus. The nature of competition is such that the capitalists must be increasingly competitive or face extinction at the hands of their competitors. The resulting increase in accumulation of capital, while essential for the maintenance and growth of capitalism, also sets in motion forces that undermine its existence. According to Marx, the unrelenting competition and accumulation have four consequences: economic concentration, the tendency of the rate of profit to fall, sectoral imbalances, and the alienation and growing misery of the working class. Together these tendencies cause crises of capitalism and its eventual demise.

As capitalism develops and becomes more competitive, only the strong firms survive, while the weak are either absorbed or decimated by the strong. Moreover, as technology improves, so too does the cost of starting a new business or operating an existing one increase. New firms cannot enter the market because of the high start-up costs, and the weaker existing firms disappear because they do not have the accumulated capital to finance the purchase of new technology. What remains are large firms, which are more competitive because of their lower per unit costs (referred to as "efficiency of scale" by economists) and their greater ability to finance the purchase of the latest technology. This process is referred to as *economic* or *industrial concentration*.

The increasing capital-intensity of production creates problems of its own. No doubt a firm introducing a new technology can make additional profits; but this increase is only temporary, lasting only until competing firms adopt the same or better technology and whittle away the windfall profits. The process continues, and no firm comes out better as a result. Another, and more ominous, consequence is the increase in the capital-to-labour ratio. The decreasing proportion of labour to capital yields a declining rate of profit because each new investment, unless accompanied by increases in labour productivity, generates the same amount of surplus value as before, simply replacing "living" labour with the "dead" labour congealed in machinery. Thus, when profits are compared to investments, higher investments produce only a similar amount of value and therefore the ratio of profit to investment declines. This leads Marx to conclude that capitalism is inherently marked by the law of the tendency for the rate of profit to fall. The tendency can be offset, or even reversed, however, by counteracting measures.

Capitalists can prevent the rate of profit from falling by increasing the exploitation of the workers, which can be done by increasing the hours or intensity of work – for example, by speeding up assembly-line production. These measures increase the level of surplus value. Similarly, the increase in the number of unemployed, partly caused by labour-displacing technology, may temporarily allow capitalists to pay wages below subsistence levels, thus also building up surplus value. Another factor offsetting the tendency of the rate of profit to fall is any decline in the price of capital goods due to increased demand, which allows economies of scale to be realized in the production of these goods. This decline enables firms to increase the volume of machinery employed in production without raising the capital-to-labour ratio. The final counteracting influence is an increase in foreign trade, which enlarges profits by opening new markets. Foreign trade also allows cheaper imports, which can reduce the cost of subsistence. Imperial expansion, so prominent until the 1950s, creates a captive market and, like international trade, increases the level of surplus value in the metropole through the exploitation of labour in the periphery.

The increasing capital-to-labour ratio in production also creates sectoral imbalances and disproportions in the economy. Replacing workers by machines means reducing workers' incomes, even though the level of production continues as before. The upshot is reduced total consumption compared to total production (called "underconsumption"), which causes economic recessions. Yet another serious impact of increasing capital-intensity in production is the disproportionate growth of the capital goods sector compared to the consumer goods sector: productive capacity expands because of the introduction of new machines while the level of consumption declines because of the increasing unemployment generated by the introduction of the labour-saving technology.

The *alienation of workers* is yet another feature of capitalism. While alienation refers to a psychological state, the condition ultimately derives from the material conditions of capitalism. Human labour is not just a mass of energy but a creative force, and it should give a sense of satisfaction to those who engage in it. But in capitalism, human labour ceases to be creative and personal. It becomes just another commodity to be bought and sold. Even the product of labour does not belong to the worker but to the employer. There is a separation between workers and their labour, which breeds alienation, which intensifies as capitalism becomes even more competitive and less personal. The flip side of the rising concentration of capital, according to Marx, is "the law of increasing misery" of the proletariat. As he puts it:

> Labour produces works of wonder for the rich but nakedness for the worker. It produces palaces, but only hovels for the worker. It produces beauty but cripples the worker; it replaces labour by machines but throws a part of the workers ... to a barbaric labour and turns the other part into madness. It produces culture, but also imbecility and cretinism for the worker. (Marx [1844], *Economic and Philosophical Manuscripts*, in McLellan, 1972, p.136)

In statements like these, Marx was not simply referring to a decline in wages or purchasing power, though he did use the word "pauperization" in his earlier pamphlet, the *Communist Manifesto*. He was also referring to an increase in alienation and general misery, understood in a psychological sense.

Before Marx other scholars and pundits had predicted the demise or increasing crisis of capitalism. Some classical political economists, such as Thomas Malthus, prophesied that the growth in production and income would cause a growth in population, which would impose increasing strains on natural resources and eventually lead to a stagnant or declining economy. Utopian socialists, such as Robert Owen (1771-1858) and Simonde de Sismondi (1773-1842), had similarly predicted that competition among capitalists would bring wages down far enough to cause a crisis of underconsumption. Marx's prediction differed in that it was based on concrete historical analysis. He had no patience with conjectural theories of increasing population based on the assumption of the lack of sexual discipline among the poor (Malthus) or the evil intentions or ignorance of the capitalists that led them to exploit workers (Owen). Marx regarded the problems of capitalism as inherent in its very nature. The purpose of production in capitalism is to make profits, not to satisfy social needs.

In the words of Marx and Engels:

> For many a decade past, the history of industry and commerce is but the history of the revolt of modern productive forces against modern conditions of production.... The productive forces at the disposal of society no longer tend to further the development of the condition of bourgeois property; on the contrary they ... bring disorder into the whole of bourgeois society. (Marx and Engels [1948], *Manifesto of the Communist Party*, in Tucker, 1972, p.340)

This is undoubtedly very different from Adam Smith's view that the pursuit of private interests in capitalism promotes the interests of an entire society.

According to Marx, the efforts of capitalists to counter declining profit levels by increasing the exploitation of workers foster increased alienation of the proletariat, which bursts into open class war. The working class finally unites and overthrows capitalism, which it correctly views as the source of its problems and misery. Marx says little about the final state of the collapse of capitalism, except that it would involve violent revolution because the capitalists, supported by the state, would use repressive forces to quell the working-class challenge, which would in turn fuel working-class violence. It should be remembered, however, that Marx was not advocating violence but merely predicting the likely final days of capitalism.

By placing economics and politics in a broad historical and social context, the Marxist theory performs brilliantly. But its insights into broad trends have been at the expense of explaining the operation of the micro-level political economy. The Marxist theory does not precisely explain – perhaps is incapable of explaining – movements in prices, profits, employment, and inflation, the incidence of taxation, or the impact of technology. These are exactly the areas in which neoclassical economics excels.

It is also difficult to reconcile Marx's notions regarding the increased immiseration of workers and the prediction of the imminent collapse of capitalism with later historical developments. Socialist political economists after Marx have grappled with these later developments in capitalist societies, especially with the notion that the competitive capitalist economy that Marx described no longer exists and has been replaced by *monopoly capitalism*, in which a few large companies control production and are able to manipulate markets to their advantage.

The theory of monopoly capitalism is that the logic and functioning of capitalism inherently lead to the development of ever larger firms, which control greater and greater amounts of production. These producing firms are integrated horizontally and vertically within their sectors and, more importantly, across sectors as well. They come to dominate the economy and can draw state apparatuses into supporting their activities. This leads to a merger of financial and production companies and governments in what the Austrian social democrat Rudolph Hilferding called *finanzkapital* and what later U.S. theorists, following on the heels of elite theorist C. Wright Mills, termed the *military-industrial complex* (Hilferding, 1981; Baran and Sweezy, 1966). Two approaches to post-Marx socialist political economy attempted to deal with the development of monopoly capitalism in the years up to and including World War I. These are the approaches put forward by the Russian revolutionary leader Vladimir Lenin and the social democratic approach developed by trade union leaders in continental Europe.

Leninist Political Economy

Lenin's two major contributions to socialist political economy were his formalization of a theory of imperialism and his analysis of the role of the labour process in capitalist society. However, his writings on the labour process were to remain less significant than his writings on the imperial system, although his analysis of the introduction of mass production and assembly-line techniques influenced the writings of the Italian socialist Antonio Gramsci in the inter-war period (Gramsci, 1972). When those labour writings were rediscovered in the 1970s by U.S. and European socialists, they were integrated into an effort to revitalize socialist political economy by "returning to the basics," much the same way neoconservative liberal political economy returned to marginalist and neoclassical thought for its own inspiration.

International political economy found a much more prominent place in Lenin's work. Writing from what was then a peripheral nation, Lenin was concerned with understanding the location and role that Imperial Russia occupied in the international system of states and theorizing about the implications for Russian political and economic practice of this location. He was especially interested in the rapid expansion of the colonial trading networks of European powers in the late nineteenth century into African and Asian territories and wanted to understand both the causes of this development and its consequences for the precapitalist economic formations or political economies of the colonized territory. As he argues in his work, *Imperialism, The Highest Stage of Capitalism*: "Imperialism emerged as the development and direct continuation of the fundamental characteristics of capitalism in general . . . imperialism . . . represents a special stage in the development of capital" (Lenin, [1916] 1939b, p.88).

Lenin defines imperialism as a stage of capitalist development marked by the decline of competitive firms and the rise of monopoly corporations. He says that imperialism as a system of production has five principal features:

1. The concentration of production and capital has developed to such a high stage that it created monopolies which play a decisive role in economic life,
2. The merging of bank capital with industrial capital, and the creation, on the basis of this "finance capital" of a financial oligarchy,
3. The export of capital which has become extremely important as distinguished from the export of commodities.
4. The formation of international capitalist monopolies which share the world among themselves,
5. The territorial division of the whole world among the greatest capitalist powers is completed. (Ibid. p.89)

Imperialism, in Lenin's view, is intimately tied to the development of monopoly capitalism and especially to the issue of foreign investment. He argues that at earlier stages of the development of capitalism, companies had exported goods to the periphery and benefited from the high returns they could earn on this type of exchange. In the imperialist stage, however, capitalist firms penetrated foreign markets through investment, taking over and manipulating existing firms and production relations to earn higher profits. He states: "As long as capitalism remains what it is, surplus capital . . . will be used for the purpose of increasing . . . profits by exporting capital abroad to the backward countries. In these backward countries profits are usually high, for capital is scarce, the price of land is relatively low, wages are low, raw materials are cheap" (ibid., p.63). Rosa Luxemburg, a German socialist writing around the same time as Lenin, has a similar analysis. Unlike Lenin, she stresses the role that a competitive and not a monopoly capitalist economy plays in creating imperialism. For Luxemburg, pressures resulting from competition in the home market drive capitalist firms to seek out foreign markets (Luxemburg, 1964).

Regardless of the mechanism at work, Lenin's conclusions are shared by both authors. That is, at a certain point in capitalist development, to maintain profitability firms require access to cheap raw materials and expanded, secure markets for their finished products. Having outgrown the domestic marketplace, these firms enlist the state's coercive machinery to undertake foreign adventures and establish large protected trade blocks. This inevitably creates two phenomena: first, the uneven development of core and peripheral countries; and, second, intercapitalist rivalry and world war (Lenin, 1939b; Luxemburg, 1964).

These two conclusions concerning the operation of the global economy had significant implications for political practice in peripheral and metropolitan countries. First, it meant that development in the periphery was not possible within the existing colonial system and that such development awaited the overthrow of the colonial regime. Second, it meant that the working class had no interest in world wars caused by intercolonial or intercapitalist rivalries. These wars were aimed not at improving the conditions of either the metropolitan or colonial working class but simply at bettering the lot of one group of monopoly capitalists over another. Based on this analysis, following the Russian Revolution of 1917 Lenin withdrew the Soviet Union from World War I. The same analysis justified Lenin's and Stalin's later efforts to promote autarchic development in the Soviet Union. It also justified the Soviet government's continued support under both Lenin and Stalin for anticolonial struggles in many nations in Africa, Asia, and Latin America and formed a major part of the political-economic analysis proffered by socialists and nationalists in these countries.

Social Democratic Political Economy

A second important element of post-Marx socialist political-economic thought also involves the analysis of the demise of competitive capitalism and the transition to a new stage of monopoly capitalism. This is the social democratic analysis of monopoly capitalism developed by individuals such as Karl Kautsky, Eduard Bernstein, and other trade union leaders in continental Europe and Scandinavia prior to World War I (Bottomore, 1978; Przeworski, 1986).

Unlike Leninism, this analysis was put forward by theorists located in the most advanced capitalist economies of the day and focused exclusively on the implications of this development for political practice at the domestic level. While variants of Marxism-Leninism informed the practices of revolutionary parties in many industrializing countries, social democratic theory has served as the basis for the kind of parliamentary socialism practised by socialist and social democratic parties in many industrialized nations (Boggs and Plotke, 1980; Esping-Andersen, 1985).

Dismissed by Lenin as "revisionists," social democrats like Bernstein and Kautsky insisted that in fact they, and not Lenin, were following the analysis put forward by Marx in *Das Kapital*. In their writings they argue that the continuing expansion of capitalism in individual nation-states would inevitably lay the foundations for its overthrow and replacement by socialism by increasing the ranks of the working class until that class became a large majority in capitalist society. Unlike Lenin, who argues that capitalists will never accede to a peaceful transition of power to the workers, social democrats maintain that workers can gain political power through the democratic process as long as they are organized to vote as a block and support workers' parties in parliamentary elections. As such, they place a great deal of emphasis in their analyses on links between the trade union movement and workers' political parties operating in a democratic electoral system.

As Kautsky puts it in his work, *The Class Struggle*: "The more unbearable the existing system of production, the more evidently it is discredited . . . the greater will be the number of those who stream from the non-proletarian classes into the Socialist Party and, hand in hand with the irresistibly advancing proletariat, follow its banner to victory and triumph" (Kautsky, [1892] 1971, p.217).

The appropriate mechanism through which this growing strength will manifest itself in the overthrow of capitalism is the democratically elected legislature or parliament, which Kautsky argues could be used by workers to liberate themselves in the same fashion that capitalists had used it to exploit them. "Whenever the proletariat engages in parliamentary activity as a self-conscious class, parliamentarism begins to change its character. It ceases to be a mere tool in the hands of the bourgeoisie" (ibid., p.188).

For early social democrats, the workers would use parliamentary institutions to achieve the transition to socialism through the nationalization of private property by the state. However, over time social democrats gradually abandoned the proposal for the eventual replacement of the market by the state and instead developed a theory and practice of market-state co-existence based on careful state monitoring and regulation of market activities. Most social democratic parties in Western Europe and North America, as a result, were early adherents to, and remain enthusiastic supporters of, Keynesian welfare state policies.

Social democrats have a different view of the welfare state than do most liberal political economists, however. Throughout the twentieth century, social democrats developed an analysis of the development of modern political economies based on the assumption that the inherent tendency of such economies is to generate large non-capitalist classes that can use the democratic parliamentary process to curb and offset the advantages capital enjoys in the marketplace. As Michael Shalev argues, this analysis seeks to explain the development of "welfare capitalism" in Western capitalist nations through four basic propositions:

1. The welfare state is a class issue. Logically and historically, its principal proponents and defenders are movements of the working class.
2. Like other dimensions of public policy, the parameters of the welfare state are defined largely by the choices of governments.
3. In the capitalist democracies the most significant partisan cleavage (both in terms of voter alignment and policy positions) is that between parties of the working class and other parties. For the most part, only reformist (social-democratic or "labor") working class parties have been serious left-wing contenders for governmental power in these polities.
4. The capacity for reformist labor parties to emerge and grow to the point of coming to power is a function of the extent and coherency of

institutionalized working class mobilization in trade unions and political parties. The potential for such mobilization is largely predetermined by certain historically given structural characteristics of a society. (1983, p.320)

Both Marxist-Leninists and social democrats share many of the same fundamental assumptions about the nature of a capitalist economy; assumptions firmly grounded in Marx's analyses of capitalism. They differ in their orientation (Leninists towards the international system and social democrats towards the nation-state); in their prescriptions for political action drawn from their economic analyses (Leninists favour revolutionary action and social democrats favour a peaceful, parliamentary transition to socialism); and in their attitude towards the market (Leninists support its abolition or replacement by the state and social democrats support its regulation or control by the state). These differences have their roots in the different analyses of the class structure of monopoly capitalism put forward by each theory and in the very different interpretations of the state each has made.

Contemporary Debates

Dependency and Regulation Political Economy

In the post-World War I era Leninist analysis, with its emphasis on the exploitative aspects of European imperialism, figured prominently in the liberation movements of many African and Asian nations (Nkrumah, 1965; Mao Tse Tung, 1961; Fanon, 1965). It also had a major impact in long-independent Latin American countries in the post-World War II era as theorists worked at understanding why those countries had failed to develop in the same fashion as other independent countries.

The Latin American theorists focus on the Leninist insight that imperialism had perpetuated the uneven development of metropolitan and peripheral countries, as surplus earned from the peripheral countries accrued to metropolitan nations. They argue that despite their political sovereignty Latin American nations became tied economically to metropolitan nations through foreign ownership either of companies or of the capital and technological resources required for industrial development. This places peripheral countries in a position of dependency vis-à-vis advanced industrial nations and, dependency theorists argue, results in a kind of truncated industrial structure in these countries. They usually refer to this as a process of "underdevelopment" (Furtado, 1964; Frank, 1970; Cardoso, 1972). As Andre Gunder Frank explains in his book *Latin America: Underdevelopment or Revolution* (1970):

The now-developed countries were never underdeveloped, though they may have been undeveloped. It is also widely believed that the contemporary underdevelopment of a country can be understood as the product or reflection solely of its own economic, political, social, and cultural characteristics or structure. Yet historical research demonstrates that contemporary underdevelopment is in large part the historical product of past and continuing economic and other relations between the satellite underdeveloped and the now-developed metropolitan countries. Furthermore, these relations are an essential part of the structure and development of the capitalist system on a world scale as a whole. (p.4)

Although they share a Leninist heritage, dependency theorists are divided on a number of issues. There are disputes, for instance, concerning the empirical question of whether or not industrialization is proceeding at all in many peripheral countries or whether these countries are "sliding backwards" (Warren, 1973; Smith, 1979). There are also theoretical disputes concerning the nature of the mechanism by which metropolitan countries dominate the affairs and development of countries on the periphery – a significant debate that directly influences political practice in many developing countries looking to promote indigenous economic development. Some dependency theorists follow an orthodox Leninist line, arguing that the mechanism of control is the multinational corporation based in the metropole. Multinationals transfer surplus from the periphery to the metropole through unequal trade relations: companies use their market dominance to buy resources at below market value in the periphery and sell processed goods back to the peripheral country at inflated prices (Prebisch, 1968; Amin, 1974; Arrighi, 1978).

Others reason that at least part of the blame for underdevelopment lies in peripheral countries themselves. They point to the nature of the social formation present in many of those countries as the problem. That is, they argue that because of colonization and prohibitions on indigenous economic activity enacted and enforced by imperial military authorities, many developing countries had their economies disrupted and transformed into capitalist forms of economic activity; but this happened without the growth of an indigenous capitalist class as had occurred in the course of the capitalist transformation of the economies of the metropolitan nations. Instead, peripheral countries developed only a small bourgeoisie involved in trade relations with the metropole. This *comprador* fraction of the colonial capitalist class relied upon its connections with the metropole to build up its wealth and power and continues in the postcolonial period to resist any local efforts to sever links with the former imperial power. While multinational corporations remain the primary vehicle linking metropolitan and peripheral countries, in this view the social and political structure of peripheral countries facilitates, if not actively promotes, dependent relations (Poulantzas, 1974; Murray, 1978). As Fernando Cardoso argues:

In countries like Argentina, Brazil, Mexico, South Africa and India, and some others, there is an internal structural fragmentation connecting the most "advanced" parts of their economies to the international capitalist system. Separate although sub-ordinated to these advanced sectors, the backward economic and social sectors of the dependent countries then play the role of "internal colonies." (1972, p. 90)

Although disputes over these and other issues remain unresolved, dependency theory itself has been challenged from within the Leninist tradition by many analysts who feel that its insights rely far too heavily on critiques of trade and international relations and that it ignores significant changes in global industrial organization. This has led many socialist political economists to return to Marx and Lenin's focus on *production relations* rather than *exchange relations* (Jenkins, 1981). A new version of Leninist political economy thus concentrates on the relations of production or *labour process* present in capitalist societies and especially on the changes that have occurred in those relations since the writings of Marx and Lenin.

The labour-process approach to socialist political economy is based on a careful evaluation of how capital and labour interact in the production of surplus value in capitalist society and especially on the techniques used by capital to control the workforce. The "labour process" indicates the means by which raw materials are converted to products having use-values, which may be exchanged for each other as commodities.

Following Marx, theorists of the labour process note that there are only two ways in which surplus value can be created or increased – either as *absolute surplus value*, in which workers work longer hours and create additional value, or as *relative surplus value*, in which work is intensified so that it takes less time to produce an equivalent amount of goods. As analysts note, once a country has developed legislation limiting working hours, any increase in surplus value must come from relative surplus value or productivity increases, which arise mainly from the reorganization of work (Palloix, 1976).

Marx initially remarked on these changes in his discussions of the introduction of steam-powered machinery into factories, which completed the transition from the cottage "putting out" system of hand production to the factory system of "manufactories." Following Lenin and Gramsci, labour-process theorists argue that two and possibly three major changes to the organization of work had occurred in more recent times. The first change was the dismantling of the craft system of production of individual goods by skilled workers and the introduction of unskilled mass-production techniques. The second was the introduction of assembly lines to speed up production even more. These two developments in the labour process are known respectively as *Taylorism* and *Fordism* after the two individuals most responsible for their implementation in the United States: Frederick Winslow Taylor in the steel industry and Henry Ford in the automobile industry (Gramsci, 1972).

Pioneering work in this field was undertaken by Harry Braverman in his work *Labour and Monopoly Capital* (1974). Braverman notes that capitalism is founded on the ability of capitalists to extract surplus labour from production activities and that in the process of the development of capitalism, any vestiges of worker control over production that might give them the ability to regulate how much surplus value is produced have been removed. The primary technique that has accomplished this has been the gradual transfer of knowledge over the production process from workers to managers. As Braverman puts it:

> The capitalist mode of production systematically destroys all-around skills where they exist, and brings into being skills and occupations that correspond to its needs. Technical capacities are henceforth distributed on a strict "need to know" basis. The generalized distribution of knowledge of the productive process among all its participants becomes, from this point on, not merely "unnecessary," but a positive barrier to the functioning of the capitalist mode of production. (1974, p.82)

As a result, skilled labour is "de-skilled," a new strata of managers comes to control the production process, and individual workers are rendered powerless and inert in the face of capitalist expertise: "Every step in the labor process is divorced, so far as possible, from special knowledge and training and reduced to simple labor. Meanwhile, the relatively few persons for whom special knowledge and training are reserved are freed so far as possible from the obligations of simple labor. . . . This might even be called the general law of the capitalist division of labor" (ibid., pp.82-83).

Although many original labour-process theorists limit their analysis to the examination of changing modes of organizing production in various countries (Braverman, 1974; Edwards, 1979; Littler, 1982; Edwards, Reich, and Gordon, 1975; Price, 1984), later theorists have expanded these insights to a general theory of global economic development based on the concept of a regime of production or of regulation. This analysis, popularized by Michel Aglietta, Alain Lipietz, and others associated with the French research institute CEPREMAP, is often referred to as the *Regulation School* (Aglietta, 1979; Boyer, 1986; Lipietz, 1984a).

The regulation approach argues that a particular and specific set of political-economic relationships exists for each different stage in the labour process. Each set of relationships constitutes a regime of production designed to facilitate capital accumulation and avoid the economic and political crises associated with this process. Each "regime," therefore, involves application of the coercive powers of the state to control labour and aid in the reproduction and expansion of capital. In the modern era, they say, the regime must also maintain a certain consumption norm to ensure that the mass production of commodities does not result in oversupply and a decline in prices and profits. Hence, Keynesianism is seen as an outgrowth of the modern, "Fordist" regime of production (Brenner and Glick, 1991).

Regulation school political economy shifts the focus of investigation away from the emphasis on the implications of the development of monopoly capitalism found in Marxism-Leninism and dependency theory and back to an analysis of the mechanisms by which surplus value is produced and appropriated in capitalist society. As Michel Aglietta argues in *A Theory of Capitalist Regulation*, such an approach provides

> a theoretical foundation to the periodization of capitalism into successive stages of historical evolution. The criterion for this periodization is furnished by the changing content of relative surplus value: in the first stage, the transformation of the labour process without major alteration in the conditions of existence of the wage-earning class; in a second stage, the simultaneous revolutionization of both the labour process and the conditions of existence of the wage earning class . . . we reject the idea that the concentration of capital is the most fundamental process in the history of 20th century capitalism. The key theoretical process rather lies in a radical change in the conditions of reproduction of capital in general. (1987, p.21)

This analysis sets up a theoretical dispute between dependency and regulation socialist political economy, and efforts to integrate the two approaches have not been entirely successful. There are also continuing internal disputes within the labour-process approach. One of them concerns the characterization of the contemporary labour process. Many labour-process theorists see a third stage emerging with robots and electronic control devices being introduced into the workplace and traditional mass-production techniques being replaced by specialized manufacturing (Morris-Suzucki, 1984; Sabel, 1982; Reich, 1983). But not all labour-process theorists agree that this is a new stage of "post-Fordism," and some suggest that it is merely a variation on the Fordist model, or "neo-Fordism" (Murray, 1979).

Alain Lipietz has made an effort to synthesize the dependency approach with the regulation approach. Although empirical studies of the labour processes in different countries have led to the conclusion that Fordism or mass production has been extended around the world – generating the concept of "global Fordism" (Lipietz, 1982) – it is generally acknowledged that conditions and "regimes" vary in developed and developing countries (Gordon, 1988). Lipietz uses this insight to point out that in the most developed countries the expansion of capital results from productivity increases that generate increased relative surplus value, with the goods produced being consumed on the home market. Workers, therefore, require a high consumption level, which is provided by governments following Keynesian demand-management techniques and by financial institutions providing easy credit. In many developing countries, however, the regime is based on the generation of absolute surplus value, because workers lack political rights and surplus is generated through the export of manufactured products to developed countries. Workers in these countries are provided with minimal consumption norms, and surplus is expropriated almost exclusively by capital, leading to social unrest and political instability (Lipietz, 1984b).

Social Democratic Political Economy

The main opposition to both the Leninist-inspired dependency and regulation schools of socialist political economy has continued to come from the analyses of social democrats. These analyses tend to lack the micro-level focus on shifts in production processes that characterizes regulation school approaches and ignore questions about imperialism and neocolonialism that characterize dependency analyses. Contemporary social democratic thought retains its traditional focus on the development of monopoly capitalism and its effects on the domestic political arena in "developed" capitalist nations.

The primary area of concern for contemporary social democrats continues to be the democratic class struggle; that is, the democratic process and the theorization of the impact that changes in class structures brought about by the development of monopoly capitalism have had on domestic class formation and voting behaviour. Unlike its traditional precursors, however, contemporary social democratic theory is no longer passive – merely awaiting the further development of capitalism to produce more workers and hence electoral success – but is concerned with obtaining political power to further the potential for the achievement of socialism and the replacement of capitalism. This has led social democratic theory into two main areas: first, the theorization of class formation and class solidarity; and second, the development of practical political policy and electoral strategies designed to achieve success at the polls and within legislatures.

Following some elements in Eduard Bernstein's works, contemporary social democrats have rejected the notion implicit in Marxism-Leninism that there are ultimately only two classes characteristic of the capitalist mode of production: the working class and the owners of capital. Social democrats argue that the development of monopoly capitalism has also generated a third or middle class. Although the exact membership in this class is contentious, all social democrats agree that, at a minimum, it is composed of managers and administrators and other individuals who neither directly own productive apparatuses nor struggle for wages (Esping-Andersen, 1985, p.29).

In most countries this class has expanded rapidly in size since World War II, with its fortunes closely tied to the development of bureaucracies in both large public sectors and large private sector corporations. Social democrats have been concerned with the effects of the growth of this class on the "democratic class struggle" between capital and labour they see being waged in parliamentary institutions. Just like social democrats before and immediately after World War I were preoccupied with the idea of forming coalitions between labour and other classes such as farmers, peasants, and small-shopkeepers and manufacturers, in the postwar period they started to concentrate on defining the new middle class and attracting it to an alliance with workers (Korpi, 1983). This stands in sharp contrast to those working in the Leninist vein, who have tended either to deny separate class status to "middle elements" in society or to argue that coalitions including those elements simply reduce the possibility for meaningful change in capitalist relations.

In some cases this focus on social alliances has also led contemporary social democrats away from the analysis of class altogether and towards the theorization of "new social movements," such as the peace, environmental, gay, and feminist movements. Much recent effort has gone into analyzing the social origins of these movements and into determining whether and to what extent such movements are "progressive"; that is to say, compatible with the aims and ambitions of the working class (Esping-Andersen, Friedland, and Wright, 1976). As George Ross and Jane Jenson have argued, however, this strategy creates conflicts in social democratic political practice:

> The politics of the peace, ecology and other movements and their electoralist propensities are often radical and progressive – in the sense of being change oriented – while simultaneously harbouring deep anti-working class feelings. At best such new middle strata politics seeks, in an interesting historical change of focus, to subordinate the workers' movement to its goals. At worst it simply disregards workers and their needs. . . . It follows from all this that a political position which advocates that the labour movement strike a deal with the "new politics" as is, invites new problems. To the degree to which the labour movement is sufficiently strong to insist upon pro-working class priorities in the alliance, the alliance will be unstable. To the degree to which out of organizational or ideological weakness it ends up "tailing" such new middle strata movements simply because they seem "radical" the result is likely to be very dangerous for workers. (1986, p.43)

The major debate found in contemporary social democratic political economy revolves around the question of whether or not the nationalization of industries and the implementation of state-sponsored welfare and other social security programs have achieved their aim of reducing the dependence of workers on capitalist-dominated market mechanisms for their income. Some social democrats argue that these activities should be continued until markets have been rendered completely superfluous. Others say that markets remain inherently more efficient than state-sector activities in allocating goods and services in society and should be allowed to function effectively. As Gosta Esping-Andersen points out:

> Such Social Democrats . . . have claimed that genuine socialism may be achieved through a blend of welfare state reforms, taxation policies, and a sophisticated use of Keynesian economic management techniques. Yet as a number of . . . Social Democrats have argued, political and social citizenship rights are only meaningful forms of working class participation if they are supplemented with full economic citizenship, which essentially implies a democratic form of control over the means of production (that is a total redistribution of economic power). (1980, p. 258)

Any dependence on the market, as Przeworski acknowledges, creates a problem for the reformist aspirations of social democrats because it places the working class and the working-class state at the mercy of capitalists:

> Without nationalization of the means of production, increases of productivity require profitability of private enterprise. As long as the process of accumulation is private, the entire society is dependent upon maintaining private profits and upon the actions of capitalists allocating these profits. Hence the efficacy of social democrats – as of any other party – in regulating the economy and mitigating the social effects depends upon the profitability of the private sector and the willingness of capitalists to cooperate. (1985, p.42)

The dilemma of social democratic political economy, therefore, is very real, and the debates have significant implications for political practice. Forming alliances with new social movements may dilute working-class demands and ambitions, while continued reliance upon market mechanisms may thwart further reforms required for the transition to socialism. In pursuing these contemporary issues, social democratic theory finds itself at a crossroads, and it must come to some resolution of these questions if it is to influence the nature of future social democratic political and economic practice.

The State in Socialist Theory

All socialist political economy integrates political and economic variables in a fashion that liberal political economy does not. That is, socialist political economy has never adopted, even for heuristic purposes, the separation between states and markets that liberal political economy espouses. Socialist economic theory never considers markets without also considering the impact of governments on those markets and the impact of market actors on governments and state activities. Nevertheless, the theorization of the role of the state, and especially the role of the democratic state in capitalist society, has caused major difficulties for socialist political economists.

The question of the role of the state in socialist political economy is made more difficult by the fact that Marx himself never completed his intended work on the question, and many early Marxists assumed that after a socialist revolution the state would simply wither away or emerge in a new form. Therefore they saw either no need or little need prior to the revolution itself for extensive analysis of this question (Bobbio, 1987).

All socialist theories of the state are based, in one way or another, on the Marxist conception of the state as an institution of class domination. Although there are numerous disagreements on questions such as the extent of economic domination of the state by large capital or the mechanisms by which capitalist economic power is translated into political power, nevertheless most socialists tend to subscribe to either an *instrumental* or a *structural* view of the role of the state in capitalist society.

The instrumental view of the state posits that the state in capitalist society tends to make decisions and develop policies that favour capital because it is thoroughly dominated and staffed by representatives of these interests (Mandel, 1970; Castells, 1980). This view of the state in capitalist society has dominated both Marxist-Leninist and social democratic political economy. The structural variant of socialist state theory, unlike the instrumentalist conception, is a "high level" theory in the sense that it abstracts from mundane and observable phenomena to make generalizations about the systemic or structural "imperatives" of a capitalist economy. According to this view, a capitalist economy has to fulfil certain functional requirements to operate effectively; and these imperatives drive political decision-making and exist outside of, or independently of, the will of political and administrative decision-makers (Althusser and Balibar, 1977).

Adherents of the structural view assume that because of the tendency of the rate of profit to fall, companies are constantly looking for methods of reducing production costs. One way to achieve this is to socialize many expenditures. Instead of a firm providing training, education, and health protection, for instance, these costs can be passed onto the population as a whole through their socialization, or provision, by the state. Regardless of who actually staffs the state – that is, regardless of their personal or class nature – the state must respond to the needs of capital in order to ensure the reproduction of the social system. Thus, for example, structuralists would explain the rise of the welfare state and welfare state expenditures by saying they aid the reproduction of capital in a capitalist political economy (Gough, 1979).

Although there are debates on the extent to which states can afford to provide such "subsidies" to business (O'Connor, 1973), the theorists usually argue that such expenditures are necessary for the preservation of monopoly capital and that the state makes them because, although "relatively autonomous" of capital, it is structured in a way that ensures the reproduction of the dominant political-economic system.

Although this view has interesting things to say about the development of social programs and state expenditures associated with the modern "welfare" state, its reliance on a kind of functional determinism has led to it being criticized for being too high level – that is, too simplistic, economistic, or telelogical (Thompson, 1978). Although the functional or structural interpretation of the capitalist state appears to continue to hold out the socialist promise of a future system of production relations replacing capitalism, it is difficult to see how this would occur because the theory lacks a precise conception of "agency." Instead, the state is viewed as responding to the systemic needs of capitalism, which in fact it must do because that is its function or role in capitalist society. This means that political activities involving the state are not likely to alter existing social relations and radical change must instead originate outside of the state, presumably in the economic sphere. However, it is not clear how these developments are expected to result in the eventual overthrow of a capitalist system. As a result, this structural interpretation of the nature of the capitalist state has been challenged by socialist political economists working both in the Leninist tradition and the social democratic tradition, since both hold out the possibility for change in capitalism occurring through the capture and use of state institutions.

Leninist and social democratic analyses have shared an instrumental conception of the state as a tool of the dominant social class. They differ in many respects, including most notably their analysis of whether liberal-democratic states can be captured by other classes through the democratic process or must be overthrown through revolution. These analyses avoid the mechanistic and technological aspects of structural approaches by concentrating on the relationship between the state and class actors in society. In doing so, they tend to ignore the structural capacity of states to influence how societies are organized and operate.

The Leninist and social democratic analyses of the nature of the state in capitalist society have significant implications for political practice and, unlike liberal political economy, justify the extensive use of state apparatuses to promote political goals. Like liberal political economy, however, both approaches to socialist political economy tend to undertheorize the state.

Marx's Theory of the State

Several different conceptions of the state can be located in Marx's writings, including *Capital*, the *Grundrisse*, the *Communist Manifesto*, *The Civil War in France*, and *Class Struggles in France*. In addition, early writings found in the *Economic and Philosophical Manuscripts of 1844* and in

Critique of Hegel's Philosophy of Right also contain ruminations on the origins and purpose of states and governments in Western society. Engels, of course, also touched on the state in many of his works, including most notably *Origins of the Family, Civil Society, and the State.*

Although these writings are often cursory, fragmentary, and contradictory, it is possible to glean a general conception of the state implicit within them. This is a notion of the state as a coercive apparatus established to perpetuate the political domination of society by an economically dominant class. The state is part of the superstructure, which also includes religion, ideology, art, and culture, constructed upon the economic base of a specific mode of production. Thus, different states exist for each existing or historical mode of production (for instance, a slave state, a feudal state, or a capitalist state), and some kind of new state will also exist in socialist or communist society.

Although there are many aspects to this argument (including distinctions that can be drawn between dominant and ruling classes or the possibility of an autonomous state developing when opposing classes are of equal strength, the key philosophical concept is of the state as an instrument of class rule), with its origins in the class structure of society and responding to changes in that structure brought about by movements of the economic base. As Marx remarks in *The Civil War in France*, the state is both the location of much of the class struggle and the prize that this struggle fights over. Thus, at a particular point in time the state can be used by an emerging social class to overthrow the previous ruling class:

> The centralized State power, with its ubiquitous organs of standing army, police, bureaucracy, and clergy and judicature . . . originates from the days of absolute monarchy, serving nascent middle-class society as a mighty weapon in its struggles against feudalism. Still its development remained clogged by all manner of mediaeval rubbish, seigneurial rights, local privileges, municipal and guild monopolies and provincial constitutions. The gigantic broom of the French Revolution of the eighteenth century swept away all these relics of bygone times, thus clearing simultaneously the social soil of its last hindrances to the superstructure of the modern state edifice. ([1871] 1974b, p.289)

However, once conquered and staffed by the new class, the state can also take on a repressive role in society, preventing or delaying other classes from attaining political power:

> During the subsequent régimes, the Government, placed under Parliamentary control . . . became not only the bone of contention between the rival factions and adventurers of the ruling classes: but its political character changed simultaneously with the economic changes in society. At the same pace at which the progress of modern industry developed,

widened, intensified the class antagonism between capital and labour, the State power assumed more and more the character of the national power of capital over labour, of a public force organized for social enslavement, of an engine of class despotism. (Ibid., p.284)

Thus, for Marx the state was an instrument of class domination, but not inherently so. Rather, it was an instrument that could, and usually was, used in the course of class struggle by the dominant class to maintain its hold on the subordinate classes. The actual form this domination would take, and the question of whether the state would be used at all, was dependent on the level of class struggle; that is, on the strength of the various classes and the extent of antagonism between them. Thus, the nature of the state was contingent on the political ramifications of underlying economic processes, in keeping with Marx's fundamental concept of base and superstructure. The questions of whether and how state structures could be used by subordinate classes to secure their control over the political economy were left open, sparking a debate between socialists who felt a revolution was necessary to overthrow the capitalist state and others who argued that a transition from capitalism to socialism could be achieved through existing state institutions and political practices.

Leninist, Dependency, and Regulation Theories of State

In the effort to transfer Marx's analysis of the social, economic, and political conditions of advanced capitalist nations such as France, Germany and England to the less developed Russian Empire, Lenin made several critical elaborations premised on the idea that a revolution was a necessary prerequisite to the achievement of socialism. Lenin's ideas, of course, were implemented in the political practice of the Russian Revolution and in succeeding revolutions in countries such as China, Cuba, Vietnam, Ethiopia, Yemen, Angola, and Mozambique. These concepts and the experience of the state in the Soviet Union were also transferred by force of arms to other countries in Eastern Europe, the Baltic states, and Mongolia. With some further variations, they have informed the political practice of dependency theorists and revolutionaries in countries such as Kampuchea, Peru, and Iran.

Leninist theory is premised on the notion that the capitalist class will not willingly relinquish its control over the state and will use its coercive powers – the military and the police – to attempt to retain control. Lenin argues that consequently only violent revolutionary action can bring about the transfer of state control from the capitalist to the working classes. Although many other socialists influenced by Marx, such as Rosa Luxemburg, felt that this revolution could be led spontaneously by the working class itself in the form of a mass or general strike, Lenin rejected this analysis, arguing that the working class tends to pursue only economic objectives if left to itself and that it requires the assistance of intellectuals and other progressive elements of society to achieve the political consciousness required to create and maintain a successful revolution. This, he argues, is the role of the Communist Party: to act as an institution capable of organizing and maintaining the revolutionary leadership of the working class.

In *The State and Revolution* (1917) and *What Is to Be Done?* (1902) Lenin, like Marx before him, elaborates a theory of political action based on an instrumental concept of the state. Lenin argues that in the monopoly capitalist stage of development, existing state structures had been captured and staffed by representatives of capital and were used by capital to exploit workers in both the metropole and the periphery. He argues that workers left to their own devices would probably conduct individual struggles with individual capitalists through trade union activities and fail to develop the political activities necessary to overthrow capitalist states. This, he says, is especially true in peripheral nations, where repressive state military and police activities actively prevent even the development of trade unionism among the working classes.

Lenin argues that the appropriate and necessary vehicle for achieving socialism in most countries is the Communist Party; that is, the development of a political party dedicated to advancing the interests of the working class through both economic (trade union) and political activities. The strategy he proposes involves a party-led mass revolution that would overthrow existing state personnel and allow the party to capture the state apparatus and institute worker's rule.

After the revolution is successful and the working class has seized power, the appropriate form of government required to bring about the transition to socialism is a "dictatorship of the proletariat" – a governmental structure dominated by the Communist Party. While, in the case of the Russian revolution, this involved replacing a Czarist aristocracy with a federal system of governments and local councils, or "soviets," in other countries this "dictatorship" has sometimes been put into practice using existing parliamentary or republican institutions under the control of the party.

Once in power, the worker's government moves to consolidate its economic power by nationalizing industries and agriculture, a move that also consolidates its political power by destroying the economic base of the capitalist and landowning classes. After destroying the basis for a market-based allocation of goods and services, the Leninist state establishes direct state allocation through the institution of central (state) planning of the economy. In the Soviet Union this series of steps in the development of the socialist state occurred in a rather ad hoc fashion and was intimately tied into specifically Soviet conditions such as the outbreak of civil war and the reconstruction of the military and state hierarchies under war communism. However, in many other countries this model was adopted holus-bolus, and the wholesale nationalization of industry and collectivization of agricultural activities were key features of postrevolutionary state activities.

This analysis of the revolutionary politics of socialist political economy had a great impact not only on nations that fell into the Soviet orbit during and after World War II by military force but also on peripheral countries that wished to emulate the economic growth and success of the Soviet Union, then the only existing example of a backward nation that had successfully industrialized and overtaken many advanced industrial nations. The Leninist formula presented an analysis of social and economic circumstances prevalent in many developing nations as well as a ready blueprint for political action and the creation of the postrevolutionary state, which made its appeal very great indeed. This theory of the state and of the necessity for revolutionary action characterizes both dependency theory and regulation political economy.

Although many developing nations emerging from the confines of the European colonial system adopted this model of the state and the political concepts behind it, many did not, preferring instead to develop their own forms of government and state structures based on the models of their former colonial masters. Most social democratic parties and movements in the developed countries also rejected the Leninist model after arriving at their own interpretations of Marx's writings and of the subsequent political practice and theory.

Social Democratic State Theory

An important aspect of the Leninist theory of the state is the notion that the mechanism for attainment of worker control over the state was the political party, and especially the Communist Party. Lenin's particular notion of what this party is like is not shared by social democrats. Lenin believed in the vanguard party; that is, a party composed of intellectuals and "advanced elements of the working class" that could transcend trade unionism and realize the true interests of the working class in achieving socialism. Social democrats, while agreeing with many aspects of Lenin's theory of the state, argue that the conception of a vanguard party reverses Marx and Engel's emphasis on the state responding to changes in the economic base.

Social democrats agree that the appropriate mechanism for attaining state power is the political party, but they insist that this party should be linked to and grow out of the trade union movement. They assert that such a party can participate in existing legislative bodies, form coalitions with other parties, and peacefully obtain power, thereby ushering in the transition to socialism. Social democrats argue that the Leninist vanguard party is elitist, at best can only obtain power through a coup d'état, and does not have the links with the working class required to create a true socialist state. It is forced to rely on the coercive power of the state to attempt to bring in socialism and would more likely transform itself into a "dictatorship of the party" than into a "dictatorship of the proletariat."

Given that social democrats believe the continued development of capitalism generates a multiplicity of classes including a substantial middle class (Nicholaus, 1967), they argue that capital can rule only with the allegiance of other classes and cannot simply rely upon force or coercion to impose its will. The state becomes the focus for class struggle as the democratic franchise is extended: first to legitimize capital's support among the middle classes; and later as property restrictions are removed to bring the working classes into the electorate (Therborn, 1977; Korpi, 1983). Eventually, through the political organization of the working class and the construction of electoral and party alliances with the middle classes (Esping-Andersen, 1980; Esping-Andersen and Friedland, 1982), the capitalist state can become a socialist state. Following this logic, social democrats see the adoption of Keynesianism and associated large public expenditures in the modern welfare state as a manifestation of this democratic class struggle for control of the state – as workers forcing concessions from capital through the operation of the democratic process (Shalev, 1983; Esping-Andersen, 1981).

While social democratic analysis represents a sophisticated appreciation of how states and markets are interrelated in capitalist democracies, it does not entirely explain the timing or content of the different welfare state programs adopted in different countries or jurisdictions. This is because while the analysis is sensitive to different configurations of political and partisan organization in different societies, it is not sensitive to the variations in state structures and organizations (Skocpol and Finegold, 1982). Compared to Leninist or Regulation political economy, both of which tend to have purely instrumental conceptions of the relationship between states and societal actors, social democratic political economy grants more autonomy to the state (Skocpol, 1985). But in viewing state policy-making as characterized by begrudging capitalist accommodation to working-class militancy, social democrats overlook the important role of states and state officials in the adoption of – or failure to adopt – social welfare and other policies in many countries (Hall and Ikenberry, 1989; Nordlinger, 1981; Migdal, 1988; Granatstein, 1982).

Socialist Political Economy in Canada

In the early era of Canadian industrial history, the dominant tendency was a kind of pre-Marxist "utopian" socialism or anarcho-syndicalism, which attempted to construct a new social order based on co-operatives and large, multi-industry trade unions (Lipset, 1971; Wood, 1975; Sacouman, 1979; Robin, 1968; Palmer, 1986; Palmer and Kealey, 1982). By the end of World War I and following the Russian Revolution of 1917, however, socialist political economy in Canada had adopted a distinctly Marxist flavour. For example, it accepted the need for a class analysis of Canadian society and the tenet of the leading role played by the economy and production relations in determining the nature and direction of political life (Avakumovic, 1975; Frank and Reilly, 1979).

A strong Leninist line was brought into Canada with the creation of the Communist Party of Canada (CPC) in 1919 (Avakumovic, 1975), while evolutionary social democratic principles emerged in the farmer-labour-intellectual coalition of the Co-operative Commonwealth Federation (CCF), forerunner of the New Democratic Party (NDP) (League for Social Reconstruction, 1935).

Although the CPC shifted its analysis several times in accordance with the positions and analysis of the international scene provided by the Soviet-led International of Communist Parties, the party always focused on the close relations existing between the United States and Canada and emphasized the need for Canadians to break away from the domination of the United States before socialism could be achieved at home. Therefore, the CPC supported the establishment of nationalist trade unions and ran candidates in federal elections espousing a nationalist line. Although it successfully influenced the direction of the union movement in Canada – until it moderated its nationalist line in the late 1930s to support the war effort and supported the affiliation of Canadian industrial unions with the U.S. Congress of Industrial Organizations (CIO) (Abella, 1973) – the CPC-backed Labour Progressive Party (LPP) was much less successful at the polls. In a bitter struggle with the CCF for electoral support, the CPC-LPP was never fully committed to the democratic process and was unable to attract large numbers of voters to its ranks.

Leninist, Dependency, and Regulation Political Economy in Canada

From 1919 to about 1969, the CPC and its political line dominated Canadian Leninist political economy. However, by the early 1960s concerns about continually increasing foreign penetration of the Canadian economy and the apparently concomitant loss of Canadian political sovereignty forced a reconsideration of the CPC line and led to a gradual shift in emphasis among both party supporters and academics towards a re-emphasis on the question of imperialism, resulting in the emergence of a distinctive "dependency" slant in many analyses and a separation of this variant of socialist political-economic analysis from the Community Party.

This trend was obvious in many works that were highly critical of foreign investment in Canada, especially U.S. investment, and its adverse consequences for Canadian indigenous development (Laxer, 1973; Hutcheson, 1978).[2] The resulting dependency approach infused the analysis of the Canadian political economy put forward by the so-called "Waffle" faction within the NDP and was the theoretical base of the group's "Waffle Manifesto" (Watkins, 1970) and other writings in the late 1960s and early 1970s.

This approach brought about the "consolidation" of some nationalist liberals and most socialists in the country by stressing the constraints of Canada's place in the international political economy on Canadian political life (Kellogg, 1989). It resulted in a powerful political movement, but by the mid-1970s many analysts were already concerned that the dependency analysis was empirically flawed and based on a misreading of Canadian economic development. They argued that it was also theoretically weak in its neglect of careful class analysis and overemphasis on elements such as geographical location, foreign ownership, and trade relations (Veltmeyer, 1978; Carroll, 1988).

Two authors working within the dependency approach summarized the debate in 1975:

> Is Canada a colony or an imperialist country? Is Canadian nationalism progressive or reactionary? Is the Canadian bourgeoisie comprador or independently imperialist? These are key questions facing the Canadian Left. They are not academic questions; for their answers determine the strategy for socialism in Canada.
>
> Those who view Canada as a U.S. colony with a comprador, non-imperialist bourgeoisie usually argue that the main contradiction is between the Canadian "people" and American imperialism. Usually, this position favours a two-stage revolution and alliances with the "non-imperialist" bourgeoisie. Since Canada is viewed as an "oppressed" nation, nationalism plays a progressive role in the class struggle (a variant of this position is held by CLM, CPC [M-L], and the former Waffle leadership). On the other hand, those who view Canada as a monopoly capitalist, imperialist country with an independent imperialist bourgeoisie argue that the main contradiction is between the Canadian working class and the Canadian bourgeoisie. (Moore and Wells, 1975, p.7)

Although some socialist political economists continued with a dependency analysis of the national economy, fewer and fewer did so in the 1980s as criticism of the applicability of this model to the Canadian situation grew (Veltmeyer, 1979). Instead, dependency analysis came to concentrate upon metropolitan-hinterland relations within Canada itself, arguing that the Atlantic, Western, and Northern regions of the country existed in a state of dependency and truncated development as a result of the actions and activities of Central Canadian capital (Sacouman, 1981; Leadbeater, 1984; Sager, 1987). Other former supporters of dependency theory began to use regulation theory in their analyses of the Canadian case (Boismenu and Drache, 1989; Boismenu, 1989). In this they were supported by labour historians working in Canadian universities, many of whom have attempted to integrate a historical analysis of the labour process with the historical development of the Canadian economy and politics (Palmer, 1986; Kealey, 1981). In doing this they provide not only much-needed insights into the social history of Canada and its process of class formation (Pentland, 1981; Kealey, 1985) but also empirical studies of the development of the labour process in the Canadian manufacturing and resource industries (Heron and Storey, 1986). The studies fit neatly with works in a regulation vein chronicling the effects that different international regimes of production have had on Canadian social and political structures (Houle, 1983; Cameron and Houle, 1985; Marchak, 1986).

Although it is far from clear that the Fordist model, with its emphasis on the mass production of durable consumer products, is applicable to the resource-dependent Canadian economy, several recent analyses attempt to venture beyond the analysis of economic and production relations to apply a Fordist analysis to contemporary Canadian political life (Bradford and Jenson, 1989).

Social Democratic Political Economy

Except for a brief period in the 1960s and early 1970s, the Leninist, dependency, and regulation approaches to socialist political economy have always been in the minority, labouring against both the confines of a capitalist economy and liberal political-economic theory and the more dominant social democratic tradition of political economic analysis.

Emerging out of the early pre-World War I socialist, labour, and workers parties, and gaining strength through the forging of electoral and partisan alliances with dissident farmers' groups in the 1920s and 1930s (Morton, 1950; Brodie and Jenson, 1988), Canadian social democrats embraced a moderate model of state planning and nationalized industrial and financial sectors based on the proposals of the British Labour Party and the Fabian Society (Young, 1969; Zakuta, 1964, Laycock, 1990). They did not broach the question of international dominance of the Canadian economy; instead they looked at the failures of the existing market and governmental system to provide for a reasonable standard of living for the workers, farmers, and middle-class elements who were expected to form the basis of electoral support for a socialist party.

In the 1933 Regina Manifesto, which signalled the formation of the social democratic Co-operative Commonwealth Federation (CCF), and in the 1935 document *Social Planning for Canada*, the CCF and its intellectual wing, the University League for Social Reconstruction, outlined a program of public works, nationalization, and creation of state planning machinery premised on the election of social democrats to power through the existing democratic process. This strategy was based on a nine-point proposal set out by the League for Social Reconstruction in 1931. The first steps "towards the realization of a new order" advocated by the league were:

1. Public ownership and operation of the public utilities connected with transportation, communications, and electric power, and of other

      industries as are already approaching conditions of monopolistic control.

2. Nationalization of Banks and other financial institutions with a view to the regulation of all credit and investment operations.
3. The further development of agricultural co-operative institutions for the production and merchandising of agricultural products.
4. Social legislation to secure to the worker adequate income and leisure, freedom of association, insurance against illness, accident, old age and unemployment and an effective voice in the management of his industry.
5. Publicly organized health, hospital and medical services.
6. A taxation policy emphasizing steeply graduated income and inheritance taxes.
7. The creation of a National Planning Commission.
8. The vesting in Canada of the power to amend and interpret the Canadian constitution so as to give the federal government power to control the national economic development.
9 A foreign policy designed to secure international co-operation in regulating trade, industry and finance, and to promote disarmament and world peace. (1935, p.x)

The CCF program was directed at overcoming the problems of late monopoly capitalism and providing for a more efficient allocation of resources and wealth and production of goods and services in Canadian society. As in the cases of many European social democratic parties, this analysis led the CCF and its adherents to quickly endorse and adopt Keynesianism in the post-World War II era. In fact, the analysis made in *Social Planning for Canada* presaged this development by several times approvingly citing Keynes's analysis of the failures of a capitalist market economy.

Having opted for a Keynesian strategy if elected, Canadian social democrats turned their attention to the question of the appropriate electoral strategy for the party. The strategy of constructing alliances with farmers' organizations and trade unions proved successful in helping the CCF gain power in Saskatchewan in 1944 and become the official opposition in Ontario and British Columbia in the postwar period. As Canadian society became increasingly urbanized and industrialized after World War II, however, the farmers' role in electoral and partisan politics dwindled everywhere outside of the prairie provinces and Prince Edward Island, leading to a decline in CCF electoral fortunes. In response, Canadian social democrats undertook two actions. First, they attempted to reinforce their links with the trade union movement; and second, they began a search for some other social group to form an electoral coalition. Links with the trade union movement were solidified in 1960 when the CCF transformed itself into the New Democratic Party (NDP) in a formal alliance with the new Canadian

Labour Congress (CLC). The alliance gave CLC unions the right to send delegates to NDP conventions and otherwise influence internal party affairs (Brodie and Jenson, 1988; Black and Myles, 1986; Myles and Forcese, 1981; Schreiber, 1980). After many of them passed through a Leninist-dependency phase in the 1960s and early 1970s, urging support for any actions that could cut the close links between the Canadian and U.S. economies, some Canadian socialist political economists looked for inspiration towards European and U.S. social democratic analyses of monopoly capital (Panitch, 1977; Grayson, 1980; Moscovitch and Drover, 1981). Although they were heavily influenced by new developments, their movement represented a return to the old social democratic emphasis on the analysis of domestic institutions, state policies, and class relations. Rather than concentrating on external causes for Canada's failure to develop a socialist system, like the dependency theorists, social democrats paid much more attention to internal factors and especially to the links between the nation's institutional structure and its class structure – between the state, public policy, and social formations (Panitch, 1977; Mahon, 1979, 1984; Cuneo, 1978, 1980).

Canadian social democrats not only have difficulty explaining their lack of success at the polls, but also have failed to grapple with the consequences at the theoretical level for their understanding of the party and state systems or, more generally, with the nature of the contemporary Canadian political economy. Most social democratic analyses continue to advocate the perpetuation of Keynesian welfare state programs, and only very recently has any thought been given to post-Keynesian alternatives (Rosenblum and Findlay, 1991; Gonick, 1987).

Notes

1 This is true, for instance, concerning the extensive literature that addresses the question concerning how "actually existing socialism" – that is, the system of central planning found in most socialist countries organized along the lines of the Soviet Union – operates. See, for example, Nove, 1983, and Brus, 1973.
2 This new emphasis on metropolitan-hinterland relations or centre-periphery relations in Leninist political economy accorded very well with the older Canadian tradition of a staple political economy and in fact allowed a "radicalization" of this primarily inductive, empirical approach to Canadian history and Canadian development.

CHAPTER 4

Staples Political Economy

The insights of a third method of studying Canadian political economy – the staples approach – have furthered our understanding of the Canadian situation and significantly influenced the work of both liberal and socialist political economists. Unlike the other two theories, this is only a partial theory – hence our use of the term staples approach. It can be applied only to examining the political economies of Canada and of other similar countries. In fact, it does not even describe the entire Canadian political economy but only selected aspects of it – a specificity that is its greatest strength as well as its greatest weakness.

Fundamental Tenets

The liberal and socialist theories both rely upon general models of the economy and politico-economic relations that are then applied to the particular circumstances of the Canadian case. In contrast, the staples approach adopts a more inductive methodology, basing its conclusions on the results of careful investigations into the particularities of the Canadian process of economic development.

The approach was developed primarily by Canadian economists and historians whose works are rooted firmly in the historical development of the Canadian economy. They describe the effects of this development on Canadian social and political life. The school derives its name from the emphasis on staples industries, which, following Gordon Bertram, are defined as those industries "based on agriculture and extractive resources, not requiring elaborate processing and finding a large portion of their market in international trade" (1967, p.75). Staples theorists view the

Canadian political economy as having been shaped by the export of successive staples over the course of Canadian history from the earliest colonial times to the modern era.

Following Gordon Laxer, we can identify four main "analytical assumptions" of the staples school (Laxer, 1989b, pp.180-181). First, staples theorists believe that the key to understanding Canadian history is to discover the export commodity that the economy depends on. They argue that the Canadian state and Canadian capital devote themselves singlemindedly to discovering and extracting bulk resource commodities or staples that have a ready export market. The money thus derived is used to pay wages to Canadian workers and finance imports of goods demanded by Canadian consumers. Canadian economic growth, then, is intimately linked to the demand for staples in the industrialized nations, and this demand has shaped economic development in Canada: any shift in demand for the staple in question, while inconsequential for the importing country, has a pervasive impact on the local economy, which is dependent on its export. An example is the fading away of the fashion in beaver-felt hats in Europe, which had a serious, debilitating effect on the early nineteenth-century Canadian economy, which was almost completely dependent on the export of furs (Innis, 1956).

Second, staples political economists argue that Canadian political life is heavily influenced by the country's staple export-dependent economy because economic wealth and political power are concentrated in Canadian business and political elites – often the same people – who act as the instruments of interests in the industrialized countries importing the staples. According to the theory, the Canadian business community has been more interested in promoting continued and expanded staples-resource exports than in acting as entrepreneurs developing an industrialized Canadian manufacturing economy.

Third, the staples school emphasizes history as a key to understanding the Canadian political economy. A study of the actual history of Canadian economic development enables these scholars to overcome the limitations of the liberal and socialist theories developed to understand the industrialized economies of Europe. They clearly understand that Canada and many other "new world" economies have unique features that the two traditional theories cannot account for.

Fourth, analysts in this school argue that the need to overcome geographical impediments to the expansion of staples exports helps explain the state's role in a staples-dependent market economy. They argue that confronting the harshness of the Canadian terrain and the physical distances that had to be traversed to get staples from the hinterland to ocean loading ports required large capital expenditures on transportation and communications infrastructure, which Canadian business could not afford to make. Instead, projects such as canals and river improvements, railway construction, and the establishment of telephone, electrical, and airline systems were all undertaken by the Canadian state.

Not all staples theorists place equal weight on all of these aspects, and significant debates exist between different groups concerning questions such as the historical time periods that the analysis can cover or whether the construction of transportation infrastructure amounts to industrial development or not. The most contentious question – one that divides staples political economy into two schools – is whether the reliance on staples exports rather than industrial manufacturing is a positive or negative development.

The Historical Foundations

The staples approach has its origins in research into Canadian social, political, and economic history carried out in Canadian universities, roughly between 1920 and 1940, by members of what were then known as departments of political economy. The two most prominent scholars following this approach were Harold Innis and W.A. Mackintosh. But numerous other scholars during the same era arrived at similar conclusions regarding the significance of the resource industries and their impact on Canadian settlement (Fay, 1934). These included, most notably, Arthur Lower, a Queen's University historian; S.A. Saunders, a Dalhousie University historian; and Donald G. Creighton, a University of Toronto historian, as well as others scattered across the country. Lower (1938) explored the origins and impact of the lumber industry on Canadian development, while Creighton [1937] (1956) adopted several staples tenets in developing his "Laurentian thesis" of Canadian history (Berger, 1976). Saunders examined the development of the Maritime provinces using a staples framework (Saunders, 1939).

Enough scholars were working in a similar vein by the mid-1930s to allow the publication between 1934 and 1938 of a nine-volume *Frontiers of Settlement* series on the history of Canadian economic, political, and social development. This series of books contains some of the finest writings in this tradition, including submissions from Lower (1938), Innis (1938), Mackintosh (1934), and Morton (1938). In 1939, major submissions by Saunders and Mackintosh to the Royal Commission on Dominion-Provincial Relations (the Rowell-Sirois Commission) presented the development of the Canadian economy in staple terms, and in 1941 V.W. Bladen relied on a staples framework to write the first textbook on Canadian political economy.

The two dominant thinkers in this tradition were clearly Innis and Mackintosh. While the two shared common theoretical premises in their emphasis on staples, they followed different lines of analysis and arrived at different conclusions in their works. Most later writings in the staples tradition can be classified according to whether they share Innis's pessimistic outlook on Canada's future or Mackintosh's more optimistic analysis.

The Innisian Approach

Harold Innis, an economist at the University of Toronto and one-time head of the American Economics Association, wrote a series of books from the 1920s to the 1940s discussing the significance of various early resource industries to the development of different parts of Canada. These included the classic works *A History of the Canadian Pacific Railway* (1923), *The Fur Trade in Canada* (1930), and *The Cod Fisheries* (1940) as well as numerous essays and edited works on related topics.

Innis argues that the political economy of Canada was shaped by the successive concentration on exports of cod, fur, lumber (and pulp and paper), agricultural products (principally wheat), and minerals, which all went to the metropolitan economies of Europe and later the United States. As Innis summarizes his staples thesis:

> The economic history of Canada has been dominated by the discrepancy between the centre and the margin of western civilization. Energy has been directed toward the exploitation of staple products and the tendency has been cumulative. The raw material supplied to the mother country stimulated manufacturers of the finished product and also of the products which were in demand in the colony. Large-scale production of raw materials was encouraged by improvement of technique of production, of marketing, and of transport as well as by improvement in the manufacture of the finished product.... Agriculture, industry, transportation, trade, finance, and governmental activities tend to become subordinate to the production of the staple for a more highly specialized manufacturing community. (1956, p.385)

Innis argues that Canada's export of staples products in unprocessed or semiprocessed forms was necessitated by the lack of technological capability to process them within the country and that exports were also essential to supporting the improved living conditions that had brought Europeans to Canada in the first place. The exportation of staples and the importation of consumer goods, while satisfying the needs of the immigrants, primarily benefited the interests of the industrialized nations, which secured a cheap and reliable supply of raw materials. The domestic commercial interests involved in the movement and financing of the export-import trade also benefited in the process.

With the passage of time, Innis argues, increasingly larger local resources had to be devoted to resource exports, which exacerbated the staples-orientation of the political economy. The railways built to transport wheat and lumber could not pay for themselves, which made it necessary to export pulp, paper, and minerals to take advantage of the railway's unused capacity (Innis, 1956). The increasing dependence on staples correspondingly widened Canada's technological backwardness, which only deepened the country's dependence on unprocessed or semiprocessed raw materials. This was different from the situation in the United States, where a less harsh geography and a larger population enabled the economy to depend less on staples exports and to develop both a large and prosperous agricultural sector capable of supporting a large domestic population and an industrial sector to serve the growing domestic market.

Climatic and topographical difficulties prevented Canada from undergoing a similar process of development, and the resulting dependence on staples exports, according to Innis, doomed Canada's chances of developing a domestic industrial base. Reliance on staples exports necessitated increasingly large investments in building a transportation infrastructure. The heavy debt-servicing charges that such investments involved diverted funds away from other areas of the economy, including manufacturing. The dependence on staples export also increasingly exposed the Canadian economy to the vagaries of international commodity markets, which tend to witness violent fluctuations as new capacity comes onstream in different countries, lowering world prices until world demand catches up with global supplies and prices rise accordingly. The "cumulative" impact of all this, according to Innis, was that the Canadian economy became caught in what Mel Watkins (1963) would later call a "staples trap." This form of economic life could provide relatively high standards of living to citizens of exporting countries, but only as long as domestic resource supplies and world demand remained constant or increased. Any declines in demand or increases in supplies would have drastic consequences for the domestic political economy, which would be poorly placed to respond to the challenge of finding a new economic base. As a result, Innis and most staples political economists following his lead are pessimistic about Canada's future as a reasonably wealthy "developed" country.

The Mackintosh Approach

W.A. Mackintosh, a Queen's University professor of economics and advisor to the federal Liberal government of William Lyon Mackenzie King, had more impact on practical political economy than most academics ever will. He served as a key researcher for the Rowell-Sirois Commission in the late 1930s, looking into problems caused in Canada by the Great Depression, and was one of the most powerful bureaucrats in the federal government during World War II – at a time when the federal government itself was powerful as a result of its war activities (Granatstein, 1982). Mackintosh was instrumental in introducing Keynesianism to Canada, and that approach formed the basis for Canada's postwar strategy of economic growth, but with the twist that full employment was to be secured through increased staples exports and an inflow of investments in further resource extraction and branch-plant manufacturing.

In his theoretical writings Mackintosh argues that in a "new" country dependence on the export of staples is an essential stage in economic growth. In his first article on the subject, in 1923, he states: "The prime requisite of colonial prosperity is the colonial staple. Other factors connected with the staple industry may turn it to advantage or disadvantage, but the staple in itself is the basis of prosperity" (Easterbrook and Watkins, 1967, p.3). In a report to the Rowell-Sirois Commission in 1939 he stands by this position: "Rapid progress in . . . new countries is dependent upon the discovery of cheap supplies of raw materials by the export of which to the markets of the world the new country may purchase the products which it cannot produce economically at that stage of its development" (1939, p.13).

Mackintosh presents economic development as a linear process in which each nation has to pass through a series of stages (Williams, 1983, pp.131-132). For him, Canada's dependence on staples reflects the nation's early stage of development, when staples were the only area in which it enjoyed a comparative advantage. Unlike Innis, he argues that eventually the technology acquired and the profits accumulated from the extraction and export of staples will lead to investment in manufacturing industries. The expansion of the domestic population and the availability of foreign capital and technology in setting up manufacturing plants to supply the growing domestic market would further facilitate the process. He cites the United States as having followed this route. If Canada had not been as successful as the United States, it was because of its harsher climate and smaller population, which inhibited the establishment of efficient manufacturing industries. The implication of his analysis was clear: there was nothing wrong in depending on staples exports, for eventually industrialization would arrive in Canada.

After slowing down during World War II, more work in the staple tradition emerged following the war. These include works by Vernon Fowke (1946) and Kenneth Buckley (1958), which both follow Mackintosh's line of reasoning. Both point out the tremendous economic spinoffs to the Canadian economy that had accrued as a result of booming wheat exports between the 1890s and 1920s. They argue that a large proportion of the benefits did not flow to the Western wheat producers but to Canadian manufacturers, most of them located in Central Canada. As John Richards concludes:

> To Fowke and Buckley, the wheat boom was necessary to Canadian industrialization because it alone provided a sustained high level of demand necessary for the Canadian manufacturing sector to "take off." Without wheat Canada would have had a much smaller domestic market and, given serious barriers to any new manufacturing exporter, manufacturers could not easily have substituted export for domestic markets; their level of activity could have been seriously curtailed. (1985)

The discovery by Fowke and Buckley that wheat exports provided the impetus for industrialization lent credence to Mackintosh's theory. Yet in

Fowke's works there is an Innisian strand: the wheat exports from the West (the periphery) primarily benefited the Central provinces (the centre), just as the industrialized nations benefited from Canada's exports of staples (Richards, 1985, p.53).

By the 1950s many different aspects of Canada's resource-dependent economy were being investigated (Easterbrook, 1959), including the impact on provincial development (Dales, 1957) and the impact of U.S. investment in key industries (Aitkin et al., 1959; Aitkin, 1961). The high point in the staples analysis in a practical political sense was no doubt in the late 1950s when the Royal Commission on Canada's Economic Prospects (the Gordon Commission) accepted Mackintosh's version of the staples thesis and focused its efforts on planning for and controlling the various effects on Canadian society of resource-led economic growth (Canada, Royal Commission on Canada's Economic Prospects, 1957).

By the 1960s the staples approach to Canadian political economy was being challenged on a number of fronts. The historical generalizations of the staple tradition were being subjected to detailed empirical scrutiny and to a demand for empirical verification on the part of quantitative economics and econometrics (Bertram, 1963; Chambers and Gordon, 1966). Secondly, the significance of the historical approach to understanding contemporary economic and political phenomena was being undermined by alternative methodologies in contemporary political science, such as the systems and behavioural approaches, which promised greater insight into discovering solutions for contemporary political problems (Easton, 1965; Charlesworth, 1962). Although the staples approach would receive its finest formulation at this point (Watkins, 1963), it would be increasingly relegated to the sidelines in academe as a conceptualization of the early developmental stages of a relatively new economy, an approach without much relevance to contemporary life.

Nevertheless, because most significant historical works on Canada's development had been fashioned by staples theorists, the approach could never be completely eliminated. Any researcher delving into Canada's past was bound to encounter the staple theorists and their powerful, inductively developed model of the Canadian political economy. This in fact occurred at the end of the 1960s as Canadian scholars rejected purposeless quantification and modelling for the broader insights offered by the staple perspective and as scholars of other nations searched for a superior approach to economic development than that provided by the orthodox liberal and socialist political-economic theories (Hirschman, 1958; North, 1961).

Contemporary Debates

The staples approach to Canadian political economy was revived at a time, towards the end of the 1960s, that was unusual in North American history, a time that had a pervasive impact on inquiries in social sciences. Civil rights activism in the United States and anti-Vietnam War protests across North America had rendered the intellectual milieu fertile for challenging established beliefs, while the anticolonial nationalist struggles in the Third World in the years following the end of World War II had given a new impetus to nationalism. It was also the time when the emerging evidence of the increasing strength of multinational corporations was inculcating fears that these corporations would enable the former colonial powers to once again dominate the world.

In Canadian political economy, an enhanced nationalism and a scepticism about the validity of established liberal and socialist theories led to the search for alternative analyses, for an approach that would be more in tune with the realities of Canadian history and provide a more pertinent guide to political practice than the deductive application of general liberal or socialist principles. Not surprisingly, this search led to a renaissance in staples theory.

However, the staples approach did not provide a clear guide for political action. Unlike the liberal and socialist theories, the staples analyses of both Innis and Mackintosh provided what were essentially descriptive evaluations of Canada's economic growth. Moreover, the two differed in the prescriptions they proposed for influencing the course of Canada's development, and in whether they felt the process had been harmful or beneficial to Canada. Before their analyses could be used to develop plans to improve Canada's lot, it was necessary to synthesize their various writings, observations, and insights into a general model of economic growth.

When this was attempted, it because obvious to most observers that staples political economy did not have the theoretical status of liberal and socialist political economy. That is, it did not reflect a completely separate theory outside of the liberal and socialist models; it existed simply as a specific case, a somewhat unique example of national development, or lack of it, within the more general theories. Not surprisingly, this led to two different revised versions of staples theory: one combined the pessimism of Innis with the pessimism of socialist political economy; the other, drawing on the writings of Mackintosh, was compatible with liberal optimism about the efficiency and creativity of market exchange. The first, neo-Innisian, perspective is sometimes referred to as the *new political economy*,[1] while the second approach can be termed the *new staples political economy*. Debate between the two continues to the present day (Pal, 1989).

The Neo-Innisian Approach

The neo-Innisian staples political economy combined, or attempted to combine, the work of Harold Innis with the theories of socialist political economy, especially the Leninist-dependency school. The resemblance of the Canadian economy to economies in the Third World – especially with respect to the high degree of foreign ownership – made such a line of analysis seem appropriate.

Two elements from Innis's thinking hit a particularly harmonious cord with scholars attempting to develop a new political economy. One was his conclusion that dependence on staples exports inhibited independent industrial development. The second, expressed in his later writings, was the fear of U.S. dominance of Canada.

The first element allowed the neo-Innisians to adopt dependency theory in their analysis of Canadian political economy (Levitt, 1970; Teeple, 1972; Laxer, 1973; Hutcheson, 1978). The second fostered the development of economic nationalism, which in the Canadian context necessarily involved a certain degree of anti-Americanism.[2] The two together inevitably led to the conclusion that the Canadian economy was suffering because of U.S. investment and that, more importantly, nationalist measures should be taken to reduce it. In other words, the "staples trap" could only be overcome through resort to economic nationalism. In the words of Daniel Drache, a significant figure among neo-Innisians, "Anti-imperialism, anti-capitalism and Canadian independence are an inseparable unity."

The neo-Innisian analyses have a number of common features. First, the scholars in this tradition attribute heavy emphasis to the need for an advanced manufacturing sector, a feature characteristic of economic nationalism (Gilpin, 1987). As Glen Williams points out, there is a "pervasive concern with the overdevelopment of the resource export sector of the economy at the expense of the industrial sector" (1983, p.138). As a corollary, they assert that the dominance of the resources sector has stifled the growth of indigenous manufacturing in Canada.

Second, the neo-Innisians believe "that foreign direct investment in Canadian manufacturing, among its other negative effects, inhibited our capacity to develop an export trade in industrial products" (Williams, 1983, p.138). The reference here is to U.S. investments, which have formed a majority of all foreign investment in Canadian manufacturing since the 1920s. This area of Canadian economic history has generated some of the finest work in the staples approach (Naylor, 1972, 1975b; Watkins, 1977; Levitt, 1970; Laxer, 1989a,b). The theorists argue that foreign subsidiaries have been more interested in making quick profits for their parent firms than in attempting to be innovative, export-oriented, or internationally competitive. What is ironic is that much of the U.S. investment arrived in Canada to evade tariff barriers against imports, a measure itself inspired at least partly by Canadian nationalism.

Third, these scholars warn that "a failure to address and correct these trade problems will result in decreasing living standards or even a descent toward 'economic underdevelopment'" (Williams, 1983, p.138). They are concerned that unless corrective measures are taken, Canada might turn into an industrial wasteland. Pessimism about Canada's social and economic prospects is indeed an enduring feature of neo-Innisian analyses, and it has received a fresh boost with the signing of the Free Trade Agreement with the United States (Cameron, 1988).

Finally, the neo-Innisians are acutely concerned about Canada's cultural identity, and they fear its assimilation by U.S. culture (Christian, 1977b; Lumsden, 1970). They take considerable pride in the fact that Canadians are not "Americans" and do not practise the same kind of heartless capitalism. They proudly note Canada's superior social welfare system and activist state tradition. They argue that closer economic integration with the United States will rapidly lead to cultural assimilation and recommend chalking out an independent course of economic development. In addition, they recommend financial assistance for the Canadian cultural industries and their protection from U.S. imports (Audley, 1983).

The publication of Kari Levitt's *Silent Surrender* in 1970 marked the beginning of a series of works combining Innis's staples approach with dependency theory. Building on Innis's conception of Canada as a staples-producing nation on "the margin" of Western capitalism, Levitt argues that the U.S. multinational corporations "organized the collection or extraction of the raw material staple required in the metropolis and supplied the hinterland with manufactured goods, whether produced at home or 'on site' in the host country" (Levitt, 1970, p.25).

Direct investments in Canada by the multinationals had enabled them to drain Canada of profits and, worse still, to increasingly buy into the economy from profits made locally. Levitt is especially critical of the Canadian capitalists who had allowed that to happen so they could make money managing or representing U.S. firms. As she puts it, "The Canadian entrepreneurs of yesterday are the coupon clippers and hired vice-presidents of branch plants of today. They have quite literally sold out the country" (Levitt, 1970, p.40). She describes this as a "silent surrender" on the part of Canada. The adverse effects of the branch-plant economy were cumulative, as Americans came increasingly to dominate the economy because of their superior technological and capital base.

Levitt's argument had an electrifying effect on the Canadian politicians and scholars on the left of the political spectrum. Her description of Canada as the "world's richest underdeveloped country" sounded radical for those looking for a radical political economy. But as William Carroll points out, Levitt's radicalism was "based not on a concept of class exploitation but of national oppression" (1986, p.5), and as such it was more nationalist than socialist. Among left-leaning scholars, it had an inspiring impact (Drache, 1977).

Another milestone in the same tradition was Tom Naylor's detailed *History of Canadian Business* (1975), which reinterpreted Creighton's (1937) earlier work. Naylor's primary thesis is that the dominance of the merchant class, which later controlled banking and finance, stifled the growth of the manufacturing sector in Canada. The profits that had been accumulated in the staples trade assisted the establishment of a robust indigenous banking sector in Canada. But these banks did not extend credit to nascent industries because of the higher risks and the longer pay-back period involved. Instead they were content to invest in staples trade and railways. As Naylor argues, the strength of Canadian capitalism in the commercial sector "was not matched by its industrial efforts. Rather the strength of the commercial sector went hand-in-hand with industrial weakness, by virtue of the absence of funds due to the twisting of the capital market so that funds flowed freely into commerce and staple movements, and away from industry, and because of the absence of independent innovative capacity" (1975, II, pp.282-283). The industrialization of Canada was left to foreign investment. The tariffs on imports imposed at the foreign investors' behest erected barriers to foreign goods, not capital. This marked the beginning of branch-plant manufacturing, which only grew as years progressed, while the commercial sectors were left to Canadian capital.

In his conclusions Naylor is entirely pessimistic, just like Innis and Levitt before him. He expects the U.S. dominance of the Canadian economy to increase and Canadian capitalists to be willing accomplices in the process. As he remarks in an article that preceded his book, "A Canadian capitalist state cannot survive because it has neither the material base nor the will to survive, the former contributing substantially to the latter" (1972, p.36).

Taking a similar approach, Wallace Clement shows in two books that the Canadian political economy is dominated by indigenous capitalists in finance, transportation, and utilities and a comprador bourgeoisie that manages U.S. branch plants (1975, 1977). The dominance of this group had shut out Canadian entrepreneurs from manufacturing because they lacked access to credit from banks or support from the government, which itself was an instrument of the dominant capitalists' commercial-financial sector.

The most extreme version of Innis's staples approach was developed by Daniel Drache (1977, 1982). Arguing that underlying Innis's approach was a "theory of rigidities," Drache uses that theory "to account both for the incomplete nature of Canada's industrial revolution and the inability of Canada to pursue a path of integrated development and become a centre economy in its own right" (1982, p.36). Indeed, Drache says that present in Innis's work is a complete account of the "staples mode of development." This mode of development has the following features:

1. The staple mode of development is defined by its commercial orientation. . . .
2. Resource development is based on monopoly. . . .
3. Infrastructure projects such as railways are designed to link the

domestic market to the imperial centre, with the result that the external market dominates industry and other core areas of the economy.

4. Direct investment gives foreign capital perpetual control of key industrial and resource sectors.

5. The rate of capital accumulation is persistently high . . . ; nonetheless [there is a] chronic capital shortage due both to the constant backflow of profits and dividends and to the capital intensive nature of resource exploitation. . . .

6. In economic matters, the Canadian state is autonomous neither in a relative nor an absolute sense; rather, as the creation of the imperial state, it functions as the instrument of foreign capital. . . .

7. The traditional neo-classical instruments of growth such as the tariff, resource exports, technology transfer and foreign investment become structures of dependency in a satellite economy. . . .

[Finally,] incomplete development is not a passing stage but a permanent condition of the periphery. (1982, pp.53-54)

This pattern of the "staple mode of development" purportedly shows how and why Canadian economic development is "incomplete" and will continue to be so unless there is a "profound realignment of class forces" (1982, p.54). While Drache does not spell out the makeup of this "realignment," he seems to be referring to an alliance between labour and indigenous capital to overthrow U.S. domination.

The New Staples Approach

Mackintosh's staple political economy did not receive the same reception as that of his counterpart, Harold Innis. His optimism that staples exports would eventually enable Canada to industrialize drew little sympathy from socialists, who saw no evidence of this occurring (Drache, 1982); but it did influence liberal nationalists concerned about Canada's apparent failure to develop into a diversified, industrialized economy following World War II. It was within a Mackintosh-inspired framework that the most systematic model of staples-led growth was developed, by Mel Watkins.

Watkins's staple theory of economic growth rests very much within the assumptions of liberal political economy: it focuses on the role played by entrepreneurs in the marketplace as a key determinant of economic development (Watkins, 1963). Although Watkins later adopted a more neo-Innisian perspective on Canada's economic development and endorsed many of the dependency arguments concerning both regional and national development in Canada (Watkins, 1977), this early work represents an excellent synthesis of the various conceptions of staples-led growth floating around in the Mackintosh-inspired staples literature at the time.

Watkins makes it clear that the staples approach applies only to "new" countries, such as those in North and South America, Australia, and New

Zealand. The distinguishing feature of these nations is their favourable ratio of natural resources (staples) to labour and capital. It is obvious from this that staples necessarily form the cornerstone of their economies.

> The limited . . . domestic market, and the factor proportion – an abundance of land relative to labour and capital – create a comparative advantage in resource-intensive exports, or staples. Economic development will be a process of diversification around an export base. The central concept of a staple theory, therefore, is the spread effects of the export sector, that is the impact of export activity on domestic economy and society. (Watkins, 1963, pp.53-54)

The extent to which the spread effects are realized depends on three kinds of "linkages" in the export of particular staples: "backward linkage, forward linkage, and final demand linkage" (ibid., p.55). The forward linkage involves investments in further processing of the staples, such as lumber into pulp and preferably paper. The backward linkage involves investments in production of the inputs required by the staples sector, such as railways to move wheat or machinery used in mining and logging. The final demand linkage is created by the expenditure of incomes generated in the production and export of staples; it exists to the extent that those incomes are used to invest in manufacturing of the goods consumed in the home country.

The establishment of these three linkages cannot be taken for granted. Much depends on the nature of the staple itself. Cod fishing afforded few linkages, because at the end of the season the fishermen tended to return to their homeland after they had caught and cured their fish; they didn't invest in backward or forward industries. Wheat, in contrast, attracted permanent immigrants who established, for example, an agricultural machinery industry (backward linkage) as well as food milling, processing, and preserving industries (forward linkage). Wheat production also automatically led to some degree of final demand linkage as industries were established to supply basic needs such as clothes, shoes, and toiletries to farmers and other members of the agricultural community.

The importance of final demand linkage is clearly the greatest if the economy is to diversify. But the full realization of this linkage remains elusive if the staples exports are in the hands of foreign investors who siphon off their profits to their home countries, leaving little behind to invest in local manufacturing. Besides, it is easier and more profitable for foreigners to supply manufactured goods to the local economy from their home country, thus making profits in both the export of staples and the import of manufactured goods. The most significant problem, however, is that staples dependence fosters an "export mentality, resulting in an overconcentration of resources in the export sector and a reluctance to promote domestic development" (Watkins, 1963, p.62). If this happens the econ-

omy is caught in the "staples trap"; it becomes dependent on the economies that receive its imports and supply its manufactured goods. Towards
the end of his article, however, Watkins indicates that he is optimistic that
eliminating the "inhibiting export mentality" is within the means of
policy-makers.

This type of new staples political-economic analysis was taken up by the
Science Council of Canada, which explicitly used the model in several of its
publications (Britton and Gilmour, 1978; Science Council, 1979, 1984),
and by the Canadian Institute for Economic Policy (Rotstein, 1984). The
objective of all of these studies was not so much to explain the development
of Canadian political economy as to provide guidelines for strengthening
domestic manufacturing. Their recommendations are based on the new
staples political economy conclusion that the high level of foreign ownership of the economy is at the root of the problems in the Canadian political
economy. As such, their project is quintessentially liberal and nationalist:
to regain control over the Canadian economy. Indeed, some of the most
widely read Canadian liberal nationalists, including Walter Gordon, have
been associated with the Canadian Institute. The analyses and proposals
put forward by the two research organizations are consistent with Watkins's
(1963) call for concerted action to overcome the staples trap.

In the Science Council's most strongly worded publication, the authors
declare: "The thesis of this study is that '. . . . the most important agent of
the industrial malaise is the way firms of foreign origin have been permitted
to operate in Canada'" (Britton and Gilmour, 1978, p.20). They point out
that foreign subsidiaries are here to maximize profits for their parent companies and not to serve the interests of Canada.

> Simply (and obviously), the behaviour of multinational corporations
> does not support the long-term aspirations of Canadians for their econ-
> omy and society. . . . The solution must, therefore, contain initial sup-
> port for Canadian firms as compensation for their more limited
> resources and must modify the economic environment in such a way that
> policies are designed to be consistent with a developing Canadian indus-
> trial sector. (p.22)

The Science Council has been particularly emphatic about Canada regain-
ing its technological sovereignty so the country does not have to rely on
foreign technology in "core" areas of the economy. To push for this objective the Council continued to recommend a host of interventionist measures. In its 1984 policy proposal, for example, it again called for subsidies
and protection from imports for domestic manufacturing. After the mid-
1980s, however, the Council watered down its proposals, perhaps because it
realized that its interventionist proposals were not appreciated by a Conservative government committed to reducing the role of the government in the
economy (see, for example, Science Council, 1988).

The publications of the Canadian Institute for Economic Policy are eclectic in character and cover a wide range of Keynesian and post-Keynesian analyses. Only a few analyze the operation of the Canadian political economy or use a formal theory to offer recommendations for improvement. The common element that binds them together is the importance they attribute to the need for overcoming dependence on staples exports and for developing a vigorous manufacturing sector.

The Institute's submission to the Macdonald Commission in 1984 represents a good example of its combination of nationalist inspirations, new staples political economy, and post-Keynesian analyses (Rotstein, 1984, pp.50-54). In typical new staples political economy fashion, it points out the perverse effects of high levels of foreign investment and the need for their reduction. It also proposes an interventionist industrial policy to promote manufacturing industries under Canadian control. Finally, in a way characteristic of the post-Keynesian literature, it opposes monetarism and proposes in its place an active fiscal and monetary policy aimed at reducing unemployment as the main priority. These policies are to be supported by an income policy negotiated with capital and labour.

The State in Staples Political Economy

The most fundamental criticism of the staples theorists is that they lack a sense of the political. That is, while working as political economists, who by definition must maintain a watchful eye on the numerous ways in which the political and the economic interact, they undermine the importance of political factors in shaping the Canadian political economy (McNally, 1981). The early staples theorists were economic or technological determinists. They ignored the importance of political institutions, political parties, elections, public policy-making, or any other of the basics of traditional political investigation.

In the early staples analysis there was no autonomous role for the state. Its actions were assumed to flow from certain economic, and primarily technological, imperatives. Its functions were defined by the exigencies of the staples trade. Policy options were limited by the constraints imposed by frontier conditions, and policies were chosen automatically by the objective requirements of staple exports (Whitaker, 1983). As Gregory Albo and Jane Jenson argue: "The nature of the state – and the particular function it performed in specific spatial and temporal locations – were derived from the needs of the staples commodity. These needs included the provision of transportation infrastructures and credit guarantees and liquidity and the promotion of staples exports in general" (1989).

Neo-Innisian staples political economists, in their concern that Canada has not developed an industrialized economy and that the country appears to be caught in a cycle of underdevelopment, suggest that the problem might lie in the conscious decision of the state and business elites to permit the dynamics of the international economy to impede industrialization in Canada. The explanations of Naylor and Clement about why the state had adopted policies that suited staple exports are explicitly political: the commercial-financial class, which controlled and benefited from those exports, had always staffed and controlled the state, thus ensuring that government policies would favour its interests (Naylor, 1975; Clement, 1975, 1977).

Like the socialist tradition that influenced them, the neo-Innisian political economists explained the role of the state in Canadian society using a theory that is characteristically instrumentalist, with all the problems that this represents. They portray Canada's industrial backwardness as a result of the dominance of the financial-commercial sector over the state. This analysis tends to ignore the role of democratic elections in the political process. Neo-Innisian analysts simply assume that the economic dominance of the commercial-financial elites is transformed automatically into political decisions favourable to them.

The new staples political economists did slightly better than the neo-Innisians in attributing due importance to the state. They allowed for the possibility of overcoming the "staples trap" through actions of the state and capital (Watkins, 1963). Unfortunately, the new staples political economists have more confidence in the ability of the state to shape the economy for the better than is warranted by its record to date. The history of state intervention in the Canadian economy is replete with examples of corruption, wastage, and making a bad situation worse. The nationalist solution of protecting and subsidizing domestic producers to promote industrialization could lead to results similar to those created by staples-led growth. A "rentier" mentality whereby the protected indigenous capitalists are content with supplying to the domestic market at great cost to the consumers might be the result (Richards, 1985, p.58). Economic nationalists cite few examples of successful cases and ignore an even larger number of unsuccessful attempts at autarchic development.

Perhaps most significantly, the proposals put forward by the new staples political economists for state action to regain control over the economy and promote industrialization do not take into account the fact that the Canadian state might be too weak to be able to heed their advice. Like the liberal post-Keynesians, they also display another misunderstanding with regard to the capacity of Canadian governments to deal with the international political economy: they tend to assume that Canada can take whatever measures it chooses to advance its own interests. This is simply not the case. Canada is bound by international agreements that it has willingly entered into and cannot violate at whim. Under international trade agreements, Canada cannot impose tariffs and quotas on imports or subsidize its exports, at least not as easily as these scholars suggest.

The Promise – and the Failure – of the Staples Approach

The staples approach to political economy enjoyed widespread popularity in Canada between the 1920s and 1950s and was revived towards the end of the 1960s under the banner of Neo-Innisian dependency theory. But its claim to be in line with dependency analysis began to be questioned in the late 1970s (Macpherson, 1979; Panitch, 1981; McNally, 1981). Socialist critics argued that the staples theorists' focus on the exchange relationships of domestic and international capital was not Marxist, because it ignored production relations and class conflict. The debate quickly became polemical, with the neo-Innisians arguing that circumstances peculiar to Canada warranted the rejection of universal Marxist formulas developed in the European context and their replacement with an indigenous socialist model that took Canada's dependence on staples into account (Drache and Clement, 1985; Drache and Kroker, 1983; Parker, 1977; Watkins, 1982).

The main strength of staples political economy is its insistence on following an inductive methodology, which largely avoids the propensity of both liberal and socialist political economy to force the world into pre-established moulds. This inductive methodology provides several avenues for further refining Canadian political economy, primarily through the pursuit of comparative studies. But until now most staples analysis has used this same methodology to argue that Canada is in some manner "exceptional." If staples political economy is to contribute further to an understanding of how the Canadian political economy operates, it must abandon its emphasis on Canadian "exceptionality." Harold Innis, the founder of the staples approach, clearly understood this point. As William Christian notes: "Innis treated Canada not as a unique phenomenon but as a particular one. . . . He worked inductively and not deductively. He drew his theory from the facts that he studied; but there was always an interpretation of facts and theory, each refining and modifying the other" (1977a, p.21).

The charge against staples analyses that they lack a comparative perspective does not apply to some recent studies in Canadian political economy, but none of these claim to be working in the staples approach (Laxer, 1989a,b; Myles, 1989; Atkinson and Coleman, 1989). Others have recognized their debt to at least classical staples theory (Williams, 1983; Richards and Pratt, 1977; Marchak, 1983; Frank, 1984; Nelles, 1974; Basran and Hay, 1988). So far the comparisons made using a staples perspective have been largely internal to Canada; that is, they are often cross-provincial or cross-regional studies.

Comparisons of Canadian economic performance with that of other developed countries have already generated insights that staples theorists could incorporate into their thinking. For example, comparative analyses have shown that Canada is not unique in experiencing an increase in foreign investment. Indeed, all industrialized nations have witnessed a tremendous increase in foreign investment (Carroll, 1986). Comparative studies have also shown that Canada's situation vis-à-vis the United States is not unique in its dependence on staples exports and imports of manufactured goods. The exports of nearly all industrialized nations to Japan consist of primary or semimanufactured products, while their Japanese imports consist almost entirely of manufactured goods. Are we to conclude, following the staples approach, that all industrialized nations are becoming Japanese "dependencies"? A comparative treatment of the Canadian political economy would also provide a useful reminder that Canada is not always the loser in its relationship with the United States: over the last several years, the flow of Canadian investments to the United States has exceeded the flow in the reverse direction (Carroll, 1986; Niosi, 1982, 1985), and not all Americans are pleased with this development.

Gordon Laxer is correct when he suggests: "To renew itself, the new political economy needs to modify several assumptions which have more to do with belief than with the reality of Canada's international position. The idea of external control of Canadian life is too rigidly held. It is easy to blame others" (1989a, p.186).

Notes

1 The Canadian "new political economy" is to be distinguished from its U.S. counterpart, which refers to the application of public choice theory, the fundamentals of which are the same as those of neoclassical economics, to the study of politics.

2 Reference to Harold Innis by the neo-Innisians as a nationalist is ironic, given his frequent invectives against it. In particularly strong language he once remarked: "Warm fetid smell of nationalism the breeding ground of the pestilences of the west, the worship of which kills its millions" (Christian, 1977b, p.62). In another instance he noted, in an inversion of Lord Acton's dictum, that "Nationalism is still the last refuge of scoundrels" (Williams, 1986, p.38). Yet it cannot be denied that Innis was acutely aware of Canada's peripheral position in world capitalism, and in his later works he pointed out that Canada had exchanged British for U.S. dominance (Christian, 1977b, p.62); "from colony to nation to colony" as he described it. Ignoring his antinationalist diatribe, his followers in the staples school emphasize his anticolonial sentiments (Drache, 1969; Watkins, 1982) because it bolsters their case against U.S. dominance of Canada.

CHAPTER 5

The Structure and Organization of the Economy

All of the approaches and theories of political economy discussed so far have this feature in common: they undertheorize the question of the role of politics and the state. Although each approach notes the interrelationships that exist between states and markets in capitalist economies, each assumes a certain role for the state based on a particular theoretical analysis of the functioning of such an economy. All the existing theories primarily analyse the manner in which markets exist and operate in capitalist society and consider the activities of the state as flowing from the fundamental characteristics of functioning market economies. They fail to investigate the manner in which states actually operate and make decisions or policies, but simply assume that governments will implement policies that will further the functional requisites of market economies and their dominant actors. None of the theories examine whether states operate in practice in the manner prescribed to be theoretically optimum or, indeed, if they are capable of doing so.

In assessing the question of the actual role played by the Canadian state in the country's political economy it is important to focus on the general nature of constraints on, and opportunities for, state activity posed by the system of market relations in which the state operates. Certain constraints are placed on state action by the system of production found in Canada, while others originate in the existing system of international trade. Moreover, other constraints are posed by the organization of the state itself and by the extent of organization of the two major societal actors that the state faces in the domestic political economy: labour and capital.

Why would a Canadian government want to intervene in a system that, for all its flaws, has generated a high standard of living by international standards? The answer to this question lies in the fact that the existing system of market-based production and allocation of wealth, coupled with the way the domestic political economy is integrated into the international political economy, generates severe inequalities in incomes, opportunities, and quality of life. These inequalities are generally unacceptable to citizens of a democratic polity, and the existence of a democratic governing process allows individuals and groups in Canadian society to demand that the state use its authority to alter market arrangements so the disparities are eliminated or reduced.

Whether or not the state recognizes these demands or eventually acts on them remains to be seen. In Canada, as elsewhere, many citizens benefit little from the operation of a market-based economy and want to see its alteration; but others receive a larger share of the benefits and don't want to lose their privileges. Thus the state is pressured to both retain and reform the status quo; and how the state responds ultimately depends on the strengths of the groups that are advocating various positions, and upon the ability of the state itself to resist societal pressures.

This question of *state autonomy*, or of the capacity or incapacity of states to undertake policies and activities independently of societal pressures, is complex. State and societal actors operate in two key contexts: the domestic political economy and the international political economy. And any theoretical analysis must take into account four significant aspects of the Canadian domestic and international political economies: first, the production of wealth in Canada has been and remains dependent on resource production and the export of resource commodities to international markets, increasingly to the United States. Second, the regions of the country are not all equally dependent on these resource exports. Third, regional economies based on resource exports are inherently unstable and there are significant inequalities in wealth and incomes in the various regions of the country. Fourth, Canadian governments can and do attempt to offset these inequalities through massive public expenditures. But in many cases the governments can do little to address the root causes of these problems, because of the way the instabilities stem from the nature of international resource trade, and because of the commitments Canadian government have made to perpetuating the existing international trading system.

The Economy in Comparative Perspective

An analysis of the economic structure of a country usually starts with a description of how many and what kinds of different goods and services are produced in that country – information that says a great deal about what people do there, how wealthy they are, and, by implication, which industries and productive activities are most significant to the nation's political economy as a whole. Examining the structure of a solitary domestic econ-

Table 1

Canadian Economic Performance in Comparative Perspective

	($000,000 U.S. -1989)
Algeria	58,500
Bangladesh	18,100
Bulgaria	51,200
Canada	513,400
Ecuador	11,500
Indonesia	88,700
Japan	1,913,400
Saudi Arabia	72,900
U.K.	817,700
U.S.	5,198,400
U.S.S.R.	2,663,700
Zaire	6,600

SOURCE: Central Intelligence Agency, Directorate of Intelligence, *Handbook of Economic Statistics, 1990* (Springfield, VA: U.S. Department of Commerce National Technical Information Service, 1991).

omy, however, does not reveal whether or not, or to what extent, that economy is typical or atypical of modern nation-states. To obtain that type of information, we need to compare the nation's performance with the record of other countries.

The best indicators of aggregate national economic performance are measures known as Gross National Product (GNP) and Gross Domestic Product (GDP). These are closely related figures that give the total costs of producing all the goods and services found in a country in a given year. They include all wages paid out, all investments made, and all the profits taken by all the companies and individuals producing goods or services in the country. As such, they are very large figures that can be broken down by region or by production activity, as need be.[1] Using GDP, Table 1 shows that the total value of production in Canada is large by international standards, outranking all of the countries listed except Japan, the United States, and the United Kingdom. The Canadian economy, though much larger than the economies of Ecuador or even Saudia Arabia, is about one-quarter the size of the Japanese economy and one-tenth the size of the U.S. economy. The figures indicate roughly where the Canadian economy stands in the world: somewhere in the middle. This middle position accounts for the fact that there are a variety of interpretations of Canada's economic performance.

Whether its performance is viewed positively or negatively depends, to a certain extent, on the countries Canada is compared to.

The aggregate production figures in Table 1 are somewhat misleading as an indication of economic performance: they reveal a great deal about general economic performance but little about the standard of wealth in a country, which must be measured not against overall economic activity but against the size of the population. To evaluate a country's standard of living we use GNP or GDP *per capita*: the country's aggregate value of production divided by its population. This figure gives an idea of the wealth of individual citizens as compared to people in other countries.

As Table 2 illustrates, while Canada is not one of the largest producing nations by international standards, it is a rich one. Canadian per capita GDP ranks among the highest in the world, much higher than most Third World countries, only slightly behind the United States, and higher than countries such as Japan and the United Kingdom which have larger economies than Canada. Although per capita GDP reveals little about the quality of life in a country or about such aspects of everyday life as the levels of crime or pollution that citizens must endure, it does provide a more accurate comparison of national wealth than simple aggregate GNP does. But even per capital GNP or GDP reveals little about the creation of wealth in society,

Table 2
Canadian Per Capita GDP in Comparative Perspective

	($U.S. -1989)
Algeria	2,350
Bangladesh	160
Bulgaria	5,690
Canada	19,600
Ecuador	1,170
Indonesia	480
Japan	15,530
Saudi Arabia	4,450
U.K.	14,300
U.S.	20,890
U.S.S.R.	9,230
Zaire	190

SOURCE: Central Intelligence Agency, Directorate of Intelligence, *Handbook of Economic Statistics, 1990* (Springfield, VA: U.S. Department of Commerce National Technical Information Service, 1991).

or its distribution. To discuss these important aspects of a country's political economy, other measures are needed.

Domestic Economic Performance

Income Distribution Between Individuals

A good aggregate measure of the distribution of wealth in society is arrived at by taking the total income of the country and determining how many families or unattached individuals receive fixed percentages of that income. The usual method adopted by national statistical agencies – such as Statistics Canada – is to rank citizens by their income and then determine how many individuals or families fall into each 20 percent group or quintile of total national income. Table 3 presents the Canadian figures for 1988, indicating a wide disparity in incomes. The top 20 percent of the population earns 47 per cent of total income while the bottom 20 percent earns about 3 percent of total income. Although some countries have a much worse record, these figures reveal the inequities of Canadian income distribution: less than one-half of the Canadian population earns about three-quarters of the country's total income.

Incomes also vary significantly in Canada by region, ethnic origin, age, and gender. Families headed by women are much more likely to live below the poverty line, as are families headed by members of the country's aboriginal peoples. In 1981, 41.8 percent or almost one-half of all families headed by women were classified as poor, and 40 percent of all Native families in the country lived with more than two families per dwelling. Aged persons, and especially aged women, also suffered from high poverty rates. Over 58 percent of elderly single women lived below the poverty line in 1983, more than four times the very high rate found among retired men (National Council on Welfare, 1983).

Income Distribution by Region

The regional, spatial, or geographic distribution of production is a particularly important aspect of political-economic analysis because of what it reveals about differences in incomes and occupations. Some countries have a more or less equal spatial distribution of production throughout the national territory and hence a more or less equal distribution of incomes and occupations. Most do not, and Canada certainly has a marked inequality in its spatial distribution of production, which results in significantly different demands being placed on governments in different parts of the country.

To investigate these regional differences we will look at the regional distribution of aggregate production and at the regional distribution of incomes. The figures in Table 4 provide a breakdown of GDP by province and the percentage that each province contributes to the national total.

Table 3
Aggregate Income Distribution in Canada – 1988

Quintile	% Total Income	Cumulative
Top 20 percent	46.9	46.9
20-40 percent	25.1	72.0
40-60 percent	15.7	87.7
60-80 percent	9.0	96.7
Bottom 20 percent	3.3	100.0

SOURCE: Statistics Canada (1988), *Income Distribution by Size in Canada*, Catalogue No. 15-207 (Ottawa: Minister of Supply and Services Canada).

Table 4
Provincial GDP and Share of National GDP – 1988

	Provincial GDP ($000,000)	Share of National Total (%)
Newfoundland	7,864	1.3
Prince Edward Island	1,762	0.3
Nova Scotia	14,814	2.5
New Brunswick	11,726	1.9
Quebec	144,031	23.9
Ontario	247,969	41.2
Manitoba	21,483	3.6
Saskatchewan	18,578	3.1
Alberta	63,489	10.5
British Columbia	68,216	11.3
NWT/Yukon	2,626	0.4

SOURCE: Statistics Canada (1990), *Provincial Economic Accounts*, Catalogue No. 13-213 (Ottawa: Minister of Supply and Services Canada).

The figures show a wide range of GDPs among provinces. More significantly, about 65 percent of Canadian economic activity takes place in the two Central provinces of Quebec and Ontario. The four provinces of Atlantic Canada account for only 6 percent of total production, while the four Western provinces account for about 30 percent. In other words, about two-thirds of Canadian production occurs in Central Canada and about one-third in the Western provinces. This means, of course, that the two Central Canadian provinces are clearly the dominant economic units in the country.

Table 5
Provincial Per Capita Incomes – 1988

	Gross Incomes	% Ontario	Per Capita Federal Transfers	Net Without Transfers	% Ontario
Newfoundland	13,850	63.4	3,095	10,755	47.4
Prince Edward Island	14,411	65.9	4,315	10,096	44.5
Nova Scotia	16,083	73.5	3,758	12,325	55.2
New Brunswick	15,062	68.9	2,526	12,536	55.2
Quebec	18,520	84.7	304	18,222	80.3
Ontario	21,861	(100)	–831	22,692	100.0
Manitoba	17,167	78.5	1,521	15,646	68.9
Saskatchewan	15,754	72.0	1,854	13,900	61.2
Alberta	19,947	91.2	–1,688	21,635	95.4
British Columbia	19,179	87.7	–645	19,824	87.4
National Average	19,517				

SOURCE: Statistics Canada (1988), *National Income and Expenditure Accounts*,
Catalogue No. 13-001 (Ottawa: Minister of Supply and Services); and
Horry, Isabella D. and Michael A. Wallace (1991), *Government
Spending Facts* (Vancouver: Fraser Institute).

As we saw in comparing Canadian GNP to that of other countries,
however, these aggregate statistics can be misleading for estimating the
relative wealth of different jurisdictions, because they do not take into
account variations in size of population. All things being equal, we would
expect Ontario and Quebec, with their large populations, to produce more
than other less populated provinces. Once again, a better measure of wealth
is not GNP or GDP alone, but GNP or GDP per capita.

As the figures in Table 5 show, including the government's corrective
measures, provincial per capita incomes vary by as much as 29 percent
below and 12 percent above the national average. When federal transfers are
deducted the variations are more severe, with the Maritime provinces ave-
raging only one-half of the per capita income of Ontario.

Not surprisingly, then, wealth and poverty have a regional dimension in
Canada because of the unequal regional distribution of production. While
about 15 percent of the Canadian population lived below the poverty line in
the early 1980s, this percentage was not evenly distributed among the
provinces. Over 18 percent of the families in Newfoundland and New
Brunswick lived below the poverty line, as opposed to only about 10 percent
of those in Alberta and British Columbia.

Again, other countries have much worse records in distribution of income, while still others enjoy much more equitable arrangements. Nevertheless, there are significant distributional inequities in Canada, and certain people and groups in Canadian society benefit more than others from the operation of the political economy.

In a democratically organized market economy these inequities can and do lead to demands for political or state action to alter the situation, and Canadian governments have responded to these demands by using a variety of redistributive means to bolster individual and regional incomes. These include provision of welfare and social security payments, transfers of federal tax revenues to provincial governments, and the provision of regional development grants and subsidies to corporations willing to locate in regionally depressed areas. Some of these efforts have been reasonably successful, while others have not succeeded in altering the existing situation. In general the programs have succeeded only in raising the average provincial per capita income in the Maritime provinces from one-half to two-thirds of the Ontario level.

The Sectoral Structure of the Economy

While a country's aggregate distribution of production and income provides important facts for any political-economic investigation, the particular manner in which goods and services are produced is also extremely important for an understanding of how the political economy operates and the constraints and opportunities that state faces. An analysis of the sectoral structure of a country's economy reveals a great deal about why certain areas of a country or certain strata of its population are rich or poor and about the types of demands governments handle when determining the extent of state involvement in the functioning of the economy.

The best way to look at the sectoral structure of the economy is to consider the amount and nature of goods and services produced in each of the three major sectors of the economy: primary, secondary, and tertiary (Fisher, 1966). The primary sector of the economy is composed of all economic activities associated with the extraction and production of natural resources. According to the United Nations system of Standard Industrial Classification (SIC), these activities include agriculture, forestry, fishing, mining, and oil and gas exploration. The secondary sector is composed of all activities associated with the further processing of natural resources and manufacturing. The tertiary sector is composed of the various goods and services provided to support or organize the primary and secondary sectors, including construction and transportation, finance, real estate and insurance, public administration, and the wholesale and retail trades.

In most countries the historical trend has been for economic activity to

Table 6
Sectoral Distribution of Canadian Economic Activity

	(% GNP/GDP)		(% Employment)	
	1880	1983	1891	1984
Primary	43.5	10.1	49.2	7.1
Secondary	18.9	19.0	14.7	17.9
Tertiary	37.6	71.2	36.1	75.0

SOURCE: Statistics Canada (1984), *GDP by Industry 1984*, Catalogue No. 61-213 (Ottawa: Minister of Supply and Services Canada). Buckley, K.A.H. and M.C. Urquhart (1965), *Historical Statistics of Canada* (Toronto: Macmillan).

shift from the primary to the secondary sectors and finally towards the tertiary or service sector (Kuznets, 1966). This same trend appears to have been the case in Canada, as the figures in Table 6 indicate.

Both the amount of goods and services produced and the numbers of people employed in each sector have shifted decisively towards the tertiary or service sector. On a national basis, the primary and tertiary sectors have shifted locations as sources of economic production. This change has been caused primarily by a rapid decline in agricultural activity and employment, which fell from 32 percent of GNP and about 46 percent of employment in 1880-91 to between 3 and 4 percent of each in 1983-84. Most of this economic activity and employment has been picked up in the tertiary sector, and especially in the provision of various kinds of services, which rose from 38 percent of GNP and employment in 1880-81 to over 70 percent in 1983-84.

This is not to say that the Canadian economy is now any less reliant on natural resource-based production to generate its wealth than it was in the past. Much of Canada's manufacturing base consists of processing resource-based commodities such as lumber, pulp and paper, and various mineral and oil-based products, which are all commonly thought of as "primary production" although the United Nations SIC system classifies them as "manufacturing industries." In 1983, $17.8 billion or about one-quarter of Canada's domestic manufacturing capacity was accounted for by the wood, paper, and allied products industries along with the primary metal, non-metallic, and petroleum and coal products industries. A further $10.2 billion of Canada's economic activity involved electricity generation. Other areas of economic activity, such as the rail and truck transportation of resources and resource products and many construction projects, are closely related to these natural-resource activities. In addition, resource activities generate indirect effects, from banking and financial arrangements associated with large-scale capital projects to the food, cars, and other expenditures made by consumers who earn their salaries in the resource sector. In all, resource and resource-based activities generate as much as fifty cents out of every dollar produced in this country.

This continued reliance of the Canadian economy on primary resources and resource-based manufacturing puts it at odds with the situation in many other large nation-states and has important consequences for the operation of the Canadian political economy. Three aspects of this resource dependence are especially significant. First, many of these resources and resource-based manufactured goods are exported; their primary markets are in international trade. Second, there is an important regional aspect, because not all parts of the country are as reliant on resources as others are. Third, the Canadian state relies on resource-based activity to generate the tax revenues and royalties required to fund its activities.

Significant Aspects of the Resource-Based Economy

The International Structure

Canada has a marked dependence on international trade for the generation of wealth. As the figures in Table 7 indicate, Canadian trade dependence is high among the nations of the Organization for Economic Co-operation and Development (OECD) and has increased over the past twenty-five years. The figures in Table 8 also show that the actual goods Canada exports to generate such a large proportion of its GNP are primarily resource goods, either in a raw state or only slightly processed.

While the level of manufactured exports increased dramatically between 1960 and 1980, most of this increase occurred in a single sector: the automobile industry, covered by a special trading arrangement, the Canada-U.S. Auto Pact. Although the Auto Pact has contributed to the increased export of cars, under its terms Canada also imports large numbers of assembled automobiles and auto parts. Canada's positive balance of trade in merchandise items remains reliant on natural-resource exports, as Table 9 illustrates.

In fact, the total primary processing sector generates an annual trade surplus of over $30 billion – a sum sufficient to pay for all the deficits incurred importing highly manufactured goods as well as the large yearly deficit on services trade incurred largely as a result of the large sums flowing out of the country in dividend and interest payments, as well as in areas such as tourism.

Although in the past Canada had two major markets for its exports – the United States and the United Kingdom – this situation has changed dramatically since World War II. Since 1940 the U.S. market has emerged as the major destination for all Canadian exports, with Canadian trade steadily shifting away from the United Kingdom.

The United States alone now accounts for more than two-thirds of all

Table 7
Canadian Trade Dependence in International Perspective

	(Exports as a Percent of GDP)	
	1965	1980
Canada	15.6	25.6
France	10.2	17.1
Japan	9.5	12.4
U.K.	13.3	22.0
U.S.	3.9	8.4
W. Germany	15.6	23.6
OECD Average	9.0	16.5

SOURCE: Canada, External Affairs (1983), *A Review of Canadian Trade Policy* (Ottawa: Minister of Supply and Services Canada), p. 20.

Table 8
Percent Exports by Commodity Group

	1960	1980
Agricultural Goods	18.8	11.6
Crude Materials	21.2	18.7
Fabricated Materials	51.9	37.6
Manufactured Goods	7.8	31.2

SOURCE: Canada, External Affairs (1983), *A Review of Canadian Trade Policy* (Ottawa: Minister of Supply and Services Canada), p. 26.

Table 9
Canadian Merchandise Trade Balances – 1983

	($000,000,000s)
Agricultural Products	4.60
Forest Products	11.91
Crude Minerals	2.06
Energy Products	7.68
Fishing and Marine Products	1.13
Semiprocessed Minerals	2.92
Automobiles and Parts	1.92
Other Highly Manufactured Goods	–18.70

SOURCE: Wilkinson, B. (1985), "Canada's Resource Industries," in J. Whalley, ed., *Canada's Export Industries and Water Export Policy* (Toronto: University of Toronto Press), p. 3.

Table 10
Direction of Canadian Export Trade – 1900-80

	1900	*(percent)* 1920	1940	1960	1980
U.S.	38.3	37.4	41.1	55.8	66.2
U.K.	52.3	39.4	35.5	17.4	4.0
Japan	0.1	0.6	2.5	3.4	5.4
Other Europe	2.9	13.8	6.3	8.3	10.7
Third World	—	—	—	7.9	11.9
Other (e.g. U.S.S.R.)	6.4	8.8	14.6	7.2	1.8

SOURCE: Webb, M.C. and M.W. Zacher, (1985), "Canada's Export Trade in a
Changing International Environment," in D. Stairs and G.R. Winham,
eds., *Canada and the International Political/Economic Environment*
(Toronto: University of Toronto Press), pp. 88-89.

Canadian exports and is by far the largest single market for Canadian
goods. The effects of this growing dependence on the U.S. market are far-
reaching, and the rules of the international trading system that govern this
trade have a very significant impact on the policies that Canadian governments can adopt.

The Regional Distribution of Sectoral Activity

Although the Canadian economy as a whole never did experience the shift
into manufacturing industries envisioned by the orthodox theory of economic development, the economies of Ontario and, to a lesser degree,
Quebec were able to make the move.

The figures in Table 11 indicate an unequal distribution of sectoral

Table 11
Distribution of Sectoral Economic Activity by Region – 1983-84

	Primary	*(% National GDP)* *Secondary*	*Tertiary*
Atlantic	4.3	3.8	7.6
Central	21.1	78.9	59.3
West	74.6	17.3	33.1
	(100)	(100)	(100)

SOURCE: Statistics Canada, *Provincial GDP by Industry, 1983*, Catalogue No.
61-202 (Ottawa: Minister of Supply and Services Canada), pp. 27-35.

Table 12
Primary Sector Component of Provincial GDP – 1980/83

	(% Provincial GDP)
Newfoundland	16.2
Prince Edward Island	12.8
Nova Scotia	6.3
New Brunswick	6.0
Quebec	3.9
Ontario	5.1
Manitoba	11.2
Saskatchewan	27.0
Alberta	28.3
British Columbia	9.8

SOURCE: Anderson, F.J. (1985), *Natural Resources in Canada* (Toronto: Methuen), pp. 16-17. Statistics Canada (1983), *Provincial GDP by Industry*, Catalogue No. 61-202 (Ottawa: Minister of Supply and Services Canada).

Table 13
Percent Regional Resource-based Manufacturing Activity – 1980

Atlantic	56.7
Quebec	29.0
Ontario	20.5
Prairies	27.5
B.C.	63.1
Canada	29.0

SOURCE: Anderson, F.J. (1985), *Natural Resources in Canada* (Toronto: Methuen), pp. 16-17.

economic activities by region. The Western provinces have a high share of Canadian primary production; that is, agricultural and natural resource production. Central Canada, on the other hand, completely dominates manufacturing activities. The Atlantic provinces, with their relatively small economies, not surprisingly remain marginal in all three sectors of the national economy. But, as Tables 12 and 13 show, these provinces still rely heavily on their natural resources and service sector to generate economic wealth.

These figures illustrate that the Atlantic region and British Columbia remain heavily dependent on resource activities for their economic well-being. Only Quebec and Ontario have diversified economies that are not entirely resource-dependent – although even in those provinces substantial economic activity is still directly associated with resource extraction and processing.

The inhabitants of the Western and Atlantic provinces gain their wealth from natural-resource and agricultural activities, which, because of their dependence on uncontrollable foreign markets and the large amounts of capital invested in them, are inherently less stable than the manufacturing activities located in Central Canada. Canada has a monopoly or near-monopoly on the production of only a few resources or agricultural goods, and Canadian producers must sell at prices set by international conditions of supply and demand. Canadians are not price-makers but price-takers in international markets. While international demand for most resources – outside of wartime – has increased at a relatively steady but low rate, world supplies of certain primary products are highly variable. A good harvest, the discovery of significant new reserves of minerals or oil, or the addition of new production capacity in the fishery or forest products sectors can greatly add to world supplies and quickly drive down world prices. Those prices stay down until demand catches up and surpasses supplies, resulting in sudden price increases, which spur additional exportation and production, and so on. These fluctuations in international supplies account for the boom and bust cycles seen in most resource industries and, by implication, most resource-based economies.

The instability of regional resource-based economies generates personal and regional disparities in incomes. Resource-dependent regions of the country can enjoy periods of high or low incomes, depending on international supply and demand factors affecting their particular resources. Given the orientation of most resource exports towards the U.S. market, in effect this means depending on the state of international supplies and U.S. demand. Any increase in international supplies or decrease in U.S. demand can devastate a regional economy; the reverse situation can bring on a wave of new-found prosperity.

Both these aspects of regional economic health remain largely outside the control of Canadian governments. Those same governments, though, will receive demands for ameliorative action from residents of affected regions whenever economic downturns occur. Because the governments rely on taxes and royalties generated from these same resource-based activities for the majority of their revenues, any funds required to offset adverse economic conditions in the regions must come from outside the region. This in itself serves as major constraint on state activity. The Canadian state is not well suited to respond to these demands because in a federal state regional demands for additional funds have the effect of pitting different governments against each other – whether it is provincial governments urging the

Table 14
Government Expenditures in Canada by Level of Government – 1985

	($000,000s)
Federal	120,440
Provincial	109,515
Local	39,279
Total	**269,234**
GDP	502,670
Government % of GDP	53.5

SOURCE: Statistics Canada (1985), *Canada Year Book* (Ottawa: Minister of Supply and Services), pp. 733, 723.

federal government to redistribute funds from one region of the country to another; or governments of "have" regions resisting transfers to "have not" regions for fear that those transfers might be permanent rather than a temporary means of getting through until the next upswing in resource prices.

Public Sector Reliance on Resource-Based Activity

The third aspect of Canada's resource-based economy is the reliance of the Canadian state on that economy to generate taxes and royalties and fund expenditures.

The resource-funded public sector in Canada is large, although not overly so by international standards. As the figures in Table 14 show, by the mid-1980s government expenditures accounted for just over 50 percent of all goods and services produced in Canada. A much larger percentage of economic activity is subject to some form of government regulation or administration.[2] By international standards the size of the Canadian public sector is about average for market economies. Many countries have larger percentages of their overall economic activity accounted for by governments, while many have less. Table 15 presents some international comparisons.

While government expenditures are an important part of Canadian economic activities, government employment is also an important element of the Canadian occupational structure. As the figures in Table 16 illustrate, Canadian governments directly employ about 20 percent of the labour force. Once again, in comparative perspective the Canadian figure is large, but it is not exceptionally so when placed against the experience of other similar political economies, as the figures in Table 17 show.

Revenues to pay for these expenditures and employees are generated from

Table 15
Canadian Government Expenditures in International Comparison

	(% Government Share of GDP – 1980-81)
Canada	41.1
U.S.	35.2
U.K.	46.5
Japan	33.6
France	47.7
W. Germany	48.8
Sweden	63.7
Australia	33.9
Spain	33.0

SOURCE: Cameron, D.R. (1986), "The Growth of Government Spending: The Canadian Experience in Comparative Perspective," in K. Banting, ed., *State and Society: Canada in Comparative Perspective* (Toronto: University of Toronto Press), p. 24.

taxes – the largest being personal and corporate income taxes, and sales taxes including the federal Goods and Services Tax (GST) – and from government borrowings on both domestic and international financial markets. While governments can carry large debt loads for long periods of time, payments of both interest and principle must eventually come from taxes. These taxes and royalties paid to governments for the use of public lands and resources – amounting to about 85 percent of the Canadian land base – largely originate in the wages and profits generated by resource-based activities. The ability of Canadian governments to undertake the delivery of goods and services to Canadian citizens, then, like everything else in Canada, is subject to the health and vigour of the resource-based primary and secondary manufacturing components of the economy. Like everything else in Canada, these activities are subject to international constraints and regional variations in economic activities.

Political Implications of the Economic Structure

An important political consequence of the resource orientation of the economy is the strong demand it generates for government relief in times of low resource prices. The demands for relief as made both by resource industries and workers tend to be temporary and involve different types of insurance schemes, such as government-administered unemployment insurance or crop insurance. Small resource producers have also sought out government assistance in preventing large companies from manipulating

Table 16
Public Sector Employment in Canada by Level of Government – 1982

Federal	General Government	351,295	
	Government Enterprise	138,281	
	Armed Forces	82,888	
	Total		**572,464**
Provincial	General Government	317,407	
	Government Enterprise	159,260	
	Total		**476,667**
Local	General Government	287,103	
	Government Enterprise	45,577	
	Total		**332,680**
Other	Education	509,006	
	Hospitals	297,195	
	Total		**806,201**
Total Government Employment			**2,188,012**
Total Labour Force			**11,743,000**
Percent Government Employment			**18.6**

SOURCE: Sutherland, S. and G.B. Doern (1985), *Bureaucracy in Canada: Control and Reform* (Toronto: University of Toronto Press), pp. 134-135.

Table 17
Government Employment as Share of Total Employment – 1982

	(%)
Canada	19.9
Australia	25.4
Sweden	31.8
U.K.	22.4
U.S.	16.7
France	16.1
W. Germany	15.6
Japan	6.6

SOURCE: See Table 15.

prices; this usually involves the creation of marketing boards in areas such as grains, fish, fur, or pulpwood.

The demand for state-sponsored redistribution also originates in the general shift in employment from agriculture to services. Although the service sector is large and encompasses a whole range of activities from finance to transportation and communications, employment gains have been concentrated in the wholesale and retail sectors and the business and personal service sectors. In these sectors employment tends to be low-wage, often involving women, since it is often available on a part-time or "casual" basis – compatible with the historically imposed family obligations of women.

Individuals in these categories, not surprisingly, demand action from the state that would help them to obtain the same standard of living available to employees of high-wage resource and resource-manufacturing activities: for instance, permanent increases in income through public provision of essential services or the creation of a "social wage" in the form of government-funded health insurance, pensions, education, public housing, or subsidized electricity. Because incomes and profits in most activities associated with services are generally low, governments must redistribute income earned in other sectors of the economy to improve the conditions of service-sector workers. Most government redistributive measures in Canada do this by taxing incomes and profits earned in the high-wage primary and secondary sectors and funnelling them to the populous low-wage workforce in the tertiary sector.

The health of the primary and secondary sectors, then, is of great importance not only to regional economies but also to the operation of the whole political economy. These activities must provide both a reasonable return for the people engaged in them and a return high enough so that governments can undertake programs to improve the standards of living of people who are unemployed, unemployable, or underemployed. In Canada the demands for interregional, intersectoral, and interpersonal redistribution of fiscal resources are specific manifestations of the more general tendency in all democratic market systems for electors to demand redistributive action from the state to offset market-based inequalities in incomes and opportunities. Conditions and circumstances vary in different countries concerning the nature of these demands for action and the ability and willingness of the state to respond to them. At a very basic level, the responses of the Canadian government to this general tendency are seriously constrained by the resource-export-dependent nature of the production of wealth in this country.

Notes

1 GNP includes investments made outside the region and investments made by non-residents in the region. GDP does not include these investments.

GNP is therefore always larger than GDP, which means that GDP is, in fact, the best measure of production within a given territory. But the difference is usually small enough that the two can be used interchangeably, which is what we will do here.

2 These figures actually underestimate the extent of government activities. Not only do they ignore government regulatory activity, but they also account only for government expenditures made from revenues actually collected. Canadian governments also strongly affect economic activities through decisions to not collect certain taxes or royalties if individual or corporate taxpayers agree to undertake specified activities in return. Although it is extremely difficult to measure this type of tax expenditure, and few studies exist on the extent of such activities in Canada, a reasonable estimate places the cost of tax expenditures at the federal level alone at about 50 percent of federally budgeted expenditures. This means, of course, that Canadian economic activities, either accounted for directly or heavily influenced by government activities, amount to a figure closer to 60 or 70 percent of GDP than 50 percent (Canada, Dept. of Finance, 1979, 1980, 1985; Woodside, 1983).

CHAPTER 6

Canada and the
International
Political Economy

The opening up of international trade – led by Britain in the nineteenth century and the United States in the twentieth century – continues to affect every industrialized nation, albeit in different ways and to different degrees. This has been especially true since the establishment of the new political-economic order under the aegis of the General Agreement on Tariffs and Trade (GATT) and the International Monetary Fund (IMF) immediately after World War II. The new order not only fostered interdependence among nations but also created imperatives for nations to resist the adverse effects of interdependence while maximizing the benefits. The result has been an unparalleled degree of openness in the world economy co-existing with the clever manipulation of international trade rules by nations seeking to turn things in their own favour.

The contemporary international political economy is both an economic and a political order. On the economic side it is based on the liberal doctrine of comparative advantage, or "free trade," which postulates that each nation should export the products that it can produce most efficiently and import the rest. This doctrine presumes the primacy of market forces, which are deemed to deliver maximum economic benefits to all participating nations. On the political side the international political economy derives from the acknowledgement that market forces do not benefit all nations equally. The nations that benefit the most promote the doctrine of free trade in its purest form while the remainder manipulate the rules as best they can. But even the states avowedly committed to the doctrine of comparative advantage intervene to check the adverse effects of open trade and to gain artificial advantage over their trading partners.

Government intervention to manipulate market forces is a common feature of the market-oriented postwar economic order. As the 1985 Canadian Macdonald Commission noted, "Governments do not serenely observe the operation of international market forces without concern for their impact on their society, economy and people, and indirectly, therefore, on the status and power of individual states in the international system." The commission also observed: "It is misleading, therefore, to view the post-war liberal international economic order as a market order. It is a political order within which national governments are prime actors in a system where they have allowed market forces considerable freedom to operate" (Macdonald Commission, 1985, Vol.1, p.31). In modern political economy the free operation of market forces co-exists with state intervention, and this is as evident on the international scene as on the domestic. Canada's participation in the new international economic order has been no different than that of other countries: professing faith in reduced barriers to trade, largely abiding by the principles but also conveniently ignoring them, even manipulating them, when convenient.

The concept of *international political economy* (IPE) as understood here is broader than international trade relations. It includes formal treaties and agreements governing the terms of trade among nations. The prime examples are GATT and the Canada-United States Free Trade Agreement (FTA). The concept also includes the relative economic and political standing of nations in the world. The sheer size of the U.S. and Japanese economies, for example, gives these two nations more power and influence to shape the international economy than a small country, such as, say, Fiji or Iceland. Canada, though no match for the United States or Japan, is more powerful economically than most other nations of the world and possesses a limited ability to manipulate trading in its favour. Another significant aspect of IPE is the historical pattern of a nation's trade, which establishes a structure of relationships that impose constraints and provide opportunities to national policy-makers on an enduring basis. For example, the open order established after World War II enhanced trade opportunities for the highly competitive Canadian resource industries, but at the same time it constrained the Canadian government from protecting its vulnerable consumer products industries from imports.

The structure of IPE is, however, far from monolithic. There is no basic law such as a constitution at the international level that governs the relations among nations. International agreements (such as the GATT or FTA) are weak substitutes for a constitution because of their voluntary character. The absence of a body such as a state with the authority to enforce the norms, rules, and agreements of international relations only aggravates the loose character of IPE, offering opportunities for manipulation depending on a country's relative economic, political, and military strength. Numerous studies have emphasized Canada's position as a middle-power in IPE (Fox and Jacobson, 1973; Fox, 1977; Lyon and Tomlin, 1979; Wood, 1988).

The main implication of this is that Canada is quite powerless in dealing with the dominant powers, the United States, Japan, and the European Community (EC).

The Canadian Position

The feature of the Canadian economy that plays the most critical role in Canada's international economic relations is its historic dependence on international trade. The Europeans colonized Canada so they could sell its natural resources in the world market. The proceeds from the exports paid for the importation of goods consumed by the settlers. So, right from the start, Canada has been a trading nation, and its economy has become dependent on trade. Reflecting the importance of trade, Canada established its Trade Commissioner Service as far back as 1892, long before the establishment of its own diplomatic service (Canada, Dept. of External Affairs, 1983, p.4). The importance of international trade to the Canadian economy has fostered the government's keen participation in most major international trade institutions such as GATT, the IMF, and the World Bank, as well as in the United Nations and its various specialized agencies.

An overwhelming, and increasing, proportion of Canada's trade for most of this century has been with one country, the United States. In 1988, while the United States absorbed more than 75 percent of our exports, almost 80 percent of our total imports also came from that country (Economic Council of Canada, 1988, p.3). Canada has traditionally maintained a trade surplus on its "merchandise account" with the United States (that is to say, it has exported more goods than it has imported), but it has run even larger deficits on its "non-merchandise account," which includes trade in services and the transfer of profits by subsidiaries of U.S. firms (Canada, Dept. of Finance, 1988). Meanwhile, the United States is not dependent upon Canada to anywhere near the same extent; only 19.3 percent of its total trade is with Canada, even though Canada remains its single largest trading partner (Macdonald Commission, 1985, Vol. I, p.63).

The dominance of resource products in its exports also affects Canada's international economic objectives. Until the turn of the century, the Canadian economy was based on exports of fish, fur, timber, and wheat. In the twentieth century, as industrialization swept the world at an unprecedented speed, the demand increased for Canada's natural, especially mineral, resources, making the country one of the world's largest exporters of natural resources. In 1986 only 43.7 percent of Canadian exports (more than half of them automobiles and parts going to the United States) were fully manufactured goods. The remaining exports were semimanufactured products (euphemistically called "fabricated materials" in government statistics), unprocessed crude materials, and farm and fish products (Canada, Dept. of Finance, 1988a, p.10). These figures, however, mask the fact that many Canadian manufactured exports are, for the most part, based on the domestic availability of raw materials. Thus, for example, Canadian exports of paper, steel, and processed food depend on the abundant availability of forestry, iron, and agricultural products.

In contrast, Canadian imports have always consisted mainly of manufactured goods. Imports accounted in 1966 for 21 percent and in 1984 for 35.8 percent of the Canadian consumption of manufactured goods. The dominance of imports is especially great in the high-technology and capital goods sectors – sectors that are often regarded as being essential to the long-term competitiveness of Canadian industries, indeed, of the economy. In such products, Canada has traditionally experienced huge trade deficits. The policy of import substitution pursued vigorously in the late nineteenth century and for most of the twentieth has made almost no difference to the strength of the Canadian manufacturing sector, except in a few industries such as automobiles and telecommunications.

The dominance of staples in Canadian exports and of manufactured goods in imports has played a critical, if contradictory, role in shaping Canada's international economic objectives. The abundance of marketable natural resources in Canada determined right from the beginning that this sector would be the cornerstone of the Canadian economy and that the reduction in foreign trade barriers to those exports would be Canada's main foreign economic policy objective. This presented a problem, because Canada's demands for reductions in foreign barriers generated corresponding demands from other countries for Canada to lower its own barriers to imports, which were particularly high on manufactured goods. Meeting this demand was difficult because Canada wanted to grow out of its role as "the hewer of wood and drawer of water" by nurturing its manufacturing industries behind tariff walls until those industries were strong enough to take on the world market. But over the years many industries – including textiles, clothing, and footwear – failed to grow out of their infancy and needed continued protection. The large number of workers employed, often in economically depressed regions in Ontario and Quebec, made the removal of protection even more difficult. Canadian policy-makers have thus been led to pursue somewhat contradictory goals: negotiating reductions in barriers to exports and attempting to retain Canada's own barriers to imports. Since World War II especially, Canada has been under increasing U.S. pressure to lower its import barriers as the price for gaining increased access to the U.S. market for Canadian exports.

The History of Canada's Trade Relations

Great Britain's move towards free trade through the repeal of the Corn Laws in 1846, with its inadvertent effect of terminating the Canadian producers' preferred access to the British market, marked the beginning of Canada's efforts to develop its own trade policy. The British action signified that Canada's interests were not a factor in the mother country's trade policies. Consequently, the five colonies forming British North America signed the Reciprocity Treaty with the United States in 1854, offering preferred access to each other's markets. The treaty was terminated in 1866 at the request of the U.S. government for several reasons, including Canada's huge trade surplus, concerted pressures from U.S. interests adversely affected by Canadian exports, and Britain's support for the South in the American Civil War, which caused resentment in the eventually victorious North.

The end of the treaty led Canadian policy-makers to search for alternative means of establishing assured access to a large market for Canadian producers, and one of the results of this search was the establishment of Confederation in 1867. At the same time, the newly established Canadian government continued to pursue another reciprocity agreement with the United States, but to no avail. Frustrated with the U.S. government's lack of interest in negotiating a trade deal, the Canadian government under Sir John A. Macdonald announced the National Policy in 1879. Its cornerstone was a drastic increase in tariffs on imports. One reason for the measure was to exert pressure on the U.S. government to negotiate reciprocal reductions in tariffs against each other's exports. Another was to foster industrial development by protecting Canadian "infant industries" from imports and by encouraging foreign manufacturers to establish plants in Canada so they would avoid tariffs. This second goal was by and large accomplished as many manufacturing plants, both Canadian and foreign (mostly U.S.), were established towards the end of the century. But the goal of negotiating reciprocity with the United States remained as elusive as ever. Undaunted by the lack of interest in the United States, the Canadians continued their efforts covertly under the Conservatives and overtly under the Liberals. An offer of preferential access for British exports in 1879 remained similarly unreciprocated by the British government.

The goal of reaching a free trade agreement with the United States was almost reached in 1911, when the Liberal government under Wilfrid Laurier announced an agreement to reduce tariffs on a reciprocal basis with the United States on a range of natural products and some manufactured products. The agreement was clearly designed to support the Western and Eastern agricultural and primary producers, while only marginally reducing the protection afforded Central Canadian manufacturers. But 1911 was an election year. The Conservatives, in an alliance with business and labour in the manufacturing sector and rabidly anti-American British Loyalists, mounted a bitter campaign that ended in a humiliating defeat for the Liberal Party. The lesson from the election was not lost on either of the main parties, and neither dared raise the topic for several decades.

The anti-American, pro-British sentiments that marked the 1911 election were out of tune with the time, for the United States was emerging rapidly as the world's foremost military and economic power. Despite the rejection of the free trade deal, Canada's trade with the United States continued to expand, and increasingly large amounts of U.S. investment continued to pour in. Canada was on the march towards closer integration with the U.S. economy, punctuated only by the Great Depression in the 1930s. In 1935 the two nations signed an agreement to lower their tariffs substantially; this was the first trade pact between the neighbours since 1854. It was followed by further attempts to reduce tariffs, and in 1938 an agreement was reached among Canada, the U.S., the U.K., Australia, New Zealand, and South Africa to provide easy access for each other's goods. The process of multilateral reductions in trade barriers had begun, a process that gained momentum after the end of World War II.

The United States emerged from the war as the dominant technological, economic, and military power in the world, and it was in its interest to organize an open world trading order. That goal was supported by Canada, which also emerged from the war as a beneficiary in economic terms. The U.S. efforts led to the negotiation and signing of the General Agreement on Tariffs and Trade (GATT) among twenty-three nations in 1947. This agreement, which has expanded considerably both in membership and scope since its inception, still forms the basis for trade among the non-Communist nations.

In 1948, immediately after the signing of the GATT, Canadian and U.S. negotiators reached an agreement to establish virtually free trade between the two countries, and there was pressure on Prime Minister William Lyon Mackenzie King to move forward and sign the treaty. But at the last minute King balked, later noting in his diary: "I stressed strongly that regardless of what the economic facts might be, the issue would turn on union with the States and separation from Britain" (Whalley, 1985, p.37). King was clearly being sentimental about Britain, for Canada's trade relations with the mother country had been dwindling rapidly and were no match for relations with the United States by the late 1940s.

The postwar international economic order has been characterized by *multilateralism*, a principle fully supported by Canada. Canadian leaders, aware of the nation's high degree of trade dependence, have recognized that a multilateral arrangement provides the best guarantee against protectionism and the economic and diplomatic powers of the larger nations. This explains the active Canadian participation in all the rounds of GATT negotiations and its support for other international institutions. While its commitment to multilateralism is beyond doubt, in practical terms the multilateral framework has worked mainly towards expanding Canadian trade with the United States.

The visibility of these relations with the U.S. is so high that it is easy to lose sight of trade with other nations. The European Community or EC (a common market for goods, services, and labour among the U.K., Ireland,

Portugal, Spain, Italy, Greece, France, Belgium, Luxembourg, the Netherlands, Germany, and Denmark) forms the world's largest trading bloc. It is Canada's second largest trading partner, although it accounts for only 7.8 percent of our total trade. As recently as the 1950s, our trade with the U.K. alone was twice as large as our current trade with all the EC nations put together. In the early 1970s Canada sought to reverse this trend, with little result.

The Asia-Pacific region – consisting of the economic superpower Japan, the Newly Industrialized Countries (NICs) of South Korea, Taiwan, Hong Kong, and Singapore, and the rapidly industrializing China, Thailand, Malaysia, Indonesia, and Philippines – has had the fastest rate of economic growth in the world over the last few decades. Much of its success derives from exports of standard-technology manufactured products. Its competitiveness and ability to erode Canada's economic prosperity, while real, are often exaggerated. Collectively, these countries supply a small fraction of our total imports, most of which, at any rate, come from Japan, a high-wage economy. While employment in many Canadian industries – most notably in textiles, clothing, footwear, toys, and automobile parts – has been eroded significantly by imports from these countries, their success is based on the principles of comparative advantage, which Canada has supported. Indeed, these countries have been able to export despite the various discriminatory practices that Canadian and other Western governments maintain against their products. They also form an increasingly important destination for exports, especially for Western Canadian producers, and bullying these countries to accept unfavourable terms of trade, which has been common in the past, will become increasingly difficult in the future.

Trade with Eastern Europe formed about 3 percent of our total exports and about 1 percent of our total imports in the late 1980s. We have traditionally had a massive trade surplus with Eastern Europe, much of it accounted for by wheat exports.

Our trade with Third World nations that are non-oil exporting and outside the Asia-Pacific region (which leaves most of Africa, South Asia, and South and Central America) is minuscule as a proportion of our total trade. One reason for the low degree of trade with these nations is that they mainly export primary products, which Canada itself has in abundance. Another reason is the barriers that Canada (along with other industrialized nations) maintains against their exports: the trade-weighted Canadian tariffs on goods from Third World countries have been about twice as high as on goods from industrialized countries (Macdonald Royal Commission, 1985, Vol. I, p.257). In the early 1970s, Canada agreed to afford preferential tariffs to Third World nations but in practice this move has been meaningless because more than 95 percent of the total goods exported by the Third World are not eligible for those lower tariffs. While Canada's foreign aid to these nations (0.42 percent of the GNP in 1982) is above the OECD average (0.38 percent), it is substantially below the level provided by the Netherlands and the Scandinavian nations (Helleiner, 1985, p.120). Moreover, much of Canada's foreign assistance is in the form of tied aid (aid tied to the purchase of Canadian goods). This approach may partly explain the trade surplus that Canada has traditionally maintained with these nations (ibid., p.104).

The General Agreement on Tariffs and Trade

When the GATT was signed in 1947 it was seen as a provisional measure that would be replaced by a more wide-ranging and permanent entity, the International Trade Organization (ITO). After the U.S. president failed to secure congressional approval for the ITO treaty, the GATT signatories agreed that the General Agreement and its secretariat would assume the proposed functions of the ITO. Since then the number of member nations in GATT has expanded to eighty-nine, with another thirty maintaining de facto application of its rules. The original provisions of the agreement have remained essentially intact, even though over the years a number of supplementary codes and agreements have been adopted to strengthen, extend, or clarify the original rules. The GATT remains a loosely worded document, reflecting its original provisional character. The flexibility resulting from this looseness has permitted the practical resolution of many trade frictions among its members; but that same flexibility has also allowed the members, especially the economically powerful ones, to bend the rules in their favour.

The purpose of GATT is to promote a liberal international economic order based on the principle of comparative advantage. It establishes reciprocal rights and obligations among its members to reduce barriers to international trade, and it offers exporters opportunities to sell in the markets of member nations. But it also imposes obligations to not erect barriers to imports, except under special circumstances provided for in the agreement – which represents a problem for Canada.

These are GATT's principal provisions:
- The Most Favoured Nation (MFN) clause in Article I guarantees the principle of non-discrimination as "immediate and unconditional" in the conduct of international trade. It specifies that any concessions or favourable treatment offered to one member nation must be made available to other members as well. There are, however, some clearly specified exceptions to this principle: nations entering into free trade (for example, the FTA) or customs union (the EC, for example) are not obliged to offer the same concessions to others; the trade measures of Third World nations; specifically exempted trade arrangements such as the Canada-U.S. Auto Pact; and the special arrangements in textiles and clothing trade under the Multifibre Agreement.

- A tariff binding provision in Article II "binds" tariffs to the existing level, which can be reduced but not increased, except after undergoing a formidable process of negotiation with the principal exporters of the product(s) in question.
- The concept of national treatment in Article III states that once a product enters the domestic market and the applicable tariffs are paid, the product must be treated the same as similar domestically produced products. The intent is to prohibit governments from discriminating against imports in favour of domestically produced goods in forms other than tariffs.
- A general prohibition against quantitative restrictions on imports (and exports), except in cases of certain clearly specified goods under specific circumstances. The exceptions include agricultural products, textiles and clothing, and the restrictions imposed by Third World nations and other nations facing serious balance-of-payment difficulties. Another crucial exception is the Emergency Action clause contained in Article XIX, which permits temporary limitations on imports to mitigate unforeseen hardships caused by imports. The restrictions cannot be imposed on a selective basis, that is to say, in a discriminatory manner.
- A provision for countervailing and antidumping duties against subsidies and dumping. In case of a government subsidy that gives exporters an unfair advantage vis-à-vis the producer in the importing country, the importing country is entitled to impose countervailing duties to the extent of the subsidy. (An example of this is the much-publicized attempt by the United States to impose countervailing duties on Canadian softwood lumber.) Similarly, if exporters sell goods abroad at a price lower than the price they sell at in their home market, the good is deemed to be dumped, and the importing nation is entitled to impose antidumping duties. A good is not regarded as being dumped just because the imported product is cheaper than the comparable domestically produced product (although the word is sometimes used in this way).
- A dispute settlement mechanism favours consultation and conciliation rather than formal adjudication. Violations of GATT rules do not automatically lead to punitive measures. Punishment (in the form of retaliation by countries adversely affected by the exports of the offending nation) is imposed only after consultations fail. Most disputes are settled between the concerned parties without calling upon the GATT machinery. When this is not possible, a "working party" or a "dispute panel" consisting of named experts is constructed to examine the complaint and recommend solutions.

Tariffs and GATT

Tariffs are reduced within the GATT system during successive "rounds" of negotiations among the members nations. There have been seven such completed rounds, with the eighth round, known as the "Uruguay Round," beginning in 1986 and scheduled for completion in 1992. For all practical purposes, the first Geneva Round (which took place at the same time as the negotiation of the General Agreement in 1947), the sixth Kennedy Round (1964-67), and the seventh Tokyo Round (1973-79) have been the most important in introducing significant changes in GATT. The Uruguay Round, if and when completed (which appears doubtful because of the sharp differences between the United States and the European Community on several key issues), is expected to be similarly important, if for no other reason than its apparent failure to resolve contentious issues related to subsidies and trade in agricultural products.

In Canada the GATT talks are preceded by intense negotiations among various competing interests to influence the positions that Canadian representatives will adopt. The exporting interests usually press the government to lower tariffs on imports as a concession for achieving reduced foreign barriers to exports. On the other hand, the import-competing industries, usually the traditional manufacturing industries in Canada, press the government to avoid tariff reductions on imports. The Canadian negotiators must pursue these two contradictory objectives. The Canadian position has for the most part favoured the interests of the exporting industries, which is not surprising given their dominance in the economy (Mahon, 1984).

Tariff reductions have been an important goal during all the rounds of GATT negotiations. The negotiations are conducted on an item-by-item basis, whereby pairs of nations bargain for reduction in each other's tariffs on particular products. The reductions agreed on are made available, under the MFN clause, to all other members. Other pairs of nations are simultaneously negotiating for similar reductions on other products of interest to them, and thus tariff reductions spread throughout the GATT system. In practice, not all members negotiate with all others with respect to every product, which would be clearly an unmanageable process. Rather, negotiations take place only between the members that are principal exporters and importers of the product in question. Canada has thus negotiated primarily with the United States, since most of its trade is with that country.

To avoid the cumbersome nature of the item-by-item negotiations, the Kennedy and Tokyo Rounds were for the most part conducted on a "linear" basis, whereby members first agreed on a formula of across-the-board reductions by a certain percentage and then negotiated only with respect to the exceptions to the formula. Canada was exempted from the linear cuts at the Kennedy Round, but not at the Tokyo Round, because it was primarily an exporter of resource products on which tariffs were already generally low everywhere and hence would have had to reduce its tariffs on manufactured imports without gaining a matching level of benefits for its exports. After the implementation of the Kennedy Round cuts, the average Canadian tariff on all industrial products was 13.6 percent, compared to 6.5 percent

Table 18
Post-MTN Average Tariffs on Industrial Products, Percentage

Country	Depth of Cut*	Raw Materials	Semi-Manufactures	Finished Manufactures
U.S.	31	0.2	3.0	5.7
Canada	38	0.5	8.3	8.3
Japan	49	0.5	4.6	6.0
EEC	29	0.2	4.2	6.9
Sweden	28	0.0	3.3	4.9
Tariffs of nine industrial countries combined	34	0.3	4.0	6.5

* Depth of cut is for all industrial products; depth of cut and average post-MTN rates are weighted on the basis of actual customs collections.

SOURCE: GATT, Director-General (January 1980), *The Tokyo Round of Multilateral Trade Negotiations, Supplementary Report.*

for the U.S., 6.6 percent for the European Economic Community (EEC), and 5.5 percent for Japan (U.S. Congress, 1987, p.31). Table 18 shows the comparative tariff rates of some of the industrialized nations on products by their level of processing after the implementation of the Tokyo Round cuts.

As the table illustrates, the tariff increases with the level of processing involved; this has been true for most countries since before the establishment of GATT and reflects governmental desires to foster domestic manufacturing by protecting domestic goods from imports. Nevertheless, it is true that Canada protects its manufacturing industries more than other industrialized nations. More than two-thirds of the total imports into Canada are effectively duty-free, but the duties that do exist tend to be higher than in other industrialized nations (Stone, 1984, p.63). While tariffs have by and large disappeared as a major impediment to trade, a handful of products are still protected by high tariffs. In Canada, textiles, clothing, footwear, clocks, glass tableware, window shades, vermouth, aperitifs, and cordial wines are protected by the highest rates of tariffs, exceeding 20 percent (Salembier, 1987, pp.107-108).

Non-Tariff Barriers and GATT

Andre W. Moroz defines Non-Tariff Barriers (NTBs) as "those policy measures that artificially manipulate the relative competitiveness of domestic and foreign supplies in a given market with the explicit intention of improving the competitive position and hence increasing the level of output and income of the domestic producers above that allowed by free trade" (Moroz, 1985, p.262). The types of instruments a government can use to discriminate against imports are too numerous to catalogue. The most commonly used NTBs are quotas on imports, subsidies to domestic industries, technical standards, and preferential government purchasing.

The underlying spirit of GATT is more opposed to quotas than to tariffs as a barrier to trade. Quotas, by setting absolute limits to the quantity of imports, establish a stronger trade barrier because imports cannot overcome a quota regardless of their competitiveness in either price or quality. Tariffs at least allow foreign exporters to keep supplying. The trade in clothing is a perfect example: the industrialized nations have not been able to stop imports despite extraordinarily high tariffs and so they have had to use import quotas as well. Despite the greater ability of quotas to impede trade, GATT has been more successful with tariffs than quotas because of the myriad forms, some subtle and others not so subtle, in which quotas appear in international trade.

Quantitative restrictions on imports, or quotas, are generally prohibited by Article XI of GATT, except for agricultural and fisheries products (Article XI), controls designed to offset balance-of-payment problems (Article XII), and barriers to trade imposed by Third World countries (Article VIII) (GATT, 1969). In addition, Article XIX allows member nations to raise tariffs or impose quotas on imports to protect domestic industries. This is meant as an emergency clause to help a signatory mitigate unforeseen hardships caused by imports, and the conditions under which it can be used are highly restrictive, as intended by its authors. In return for limiting imports, the country is expected to offer compensation to countries with "substantial interest" in the product as exporters. Another restriction is that the measure be temporary, which, while not defined, generally means no longer than five years. Moreover, the quotas must be applied on a global basis, that is to say, against all nations on a non-discriminatory basis.

Given the difficulties associated with its use, Article XIX has been applied infrequently, including twenty-two times in all by Canada (GATT, 1987b). Most of the Canadian applications have been on agricultural, textile, and clothing products, all of which enjoy special treatment under GATT. Instead of using global quotas under Article XIX, most industrialized nations impose quotas on imports outside the provisions of GATT. The agreement is silent on arrangements whereby an importing nation enters into a bilateral agreement with the exporting nation to limit its exports of specified products to a certain level. Such arrangements are called Voluntary Export Restraint Agreements (VERA) or Orderly Marketing Arrangements (OMA). Since they are entered into entirely outside the provisions of GATT, they are not bound by the conditions of Article XIX. Textiles and clothing products are the only goods that have legal sanction under GATT, under the Multifibre

Agreement, to be dealt with in this way. VERA does not technically contravene the provisions of GATT, because GATT does not explicitly prohibit it. But it does violate the spirit of GATT to the extent that it is applied on a discriminatory basis, does not involve payment of compensation, and is not temporary.

In recent decades, countries seeking to impose quotas on imports have resorted to VERA/OMA more often than to Article XIX (GATT, 1987c). The reasons why countries agree to restrain their exports in this fashion are political and economic. First, they do not want to weaken their general relations with nations that are important destinations for their exports and that seek VERAS or OMAS to restrict imports. Second, there are economic benefits for nations that agree to VERA, such as assured market access for other exports and the ability to collect export quota price premiums caused by artificially limited supplies (GATT, 1987a). Nevertheless, unlike actions under Article XIX, which can be taken unilaterally, VERA/OMA requires the consent of the exporting countries. Since those countries can refuse to enter into such an agreement, as often happens, the ability of an importing country to use this instrument depends largely on its bargaining power.

To control imports effectively through VERA/OMA, the importing country must have the capacity to persuade the major exporting nations to restrain their exports. At the same time, the exporting countries must see some benefits in doing so; otherwise they would refuse to enter into an arrangement. Canada's capacity to negotiate VERA is, generally speaking, low. Canada is not large enough to provide exporting countries with the incentive to restrain their exports in return for assured access to its market. Exporting countries are also apprehensive that agreeing to such arrangements with Canada would invite pressure from other countries to enter into similar arrangements. Australia finds itself in a similar position, reflected in the fact that it has had to resort to Article XIX more than any other country. The U.S. and the EC, with their tremendous diplomatic and economic resources, are in much stronger positions in this regard. It often helps Canada to join with the U.S. in such actions, as was clearly the case in VERA with Japan on automobiles. Yet, even though Canada is not strong enough to pressure other nations to accept export restraints, it is also not weak enough to enable other nations to force restraints upon it.

Canada has used Article XIX quotas or VERAS less frequently than the U.S. or the EEC (GATT, 1987b). One reason is that Canadian tariffs are generally higher than tariffs in other industrialized nations, thus reducing the need for protection through quotas. As well, Canada, unlike most other industrialized nations, has never had a large manufacturing sector, which is often the intended recipient of quota protection. Finally, the high dependence of the Canadian economy on exports ensures that Canada will use caution imposing import controls, lest its own exports be subjected to similar controls abroad.

Table 19
Subsidies to Canadian Industry: 1978, 1981, and 1984[1] (millions of current dollars)

Industry	Direct Current Subsidies[2]			Conditional Indirect Subsidies[3]			Capital and R&D Subsidies[4]			Total Subsidies		
	1978	1981	1984	1978	1981	1984	1978	1981	1984	1978	1981	1984
Agriculture	649.47	1229.37	436.52	473.15	566.03	643.75	39.44	93.60	36.69	1162.06	1889.00	1116.96
Forestry	4.07	74.56	14.74	7.73	2.18	2.45	0.85	32.00	3.62	12.65	108.74	20.81
Fishing, Hunting, and Trapping	19.50	78.96	183.88	2.54	14.17	3.72	6.18	12.44	16.19	28.22	105.57	203.79
Petroleum and Gas Wells	39.52	66.77	8.83	n/a	32.93	92.63	10.50	101.02	24.99	50.02	200.72	126.45
Mining	19.28	67.61	1.67	4.38	698.30	0.00	37.33	1.17	1737.56	60.99	767.08	1739.23
Food and Beverage	133.53	174.71	123.16	12.61	18.47	16.15	28.18	18.48	37.89	174.32	211.66	177.20
Rubber	2.12	3.54	2.73	0.97	1.22	1.37	7.96	5.80	19.85	11.05	10.56	23.95
Textiles, Leather, and Clothing	7.86	11.95	9.22	1.63	1.93	2.17	9.67	19.15	40.01	19.16	33.03	51.40
Wood and Paper Products	21.78	69.83	36.78	35.02	39.69	79.06	59.17	146.20	116.23	115.97	255.72	232.07
Primary Metal Products	62.09	18.68	4.80	2.13	2.62	2.95	31.73	21.60	11.63	95.95	42.90	19.38
Metal Fabricating	8.53	22.55	12.64	1.22	2.24	2.09	12.57	24.43	30.21	22.32	49.22	44.94
Machinery and Equipment	3.29	6.73	6.64	0.35	0.80	0.69	28.09	40.01	43.71	31.73	47.54	51.04
Transportation Equipment	77.20	83.89	28.04	1.13	1.76	1.77	63.29	152.12	181.05	141.62	237.77	310.86
Electric Products	3.07	6.25	4.74	0.64	0.80	0.90	35.25	77.42	67.27	38.96	84.47	72.91
Non-metal Mineral Products	2.63	8.72	1.78	1.07	1.33	1.50	9.16	3.78	9.21	12.86	13.83	12.49
Petroleum/Chemical Products	4.66	8.78	33.47	2.80	3.49	3.93	44.75	20.91	27.61	52.21	33.18	65.01
Other Manufacturing	3.70	8.00	3.39	1.28	1.67	1.86	8.74	18.25	13.96	13.72	27.92	19.21
Services	1745.82	3002.25	1760.35	n/a	1.60	16.51	16.50	571.62	714.25	1762.32	3575.47	2491.11
Total	2808.12	4943.15	2673.38	548.65	1391.23	873.50	449.36	1360.00	3131.93	3806.13	7694.38	6678.81

Table 19 — *(Continued)*

NOTES: 1 This is the pretax value to the industry. Most subsidies are taxable; consequently, the net value to the producer is lower. Estimates for 1978 and 1981 include federal and provincial grants; estimates for 1984 *do not* include subsidies from provincial governments.

2 Direct current subsidies are current subsidies that are paid directly to the industry benefitting from the subsidy. Included in the estimates are all federal and provincial current production subsidies provided in the form of grants for purposes of subsidizing income deficiencies, labour inputs, other current inputs, and transportation and other distribution costs.

3 Under certain programs, the industry directly receiving the subsidy – the recipient industry – is not the industry ultimately benefitting from the subsidy – the beneficiary industry. When the recipient industry does not retain the subsidy but passes it on fully and exclusively to a second, specifically targetted industry, then the latter (beneficiary) industry is provided a conditional indirect subsidy. In certain instances, a conditional indirect subsidy is provided through government regulations. Included in the estimates are transportation subsidies provided under the Maritimes Freight Rates *Act*, the Atlantic Region Freight Assistance *Act*, and the lower postal rate for Canadian magazines and periodicals, and the Crows Nest Pass Agreement.

4 Capital subsidies are grants paid to industries to subsidize the construction of buildings and facilities, the purchase of machinery and equipment, or the undertaking of research and development (R&D). Estimates include the following programs: Regional Industrial Development Act, Defence Industry Productivity Program, Enterprise Development Programs, Regional Industrial Development Act, Defence Industry Productivity Program, Enterprise Development Program, Industrial Research Assistance Program, as well as other, smaller federal programs, and, for 1978 and 1981, certain provincial programs.

SOURCE: Salembier, G.E., Andrew R. Moore and Frank Stone (1987), *The Canadian Import File: Trade, Protection and Adjustment*, Table 2.3 (Montreal: Institute for Research on Public Policy), pp. 37-38.

The second government instrument for controlling imports, subsidies to domestic industries, are of various kinds; but they all have the common effect of artificially increasing the competitiveness of the recipient industry. In the home market, the subsidized domestic products have a price advantage over imports to the extent of the subsidy. In export markets, the subsidy permits a price advantage over other nations' exports of the same product and over the products made in the importing country. Consumers, of course, gain from buying subsidized products, the bill being footed by taxpayers in the country providing the subsidy. Liberal economists argue that subsidies misdirect economic resources to uncompetitive rather than competitive industries. In addition to the inefficiencies that subsidies cause in the domestic economy, their adverse effects are transmitted to the world economy through international trade.

Nevertheless, all governments provide numerous varieties of subsidies to domestic producers and exporters. These can take the form of cash grants for workers' training, the purchase of capital equipment, or conducting research and development. The intended effect is to reduce the firm's cost of production. Instead of cash grants, governments sometimes provide loans at reduced interest or none at all, which again has the effect of reducing production costs. Tax credits or tax breaks have a similar impact on the recipient firms. The total cost of the subsidies provided by the Canadian government fluctuates rapidly but always runs in billions of dollars, as shown in Table 19.

Despite the severe trade-distorting effects of subsidies, GATT has surprisingly little to say on the subject. Its only reference to subsidies occurs in Article VI, which entitles a member nation to impose countervailing duties equivalent to the extent of a subsidy. While the provision is designed to protect domestic producers from unfair foreign competition, it also permits nations to harass foreign producers. In light of this weakness the Tokyo Round agreed to provisions that, to some extent, clarify the circumstances under which countervailing duties can be imposed. This has not, however, prevented their abuse, as many suspect was the case with the U.S. attempts to impose countervailing duties on Canadian softwood lumber exports. GATT is silent on subsidies to industries that do not export and sell only in the home market. In fact, there has been no attempt to control such subsidies, even though they discriminate against imports by lowering the domestic industry's costs of production and hence give its products a price advantage over imports in the domestic market.

Government assistance that is available generally to the population and not directed at a particular industry is not usually considered a subsidy for the purpose of levying countervailing duties. For example, the U.S. government cannot impose countervailing duties on Canadian exports on the ground that the government subsidizes the cost of production by contributing to education and health services, unemployment insurance, old age pensions, and so forth. On the other hand, the Canadian government's regional development grants to Michelin Tyres to aid its location in Nova Scotia prompted countervailing duties in the United States because the grants were directed at a specific firm, which lowered its costs of production and hence the prices of its exports.

Government procurement of domestically produced goods is another means of discriminating against imports. The importance of this instrument can be better appreciated if we remember that the total purchases by federal and provincial governments in Canada account for well over 10 percent of the total GNP. The figure rises to over 20 percent if purchases by semigovernment bodies such as crown corporations, hospitals, and educational institutions are included (Moroz, 1985, p.251). All nations use this measure to a greater or lesser extent. The GATT Code on Government Procurement, negotiated during the Tokyo Round, is relaxed in its restrictions: it requires that purchases over $220,000 be open for international bidding but permits numerous exceptions to this general rule. Only an estimated one-sixth of the federal government's purchases in Canada are open for international bidding (ibid.).

In many countries in the mid-1970s some highly visible uses of import quotas affecting textiles, clothing, footwear, colour televisions, automobiles, motorcycles, and steel, among others, led commentators to conclude that the world was entering an era of new protectionism. Now this clearly seems an overreaction. Many industrialized nations were encountering severe economic difficulties in the late 1970s and early 1980s, prompting them to impose non-tariff barriers to imports, but the more recent upturn in economic fortunes led to a reversal of this trend. Even before economic recovery began, the general tendency was for levels of protection to decline (Moroz, 1985, p.258). The average level of tariffs in the industrialized nations decreased from 9 percent to 4 percent between 1965 and 1980 (Blais, 1986, p.7). The use of quotas no doubt increased, "although their effect is less extensive than generally claimed" (ibid.). In the manufacturing sector quotas have been applied on goods that already have high tariffs; hence, the additional protection offered is not great. Subsidies to domestic industries, however, increased considerably in the industrialized nations, rising from 1.8 percent to 3.1 percent of those countries' GDP between 1965 and 1980 (ibid.). The increase in subsidies might well be the result of a reduced level of protection in international trade, which necessitated government financial assistance to domestic industries to become competitive against imports.

The Future of GATT and the Rise of the FTA

GATT, born in the context of steep pre-World War II trade barriers, has been remarkably successful in reducing those barriers and introducing a modicum of uniformity and security into the conduct of international trade. As a result, international trade is now freer than at any time in the last one hundred years. More importantly, GATT has reduced the risk of any sudden or sharp increase in trade barriers.

Since GATT's establishment, the value of world trade has increased more than six times (Macdonald Commission, 1985, Vol.I, p.281). During this period, the growth in exports has been higher than the rate of economic growth in most industrialized and Third World nations (ibid., p.280). In the OECD, the average value of exports and imports as a percentage of the GDP increased continuously: from 52 percent in 1970 to 58 percent in 1975; 66 percent in 1980; and 67 percent in 1982 (Blais, 1986, p.7).

While GATT cannot be credited for all the expansion in international trade, it has certainly played a key role in supporting the expansion. As the Macdonald Commission concluded: "The performance of GATT to date has been without historical precedent and generally satisfactory, not in any absolute sense of perfection, but in comparison with that of earlier periods. Without GATT, it is unlikely that Canadian exports would have grown at a faster pace than the national economy during the post-War years" (1985, Vol.1, p.281).

While the role of GATT has been critical in promoting international trade and increasing the economic prosperity of trade-dependant nations such as Canada, there are some justified fears about its future. For one thing, its membership has increased fourfold since its inception, making multilateral negotiations difficult because of the wider variety of interests that must now be accommodated. Moreover, there is now no nation that can act as the United States did in the period between the 1940s and the 1960s to prod negotiations and enforce discipline. In fact, the gigantic U.S. trade deficit in recent years has made protectionism politically popular in that country, although the U.S. was the architect of GATT and the modern liberal trading order. The EC's preoccupation with integration within Western Europe and its disregard for the interests of the nations outside the region also does not bode well for GATT's future.

The fear that GATT might not be as effective in the future as it has been in the past has led many, including the current Canadian government, to look for alternatives. Without abandoning GATT, Canada's focus has shifted towards solidifying and furthering the already relatively open trade relations with the United States. The reasoning behind this shift in Canadian policy is that the principal effect of trade liberalization under GATT, as far as Ottawa was concerned, was to increase Canada's trade dependence on the United States. As the Macdonald Commission remarked: "For Canada, the post-War opening up of the international economic order has not been accompanied by a diversification of our trading partners. The reverse has happened: our post-War participation in the global economy has led to an increasingly continental economic integration of our trade partners" (1985, Vol.1, p.58).

In fact, the recognition that dependence on the United States was an unchangeable reality dawned upon the Canadian policy-makers even before the Macdonald Commission reported or the Conservative government assumed office. The same Trudeau government that in the early 1970s had declared its intention to move away from the United States and Britain and pursue the "Third Option" had by 1983 opened negotiations, which eventually failed, with the Americans to arrive at free trade in specific sectors (Economic Council, 1988b, p.4). It was in the context of this failure to negotiate sector-specific free trade arrangements with the United States and the scepticism about the prospects of further trade liberalization under GATT that Canadian policy-makers began to contemplate a general free trade agreement with the U.S. The Macdonald Commission made the point rather well:

> Thus, while Commissioners support continued efforts to work through the GATT, we are not sufficiently optimistic about the possibilities of major breakthroughs in the short term to advocate an exclusive preoccupation with the multilateral GATT system. Further, the major benefits for Canadians of a successful GATT reduction of non-tariff barriers would be increased access to the U.S. market. The United States will be our major market, whether or not there is another successful round of GATT negotiations. The fact is, therefore, that the multilateral route which we prefer has, as a primary objective, an increase in the security of our dominant trade relations with the United States. (Macdonald Commission, 1985, Vol.1, p.60)

Following the same line of reasoning, the Mulroney government soon after its election in 1984 declared its intention to pursue free trade with the United States, pending the outcome of the Uruguay Round negotiations. The agreement was reached in October 1987 and came into effect on January 1, 1989. The Free Trade Agreement signifies the de facto recognition of Canada's special trade relations with the United States, which have existed for almost a century, and reflects a sense of resignation among policy-makers that it is not possible to use state actions to diversify Canada's trade relations to any substantial degree and avoid the pattern imposed by the international marketplace.

The Canada-U.S. Free Trade Agreement

Canada may regard moderation and willingness to compromise as an integral part of its national character, but it has not displayed either quality in its debates on free trade with the United States. This was true in the 1911 election campaign, and it was true during the federal election in 1988. In both those elections free trade was the key issue. Even the scholarly commentaries on the subject tend to exaggerate either the beneficial or the adverse effects of free trade with the United States. But the present FTA is not likely to provide all the material benefits claimed by its supporters, or destroy Canada as alleged by its opponents.

When Canada entered into negotiations with the United States, the minister for international trade, James Kelleher, stated that Canada had four objectives:

- *security of access* to the United States market, particularly by reducing the risks inherent in the U.S. system of restrictive trade measures (for example, quotas, surtaxes, and so forth) and the constitutional powers of Congress to pass protectionist legislation affecting Canada;
- *expanded access* to the United States market in order to provide Canadian industry with a market large enough to realize economies of scale and specialization and to carve out niches for specialty products;
- *a stable North American trading system* that would encourage an orderly transition in Canada towards an economy more competitive at home and in world markets and provide increased incentive for investment from all sources;
- *an ordered and more predictable system* for managing the trade relationship and resolving disputes. (Lipsey and York, 1988, pp.10-11)

Main Provisions of the Agreement

Tariffs. While about 70 percent of the Canadian exports to the U.S. and 65 percent of U.S. exports to Canada were already exempt from tariffs in 1988 (Economic Council, 1988b, p.7), the agreement provides for the elimination of all tariffs by January 1, 1999. Many tariffs were removed when the agreement came into effect on January 1, 1989, and the rest would be eliminated in two stages, in 1993 and 1998. Tariffs on products protected by the highest levels of tariffs will be the last to be eliminated. Since Canadian tariffs are on average higher than the comparable tariffs in the U.S., the adjustment pressures resulting from their removal is likely to be greater for the Canadian producers than for U.S. producers.

National Treatment. The agreement requires, like Article I of GATT, that the two countries will not discriminate against the others' exports. There are, however, numerous specified exceptions to this general principle. This provision does not stop either country from adopting particular measures that discriminate against imports from the other country; it just requires that the adopted measure be equally applicable to goods and services from both countries.

Agriculture. All tariffs on agricultural products will be phased out over ten years, but temporary increases in tariffs on fresh fruits and vegetables will be allowed during peak growing seasons for twenty years. The agreement also provides for termination of export subsidies in bilateral trade, exemptions from laws controlling imports of beef and veal, harmonization of some technical standards, and a commitment to make standards more uniform. Most of the non-tariff barriers remain untouched. The agreement allows, as does GATT, the continuation of import quotas to support supply management schemes for poultry, eggs, and dairy products. This is to prevent imports from flooding the market because of high domestic prices maintained purposely by various management schemes in both countries.

Automobiles. Since 1965 there has been managed trade in automotive products between the two countries under the Auto Pact. The FTA essentially maintains the Pact for the existing firms covered by it. However, there are several provisions in the agreement that eliminate or reduce Canada's ability to offer incentives to foreign producers to locate manufacturing facilities in Canada. The agreement will also phase out Canada's ban on the importation of used cars over five years.

Energy. The FTA's provisions regarding the energy sector have been among the most far-reaching and contentious in Canada. Energy is a vital sector in the Canadian economy: about 14 percent of total Canadian investment is in this sector, which accounts for about 10 percent of total Canadian exports (Economic Council, 1988b, pp.11-12). The U.S. is the world's largest energy consumer and importer, as well as producer, and Canada is its largest foreign supplier. Many of the Trudeau government's measures to Canadianize the sector were a major irritant for the U.S., and it is doubtful whether the U.S. government would have signed the FTA without an assurance that such measures would not be repeated.

The energy sector as defined in the agreement includes oil, natural gas, light petroleum gas, coal, uranium, and electricity. The FTA eliminates almost all barriers to trade in these commodities. It explicitly prohibits – and this is the feature that riles the critics of the FTA the most – the use of measures that make export prices higher than domestic prices, such as the export tax imposed under the National Energy Program by the Trudeau government. Moreover, the FTA, while not prohibiting restrictions on the amount of energy exports to the U.S. in times of shortage, requires Canada to permit U.S. importers to purchase an amount no smaller than the "proportion prevailing in the most recent 36 month period." The U.S. government wanted this provision to make absolutely sure that in times of shortage the Canadian government would introduce cuts affecting consumers on both sides of the border equally. While this is in keeping with the provisions implicit in GATT (Article XX) and Canada's obligations under the International Energy Agreement pertaining to oil, the FTA goes further by explicitly specifying the proportion in which supplies will be shared. Critics allege that insofar as the Canadian government cannot reduce supplies to the U.S. consumers in times of shortages without hurting Canadian consumers as well, this is a serious erosion of Canada's sovereignty.

Services. The role of services in the economies of the industrialized nations, especially in Canada and the United States, has grown rapidly in recent decades. Over two-thirds of the GNP and employment in both countries is now concentrated in this sector, which is significantly higher than the average for industrialized nations (Radebaugh, 1988, p.20). Services also occupy an important place in the trade between the two nations. In 1986 Canada imported $18.6 billion of services from the U.S. and exported $7 billion worth of services to it (Schott and Smith, 1988, p.137). Not surprisingly, the FTA contains two long chapters covering 150 specified services, including financial, agriculture and forestry, mining, distributional trade, construction, and commercial services (Radebaugh, 1988, p.27). The agreement explicitly excludes transportation, basic telecommunications, doctors, lawyers, childcare, and government-provided services such as health, education, and social services. The agreement also "grandfathers" – that is, it permits the continuation of all existing laws and regulations in the covered services. The principal effect of the agreement is to prevent the erection of new barriers to trade in covered services. The agreement does not prevent either nation from enacting new policies, so long as the particular policy does not discriminate against the other nation.

The agreement treats financial services separately from the other services. Unlike the other services, the trade in financial services was subject to numerous barriers, especially in Canada. Hence, the intent of the agreement is to eliminate some of the existing barriers as well as prevent the imposition of new ones. Under the agreement, U.S. firms are exempt from limitations on ownership of Canadian financial institutions applicable to firms from other countries (for example, the limitations that foreign firms cannot acquire more than 10 percent of a Canadian insurance firm and that foreign subsidiaries, as a group, cannot hold more than 16 percent of the total capital of the Canadian banking industry).

Investment. The FTA eliminates cross-border barriers to investments in all sectors except financial services, transportation, basic telecommunications, cultural industries, oil and natural gas, uranium mining, and the non-covered services such as childcare, health care, and education. The agreement also "grandfathers" all existing rules, except those explicitly mentioned. Under the agreement Canada reserves the right to review direct acquisition of Canadian firms by U.S.-owned firms, but the threshold value of the company acquired has been raised from $5 million to $150 million. The review of indirect acquisition, which occurs when a foreign firm purchases another foreign firm that has a Canadian subsidiary, will be phased out. Canada is prohibited from applying new conditions relating to the performance of U.S. firms that do not also apply to Canadian firms. The Economic Council has calculated that the takeover of two-thirds of all Canadian-controlled non-financial assets by U.S. firms will still be reviewable under the agreement (Economic Council, 1988b, p.14). The FTA does not prohibit the nationalization of firms. It rather prohibits nationalization targeted against the other country's firms; in other words, the government must undertake nationalization in a non-discriminatory manner.

By grandfathering most existing restrictions and prohibiting only new ones, the FTA is more restrictive towards the United States, which currently has almost no restrictions on foreign investment (except in telecommunications and maritime shipping) but might have considered imposing them in the future, given the recent increase in foreign investments into the country. In such an eventuality, Canadian investments would be exempt under the FTA. This is significant for Canada because in recent years its investments in the U.S. have grown faster than the investments of U.S. firms in Canada. Between 1982 and 1986, Canadian direct investment in the U.S. grew by 56.4 percent whereas U.S. investment in Canada grew by only 15.3 percent (Schott and Smith 1988, p.135). In aggregate, however, Canadian investments in the U.S. are still less than half the amount of U.S. investments in Canada.

Government Procurement. The agreement opens federal purchases of goods (but not services) in both countries to all Canadian and U.S. suppliers on contracts exceeding U.S.$25,000, as opposed to U.S.$171,000 under GATT. But the provision excludes many government departments and agencies in both countries and applies only to procurement at the federal level, leaving out the major expenditures of provincial, state, and local governments. Important exclusions also include procurement of defence, transport, and telecommunications goods at the federal level. All in all, the agreement makes little difference to the pre-existing situation in this area.

Dispute Settlement. One of Canada's most important objectives for entering into the negotiations was to gain security of access to the U.S. market. This meant establishing an independent mechanism for adjudicating trade disputes and enforcing its rulings. The FTA makes only minor improvements, if any, on the existing situation.

In case of disputes over the use of the antidumping or countervailing measures, either country is entitled to appeal the other's decisions to independent binational appeal panels instead of the federal courts that used to be the appellate body before the agreement came into force. The panels consist of five persons, two nominated by each side and the fifth chosen by the four members of the previous panel or by lot if this is not acceptable. The Antidumping and Countervailing Duty Panel is merely required to rule on whether the Canadian Import Tribunal or the United States International Trade Commission, as the case may be, fairly applied the country's trade remedy laws. The panel is required to issue its ruling within 315 days. The agreement also sets a seven-year deadline for developing new rules governing antidumping and countervailing duties that would be mutually acceptable to both countries. Until the new rules are agreed upon, the panels will be applying existing laws, and hence decisions are not likely to be substantially different from the judicial precedents. The U.S. producers' ability to initiate actions on rather frivolous grounds will also continue as before. Perhaps the only beneficial impact of the dispute-resolving mechanism is the newly imposed ten-month time limit to the resolution of disputes – in contrast to the several years this could once take.

The agreement provides for a separate mechanism for resolving general disputes, that is, those disputes related to the implementation of the agreement but excluding countervailing and antidumping measures:

- A dispute between the two countries that cannot be resolved by mutual consultation is referred to the Canada-United States Trade Commission, a permanent body jointly established to oversee the implementation of the agreement.
- If the commission fails, the dispute is referred to a Binational Arbitration Panel, whose composition and functioning is similar to the Appeal Panel. The panel must submit its report to the commission within eight months.
- If the commission does not accept the panel's report or otherwise fails to resolve the dispute, the aggrieved party is authorized to retaliate by withdrawing "equivalent benefits," which in trade parlance means erecting import barriers to the targeted country's exports.

This mechanism is similar to the one provided for in the GATT, but it is somewhat of an improvement in that it provides for a faster resolution of disputes.

Cultural Industries. Canadian cultural industries are excluded from the agreement. Thus, the "national treatment" provision for trade and investment does not extend to the cultural industries. Canada can discriminate against U.S. firms in the cultural sector in the future, although doing so will trigger the U.S. right to retaliate against Canadian exports in other sectors by imposing "measures of equivalent commercial effect." This means that Canada will have to compensate the United States to the equivalent of the level of discrimination. This applies only to new measures, because all existing measures (such as the condition that all television and radio broadcasting should be fully Canadian-owned) are grandfathered. The existing Canadian control over its cultural industries is guaranteed, but an increase in the level of control, while permitted, will have to be counterbalanced.

Termination of the Agreement. Either nation can choose to terminate the agreement upon six months' notice. While this appears simple enough, the decision will be anything but easy, especially for Canada. The adverse impact of the termination on firms that have adjusted to the FTA or been established to sell in the continental Canada-U.S. market would have to be taken into account. The decision will be relatively easy for the U.S. because a comparatively small percentage of its economy is dependent on trade with Canada, and hence it is less affected by the free trade agreement.

Expected Impact of the FTA on Canada

Earlier studies on the likely impact of free trade with the United States showed Canada benefiting by as much as a 10 percent increase in GNP.

These studies, conducted before the FTA was signed, assumed the complete elimination of barriers to trade between the two nations, but the agreement reached provides for the continuation of many barriers. Consequently, more recent studies on the impact of the FTA predict much smaller benefits. The Economic Council of Canada, in its prediction of the "most likely outcome," states a real (that is, adjusted for inflation) increase of 2.5 percent in GNP when the agreement is fully implemented in 1998 (1988b, p.18). The federal finance department's study, using a totally different model, similarly predicts an increase of 2.5 percent in real income in the long run (Canada, Dept. of Finance, 1988b, p.108). The Council's long-term forecasts also show an increase of 1.8 percent in employment, or a 251,000 net gain in jobs, a 0.7 percent increase in productivity, a 5 percent increase in investments, and increases of 2.2 percent in exports and 3.9 percent in imports (Economic Council, 1988b, p.18). Both studies indicate that the gains will be spread almost evenly across all regions in Canada (ibid., p.24; Canada, Dept. of Finance, 1988b, p.34).

The two studies disagree about the sectoral impact of the agreement. The Council expects most of the gains in output to accrue from the service (2.6 percent increase) and primary (1.8 percent increase) sectors and the construction industry (6.8 percent increase), with the average increase in output for the manufacturing sector being only 1.2 percent (Economic Council, 1988b, pp.22-23). In contrast, the finance department's forecast predicts the gains in output to derive mainly from the manufacturing sector (10.6 percent increase), with only a negligible (0.9 percent) increase for the service sector (Canada, Dept. of Finance, 1988b, p.31). We must wait until 1998 to find out which, if either, forecast is correct. The Economic Council further predicts that in the manufacturing sector the wood, primary metals, and printing and publishing industries will be the primary beneficiaries (Economic Council, 1988b, p.21). The greatest decline in output and employment in the manufacturing sector will be experienced by the rubber and plastics, leather, textiles, and electrical products industries (ibid.).

The Economic Council's forecasts would seem to indicate that the expected gains of the FTA are rather small, hardly the stuff to get excited about. The expected increase of 2.5 percent of the GDP over a ten-year period is nothing when we realize that in each of the decades between 1951 and 1981 the country's real increase in GDP was well over 33 percent (Canada, Dept. of Finance, 1988b, p.7). No doubt, the 2.5 percent increase will be in addition to the growth that would have taken place without the agreement, but still to call an average additional increase of only 0.25 percent per year anything but small is an exaggeration. Between 1984 and 1987 alone, the average real GDP in Canada increased by 4.4 percent (Canada, Dept. of Finance, 1988b). A close look at the figures for employment gains also makes one wonder about the exuberance of the FTA supporters.

While the critics of FTA show a great divergence in their views, some of them have almost nothing good to say about it (for a comprehensive cata-logue of the alleged demerits of the FTA see Cameron, 1988). They see the elimination of all tariffs as a death-knell for the manufacturing industries in Canada, because of the flood of U.S. imports that will ensue as a result. They foresee an exodus of the U.S. multinationals and an attendant loss of the jobs whose primary reason for locating in Canada was the avoidance of tariffs. The removal of those tariffs will eliminate their reason for being here. They are equally opposed to the energy provisions of the agreement. They view the relaxation of controls on investment as ceding control over our own economic destiny as a nation, and they point out that the minor changes to government procurement have accomplished nothing. They also argue that contrary to the government's claim, the cultural industries are not excluded from the agreement because new measures against U.S. cul-tural imports and investments will have to be counterbalanced. They see the dispute settlement mechanism as inconsequential because it does not con-tain effective sanctions or guaranteed results.

The critics are as much opposed to the hidden agenda behind the agree-ment as to its specific provisions. They charge that by signing the agreement Canada has committed itself to the laissez-faire liberalism practised in the United States. They find it especially disturbing that Canada should have committed itself to this course at a time when the market approach to economic management has been discredited, as the United States' own weakness shows, and the success resulting from government intervention in the Japanese economy confirms. The principle of national treatment present in the agreement is seen as reducing our ability to discriminate against U.S. imports and investments to control their adverse effects. The critics are also apprehensive that free trade will lead to pressure on the Canadian government to reduce both "social wages" (for example, govern-ment expenditures on education or health care) and environmental stan-dards to the lower U.S. standards so that Canadian producers will become competitive with their counterparts south of the border.

Many of the criticisms of FTA are undoubtedly inspired by Canadian nationalism, the understandable target of which is the United States. How-ever, the underlying theme of these criticisms – that the FTA, unlike any-thing in the past, will erode Canadian nationhood – is an exaggeration. In the past the country has shown great resilience in the face of increasing economic integration with the United States. The facts speak for them-selves. Canadian trade with the U.S. increased from 38 percent of total exports in 1947 to over 70 percent in 1989, an average increase of almost one percentage point every year. Our imports from the U.S. increased similarly. More than three-quarters of the television-viewing in Canadian homes is of American-produced programs. Yet Canada has survived as a nation. In all likelihood, the future increase in trade with the U.S. will be much smaller than that experienced over the past few decades. Electronic goods will continue to come from Japan, clothes from Hong Kong and Korea, shoes from Italy, and wine from France – FTA or not.

Political Implications of National-International Integration

The aspect of Canada's position in the international political economy that is most significant for our purposes is the open nature of the Canadian economy. Canada is one of the most trade-dependent nations in the world, despite its numerous import barriers. This high degree of trade dependence coupled with its economy's small size compared to some other nations make it vulnerable to international political-economic factors. The goods produced and the prices they are sold at are often determined by international market forces, which diminishes Canada's capacity to control its political economy. As such, the international arena imposes an enduring constraint. The fluctuations and uncertainties endemic to the international economy further weaken Canadians' control over their own political-economic destiny.

Another crucial feature of Canada's place in the international political economy is its high degree of dependence on the United States as a destination for exports and a source of imports. The FTA is a concrete acknowledgement of this dependence. In fact, Canada embarked on the road to continental free trade with the U.S. as early as 1935. The pace accelerated with membership in the U.S.-sponsored GATT. By signing the General Agreement, Canada agreed to accept limitations on its policy options. It also agreed in principle to lower its trade barriers and not to subsidize its exports. And it agreed to broadly accord "national treatment" to imports. The limitation of options may also be the case with the proposed extension of the Canada-U.S. Free Trade Agreement to Mexico. However, as the figures in Table 20 show, Canada's trade with Mexico is small.

What are the political implications of all of this? We know that interregional, intersectoral, and interpersonal disparities in Canadians' incomes exist (Chapter 5) and that the operation of the Canadian political economy, on an aggregate national basis, has failed to result in an even distribution of benefits across different sections of the population. We know that certain groups have consistently benefited less than others from the operation of the existing domestic political economy. The significant question is why this has occurred, given the belief that liberal market economies work to equalize wealth and opportunities across the population. The persistence of inequalities in Canada has not only caused theorists and members of the public to question the main tenets of classical liberal political economy but has also led to demands for government actions that have violated the principles of the dominant liberal political-economic theory.

The root cause of many of these inequities lies in the resource-export-dependent nature of the Canadian economy, but the governments' abilities

Table 20
Canada-Mexico Trade – 1990

Rank	Commodity	$000,000	Percent of Total Exports
Canadian Exports			
1	Dairy Products	72.8	12.3
2	Vehicle Parts	64.6	10.8
3	Electrical Machinery & Equipment	60.2	10.1
4	Machinery	57.4	9.7
5	Iron & Steel	56.5	9.5
	All Exports	**593.7**	**100**
Canadian Imports			
1	Machinery	549.4	31.7
2	Vehicle Parts	404.8	23.4
3	Electrical Machinery	320.4	18.5
4	Vegetables	78.5	4.5
5	Fuels & Oils	56.8	3.2
	All Imports	**1,729.8**	**100**

SOURCE: Statistics Canada (1991), *Exports by Country, January-December 1990*, Catalogue No. 65-003; *Imports by Country, January-December 1990*, Catalogue No. 65-006 (Ottawa: Minister of Supply and Services).

to alter this situation are limited. Instead, to guarantee markets for its resource and resource-based exports, Canada relies on a liberalized international trading environment and on special arrangements with its major trading partner in areas such as automobiles and services. These international political-economic arrangements and institutions greatly constrain the ability of Canadian governments to deal with the root causes of many Canadian political and economic problems.

CHAPTER 7

The Structure and Organization of the State

States are constrained both by the nature of the domestic political economy and by how that political economy is integrated into the international political economy. But although these two sets of constraints determine how states work, they are not the only limitations on the capacity of states to influence markets. An equally important constraint concerns the nature of the societal actors working to influence the state's direction – and the extent of the state's autonomy from these social forces (Skocpol and Finegold, 1982).

The various theories of political economy contain numerous different conceptions of the state and its actual and proper role in society. They range from the liberal notion of a "neutral" state promoting the general interest of all members of society to the socialist notion of the state as an instrument of class domination.[1] The approaches differ primarily in their evaluations of *state autonomy*, that is, in their evaluations of how independent the state is from societal pressures. Some analysts argue that the state is inherently highly autonomous, enjoys a vast sphere of independent activity, and is capable of judging between proposals and demands made by various societal groups on their merits or according to the state's own criteria. Other analysts regard the state as much less autonomous and greatly restricted in its ability to choose a course of action because of the pressures of powerful societal groups. Yet other analysts argue that the state is relatively autonomous, enjoying a wide range of independent decision-making capability in some areas of government activity and much less in others.

In our investigation the question of autonomy generally refers to the extent of the state's separation from either capital or labour – the two major societal actors in a capitalist economy. Whether the state is autonomous from both groups, is an instrument of either one, or enjoys some circum-scribed sphere of independence from both depends on a variety of factors. The relationship is a function, first, of the organizational coherence and capability of the state – that is, of the state's own ability to formulate and promote an autonomous or independent course of action. Second, it is a function of the organizational coherence and strength of labour and capital and of their ability to influence state plans and activities. Some societies are "strong" and states "weak," while other societies are "weak" or poorly organized and states "strong." Other variations also exist, such as strong states and strong societies or weak states and weak societies. How states are able to affect markets varies according to the strength of each actor in society (Migdal, 1988).

This means that the question of state autonomy is not so much a subject for theoretical dispute as a matter of empirical investigation. That is, it is a question that can be determined by examining the internal strength of the state and comparing that strength with the internal strength and coherence of other societal actors. We would expect an autonomous state to exist when the state is well organized and united and societal or market actors are disunited and fragmented. We would expect a non-autonomous state to exist when state organizations are fragmented and faced with united and cohesive societal actors. In between these two conditions are a variety of other situations in which the state is only relatively or partially autono-mous. In fact, eight possible situations exist.

As Figures I and II illustrate, states enjoy full autonomy from labour and capital in only one circumstance: when a strong state faces both weak labour and weak capital. States are relatively autonomous in four circum-stances: when a strong state faces either one of strongly organized capital or labour, or both, and when all three actors are weak. A state lacks autonomy in the three circumstances when a weak state faces either one of strongly organized labour or capital, or both.

The Organization and Operation of State Institutions

In a democratic-political economy, the state's relative strength depends largely on its capabilities for undertaking timely, effective actions that realize the aims and ambitions of popular representatives in government. To assess these capabilities we must look in turn at the nature and function-ing of the representative and legislative systems that link the state to society, as well as at the nature and functioning of the administrative systems charged with the execution of legislative decisions.

The two most important points to note about the Canadian state from an institutional perspective are that it is a *parliamentary democracy* and a *federal system*. Understanding these two aspects of the Canadian state in their historical contexts is essential to understanding the political-

Figure I
Extent of State Autonomy When State Strong

		LABOUR	
		Strong	Weak
CAPITAL	Strong	Relatively Autonomous	Relatively Autonomous
	Weak	Relatively Autonomous	Autonomous

Figure II
Extent of State Autonomy When State Weak

		LABOUR	
		Strong	Weak
CAPITAL	Strong	Non-Autonomous	Non-Autonomous
	Weak	Non-Autonomous	Relatively Autonomous

economic linkages that influence and determine resource allocation in the country. The Canadian state emerged out of a gradual process of decolonization as successively more and more tasks undertaken by the British government were transferred to the domestic state. This process took well over a hundred years to complete, with the final British powers over amendment of the Canadian constitution only being transferred to the domestic institutions of government in 1982.

The first major step in this decolonization occurred in 1867 with the enactment of the British North America (BNA) Act or Constitution Act. This act of the British Parliament established the basic constitutional structure of the country but left several major areas of state authority under British control, including powers to conduct Canada's international relations with other states and to negate any Canadian laws that might interfere with British foreign policy.[2] Until the BNA Act, Canada existed as a collection of separately governed British colonies and a substantial parcel of Hudson's Bay Company land known collectively as British North America.

Under the terms of the act, the Maritime colonies of New Brunswick and Nova Scotia were united with two new provinces, Quebec and Ontario, created out of what had been the United Province of Canada. In addition, a new central government – the federal government of Canada – was created. Subsequently, the federal government purchased the Hudson's Bay lands in

1869 and eventually created three new provinces in the area: Manitoba in 1870 and Alberta and Saskatchewan in 1905. Meanwhile, through a variety of financial incentives linked to railway construction and debt allowances, the federal government induced two other British North American colonies to join the new nation: British Columbia (1871) and Prince Edward Island (1873). The last remaining colonial holdout, Newfoundland, was finally cajoled into Confederation in 1949 after its local government had been forced to declare bankruptcy and placed in "receivership" by the British prior to World War II. Many of the provinces, including Quebec, Ontario, and Manitoba, entered into Confederation with much smaller territories than they now possess and were expanded into territorial lands in a series of agreements negotiated between the federal and provincial governments from 1879 to 1912 (Nicholson, 1964).

All of the original provinces joined Confederation under the same terms, although several of the later additions did not. The three prairie provinces did not receive control over their lands and natural resources until 1930 (Lingard, 1946; Martin, 1920). The original terms of Confederation were set out in various sections of the BNA Act, especially Sections 91 to 95 and 102 to 126. Section 91 set out the powers of the new federal government, and much of the rest of the document dealt with how the new federal government institutions were to be staffed and organized. The BNA Act essentially provided for a single political and economic unit to be created among the territories of the formerly separate colonies and gave the federal government adequate powers and sources of revenue to ensure that this common economic market and political entity would be maintained. The provincial governments were given jurisdiction over most of their lands and local matters, and they were expected to generate enough revenues, through a combination of federal grants and provincial natural-resource income, to finance their affairs (Resnick, 1987; Vipond 1989).

The BNA Act also specified the types of fundamental political institutions to be established in the new country. Canadian governments were to follow the British, or Westminster, parliamentary model but the Canadian state was to be structured as a federal system – which led to important modifications of the British model.

The Federal System

In a federal system of government a country has not one, but two, sovereign levels or orders of government. One of these levels is generally known as the central or federal government; the other level is known by a variety of different names in different federal countries of the world – for example, as "lander" in West Germany, "constituent republics" in the Soviet Union, or "states" in the United States, Brazil, and Mexico. In Canada the second level of government is known as the provincial. Federal states differ from more unitary forms of states in that the two "levels" of government are sovereign or independent of each other in their specified areas of jurisdiction (Wheare, 1946).

The principle of *divided sovereignty* embodied in a federal system is significant for political-economic analysis, for a number of reasons. First, it means that the state in a federal system is in actuality a number of states, each with its own procedural nuances and institutional arrangements. Second, it means that considerable attention must be paid to the specific areas over which the different levels of government have jurisdiction. In a federal system, for example, it makes a great deal of difference whether the central government or the state governments control important areas such as banking, social insurance, or labour law; this control will help determine which interests and actors are involved in the policy process, how those interests and actors are structured internally, and how they interact with each other in the allocation of goods and services in society.

An important variable in the analysis of the state in Canada, then, is the distribution of legislative powers between the two levels of government. In most federal systems, and here Canada is no exception, the distribution of legislative powers between the two component levels of government is established in a written constitution. Under the terms of the BNA Act, the federal government obtained several important economic powers, including exclusive jurisdiction over trade and commerce, interest, banking, and currency; the provinces obtained jurisdiction over important areas of social concern, including matters relating to health, education, municipal government, and private property (Mallory, 1971; Dawson, 1947); and over public lands and resources.

Although provincial resource royalties were capable of generating adequate revenues to finance provincial activities in these areas at the time of Confederation, they proved woefully inadequate as the areas of governmental activity expanded in the early years of the twentieth century. This situation was brought to a head by the economic depression of the 1930s and led to several unsuccessful attempts to restructure the division of powers and revenues to enable the two levels of government to carry out their constitutional responsibilities. After World War II, some success was achieved in this area when various forms of federal government transfer payments to the provinces were established (Lynn, 1967; Moore, Perry, and Beach, 1966).

The original division of powers contained in the BNA Act remained in place with very few changes for over 115 years because the act did not contain any method or formula for constitutional amendments.[3] Nevertheless, the division of powers did change drastically as a direct result of the practice of judicial interpretation of constitutional statutes. Until 1949, when the Supreme Court of Canada achieved the status of final constitutional arbiter, constitutional decisions for Canada were made in London by the Judicial Committee of the Privy Council (JCPC), a committee of the

British House of Lords. The JCPC was involved in many constitutional conflicts between the federal and provincial governments before 1949 and made many, sometimes contradictory, decisions. Although the JCPC tended to rule in favour of the federal government in the first few years after Confederation, by the 1890s it had reversed itself and tended to side with the provinces in their disputes with Ottawa (Cairns, 1971; Browne, 1967). This situation was maintained until after 1949, when the Supreme Court of Canada started to favour the federal side in many constitutional cases (Russell, 1977). In general the provinces were given great powers in dealing with matters within provincial boundaries and the federal government was given great powers in dealing with interprovincial and international matters. Although this division of powers worked well enough in the early era of Confederation, such a "watertight" scheme is largely unworkable in the modern era because many actions of provincial governments affect interprovincial and international areas of federal jurisdiction, and vice versa.

Like the problems with fiscal relations and a lack of an amendment formula, the problems of divided federal and provincial jurisdictions have resulted, in practice, in the need for extensive and frequent federal-provincial consultation on virtually every significant issue of Canadian political and economic life. This has given rise at both the administrative and executive levels to a complex and somewhat time-consuming process of intergovernmental negotiations, sometimes referred to as *co-operative* or *executive federalism* (Smiley, 1987). It has also led to proposals to alter the fundamental constitutional structure of the country in a way that would institutionalize federal-provincial consultations, either through the institutionalization of first ministers' conferences or through a revamped Senate that would represent the provinces in federal policy-making (Smiley and Watts, 1987; Thorburn, 1984).

Although the courts do not have the power to make legislation and can only strike down legislation found to be *ultra vires*, or beyond the powers of a given level of government, both levels of government must take court rulings into account if they are to be sure that their legislation will remain valid. The inclusion of a Charter of Rights and Freedoms in the Canadian constitution in 1982 has further reinforced and expanded the powers of the courts by allowing them to strike down legislation that in their judgment contravenes the fundamental rights and freedoms established in the charter. Although governments can temporarily override some elements of the charter by invoking a "notwithstanding" clause contained within it, there is no doubt that the powers of the courts have been expanded (Russell, 1982, 1983).[4] The courts operate on the legal principle of *stare decisis*, or of adhering to precedents set by earlier decisions, but exactly how each court will decide any particular issue is unknown. Therefore, Canadian governments can never be sure that legislation they pass will actually take effect, and in many cases they must wait for a court ruling on the validity of the legislation before they can utilize it effectively. Again, this is a time-consuming process and does not contribute to the ability of governments to move quickly and decisively in many areas of state activity.

Under the rules of a federal system, state structures are purposely divided and fragmented into national and constituent governments, while the judiciary, as the arbiter of constitutional disputes, is elevated to an important role alongside the traditional legislative and executive bodies of government. This fragmentation reduces the state's capacity to establish and follow an independent course of action.

Parliamentary Democracy

The Canadian decision to establish a parliamentary form of government and a federal state structure was not entirely novel. The colonies of British North America had already developed political institutions following British parliamentary practices and had existed as separate colonies or provinces for many years. But the decision to continue with this type of arrangement would have serious ramifications for the cohesiveness and organizational solidarity of the Canadian state. It would also affect its ability to chart a course of action autonomous from the positions and prescriptions of other societal actors.

Developed over a thousand years in Britain, the parliamentary form of government is characterized by the existence of a central representative institution or Parliament, which controls the spending and raising of revenues (Jennings, 1952; Dicey, 1908; Bagehot, 1920). Parliamentary systems are quite different from congressional or republican systems, in which a representative legislative body has the exclusive ability to make laws (Stewart, 1974). Congressional or republican systems, like those of the United States and France, were created to replace a monarchical form of government with a form of representative government. Parliamentary systems, on the other hand, developed with the intention not of replacing the law-making power of the Crown but of ensuring that the Crown's power would not be abused. In parliamentary systems a great deal of law-making power rests with the government or cabinet, and to a very great extent the deliberations of Parliament are intended to publicize and monitor the government's activities.[5]

The colonies of British North America did not achieve *responsible government* until the 1840s.[6] Before that the colonies were governed by a representative of the British Crown, the governor or governor-general, with the aid of an appointed legislative council. Elected colonial houses of assembly had existed for some time but had only limited rights to consultation over the raising of government revenues. The Rebellions of 1837 in Upper and Lower Canada were fought largely over the issues of *representation by population* for the lower houses and the need for responsible government. These demands were achieved following the submission of Lord Durham's report on the rebellions and their causes when the British government instructed the colonial governors to appoint to their legislative councils only those individuals who had the confidence of the colonial assemblies.

Although the names have changed and the government today consists of a cabinet composed of the premier or prime minister and other ministers of the Crown, these individuals are still appointed by the governor-general (or lieutenant-governor in a province) under the convention that they must enjoy the confidence of the House of Commons or provincial legislature. With the development of an established party system contesting elections to the legislature, this means that these individuals are the leader of the majority party in the House and other individuals chosen by the premier or prime minister from among other members of that party in the legislature. From a legal standpoint, the government of the country continues to be appointed by the Crown and the government still controls the agenda and timetable of Parliament as long as it enjoys the support of a majority of members of Parliament. Under the system of responsible government, if the government no longer enjoys the confidence of the House of Commons and its legislation is defeated, it is no longer the government and the Crown will replace it, either by calling on a new group within the existing Parliament to form a government or by dissolving Parliament and calling an election to see if a new government can be formed from among a new set of members of Parliament.

The existence of a parliamentary system of government in Canada partially offsets the difficulties encountered by the state as the result of the operation of a federal system of government. That is, unlike republican or congressional systems, which purposely separate and divide the legislative and executive functions of government, parliamentary systems provide the political executive with a great deal of control over their "legislatures."

The Electoral System

Canada is not only a parliamentary system; it is also a parliamentary democracy. Many important positions in the Canadian political structure, however, are not elected but appointed, including the governor-general and provincial lieutenant-governors, court justices and regulatory commission members, the prime minister, premiers, and cabinet ministers, and all civil servants. But with one exception the legislative bodies of both levels of government are elected. The exception is the federal Senate, which is appointed by the Crown on the advice of the federal cabinet and in accordance with constitutional provisions regarding its regionally representative membership. Although most other legislatures have always been elected, the nature of the electoral suffrage – or right to vote – and the qualifications required to run for office have changed significantly since Confederation

(Van Loon and Whittington, 1987; Qualter, 1970). The nature of the Canadian electoral system and the changes in the right to vote have had a significant impact on the operation of the Canadian parliamentary system and on the operation of the Canadian political economy.

The general pattern in Canada has been for the electoral franchise to be gradually extended to the point where Canada now has a universal adult franchise – every Canadian citizen over the age of eighteen has the right to cast a single ballot in elections held in the constituency where that person lives. Only officials who are part of the electoral process itself, and especially those involved in the counting or recounting of ballots, do not have the right to vote. This includes chief electoral officers in each constituency and returning officers at each poll where ballots are cast. In addition, federally appointed justices, who may be involved in judicial recounts of contested election results, are also not entitled to vote.

Until the passage of the Dominion Elections Act in 1920, provincial rules prevailed, and even national elections were carried out according to regulations that varied considerably from province to province in terms of who was entitled to vote.[7] Usually only male Caucasian British subjects with a certain level of property holdings were enfranchised. This greatly restricted the number of individuals actually casting ballots in elections, as did several provincial statutes insisting that prospective voters pass literacy tests. Although the property qualification was gradually reduced and the literacy tests were eliminated in most provinces, significant elements of the populace remained disenfranchised until recently. It was only in the 1970s that the provision allowing British subjects to vote was dropped and the franchise limited to Canadian citizens. At the same time, the voting age was lowered to eighteen from twenty-one.

The first major extension of the franchise occurred in 1918 when women obtained the vote. Although not all women were originally given the vote, universal adult female suffrage was instituted shortly afterwards in federal elections. In many provincial elections, however, women remained disenfranchised. In Quebec women did not receive the right to vote in provincial elections until 1940. Along with gender discrimination, ethnic and racial discrimination also continued to exist at both the federal and provincial levels. In British Columbia, persons of an "oriental or Hindu" background were disenfranchised until 1945, while at the federal level status Indians and Inuit peoples remained without the vote until 1960-61.

These limitations on the right to vote were of great significance in the first fifty years of Confederation when the system of adult male propertied suffrage existed. Although technically a democracy in that its legislature – and, in effect, government – was determined by means of ballots cast at periodic elections, in practice the composition of the legislature reflected the concerns of only a restricted section of the populace and not the entire public. It should not be surprising, therefore, that many of the actions of government in this early period should have been biased towards these sectional, propertied interests.

Another significant component of the Canadian electoral system is the constituency-based, plurality electoral system based on territorially defined representation by population. While there are numerous different types of electoral systems in place in different countries around the world, most British-style parliamentary systems have a system of *territorial constituencies* from which representatives are chosen according to the *plurality principle* – that is, the winning candidate is the one who gets the most votes regardless of the margin of victory or the proportion of total votes received. This is the case with all federal and provincial elections in Canada.

This type of system has an electoral bias built into it. Although great efforts are made to ensure that each constituency has roughly the same number of voters and, thus, that any single vote cast in an election is "worth" the same amount as any other – or has the same impact on the electoral outcome – this is difficult to achieve in practice, especially when the population of a country is concentrated in urban centres and rural areas are large with widely dispersed populations. This situation has existed in Canada since urban populations began to grow in the late nineteenth century. In such circumstances, an equitable distribution of population among constituencies involves a choice between either very few geographically large rural ridings to match the population numbers present in reasonably sized urban constituencies or very many relatively small urban ridings created to match the populations present in geographically smaller rural constituencies. Whichever system is chosen, territorial biases are built into the electoral system.[8]

The Party System

The operation of the party system adds to this representative bias. Organized political parties in Canada are a relatively new phenomenon, having their origins in parliamentary alliances and social protest movements of the late nineteenth and early twentieth centuries (Duverger, 1965). Contemporary parties such as the Liberals and Conservatives had their origins in parliamentary alliances of MPs, while others such as the New Democratic, Social Credit, Green, and Parti Québécois originated in social movements of the 1930s and 1960s at either the provincial or federal level (Van Loon and Whittington, 1987; Thorburn, 1985; McCormick, 1989). The idea behind the creation of a political party, whatever its actual origins, is to obtain power: that is, in a British parliamentary system, to obtain a majority of seats in the House of Commons or provincial legislature and thereby be called upon to form a government.

Parties such as the Liberal Party of Canada and the Progressive Conservative Party of Canada have their roots in decisions of members of the federal Parliament who were not elected in partisan contests to vote collectively and consistently in order to provide the parliamentary support required to maintain a government. As these coalitions became more and more formalized and the principles behind the decisions to vote collectively became clear, elections began to be contested along party lines, with representatives of established parties running against each other in established constituencies. Protest parties emerged at various times when sections of the populace felt that their interests were not being adequately served by existing parties. Examples are the United Farmers' parties in several provinces and the national Progressive Party, which articulated the views of farmers and labour in the elections following World War I (Morton, 1950).

The establishment of national and provincial party systems had significant consequences for the operation of Canadian governments. First, the attainment of a parliamentary majority became a simpler task for political leaders who could count on a stable voting block in the legislature to back the government – a phenomenon known as party discipline in the House. Because of party discipline, the governor-general or lieutenant-governor can simply call on the leader of the majority party to form a government, knowing that this government will enjoy the confidence of the legislature.

The emergence of parties to contest elections intensified and made much more obvious the territorial and representative biases present in the electoral system. Parties with diffuse national support are penalized under a constituency-based system while parties with concentrated territorial support are rewarded. A party that achieves, for example, 25 percent of the total vote but obtains this by winning 25 percent of the vote in each riding will not win very many seats. On the other hand, parties that can muster 25 percent of the total vote but do so by winning 50 to 60 percent of the vote in each constituency in specific regions of the country or province can win a large number of seats (Cairns, 1968; Lovink, 1970).

The result of the combined workings of the Canadian parliamentary, electoral, and party systems, then, has been for first propertied interests and later territorial interests originating in the regional structure of the Canadian economy to have their demands and prescriptions for government action easily translated into conditions of parliamentary support for governments. Although property considerations have been eliminated through the extension of the franchise, the operation of the electoral system as a whole ensures that parties will be formed to express territorial interests and that governments will be formed on the basis of territorially based party support.

The operation of all three systems together, moreover, serves to limit the extent to which national or non-territorial issues will come to prominence in political deliberations. In many countries with similar systems of government, the tendency of the political system to accentuate territorial issues is less significant because the homogeneous social and economic structures of those countries cause similar concerns and conflicts to arise in different parts of the country. In the Canadian case, territorial differences are significant because the areas of the country have different economic bases, which engender different, and often contradictory or conflicting, sets of concerns in each region – and Canadian governments must respond to these varied concerns.

The Administrative System

All modern countries have extensive administrative apparatuses designed to carry out the continuing tasks of day-to-day governance according to the wishes of the political government. In different countries the size and range of issues that administrators handle vary, as do the systems that ensure *administrative accountability* – making sure that the administration follows practices and policies approved by the political government.

Canada has a number of distinct administrative and politico-administrative characteristics that influence the operation of the Canadian political economy in diverse and significant ways. The most crucial of these relates to how parliamentary systems transfer control over government decision-making to administrative officials. In parliamentary systems the political executive (cabinet) controls the agenda and timetable of Parliament and can in most circumstances guarantee passage of its legislation in the form in which it is introduced. Much political debate in parliamentary systems, therefore, occurs outside of the legislature in the process of formulating policy proposals, rather than in the debates on the proposed legislation (Pross, 1986). In this process of policy formulation civil servants play an important role, which raises questions about the extent to which the administration is responding to its own desires and needs rather than to the elected politicians.

Canada's public bureaucracy is composed of three main types of administrative agencies at three levels of government: federal, provincial, and local. The three general types of agencies are the traditional *departmental* form of organization, the government-owned enterprise or *crown corporation*, and the *independent regulatory commission* (Kernaghan and Siegal, 1987; Adie and Thomas, 1987). Each of these agencies has a different structure and a different relationship to the political government, and each has experienced growth in recent years at all three levels of government.

The traditional departmental form of organization is the most important for influencing policy formulation. This type of organization involves large numbers of public servants working in a hierarchically structured organization funded by legislative appropriation and carrying out duties assigned to them by legislation or statute. Each department is headed by a senior official or deputy minister and is responsible to a senior politician or cabinet minister for its activities. Although the number and size of departments vary considerably depending upon jurisdiction and the responsibilities assigned to the department by a legislature, collectively departments make up the backbone of the Canadian administrative system and have always been the primary device that political governments use to carry out their wishes (Hodgetts, 1973).

Government enterprises or crown corporations are publicly owned corporations that operate like any private sector corporation, with the exception that their shares are held by governments. Governments thereby control appointments to their boards of directors and are in a position to influence the general policies of the corporation if not its day-to-day activities. Although Canadian governments at all levels have used this form of administration, this use grew dramatically during wartime at the federal level and after 1960 at the provincial level (Prichard, 1983). The largest crown corporations, especially provincially owned utility corporations such as B.C. Hydro, Hydro-Québec, and Ontario Hydro, are among the largest corporations of any kind in the country.

Finally, independent regulatory commissions are small institutions with enormous legal powers that belie their size. Based on the model of the U.S. Interstate Commerce Commission established in the late nineteenth century, independent regulatory commissions are created to monitor and control the activities of private sector industries to ensure compliance with government objectives and avoidance of partisan political manipulation. Legislatures usually give them broad powers to investigate and modify private sector behaviour using hearings and regulation. Although the details and mandates of these agencies differ substantially according to the activity regulated and the jurisdiction granting regulatory authority, they all operate in much the same manner. Once again, the number of agencies and the areas of economic activity they regulate have been growing at both the federal and provincial levels throughout this century (Economic Council of Canada, 1979; Baggaley, 1981).

The growth in the size and complexity of government administration in recent years has called into question the ability of parliaments and legislatures to control government expenditures, challenged the ability of cabinets to control the decisions and regulations issued by administrators, and undermined the links between the administration, cabinet, and legislatures maintained through the parliamentary convention of ministerial responsibility (Kernaghan, 1979, 1985; Dwivedi, 1982). As a result critics have proposed a variety of reforms to bolster political control over the administration, including dramatically reducing the size and scope of government expenditures and regulatory activities through privatization, deregulation, hiring freezes, and tax reform (Kamerman and Kahn, 1989). Some of these proposals have been put into place. Other proposals have involved bolstering ministerial responsibility through the creation of larger ministerial staffs and staff agencies, strengthening parliamentary surveillance through allocating more resources and powers to parliamentary committees, and allowing individual citizens greater control over administrative activities through enhanced Freedom of Information legislation, judicial review, and the creation of offices of the ombudsman (Kernaghan, 1979). Despite these changes, administrative accountability remains a major issue at all levels of the Canadian state.

The Political-Economic Significance of State Fragmentation

The state in Canada is fragmented in three principal directions. First, and most significant for the nation as a whole, the state is fragmented as a result of the division of state authority between two levels of government as a result of the workings of the federal system. This is a significant division that affects the ability of the state to develop consistent and coherent policies in any area of state activity. The effects of this division permeate the operation of Canadian governments.

The second division concerns the manner in which the operation of the electoral and party systems promotes the enunciation of sectional and territorial interests over the enunciation of broader "national" interests.

The third division is between the political and administrative branches of Canadian governments in all jurisdictions. Administrative organizations in Canadian governments are sophisticated and well funded, and they enjoy considerable independence from elected political officials. This allows them considerable discretion in their choice of activities and further fragments the state's capability for undertaking a consistent and coherent set of actions affecting the allocation of goods and services in society.

The Canadian political economy has been strongly influenced by the federal constitution and the existence of two sovereign levels of government. Both levels of government have important powers over different economic activities. The development of a consistent and coherent set of political-economic policies has become more difficult in Canada than in many other countries because of the need to both secure intergovernmental agreement and co-ordinate governmental activities.

This problem of political co-ordination has been complicated by the regions' different economic bases. The economics of most of the provinces outside of Central Canada, and even a significant component of the Quebec economy, are reliant on natural-resource industries that fall largely within provincial jurisdiction. But trade in these goods, both on the interprovincial and the international level, falls within federal jurisdiction.

The federal government also has exclusive powers over money and banking, including the establishment of such important monetary tools as interest and foreign exchange rates. Similarly, it has exclusive powers over unemployment insurance and jurisdiction over employees involved in federally owned and regulated industries, while labour relations more generally fall within provincial powers. On the corporate side, the federal government has jurisdiction over such matters as competition and mergers, or antitrust and anticombine measures, while the provincial governments exercise control over such important matters as securities and exchange regulation. Finally, both levels of government exercise control over important tax matters involving income and corporate taxes. The formulation and implementation of a consistent and coherent set of state actions in the realm of state-market relations are made extremely complex by the fragmented nature of political controls exercised by the Canadian state.[9]

The workings and fundamental structure of a federal parliamentary democratic system, then, have a number of significant consequences for the process and nature of government decision-making within the Canadian political economy. There are at least two significant structural and procedural aspects of the Canadian system of government:

- Control over the legislative process in the parliamentary system is concentrated in the cabinet but is fragmented by the existence of autonomous levels of government created by a federal constitution.
- Political governments have responded to the gradual extension of democratic rights among the citizenry, but significant powers remain vested in appointed positions in the courts, the Senate, and public bureaucracies.

Thus, state power in Canada is only partially responsive to democratic controls, yet it is structurally limited in its ability to formulate coherent and consistent national policies by the existence of a federal system of government and the operation of a territorially based plurality electoral system. A number of important consequences for Canadian government decision-making result from these characteristics of the Canadian state:

- National policies in most areas require intergovernmental agreement. This involves Canadian governments in complex, extensive, and time-consuming negotiations between federal and provincial governments on most issues, with no guarantee that negotiations will be concluded in the manner envisioned by the initiating government. Similarly, both levels of government are subject to unpredictable judicial review of their legislative activities.
- The operation of the party and electoral systems tends to promote the enunciation of territorial grievances at the expense of national ones within the Canadian political process, a phenomenon that only exacerbates the structural tendency of the federal system to require intergovernmental (that is, territorial) agreement on key issues.
- The cabinet's ability to control a growing public sector is limited, and public bureaucracies retain a great deal of control over government decision-making. This means, in many cases, that the "resolution" of territorial or regional grievances takes place within the public bureaucracy and not within a democratically influenced or constructed legislative process.

What this means for the operation of the Canadian political economy, then, is that many conflicts in the country over the allocation of resources are territorially defined and resolved outside of the democratic political process in the context of administrative or executive federalism. Both the problems posed and the solutions proposed therefore tend to reflect the desires and demands of federal and provincial cabinets responding to sectionally based electoral imperatives or of officials responding to administrative concerns rather than to national "public opinion," as one might expect in a democratic state.

Notes

1 For good overviews of the various interpretations of the state generated by political theorists, see Alford and Friedland (1985), Skocpol (1985), and Przeworski (1990).

2 During the colonial era the Imperial government in London retained the right to overturn colonial legislation and did so usually through the powers of reservation and disallowance of colonial legislation exercised by the colonial governor or governor-general. Even after Confederation this power was retained by the British Crown in the form of the Colonial Laws Validity Act, an act of the British Parliament declaring that any law passed in a colony or Dominion of the British Empire that contradicted Imperial policy could be declared invalid. Canada and the other self-governing dominions were only exempted from this law by the Statute of Westminster in 1931 (Dawson, 1947).

3 For the first 116 years of Confederation, amendments to the BNA Act were passed by the British Parliament only when all of the provinces and the federal government could agree that changes were required. Although the need for unanimity made such changes difficult to achieve, several were in fact made, including the adoption of responsibility for unemployment insurance by the federal government in 1940 and for old age pensions in 1951 (Canada, Dept. of Justice, 1965). In 1982 the entire situation changed when a major set of constitutional changes was passed by the British Parliament, which then transferred responsibility for further changes to the Canadian governments. Included in the Constitution Act, 1982 were such elements as a Charter of Rights and Freedoms specifying the fundamental legal, political, and equality rights enjoyed by Canadians; a new section restating provincial rights to regulate natural-resource industries; and a variety of other provisions concerning such matters as aboriginal rights, the renaming of various constitutional documents, and the inclusion of several new formulas for amending parts of the constitution itself (Romanow, Whyte, and Leeson, 1984; Sheppard and Valpy, 1982).

4 The fact that the constitution gives the federal government the right to appoint Supreme Court and most other justices has been the subject of major federal-provincial disputes and has resulted in a number of proposals to provide provincial governments with additional powers to

appoint judges, including powers contained in the failed 1987 Meech Lake constitutional accord (Swinton, 1988; Russell, 1988).

5 Although modelled on British institutions, the Canadian state does not maintain a set of parliamentary institutions identical to those found in the United Kingdom. In both Britain and Canada, Parliament is a *bicameral* body – that is, composed of two houses or chambers. In Britain, because of the aristocratic origins of the British system of government, Parliament is composed of an appointed House of Lords and an elected House of Commons. In Canada, because of the federal nature of the country, two sets of parliaments exist. Although most were originally bicameral, at the provincial level the appointed second chambers or legislative councils were eliminated within the first hundred years of Confederation, leaving the present *unicameral* elected provincial legislatures or legislative assemblies. At the federal level, Parliament remains bicameral with an appointed Senate and an elected House of Commons. The Senate continues to exist at the federal level partly to ensure regional representation in central government decision-making, and it is structured to ensure more or less equal representation of the eastern and western regions of the country and Quebec and Ontario.

6 In Britain the long transition of the parliamentary system from its aristocratic origins to its democratic status concerned the gradual development of what is known as responsible government – the establishment of the convention that the government be responsible to Parliament for its actions. Responsible government was a major issue during the English Civil War of the 1640s and one of the key issues in the popular rebellions of 1837 in Upper and Lower Canada. It involves a specific relationship between the Crown and Parliament that is essential to an understanding of the present-day operation of parliamentary systems.

At its outset the British Parliament was an assembly of landlords who had forced the English monarch to consult with them before raising any new taxes. In English constitutional history the pivotal document establishing this relationship was the Magna Carta, signed by the landlords and the English King in 1215. The actual government of the land was still undertaken by the King and his court of appointed advisers, the King's Privy Council. Parliament was consulted only very infrequently when major new taxes were proposed, such as those needed for the financing of foreign wars. Although the Lords in Parliament attempted to extend their right of consultation to the consideration of other government expenditures, the monarchy resisted, and Parliament only gained this right after the defeat of the monarchy by parliamentary forces during the English Civil War.

The most important concession gained by Parliament from the monarchy as a result of the Civil War was the agreement that the monarch would henceforth appoint to government positions only those people who enjoyed the confidence of Parliament. In effect, this meant that normally members of the government would be elected members of the House of Commons. This convention – that members of the government be responsible or accountable for their actions to Parliament – constitutes responsible government.

7 At Confederation the power to control elections was vested in the federal government with the provision that existing provincial rules would remain in effect until the federal Parliament specifically overrode them. This did not occur until 1920, when the Dominion Elections Act was passed.

8 This territorial bias is further exacerbated by the lack of correspondence of seats in the legislature and popular votes received, which is usually brought about by the operation of the plurality criterion for choosing winners in constituency contests. To form a government under the rules of a parliamentary system of responsible government in Canada, it is only necessary for a government to have the support of a majority of the members of the House of Commons or provincial legislature. Because representatives to the House are selected in accordance with a plurality principle, it is not necessarily the case that the majority in the House actually represents a majority of the popular vote. It may well be that each representative on the government side gets elected by a very narrow margin in multiple-candidate contests; as a result the government, as a whole, would enjoy only the support of a very small percentage of voters. Similarly, opposition members may have won their contests by large margins and, in total, have gained a much greater percentage of the popular vote than the government. This would mean that the government actually represents and brings to its legislative agenda the ideas and concerns of a relatively small proportion of the populace. When the franchise itself was limited, as it was before 1920, this phenomenon was intensified.

9 For examples of the difficulties encountered in the formulation of economic policy as a result of divided jurisdictions and different economic bases in the provinces, see Jenkin (1983) and Savoie (1986).

CHAPTER 8

The Structure and Organization of Labour

Under capitalism, individual labourers – because of their dependence on continued employment for day-to-day sustenance – are in a weak position to influence the operation of the labour market and at a severe disadvantage when it comes to bargaining with capital for better terms. Collectively, well-organized labourers can deprive capital of a workforce through strikes or work stoppages, thus restricting production and profits – greatly increasing their ability to gain concessions from the owners of the means of production (Taylor, 1987).

Successful collective organization, or "unionization," of labour is no simple task because capital can single out and penalize individual workers for advocating and promoting such activities. For unionization to occur, workers must be willing to risk individual penalties for future collective benefits. Conversely, union strength stems from the collective withholding of labour from capital, but such a withholding encourages capitalists to pay more for scarce labour, which in turn provides an increased incentive for individual workers to break ranks and return to work. Once again, successful organization means workers must place the collective good ahead of their individual good or, at least, place long-term prospects ahead of short-term gains.

Alternatively, unionization and collective organization can be abetted by the state, which can use its authority to prohibit employers from penalizing workers or to prohibit strike-breaking activities. In most modern nation-states, through the working of the democratic process, governments have undertaken such activities in order to gain the electoral support of workers. This has resulted in the existence of a complex system of labour or "industrial" relations in which the state regulates the relationship between labour and capital.

For workers to achieve more than this from governments requires a further stage in labour organization in which unions combine into central labour organizations. These larger organizations, theoretically, then have the capacity to influence government decision-making in areas of social life that affect workers' interests. They can work, for instance, at influencing the redistribution of income through the tax system or at otherwise altering the market advantages enjoyed by the owners of the means of production. The emergence of these united and cohesive central labour organizations in different countries has depended on numerous factors, including the various origins of the labour unions, the principles upon which they were organized, and, especially, their history of past rivalries or co-operation in organizing workers. Once again, some unions individually may prosper while others founder, and the short-term interests of improving wages and working conditions may outweigh the long-term advantages of improving the general position of labour vis-à-vis capital. In some countries labour has emerged as a powerful force influencing government activity, while in others labour remains fragmented and disorganized and relatively ineffectual in its efforts to influence government policy. Because the organization of labour is a significant determinant of the actual nexus of state-market relations that exists in any country, it is an important element of political-economic analysis.

The Emergence of Wage Labour

Capitalist systems did not emerge fully formed in any nation but rather grew slowly over several hundred years as earlier systems of production were gradually transformed. These earlier systems, most notably feudalism, were based not on the production and exchange of industrial commodities by wage earners but rather on the production of agricultural goods by independent or semi-independent producers who retained rights to some portion of their produce for subsistence. The remaining portion of goods produced was appropriated by property owners in the form of rents or tithes charged to the producers.

The appropriated surplus provided the basis for the growth of aristocratic and monarchical forms of government dominated by large landlords. The aristocratic or monarchical state used some of this social product to fund its military ventures, while individual landlords used their share to finance extravagant lifestyles and further accumulation. Both these activities – military spending and luxury consumption – allowed some commodity markets to be established, initially based on small handicraft-production ventures owned by workers or families. As the ventures grew to exceed this form of independent commodity production, they required additional labourers, who came either from the surplus farm population or from the ranks of failed farmers or farmers forced off the land by landlords more interested in raising livestock than in tenant-farming. Eventually, larger and larger proportions of the populace found themselves employed as wage labourers. This was the general pattern followed in England and several other European countries, although other countries such as Japan and Germany underwent a slightly different process of development led by state encouragement of large-scale factories and workshops and the rapid creation of a wage-labour force (Moore, 1966).

Other countries, including Canada, originated as settler colonies or resource outposts of metropolitan empires and underwent yet another process. British North America was populated by people of European origin at a time when feudal structures were breaking down in Europe and a capitalist economic system was emerging. The hallmark of this emerging capitalist system was its reliance on *wage labour* (Dobb, 1964; Weber, [1904] 1958). This wage-labour system was exported to North America, and it was an important element of the first commercial fishery enterprises in British North America (Innis, 1940). It was embodied in the policies adopted by colonial authorities for the distribution of land for farming and forestry purposes (Teeple, 1972; Lambert and Pross, 1967). Although the aboriginal population of North America had a very different system of allocating wealth based on collective or communal appropriation of surplus under a hunting-gathering economy, they were drawn into the wage-labour system by their extensive involvement in the European fur trade (Innis, 1956).

Thus, virtually from its inception as a colony Canada had a wage-labour economy. The only exceptions were the early French efforts in New France and Acadia to recreate certain elements of feudal landlord-tenant relations characteristic of the French *ancien régime* (Lower, 1946). The *seigneurial* system involved the payment of various types of tributes to landlord and the church by peasant farmers. The system largely disappeared with the expulsion of the Acadians to Louisiana in the 1750s and the fall of New France to the British in 1763. Although seigneurial titles were retained until the 1850s, the British replaced the feudal rent-based system with a wage system.

British colonial authorities were worried, however, that the presence of large areas of unclaimed cultivable land would draw immigrants to the British North American colonies into independent agricultural production and undermine the wage system in the timber and fur industries. In their efforts to ensure that a low-wage system prevailed, the British granted large areas of land to various land companies, which would then sell property only to farmers who could afford the purchase price. This made farm land less accessible to poor immigrants, who were then forced into the labour market. In addition, British authorities encouraged the massive immigration of poor workers into the colonies in an effort to sustain a wage-labour economy.

Table 21
Canadian Net Migration – 1851-1921

	(000's)
1851-1861	+ 123
1861-1871	− 191
1871-1881	− 85
1881-1891	− 205
1891-1901	− 181
1901-1911	+ 715
1911-1921	+ 233

SOURCE: Buckley, K.A.H. and M.C. Urquhart (1965), *Historical Statistics of Canada*, Series A244-253, 22 (Toronto: Macmillan).

The first such major immigration consisted of over 900,000 Irish Catholics and Protestants (mostly poor farmers) fleeing the Irish potato famine and British enclosure movements. They landed at Quebec City in the decade between 1846 and 1854 and were responsible for an increase in the Canadian population from about two million in the late 1840s to about 3.2 million in 1861 (Lower, 1946; Palmer, 1983; Buckley and Urquhart, 1965). Through massive immigration and restrictive land policies, the British managed to keep wage levels down in British North America.

The relatively open U.S. border was a major impediment to Imperial efforts to create a wage-labour force. In times of economic downturn, like the one in Canada both before and shortly after Confederation, workers could simply emigrate to the United States to find better conditions. In fact, as the figures in Table 21 show, this emigration throughout the latter half of the nineteenth century consistently undermined Canadian government efforts to increase the labour force through immigration (Porter, 1965).

Net out-migration from Canada was not reversed until the dominion government embarked on a major project of populating the recently purchased Northwest Territories for agricultural purposes following the completion of the Canadian Pacific transcontinental railway in 1886. Although a substantial proportion of those immigrants were from Britain, Ontario, and the United States, the majority were of Scandinavian and Eastern European origin. Two very large waves of immigrants – or, rather, one large wave interrupted by World War I – swept into the prairies in 1905-15 and 1920-30. The three to four million newcomers brought in by the lure of cheap farm land and cheap ocean passage were the main cause of the rise in the Canadian population from 4.8 million in 1891 to about 10.3 million in 1931, and this group formed a major addition to the Canadian wage-labour force.

The Growth of Labour Unions

The creation of a wage-labour force in the country also provided the possibility that people in the labour force would create unions and other organizations dedicated to improving their market position. This phenomena did in fact occur. But the way it happened greatly reduced the ability of the resulting labour organizations to proceed to the third stage and form labour centrals capable of influencing state activities.

The formation of union organizations was resisted by capital and discouraged by government legislation until 1872, when the dominion government made its first efforts to regulate an increasingly bitter and disruptive struggle between labour and capital in the existing resource and newly formed manufacturing industries. Even following the establishment of a more favourable legislative climate for union organization, however, the different forms of organization adopted by workers in different regions and sectors of the economy severely restricted the development of united labour central organizations.

Before the adoption of more permissive legislation following Confederation, worker efforts to improve wages and working conditions took the form of local and site-specific strikes and work stoppages. Landless immigrants employed on large-scale canal projects on the Ottawa and St. Lawrence river systems organized the first large-scale collective labour resistance to capital. The workers, mainly Irish immigrants, protested appallingly poor working and living conditions, and their work stoppages and strike activities rapidly spilled over into other areas of economic activity, including the timber trade, which employed large numbers of Irish and Québécois workers (Cross, 1973; Pentland, 1981).

This form of working-class revolt laid the groundwork for community-based organization carried out by the Canadian branches of the U.S.-based Knights of Labor in the early years of Confederation (Palmer, 1983; Palmer and Kealey, 1982). The Knights of Labor had some initial successes organizing strikes in Ontario manufacturing industries and lumber towns, but it was unable to prevent employers from offering higher wages and better conditions to strikebreakers. It also had neither the membership solidarity nor the financial resources necessary to conduct prolonged job actions. By the turn of the century the organization had disappeared from the Canadian labour scene.

Actual trade unions based on the craft principle of organization had been formed in Canada by weavers, printers, cigar-makers, dock workers, bakers, and other skilled workers before Confederation. Beginning in the years immediately before Confederation, however, many of these unions began to affiliate with larger craft unions based in the United States. Although motivated to some degree by international solidarity, the unions were also responding to the poor economic circumstances in Canada. Membership in

U.S. unions allowed Canadian craft workers access to jobs south of the border (Logan, 1948, 1928; Lipton, 1967).

This process of affiliation with U.S. unions would eventually cause a great deal of difficulty for Canadian union organization. But it was a significant factor in Canadian labour organization only after the turn of the century, when many Canadian unions became affiliated to the U.S. labour central, the American Federation of Labor (AFL). In the earlier years of Confederation, struggles between employers and employees over such items as the twelve-hour and nine-hour day were successfully led by indigenous skilled labour organizations, including, especially, the unions in Ontario affiliated with the Toronto Trade Assembly. These groups were able to create monopolies or near monopolies in specific skilled activities. They could discipline strikebreakers by removing their credentials or certifications, and they governed admittance to the trades through apprenticeship requirements. As a result these unions were able to compel owners to improve wages and working conditions in specific sectors. The great majority of workers, however, possessed few skills and were employed in activities requiring few skills. The craft-based labour organizations saw little advantage for their members in organizing other less skilled workers, who tended to be left to their own devices.

Regardless of their occupations, workers in Canada – providing they owned some property – did have the vote and could influence the state's activities in the labour sphere through the exercise of their franchise. But only the most successful craft workers possessed the necessary property requirements, and to placate these individuals the Conservative government of John A. Macdonald introduced the Trade Unions Act of 1872. Following earlier British precedent, the act legalized trade unions or, rather, decriminalized trade union activity, which had previously been regarded as illegal action in restraint of trade (Coats, 1914).

The 1872 act did not make union recognition by employers mandatory, nor did the government recognize the workers' right to strike as a legitimate method of pressuring employers to improve wages and working conditions. Individual unions still had to find their own means of securing employer consent to enter into collective bargaining arrangements with workers – a situation that continued to favour unions organized along craft lines, which were concentrated in the manufacturing sector. Workers in the resource and agricultural sectors continued to face severe impediments to collective organization. Much of the agricultural production was the work of owner-operated family farms or independent commodity producers; large-scale farming using a wage-labour force only developed later on as farms grew in size and output. Owner-operators, or farmers, tended to organize not into trade unions – which are institutions created to improve the market conditions of wage-labour vis-à-vis employers – but into co-operative organizations created to challenge the unequal market advantage enjoyed by refiners, grain handlers, and transportation companies.

In the resource industries, workers had long resorted to strikes and work stoppages to press their demands for better wages and working conditions (Hamelin, Larocque, and Rouillard, 1970). But they began to form separate trade unions only after 1900. Disdained by craft unions for their unskilled membership and in turn disdaining craft unions for their "aristocratic" pretensions, in English Canada workers in the resource sector began to form unions with a decidedly militant, socialist, and internationalist flavour, such as the mass-based Industrial Workers of the World (IWW) and the One Big Union (OBU), which led strikes among resource workers in both Western and Central Canada before and immediately after World War I (Logan, 1948; Lembcke and Tattam, 1984). These industrial unions clashed repeatedly with both employers and craft unions. The craft unions were much more moderate in their approach to collective bargaining and tended to side with employers on many key issues.

In Quebec the situation evolved differently because of the influence of the Catholic church. Workers there also formed nationalist industrial unions, but these were oriented towards the Quebec nation and decidedly less militant than their English-Canadian counterparts. Established first in the Quebec pulp and paper sector towards the end of World War I, federations of Québécois Catholic workers challenged the religious neutrality and socialist secularism of established Canadian industrial unions. Following the blueprint set out by papal dictates on the labour question, these Quebec unions, like their European Catholic counterparts, adopted a less antagonistic attitude towards management (Latham, 1930).

The militancy of the English-Canadian industrial unions nevertheless forced the dominion government to alter the pattern of labour regulation it had adopted under the 1872 Trade Unions Act. Work disruptions, including a major series of work stoppages in the railway and resource sectors at the turn of the century, led to the creation of a federal royal commission looking into labour-management relations. This in turn resulted in the federal government, under the deputy minister of labour, William Lyon Mackenzie King, passing the Industrial Disputes Investigation Act (IDIA) in 1907 (Kealey, 1973). The IDIA legalized strike activity, but only after a compulsory investigation by a conciliation board of the reasons behind the dispute. This legislation was to provide a relatively stable system of industrial relations throughout the economic expansion of the 1910s and 1920s, while the poor economic conditions of the 1930s served to "discipline" workers through the threat of unemployment.

The system only fell into disarray during World War II, when full employment coupled with the extension of the franchise after the revisions of the Dominion Elections Act of 1921 provided labour with an exceptionally strong position vis-à-vis both employers and governments. Faced with severe industrial unrest and the rapidly expanding support of workers for the new labour-farmer party, the Co-operative Commonwealth Federation (CCF), under the authority of the War Measures Act the federal Liberal government of Mackenzie King created a new system of state regulation of labour-management relations under Privy Council Order 1003. Based on the model provided by the U.S. National Industrial Relations Act (the Wagner Act) of 1935, P.C. Order 1003 exchanged union recognition by employers following a certification vote among employees for recognition by unions of orders issued in conformity with statutory labour codes by quasi-judicial labour relations boards (Heron, 1989). With some variations, P.C. Order 1003 remains the basic model for Canadian industrial relations.

In the modern era the most significant development in Canadian union organization occurred in the 1960s with the creation of unions of government workers. Collective bargaining rights for public sector employees were only recognized in legislation in the mid-1960s, yet because of the large growth of the public sector these unions have become some of the largest in the country (Kumar, 1986). Teachers and hospital workers also joined union ranks in the mid-1970s, and the affiliation of public sector workers to trade unions was responsible for most of the general growth of unionization throughout this period.

In 1961 there were only fifteen public sector unions. By 1981 there were over seventy-one, and total membership in those unions had risen from 183,000 to 1.5 million. As a proportion of unionized workers, public sector members in 1961 accounted for only 12.5 percent of union members; by 1981 the figure was close to 40 percent. By 1981 the three largest public sector unions at the local, provincial, and federal levels, the Canadian Union of Public Employees (CUPE), the Public Service Alliance of Canada (PSAC), and the National Union of Provincial Government Employees (NUPGE), had 267,000, 210,000, and 155,000 members respectively. This growth had a significant impact on the balance of power within the labour movement.

Public sector unions now dominate the Canadian labour scene, ranking individually among the largest unions in the country and collectively as the largest group of unions. These unions do not share the internationalism of many of their private sector counterparts, although many of them are oriented towards the provincial level and, therefore, tend to reinforce provincial rather than national political aspirations. This is especially true in Quebec where recent elections have turned on the shifting loyalties of Quebec public sector workers (French, 1985).

In most jurisdictions labour-management relations in the public sector are regulated in a different fashion than in the private sector. Public sector workers did not gain the right to strike or form unions until much later than their private sector counterparts, and the extension of these rights to the

Table 22
Canadian Union Membership Growth by Sector – 1951-82

	(000's)		
	1951	*1963*	*1982*
Six Major Industrial Unions	245.6	360.0	674.2
Thirteen Building Trades Unions	92.9	185.7	370.3
Five Public Sector Unions	30.7	103.6	1,144.4

SOURCE: Kumar, P. (1986), "Union Growth in Canada: Retrospect and Prospect," in W.C. Riddell, ed., *Canadian Labour Relations* (Toronto: University of Toronto Press), pp. 188-119.

public sector was usually carried out through the creation of a separate system, with severe limitations imposed on the right to strike. In most jurisdictions public sector workers are not covered under labour codes regulating private sector workers but under a separate statute, and they are governed by the decisions of a separate regulatory board or agency. In the federal government, for example, workers in federally regulated industries are covered by the Canada Labour Relations Board while public sector workers are governed by the Public Service Staff Relations Board (Swimmer, 1987).

Despite large gains in union membership, great numbers of Canadian workers, especially in the growing non-governmental service sector, remain unorganized. Workers in the resource and manufacturing sectors had already reached levels of over 70 percent unionization by 1965 while workers in the public sector had reached over 90 percent unionization by 1981. In the service sector, only about 30 percent of workers were unionized. As a result, total unionization rates in Canada, although growing, remain in the 30 to 40 percent range. Although union growth has been more rapid than the growth of the civilian labour force, some two-thirds of Canadian workers remain unorganized. Not surprisingly, this tends to limit the ability of unions to influence market exchange in a way that would offset the advantages enjoyed by capital.

The Role of Labour Central Organizations

The union movement's ability to proceed beyond issues of wages and working conditions and affect the pattern of state organization of market activities is conditioned by another set of factors relating to the cohesiveness and organizational capacity of the movement as a whole. Especially significant are two factors: the ability of labour to cohere into powerful central organizations that can directly influence the nature of state policy-making; and the ability of labour to influence the composition of the government itself directly through the democratic electoral process.

Table 23
Unionization of Canadian Workers – 1921-81

	Locals	Union Membership (000's)	Percent Non-Agricultural Paid Workers
1921	2,668	313	18.4
1931	2,772	311	15.3
1941	3,318	462	18.0
1951	5,458	1,029	28.4
1961	6,945	1,447	31.6
1971	10,056	2,231	33.6
1981	15,555	3,487	37.4

SOURCE: Kumar, P. (1986), "Union Growth in Canada: Retrospect and Prospect," in W.C. Riddell, ed., *Canadian Labour Relations* (Toronto: University of Toronto Press), pp. 108-109.

Influence on the electoral process is best achieved through the use of labour parties, which exist in many countries under a variety of names. In Canada early political alliances between workers and farmers enjoyed successes in Ontario and the prairie provinces, although these coalitions – in parties such as the United Farmers of Alberta, the United Farmers of Manitoba, and the United Farmers of Ontario – were dominated by farmers. The same was true of the Progressive Party and the Co-operative Commonwealth Federation, which contested elections at the federal level after 1920. As the significance of farmers declined with the industrialization of Canada, so too did the fortunes of these parties. As a result of its declining electoral fortunes, the CCF reconstituted itself as the New Democratic Party (NDP) in 1960 and formed a formal electoral alliance with organized labour.

Unlike the situation in many European countries, in Canada the mainstream political parties at both levels of government have been able to use their positions in government to disarm both agrarian and labour protest. Through the passage of "progressive" legislation and the expenditure of state funds on social programs, these parties successfully attracted many former members of agrarian and labour protest movements into their ranks. At the federal level this has left only a hard-core 15 to 20 percent of electoral support for the NDP (Young, 1969; Morton, 1974). Thus, while workers in Canada have obtained a greater state presence in activities that benefit them, this presence has been accomplished not so much through the creation of specific workers' parties as through more diffuse electoral activity. Voting, clearly, has been significant in influencing Canadian governments to address workers' interests, and partisan political activity has been much less so.

Canadian workers have also failed to develop unified labour centrals capable of directly influencing government decision-making. In Canada, a single cohesive and unified labour central organization like those existing in many European countries has not developed. Virtually from their inception, labour central organizations in Canada have been divided along a number of lines reflecting the major divisions in trade union organization: craft or skill versus plant or industry; public versus private sector membership; and (overlapping with the first two) provincial, national, or international interests.

The organizations of skilled workers such as printers, coopers, or lasters in the various manufacturing industries were usually affiliated with larger U.S. unions in the craft-based American Federation of Labor (AFL). Workers in the agricultural and resource sectors, who composed the majority of the workforce, tended to be organized into unions or co-operative associations organized on a national rather than international basis. Farmer co-operatives formed the basis for political associations that promoted the interests of the agricultural sector; these included the Grange and United Farmers' parties (Macpherson, 1953). Although these organizations formed alliances with organized labour in political associations such as the Progressive Party and later the CCF (Morton, 1950), they remained distinct from the rest of organized labour, befitting the status of most farmers as both owners and operators, or employers and employees. In the resource sector by the mid-1920s the various industrial unions in English Canada united to form a national, industrial central, the All-Canadian Congress of Labour (ACCL) (Lipton, 1967; Palmer, 1983). This organization competed with the AFL-affiliated, craft-based Trades and Labour Congress (TLC) for the allegiance of the country's English-speaking workers.

In Quebec, following the creation of Catholic trade unions, a separate Catholic trade union central was formed during World War I and represented many Québécois workers – although a significant number of them remained in AFL-affiliated craft unions. The National Central Trades Council, formed in 1918, became the Confédération des travailleurs catholiques du Canada (CTCC) in 1921. Although originally organized by skill, the Catholic movement allowed for industrial organization and eventually came to have a large number of unskilled workers within its ranks. Throughout its history, however, it has been challenged by non-religious trade unions for the right to represent these workers. By 1960 it had dropped its Catholic orientation and become the secular, nationalist Confederation of National Trade Unions (CNTU). But it is still challenged in Quebec by the unions belonging to the Quebec Federation of Labour (QFL) affiliated to the Canadian Labour Congress (CLC) and more recently by radical unions belonging to the Centrale des syndicats démocratiques (CSD) (Dofny, 1968; Kumar, 1986).

In the rest of Canada the dispute between craft and industrial unions came to a head during the Depression when the new Congress of Industrial Organizations (CIO) was formed in the United States by a group of dissident AFL union leaders led by United Mine Worker head John Lewis. Many Canadian industrial unions affiliated with the CIO, while the CIO aided in the creation of several new unions in Canada's growing manufacturing industries (Abella, 1973). These Canadian CIO unions merged with the remaining, more radical, ACCL industrial unions to form the Canadian Congress of Labour (CCL) in 1940. In 1956, following the merger of the AFL-CIO in the United States, the CCL and the TLC merged to become the Canadian Labour Congress (CLC).

With this merger the Canadian union movement finally overcame some of the divisions between craft workers and unskilled labour that had plagued it from its inception. But it remained divided on other lines. At the national level many union leaders and rank-and-file members were not satisfied with the U.S. leanings of many CLC unions that remained affiliated to the AFL-CIO. In the mid-1960s this resulted in the emergence of a new national union movement, primarily in the Western resource industries, and the creation of a new labour central, the Confederation of Canadian Unions (CCU). It also resulted in the separation of many CLC unions from their AFL-CIO ties, including the large Canadian Paperworkers Union (CPU), the Canadian Autoworkers Union (CAW), and the International Woodworkers of America (IWA). These moves towards establishing a nationalist CLC sparked the withdrawal of many U.S.-based building-trade unions from the CLC in the early 1980s to form yet another central organization, the Canadian Federation of Labour (CFL) (Wood and Kumar, 1981).

As a result the existing trade union movement in Canada remains fragmented, mainly along nationalist lines. The CFL is closely tied to the U.S. AFL-CIO, the CLC is moderately nationalist, the CCU more militantly nationalist, while the CNTU and CSD promote moderate and militant Quebec nationalism respectively.

The Political-Economic Significance of Labour Fragmentation

Although the old craft and religious divisions have largely disappeared, labour unions in Canada are still unable to agree on common courses of action or common directions for government policy-making. Continuing divisions along national/international lines have resulted in multiple union centrals. In addition the Canadian system of industrial relations is fragmented along federal-provincial and public-private sector lines and into many independent or semi-independent local bargaining units; together these additional aspects diminish the capacity of organized labour to alter market relations or influence state activities.

The fragmentation of the collective bargaining process in Canada is partly a result of the evolution of the country's legal system of industrial relations. This system, like most other aspects of Canadian life, has been and still is affected by the existence of a federal system of government. Until 1925 labour-management relations were considered to be an area of exclusive federal jurisdiction. In that year the Judicial Committee of the Privy Council ruled in the case of *Sniderman vs the Toronto Board of Electric Commissioners* that labour-management relations were contractual relations that fell within provincial jurisdiction. From 1925 to 1939 the provinces, led by Ontario and British Columbia, began to implement their own systems of industrial relations. The federal government retained authority over its own employees and those in federally owned or regulated industries. This dual system was temporarily united during World War II when the federal government assumed jurisdiction over labour-management relations under its wartime emergency powers. P.C. Order 1003 applied equally across the entire country. In 1948 jurisdiction was returned to the provinces, which proceeded to alter their previously existing systems of industrial relations to bring them into line with the new system. At present a fragmented system of industrial relations exists in the country, with each province retaining jurisdiction over its own system of labour-management relations and the federal government also maintaining a different system (Riddell, 1986).

The operation of this federal system of labour relations leads to workers and unions facing different rules and regulations in different jurisdictions, which greatly complicates a union's organizational tasks. The job is made even more onerous by the fact that these legal systems all promote unionization and collective bargaining at the plant or local level. As the figures in Table 24 illustrate, Canadian unions tend to be divided into numerous small locals that engage in collective bargaining at the firm or plant level.

Most unionized workers are represented by a single union in a situation involving a single employer operating either one plant or a multiple-establishment enterprise. However, almost half of the bargaining units in Canada are found in single-establishment, single-employer operations. This aspect of Canadian industrial relations contrasts with the situation in many other countries where bargaining takes place on an industry or even country-wide level, so that less time is devoted to local organizations and the necessities of multiple contract bargaining and more time is spent on issues related to the general health of the union movement and the promotion of labour's interests in policy formation (Esping-Andersen and Korpi, 1984; Hibbs, 1987b).

As a result, labour in Canada has never achieved the same organizational coherence, participation, or extent of unionization as it has in many other countries, as the comparative statistics in Table 25 illustrate.

Given its fractured state, the most significant political tool left to labour in Canada has been neither the political party nor the central labour organization but, befitting its fragmented and decentralized nature, the

Table 24
Canadian Collective Bargaining Structure – 1982
(Agreements Covering More Than 200 Workers)

Negotiating Structure	Units	(Percent) Workers
Single Employer		
Single Establishment		
Single Union	46.2	18.3
Multi-Union	0.9	0.4
Multi-Establishment		
Single Union	39.1	51.1
Multi-Union	5.2	5.3
Multi-Employer		
Single Union	7.5	14.1
Multi-Union	1.1	10.9

SOURCE: Davies, R.J. (1986), "The Structure of Collective Bargaining in
Canada," in W.C. Riddell, ed., *Canadian Labour Relations* (Toronto:
University of Toronto Press), p. 214.

grassroots protest. The pattern of industrial strife erupting periodically
over wages and working conditions throughout the country, though necessarily in a somewhat crude and inarticulate manner, has been the best
demonstration of labour's interests in resource allocation and distribution
(Hibbs, 1976, 1978; Lacroix, 1986).

Table 25
Canadian Union Membership and Participation in Comparative Perspective – 1981

	Membership (000's)	Percent Wage/ Salary Earners
Australia	2,994	55.8
Canada	3,487	35.3
Japan	12,355	30.6
Sweden	3,055	88.8
U.K.	12,182	57.5
U.S.	22,396	24.7
Germany	9,340	41.9

SOURCE: Kumar, P. (1986), "Union Growth in Canada: Retrospect and Prospect,"
in W.C. Riddell, ed., *Canadian Labour Relations* (Toronto: University of
Toronto Press), p. 127.

CHAPTER 9

The Structure and Organization of Capital

The Canadian state, originally divided along Imperial and colonial lines, is now divided along federal and provincial lines as well as political and administrative lines. Canadian labour, originally divided along craft and industrial lines, is now divided along unionized and non-unionized lines as well as federal/provincial, national/international, and public/private lines.

Canadian capital is no exception to this rule of fragmented organization. Capital has been and remains divided along small and large business lines, national and international lines, and sectoral lines. Like labour and the state, capital too suffers from fragmentation along federal-provincial lines, and as a result it is unable to articulate a national strategy and a national series of goals with an essentially united front. Nevertheless, Canadian capital has produced a number of powerful and well-funded business associations that can and do present detailed sectoral policy prescriptions to governments. Because the Canadian political system responds well to territorially based demands and the various sectors of the economy tend to be territorially differentiated, capital has many entrance points into the political system and the governmental decision-making process.

The Role of Capital in a Capitalist Economy

The decisions made by the owners of the means of production by and large determine not only what goods and services are produced in society but also when and where labour will be used in their production. Whether or not these production decisions are effective is of great importance to society as a whole because the decisions affect the lives and livelihoods of more than just a small group of capitalists. They also directly affect the lives of workers and their families and, in so doing, the lives and livelihoods of all those elements of society that produce other goods and services intended for consumption.

In a capitalist economic system, then, capital enjoys several advantages over labour stemming from its ownership of the means of production. Labour can offset some of these advantages through the democratic process, since in any capitalist economy workers always form the majority of the population and, at least theoretically, can exercise the franchise as a means of persuading governments to enhance their market position. But, although labour cannot always achieve in practice what is possible in theory, even a unified and cohesive labour organization that is capable of obtaining some redress in the marketplace through state action is not able to overcome all of the advantages that capital enjoys in a capitalist economy. Capital's additional advantages directly influence the state's ability to alter market relations and offset labour's democratic electoral advantages (Przeworski, 1990).

First, capitalist productive activities do more than simply regulate the level of employment and consumption in society or contribute to the general functioning of the economy. Capital's productive activities directly affect the fiscal health of the state, which, in a capitalist system, must rely for its revenues on taxes paid by corporations and individuals. Any decrease in capitalist productive activity, all other things being equal, reduces the state's ability to obtain revenues through taxation of individual incomes or corporate profits. Although states have other means of obtaining revenues – for example, through royalties, licence fees, inheritance taxes, or customs duties – in the modern era all nation-states rely heavily on income and sales taxes for their revenue needs. To make sure they don't "kill the golden goose" that provides them with a ready source of income, states must be extremely cautious about regulating or otherwise restricting capitalist decision-making.

Second, capitalist profits are highly mobile and not bound by national boundaries. Various mechanisms exist for taking profits from one country and investing them in another; and business can respond to any unwanted state "intervention" in the market by removing its capital to another location. Although this theoretical mobility is limited by a variety of factors – including possible restrictions on investment opportunities in other countries or jurisdictions – the potential loss of employment and revenues is a threat that both labour and the state must contend with in making decisions. Any attempt by the state to limit or remove this mobility – for example, through a ban on expatriation of profits – can have adverse consequences for investment in the domestic economy by non-resident capitalists. Because of the negative consequences this entails for state revenues, capitalists – both domestic and foreign – have the ability to "punish" the state for any actions it takes that meet with their disapproval.

Third, capitalist profits can be and are used as an important source of funding for modern political parties, greatly outweighing the funding available to labour parties through union dues. In many countries, including Canada, the attachment of workers to labour parties is tenuous, and there are many other countervailing influences on workers' voting behaviour. In many countries modern elections often turn on relatively short-term issues or personalities, and parties require large budgets to influence voters through extensive media advertising campaigns. Although labour parties may be able to turn out large numbers of campaign workers, they often lack the financial wherewithal required to conduct media-extensive campaigning. Parties funded out of capitalist profits have precisely the opposite advantages and disadvantages, and in many countries they have successfully used these techniques to neutralize, if not overpower, labour's numerical advantages at the polls.

Finally, capitalist profits can be used to legitimize the unequal distribution of political and economic power enjoyed by capital – to present the existing order not only as the "natural" outcome of the historical development of modern societies but also as the "optimum" outcome. Profits are used to fund research institutes and individual researchers and to publicize findings, results, or prescriptions for government action that favour the continuation or extension of the society's mix of state-market relations – that is, that favour the continuing dominance of capital in society.

Like the other political-economic actors, capital must also be organized, united, and cohesive if it is to successfully use these various advantages to shape state activity in its favour and/or offset labour's advantages in the electoral system. If capital is not well organized, or if it is divided in its aims and ambitions, it will only be able to exercise its capabilities partially or unsystematically. In such circumstances capital may well be overcome by state or labour political or economic activities, although this too depends on the organization and cohesiveness of those other two political-economic actors.

And like the organization of labour and the state, the organization of capital is a significant determinant of the pattern of state-market relations in any country. In many countries capital exercises political and economic power not only through the actions of individual businesses but also through the activities of large and united business associations that undertake a variety of political activities to promote the interests of capital as a whole. Determining the nature of these capitalist firms and associations, then, becomes a key element of political-economic analysis.

The History of Business Organization

Capital Accumulation

Business has been a part of Canada since the country's very inception. In fact, business preceded settlement in North America's northern half, which was first exploited for its fish and fur resources by great trading and fishing monopolies established by the British and French crowns and operating under the mercantilist system. At first these companies actively prevented permanent settlement of the areas under their control, although in most cases they were unable to stem the tide of immigration and permanent settlement for more than fifty years.

In Newfoundland, rich fishing grounds had been harvested by Basque fishermen in the thirteenth and fourteenth centuries and later by a variety of French, English, and Spanish fishing fleets until the British gained control of the island and the Labrador coast in the eighteenth century. Almost immediately the British extended a monopoly over the fishery to a group of Kentish fishing interests. The monopoly proved difficult to enforce in practice but remained in law until the mid-nineteenth century (Hiller and Neary, 1980).

In New France, a monopoly over the fur trade was granted to the Company of New France or the "One Hundred Associates" in 1627. Although that charter was taken over by the Compagnie des Habitants in 1645, it remained in effect under the Compagnie du Canada and the Compagnie d'Occident until 1742 (Lower, [1946] 1977). The monopoly was challenged by the English through the East India Company in 1664 and most significantly through the creation of the Hudson's Bay Company in 1670 (Rich, 1960).

All of these companies viewed permanent settlement as a threat to their exclusive access to New World resources. In New France the French Crown changed the charter of the fur trade monopolies to allow for agricultural settlement, primarily for military purposes. In Newfoundland the offshore fishing interests could not prevent permanent colonization of the island and Labrador coasts. In the Hudson's Bay Company territories the arctic or semi-arctic lands immediately surrounding the Bay forts were unfit for cultivation, while settlement of the southern limits of company lands awaited the push into the area by rival fur traders of the Montreal-based North West Company in the early nineteenth century. The lack of permanent settlements in early Canada was significant since, in the absence of a domestic market, business was limited to activities aimed at export.

It was only with the development of the lumber industry after 1806 – when British North America was supplying masts and spars for the British Navy after the imposition of Napoleon's continental blockade (Albion, 1926; Lower, 1967, 1938, 1973) – that the agricultural frontier was extended throughout the Maritime provinces, Quebec, and Ontario, bringing in permanent settlements and creating the conditions for the development of domestic businesses to serve the needs of local populations (Lower, 1936; Wynn, 1981). The timber trade not only cleared land for later agricultural settlement but also provided early settlers with a ready source of capital and a wintertime occupation. Loggers and river rafters also provided the first domestic markets for agricultural goods, allowing many farming settlements to survive and thrive in a precarious climate (Minville, 1944; Cross, 1960).

The timber trade, then, played a major role both in the process of domestic capital accumulation and in the establishment of permanent agricultural settlements in the colonies of British North America. These agricultural settlements in turn provided the basis for future large-scale food exports, especially of wheat and other grains, which accompanied the settlement of first western Ontario and later the prairie provinces in the second half of the nineteenth century and the first quarter of the twentieth (Fowke, 1978).

From the very beginning of settlement in Canada, significant capital was invested in the resource and agricultural sectors with the intention of promoting exports to international markets. In the resource sectors, business was dominated by large foreign capital until the growth of the timber trade, which provided an avenue for small domestic operators to enter into the business world. Although many enterprises were small, part-time affairs, large concerns quickly emerged. Some of these, in different form, still exist today.

The accumulation of capital by domestic interests and the establishment of permanent large-scale communities had two further effects. First, the retention of some profits within British North America led to the development of a rudimentary banking and financial industry; second, the creation of permanent communities led to a demand for manufactured consumer and capital goods.

The first permanent domestic banks, established in Canada at the beginning of the nineteenth century, were intimately involved in the timber trade. They included the Bank of Montreal (1817), which followed other efforts to establish domestic banks beginning in 1792 (Hammond, 1957; Shortt, 1896). The growth of these banks was aided by the influx of funds required to sustain the British war effort during the War of 1812. The war, like the timber trade, also served to provide a domestic market for Canadian agricultural production. The banks were originally founded by rival merchant groups in cities such as Halifax, Montreal, Kingston, and York (now Toronto) to help finance the export trade, and they were generally opposed by the agrarian interests, which faced the burden of mortgage and interest payments. Although these agricultural interests continued to press for the establishment of "free banking" along U.S. lines, the colonial governments generally refused the requests and instead established a pattern of chartered banking that continues in Canada to the present day.

The result has been, not surprisingly, the creation of only a few very large banks in this country, which service local communities through branches controlled by head offices located in one of the larger cities. At various points in Canadian history, including during the rebellions of 1837 and the farmers' reform movement of the 1920s and 1930s, the size and power of the Canadian banks have aroused discord. Many proposals for their reform have been enunciated, although few have been put into practice.

The development of manufacturing activities in Canada was a slow process, encumbered first by British colonial practices that attempted to preserve the British North American market for British goods and later by the competition that domestic producers faced from U.S. imports. Manufacturers in Canada enjoyed some comparative cost advantages over British goods, primarily because of the costs of transportation between Britain and North America. High tariffs raised by the British against U.S. goods to protect the Canadian market for their own exports also allowed indigenous manufacturers the same protection (Forster, 1986). Even so, Canadian producers could not compete – with either mass-produced and well-financed British goods or cheap U.S. products. They could only survive in businesses that required small capital investments and where manufacturing relied on abundant Canadian resources. These fields included tanning and shoemaking as well as furniture and other wood-working activities, all based on the flourishing agricultural and resource industries.

When the British began dismantling their protective tariff system in the 1840s so they could provide cheaper raw materials for their own manufacturing industries, Canadian manufacturing interests wanted to replace the British tariffs with Canadian tariffs in an effort to keep out U.S. goods. The much more powerful resource sector was also threatened by the loss of British markets and wanted to replace those lost markets with new buyers in the United States. As a result, domestic manufacturing interests were sacrificed to the needs of resource capital in the establishment of the free trade Reciprocity Treaty with the United States from 1854 to 1866. This was not to be the last significant division between domestic manufacturing capital and internationally oriented resource capital in Canada (Naylor, 1975b, 1972).

When the United States abrogated the Reciprocity Treaty in 1866 the Canadian economy suffered relatively little, although Canadian politicians searched frantically for an alternative economic arrangement. They finally settled on the Canadian common market established through the Confederation of the British North American colonies and oriented towards the expansion of Canadian capital into the northwest hinterland. The economic policy followed by the new government attempted to please all three currently existing factions of Canadian capital: manufacturing, resource, and finance.

Although economic policy awaited formalization in Sir John A. Macdonald's National Policy in 1878, the outlines of the policy were clear from the outset of Confederation (Forster, 1986):

- The provision of government aid to the resource sector through the extension of financing and traffic monopolies to private companies involved in the extension of a transportation infrastructure into the peripheral regions (this included most notably the Canadian Pacific Railway) and connecting the existing colonies (especially the Grand Trunk Railway linking Quebec and Ontario and the Intercolonial Railway linking Central Canada and the Maritime provinces).

- The rescue of existing financial institutions through the takeover of provincial debts by the federal government. (Many of these debts were railway connected.).
- The creation of high tariff walls protecting Canadian manufacturing industries from both U.S. and British imports (Fowke, 1952).

The expansion of the domestic market was established by creating a common market and extending it through the incorporation of new areas into Confederation – most significantly, the purchase of the Hudson's Bay Company lands by the federal government and the encouragement of immigration into that area following the completion of the Canadian Pacific and later the Canadian Northern and Grand Trunk Pacific railways. In conjunction with the policy of tariff protection for domestic manufacturing industries, this expansion succeeded in creating a thriving domestic manufacturing sector, albeit with a substantial foreign ownership.

The Concentration of Capital

Capitalist firms and a capitalist market economy were well established in Canada before 1880 and got a boost with Macdonald's National Policy, which dedicated state activity to the perpetuation and intensification of these activities. Since 1880 capitalist development in Canada has been characterized by two phenomena, one characteristic of all capitalist political economies and the other more particular to Canadian circumstances. Characteristic of capitalist political economies has been the increasing concentration of capital as individual firms merge with each other and fewer firms come to control more and more of a nation's corporate assets. More particular to Canadian circumstances has been the development of extensive foreign ownership of corporate assets, in this case the increasing U.S. ownership of corporations operating in the country. Both phenomena have led to the development of further cleavages among an already fractured Canadian business community, and they have had an important influence on the formation of business associations in this country.

Concentration of production facilities has been increasing in Canada in most sectors, especially the manufacturing sector, since the turn of the century. In 1890, 2,879 plants accounted for 63 percent of manufacturing output in the country. By 1922, 936 plants accounted for 66 percent of manufacturing output (Rosenbluth, 1957, pp.94ff). Although this tendency towards increasing plant size continued until 1930, it declined in many industries during the 1930s and 1940s – a phenomenon explained by the tendency of companies first to adopt labour-saving technologies in the period 1900-30, resulting in the establishment of plants of increasingly larger scale, and then to adopt capital-saving technologies in the period 1930-50 to offset this tendency (Rosenbluth, 1957, p.102). This trend continued into the 1960s, as the figures in Table 26 illustrate.

Plant size is only one method of measuring industrial concentration.

Table 26

Plant Concentration in Canadian Manufacturing – 1948 and 1965

Number of Largest Units Accounting for 80 percent of Employment	Percent of Industries	
	1948	1965
1-2	20.8	8.44
3-6	19.8	18.18
7-12	15.6	18.83
13-24	14.6	22.72
25-100	14.6	23.37
Over 100	14.6	8.46

SOURCE: Canada (1971), *Concentration in the Manufacturing Industries of Canada* (Ottawa: Consumer and Corporate Affairs), p. 44.

Although informative, it tells us little about the financial concentration of industry, that is, about the concentration of ownership and economic power into the hands of fewer and fewer companies and individuals. In this sense, concentration also refers to the extent of vertical or horizontal integration present in an industry and across industrial sectors.

Vertical integration refers to the extent to which individual firms in an industry control other firms producing inputs to or controlling outputs from production activities. For example, in the steel industry a company might produce steel and also control companies providing iron ore for steel production and selling steel products in the marketplace. It might also control companies shipping raw materials and finished goods to markets. *Horizontal integration* refers to the ownership of different companies involved in the same productive activity. Thus, for example, one steelmaker might own shares in or control other steelmaking companies. These relationships are not apparent in statistics on plant and enterprise dominance. As a result, we must consider not only the concentration of plants and employment but also the concentration of corporate assets in the economy. Table 27 provides statistics on the merger and acquisition activity of Canadian firms.

As the figures illustrate, merger activity in Canada has involved both horizontal and vertical integration as well as the acquisition of non-related companies, but it has displayed different patterns at different points in history. Horizontal mergers have always been high in number, but they were especially dominant as companies moved to control markets between 1900 and 1950 (Weldon, 1966). After 1950 companies tended to integrate backwards and forwards (Reuber and Roseman, 1969); in the most recent period, after 1968, they tended to purchase non-related companies (Lecraw

Table 27
Percentage of Mergers by Type – 1900-73

	Horizontal	*Vertical*	*Conglomerate*	*Total*
1900-09	90	4	6	100
1910-19	85	10	5	100
1920-29	85	11	4	100
1930-39	88	7	5	100
1940-48	73	19	8	100
1945-61	64	23	13	100
1960-68	63	19	18	100
1968-73	57	18	25	100

SOURCE: Lecraw, D.J. and D.N. Thompson (1978), *Conglomerate Mergers in Canada* (Ottawa: Minister of Supply and Services), p. 64.

and Thompson, 1978). This tendency has contributed to the pattern of high concentration of industrial activity in the hands of a relatively few firms.

Small firms and workers in Canada have consistently objected to this increasing concentration of control over production and production decisions in the hands of fewer and fewer individuals. Both groups have been concerned with the development of *oligopolies* – where a few large firms control the market – or *monopolies* – where one firm controls the market. Such developments exacerbate the market advantages already enjoyed by capital vis-à-vis labour and simultaneously allow large firms to exclude small firms from the market through the use of collusive pricing techniques. Not surprisingly, this development has led to repeated demands by these groups for state action to curb the process of financial concentration.

Canada's first legislation opposing business combinations in restraint of trade was passed in 1889, one year before the Sherman Anti-Trust Act in the United States. This act remained in force until 1910, when it was replaced by the Combines Investigations Act (Gorecki and Stanbury, 1984), which itself was only replaced by new legislation in 1988. The 1889 legislation was passed following a report in the previous year from the Select Committee of the House of Commons to Investigate Alleged Combines in Manufacture, Trade, and Insurance in Canada. The act was designed to be enforced by provincial attorney-generals and was intended to protect consumers, especially farmers, from price-fixing by manufacturers and financial institutions. It was also meant to protect small producers from predatory pricing practices followed by larger producers and cartels (Bliss, 1973).

The first anticombines act, the "Act for the Prevention and Suppression of Combinations Formed in Restraint of Trade," like similar acts passed at other times in Canadian history, did not oppose the concentration of capital or

Table 28

Net Assets of 100 Largest Non-Financial Companies by Size Class – 1933

Class Size by Net Assets ($000,000's)	Total Net Assets ($000's)
Greater than 100	5,093,580
75.0-99.0	77,016
50.0-74.9	512,398
25.0-49.9	782,086
10.0-24.9	767,542

SOURCE: Canada (1971), *Concentration in the Manufacturing Industries of Canada* (Ottawa: Consumer and Corporate Affairs), p. 41.

attempt to keep markets open for small capital. Rather, it simply attempted to protect consumers and producers from the excesses of monopoly behaviour in the marketplace. The courts upheld the power of the legislatures to prevent the abuse of market power by monopolies or oligopolies and steadily convicted price-fixers when their schemes were uncovered and prosecuted under the various acts. However, the courts did not uphold any vestigial anticoncentration elements that remained in the acts, refusing to label mergers and business takeovers as actions in restraint of trade if that was not their sole object. Only five convictions were obtained under the first act between 1889 and 1910, and the second act of 1910 created a Combines Investigation Branch to replace provincial governments as prosecutors in future cases (Gorecki and Stanbury, 1984, p.20). This act was ruled unconstitutional by the Judicial Committee of the Privy Council in 1921.

In 1923 a new Combines Investigation Act was passed. It was modified during the Depression when farmers and consumers again complained of the predatory practices of both manufacturing and finance capital. These complaints received detailed investigation by the federal Royal Commission on Price Spreads in 1935. By that time, the commission had already found a significant concentration of Canadian industrial assets in a few large companies (see Table 28).

The two largest companies in the country in 1935 – the Canadian Pacific and the government-owned Canadian National railways – had assets of about $3.7 billion and dominated Canadian non-financial corporations. As the economy grew, more companies joined the ranks of the largest corporations, and the domination of the railway companies waned (Carroll, 1986). Still, the division between small and large businesses remained distinct (see Table 29).

Activity undertaken on the part of the federal government to prevent mergers and acquisitions was inconsequential and failed in any way to stop the process of concentration. Although several elements of its anticombine

Table 29
Corporate Concentration of Assets – 1965-73

Asset Size ($000,000's	Number of Companies 1965	1973	Percent Assets 1965	1973
Over 1,000	11	29	25.5	35.1
500-1,000	13	40	6.1	8.3
100-500	135	297	18.7	17.1
1-100	9,462	18,909	35.5	29.5
Under 1	155,638	239,226	14.2	10.0

SOURCE: Marfels, C. (1977), *Concentration Levels and Trends in the Canadian Economy 1965-1973* (Ottawa: Minister of Supply and Services), p. 42.

program failed because of federal-provincial wrangling, the commitment of the federal government to the policy was never more than half-hearted. Between 1910 and 1960 the federal government prosecuted only four merger cases, all unsuccessfully (Brecher, 1981, p.5).

Canadian industry has thus retained its bifurcated structure since the early part of the century. That is, the economy is dominated by a small number of large companies owning over 50 percent of all assets, with a plethora of small companies owning the remainder. Significantly, the economy lacks an intermediate strata of medium-sized businesses and has always done so. The reasons for this lie in the nature of Canadian production, which is destined either for large international markets or for relatively small local, regional, provincial, or national markets. Export industries, and especially resource-exporting firms, developed early and had access to large pools of foreign capital. They were able to obtain large economies of scale that served as barriers to the entry of new firms (Bain, 1968). They quickly established and held their market dominance. Companies providing goods and services for the domestic market, especially the Canadian manufacturing industries, have also been divided into large and small enterprises. Canadian federal governments have consistently upheld the interests of large capital, as the failure of the government's anticombines activity amply demonstrates.

The attitude of the federal government towards concentration was most consistently illustrated by the findings of the federal Royal Commission on Corporate Concentration (the Bryce Commission) in the mid-1970s. Discontent with the existing policy was voiced once again by small business and labour when the country's two largest conglomerates – Argus Corporation of Toronto and Power Corporation of Montreal – proposed a merger. The commission made the most eloquent statement of the government's position in favour of the development of large pools of capital in Canada, stating that these corporations were required if Canadians were to compete in international markets. It reaffirmed the need only to ensure that domestic consumers were not unjustly penalized by monopolistic behaviour on the part of the large firms (Canada, 1978). Although criticized vigorously by proponents of a more competitive marketplace, the commission's findings and recommendations were consistent with both historical and current government practices (Gorecki and Stanbury, 1979).

Foreign Investment and Canadian Capital

A second, and related, area of concern to labour and the state – and a site of a major cleavage within Canadian capital – has been the question of foreign investment and specifically foreign ownership of Canadian companies. This cleavage crosscuts the division between large and small capital and between resource-financial and manufacturing capital. This is because in Canada many large manufacturing enterprises are branch plants or subsidiaries of foreign companies. Their access to foreign capital and technology allows them to establish and retain large market shares, which distinguishes them both from large Canadian-owned companies, which tend to operate in less specialized areas of economic activity, and from the many small domestically owned companies that operate in a competitive marketplace serving local needs (Khemani, 1980).

At various times in Canadian history both large and small Canadian-owned firms have objected to the dominance of large, foreign-owned firms in the Canadian marketplace, as have nationally based Canadian labour organizations. But these groups were only able to obtain some state regulation of these activities in the mid-1970s. Then, faced with the threat of foreign-owned firms to invest elsewhere, the federal government quickly rescinded the policies, which largely disappeared with the establishment of the Canada-U.S. Free Trade Agreement in 1989.

The issue of foreign investment and foreign control of domestic industry has a long history in this country. The initial investments made in export industries were largely foreign – especially British – in origin. While much of the initial investment in Canadian manufacturing came from domestic sources, by the turn of the century a great deal of it was foreign and involved direct foreign ownership of firms producing for the Canadian market.

U.S. investment in Canadian industries had begun in the lumber trade, and many prominent people engaged in that trade – including Henry Franklin Bronson, D.D. Calvin, E.B. Eddy, and Henry Rathbun – were immigrants from the United States. However, U.S. involvement in resource development was limited by rules restricting ownership of lands to British subjects. In the minerals sector, for example, Nova Scotia's coal resources were exploited by British capital, although Americans were involved in gold, copper, and manganese extraction – often extending mining activities begun on the U.S. side of the border to follow seams across the international boundary (Marshall, Southard, and Taylor, 1976).

In the manufacturing sectors, British and European capital was often involved in early industrial projects, including the construction of steelmaking facilities in Nova Scotia and the establishment of pulp and paper plants in Quebec and Newfoundland. Investments in these areas were soon taken over by U.S. interests. At first U.S. investment was made by emigrants from the United States to Canada, people who became, in effect, domestic Canadian capitalists. By the 1870s and 1880s U.S. companies began to establish branch plants in Canada – that is, wholly owned subsidiaries of U.S. parent companies producing for the Canadian market in competition with domestic capital.

Significantly, fifty of these U.S.-owned or U.S.-controlled firms were located in Ontario and twenty-five in Quebec; only six were established in the Maritimes and one in Western Canada. This development was interpreted favourably at the time, as confirmed by an 1885 inquiry into manufacturing industries that noted with great satisfaction the influx of U.S. capital into Central Canada (Canada, 1885).

Canadian manufacturing activity accelerated after 1878 in both the primary and secondary manufacturing sectors, and foreign, primarily U.S., direct investment grew with it. Table 30 gives figures for total manufacturing activity in the period 1870-1910, and Table 31 gives figures for U.S. investment. By the early 1930s, U.S. investment dominated many important sectors of the Canadian economy, as Table 32 demonstrates. Domestic capital retained an important presence in smaller firms (see Table 33).

By the 1930s a deep division existed between domestic and international capital in the U.S.-dominated resource and manufacturing sectors. In both of these sectors this division was exacerbated by extensive Canadian participation in small enterprises that found themselves at a competitive disadvantage when facing well-financed foreign firms. In the financial sector, U.S. and other foreign investors could not obtain charters to carry on banking activities in Canada until recently. Various large U.S. manufacturing companies did pursue their own lending and financial requirements in Canada in the form of finance or "acceptance" corporations, although these firms could not accept deposits from the public and posed no threat to established Canadian banks and other financial institutions.

Beginning in the 1950s, the Canadian federal government began to promote enhanced domestic participation in many resource and manufacturing activities either for regional or national development purposes. Similar activities were undertaken by provincial governments at the provincial and local levels. To aid these activities, the federal government began to institute restrictions on foreign ownership of Canadian firms. This became an issue in Canada in the late 1950s and early 1960s when the full impact of U.S. investment in the post-World War II period became apparent (Safarian, 1966). The Royal Commission on Canada's Economic Prospects (the Gordon Commission) pointed out the possible divided loyalties of branch-plant

Table 30
Gross Value of Manufacturing Production in Canada – 1870-1910

	($000,000's)		
	Total	*Primary (%)*	*Secondary (%)*
1870	219.2	37.2	62.7
1880	303.5	33.9	66.1
1890	452.6	34.5	65.4
1900	534.6	37.3	62.7
1910	1,198.8	35.7	64.2

SOURCE: Bertram, G.W. (1962), ''Historical Statistics on Growth and Structure of Manfacturing in Canada, 1870-1957,'' *Canadian Political Science Association, Conference on Statistics* (Ottawa: Canadian Political Science Association).

Table 31
U.S-Owned or Controlled Firms – 1900-30

	(Cumulative Total)
Prior to 1900	66
1900-1910	213
1910-1920	534
1920-1930	1,075

SOURCE: Marshall, H., F. Southard and K.W. Taylor (1976), *Canadian-American Industry: A Study in International Investment* (Toronto: McClelland and Stewart), p. 21.

Table 32
U.S.-Controlled and U.S.-Affiliated Companies in Canadian Production –
Capital $1,000,000 and Over – 1932 (percentages)

	Companies	*Capital Employed*	*Value of Products*
Manufacturing	14	82	75
Mining	47	96	96
Utilities	56	98	98
Merchandising	18	88	78
Miscellaneous	21	75	50
Total All Sectors	19	90	79

SOURCE: Marshall, H., F. Southard and K.W. Taylor (1976), *Canadian-American Industry: A Study in International Investment* (Toronto: McClelland and Stewart), p. 27.

Table 33
U.S. Companies in Canadian Production – Less than $1,000,000 Capital
Employed – 1932 (percentages)

	Capital under $50,000	*Capital $50,000- $199,000*	*Capital $200,000- 499,000*	*Capital $500,000+*
Manufacturing	1.0	3.0	6.0	8.0
Mining	1.0	1.0	1.0	3.0
Utilities	1.0	1.0	1.0	1.0
Merchandising	1.0	3.0	4.0	4.0
Miscellaneous	1.0	2.0	8.0	14.0
Total All Sectors	1.0	2.0	3.0	5.0

SOURCE: Marshall, H., F. Southard and K.W. Taylor (1976), *Canadian-American Industry: A Study in International Investment* (Toronto: McClelland and Stewart), p. 27.

managers, who would work to defeat any Canadian government schemes to develop the national economy (Canada, 1957), while in the mid-1960s the impact of U.S. ownership of key sectors of the economy became a *cause célèbre* when Liberal finance minister Walter Gordon attempted to restrict foreign investment in his 1963 federal budget (Rugman, 1980, p.125). In 1968 a Privy Council task force on the structure of Canadian industry (the Watkins Task Force) looked into the issue, as did a 1970 Parliamentary standing committee (Watkins, 1968; Levitt, 1970). In 1972 yet another task force investigated the situation, resulting in the creation of the Foreign Investment Review Agency (FIRA) in 1974 (Canada, 1972; Rugman, 1977).

FIRA remained in operation for only ten years. Foreign investors objected to the restraints placed on their activities by the Canadian government and appeared to withhold investment from Canada in protest. Following the recession of 1981-82, FIRA was replaced in 1984-85 by a new and less powerful review agency, Investment Canada. Finally, in 1989, the U.S.-Canada Free Trade Agreement raised the limits on reviewable investments to $150 million, effectively exempting all but the largest takeovers from government surveillance (Laxer, 1989a).

The Growth of Business Associations

The divisions among Canadian capital are often overcome at the board level, the site of extensive corporate directorship interlocks (Ornstein, 1989). But, in terms of political organization, the divisions are manifested in the associations that represent the interests of capital to governments.

Sectoral Organization and Activities of Business Associations

Before Confederation, business associations in Canada were linked with particular industries, but they tended to represent general business interests at the local level. During this era municipal boards of trade, such as those located in Montreal, Quebec, Saint John, Halifax, Kingston, and Toronto, were especially important (Coleman, 1988, p.19). Other associations existed on a regional basis during times of crisis in an industry and attempted to regulate supply or entry into the field, but they usually ceased to exist once market conditions improved (Forster, 1986, p.110). Still other associations emerged in response to unionization in the effort to keep wages down in a particular industry; these included the Lumbermen's Association of St. John and the iron founders' associations in Quebec and Ontario (ibid., p.111). By the time of Confederation, the number of "nationally relevant" business associations was under fifteen, according to W.D. Coleman (1988). This number increased rapidly after Confederation, and an additional fifty-five such organizations existed by 1900. Between 1900 and 1980 the number grew to over seven hundred; the major periods of growth were 1915-19 and 1940-45 (Coleman, 1988, 1985a).

Several of the most significant national business interest associations were formed before 1900, including the Canadian Manufacturers' Association, which grew out of the Ontario Manufacturers' Association to become an independent agency between 1879 and 1899, and the Canadian Bankers' Association in 1891. In the transportation sector, the dominance of the Canadian Pacific Railway obviated the need for a separate business association until the emergence of highway and air transportation in the 1930s and 1940s. In the agriculture sector, the numerous associations that existed among producers of different products at the provincial level eventually merged to form the Canadian Council of Agriculture in 1910. In the resource sector, permanent organizations did not emerge until the 1920s and 1930s and then only at the provincial level, reflecting the dominance of provincial governments in resource regulation. National associations operating on a federal principle emerged in some resource industries, such as the 1917 Canadian Pulp and Paper Association and the 1935 Mining Association of Canada. In others they were not formed until much later – the 1952 Canadian Petroleum Association and the 1984 Canadian Forest Industries Council, for example. In many resource sectors dominant provincial associations, such as the Council of Forest Industries of British Columbia, often acted as national representatives in liaison with the federal government.

Much of the growth immediately after World War I and during World War II can be attributed to government encouragement of industry organization. During both world wars the federal government took over price and supply regulation of most major industries and demanded that industrial producers choose between government regulation and self-regulation.

Many industries, of course, preferred self-regulation and formed industry associations to interact with government officials and monitor industrial performance (Coleman, 1988, pp.24-26; Traves, 1979).

By 1980, about 500 national business associations and 125 farmers' organizations were active in Canada. Associations representing manufacturing firms accounted for about 40 percent of national business associations. Significantly, 480 of the associations represented firms engaged in only one sector or subsector of the economy. About 45 percent of these associations were organized on a federal basis; that is, with national associations acting as the collective voice of provincial organizations.

National Organizations and Activities

Most of these associations have weak links with each other and tend to look after only the affairs of their own sector rather than promoting the interests of capital as a whole. However, several groups do attempt to enunciate national positions for business. While not divided sectorally, nonetheless they are divided along other lines, principally between large and small capital. Given the nature of Canadian corporate ownership, this first division also involves a division between domestic and export orientation and differences in foreign and domestic ownership. These associations include the Canadian Chamber of Commerce, the Canadian Federation of Independent Business, and the Business Council on National Issues.

The Canadian Chamber of Commerce is a relatively small organization established as the federal voice of multiple local, regional, and provincial chambers. Although the Chamber represents both small and large businesses, it is dominated by its provincial wings and serves primarily as a spokesperson for small business interests at that level. At the national level, those interests are represented by the Canadian Federation of Independent Business, an association that grew out of small business protests against the proposed federal tax reforms of the 1970s.

Until 1976 large capital tended to be represented by major sectoral associations at the federal level (especially the Canadian Manufacturers' Association and the Canadian Bankers' Association). At that time, the Business Council on National Issues was formed, partially in response to the imposition of federal wage and price controls in 1975. The Business Council unites large corporations in the resource, financial, and U.S.-controlled manufacturing sectors and represents the interests of the internationally oriented business community to government decision-makers (Coleman, 1988, pp.81-99).

The Political-Economic Significance of Business Fragmentation

Canadian capital is divided along several lines, the most important of which are:

- small vs large,
- resource-financial vs manufacturing,
- domestic vs foreign ownership, and
- international vs domestic market orientation.

Although alliances between these various factions are possible, the organization of business interests has so far tended to reflect rather than overcome these divisions.

Canadian business associations reflect the divisions in the structure of the economy and the structure of trade and ownership of Canadian firms. Most associations are sectoral or subsectoral in nature, and the few national multisectoral associations tend to reflect divisions between large and small or domestic and foreign capital. In addition, the federal nature of the country has also contributed to the promotion of two levels of interest associations, with many national associations existing as weak voices for powerful provincial groups.

Not surprisingly, this fragmentation of business interests has muted the ability of capital to press governments to promote policies favourable to the interests of business as a whole, although they have been able to obtain policies favourable to their sectoral or subsectoral interests. This failure has significant implications for the operation of the Canadian political economy. It means that the Canadian federal state enjoys relative autonomy from capital because it does not face a united and coherent front of business interests, while provincial governments, reflecting the dependence of provincial economies on sectoral activities, are much more subject to the pressures of capital. Although this tendency might seem to enable labour to pressure the federal state to pursue policies geared towards the promotion of its own interests, this also does not occur because of the fragmentation of labour organizations.

The Canadian state, therefore, faces both weak capital and weak labour. In other countries this situation has resulted in states promoting their own interests, however politically defined, aimed at shaping the society's mix of state-market relations. In Canada this does not occur because of the fragmentation of the state itself. Instead, the Canadian state pursues ad hoc, incremental interventions into the market – interventions that reflect the conjunctural strengths and weaknesses of different actors at different times and in different areas of economic activity. These interventions often lead to the establishment of contradictory policies at the different levels of government and, in most instances, to the failure of state policies aimed at managing the micro- and macro-political economies.

CHAPTER 10

The Macro-Political Economy: Monetary and Fiscal Management

Although states and markets are intertwined there are distinct differences in the types of state-market relations that exist at the micro-level and macro-level of a nation's political economy. At the micro-level, extensive state-market interactions have an effect on the specific production and distribution decisions made by individual producers. While the market is the primary mechanism for making these decisions, the state is also actively involved in the process, most often through the use of subsidies or the manipulation of tax systems. The state can also regulate individual producers and, in some cases, directly provide goods and services through public enterprises. But these sorts of activities do not exhaust the potential of state actions to influence the market behaviour of individual producers and consumers. State actions at the macro-level also work to determine the behaviour of individual producers and consumers by altering the cost of credit in the domestic economy and by changing the value of a nation's currency in international markets.

The Instruments and Ends

The Rationales for Fiscal and Monetary Management Efforts

States are concerned at the macro-level with altering the basic framework of market decision-making by controlling the value of the currency, the supply of money circulating in the society, and the ease of access of investors to investment funds. The general aim is to control the aggregate rate of growth of domestic production, but attainment of this goal is subject to many constraints. One constraint is constant international pressure on the terms of trade of the nation's exports. Others are questions about political stability (which can alter foreign and international investment behaviour) or about the propensity of producers to produce and consumers to consume different amounts of different products at different prices. As a result, the effectiveness of the state's efforts to manipulate the market is never certain. Nevertheless, all modern nation-states do make these efforts.

Governments in Canada have always followed some sort of fiscal and monetary policy but until the post-World War II era the notion of fiscal and monetary management was absent from government deliberations. Traditionally government fiscal policy was simple and completely determined by the notion of balancing the government budget: to ensure that government revenues from all sources matched government expenditures and that government budgets were balanced on an annual basis. The logic behind this approach was to treat government spending just like any other economic "enterprise" and to avoid debt payments wherever possible. Any debts forced on governments by unexpectedly high expenditures or lower revenues than anticipated were retired immediately; taxes were either raised or expenditures cut to ensure that the problem did not repeat itself in the following year.

This kind of fiscal policy held sway in Canadian governments for the first seventy years of Confederation, until governments realized that their expenditures and tax policies had a major impact on the general functioning of the economy and could, at least in theory, be manipulated or managed in a fashion that would spur economic activity or decrease it. This realization, codified in Keynesian economic theory, led to a continuing debate between advocates of the pre-Keynesian balanced budget orthodoxy and advocates of Keynesian fiscal management techniques – a debate that has continued to characterize Canadian fiscal policy to the present day.

At the same time there was a similar evolution of thinking about monetary policy and monetary management efforts, involving most of the same participants. Before World War II, monetary policy in Canada was restricted to government efforts to control inflation by controlling the issuance of credit and the printing of bank notes and by protecting the value of the Canadian dollar on international exchange markets.

Governments initially encountered difficulties in these policies because credit control and the issuing of banknotes were in the hands of private banks. Ostensibly as part of their effort to ensure public confidence in the banking system, the federal government of Canada began to take over responsibility for regulating the money supply, although it did not consider actually manipulating the money supply to help expand or contract the economy until much later. Similarly, Canadian governments were always involved in efforts to ensure stability of the domestic currency in foreign exchange markets, but they did so for the first seventy years of Confederation through adherence to fixed exchange rates for the Canadian dollar against international gold and silver standards.

These monetary orthodoxies also succumbed to problems encountered in the Depression as governments failed in their attempts to maintain fixed exchange rates against gold and silver specie and began to embrace the idea embodied in Keynesian economic theory that the supply of money and credit in the economy could be manipulated to boost or restrain economic activity. As in the case of fiscal policy, however, adherents to the pre-Keynesian orthodoxy contested the efficacy of government monetary management efforts, arguing that these efforts were ineffective or inflationary, or both. Debates between adherents of the two views continue to the present day.

Contemporary Canadian debates in both fiscal and monetary policy take place within the dominant liberal political-economic discourse centring on the question of market failures and the effectiveness of government activity designed to correct those failures. Adherents to the neoclassical orthodoxy, including the modern neoconservatives, argue with Keynesians and post-Keynesians, saying that markets should be given priority and that government fiscal and monetary management efforts should eschew attempts to manipulate markets. Instead, they maintain that governments should only "manage" their expenditures to ensure that they are matched by revenues and, in this sense, remain "neutral" in their effect on private sector production. Concerning monetary policy, the monetarist wing of this group argues that, again, governments should avoid attempts to manipulate the economy and simply limit their management efforts to combating inflation by linking the growth in the money supply to growth in national production or GNP.

On the other hand, Keynesians among both mainstream liberal and social democratic thinkers argue that fiscal and monetary tools and instruments play an important, if not absolutely essential, role in managing modern capitalist economies, and that these tools are required to iron out fluctuations in the economy caused by the oversupply and undersupply of goods and services, or overdemand and underdemand. This view is the one favoured by most Canadian social democrats, who argue that such macro-economic interventions by governments stabilize employment and incomes of workers and hence counteract the unequal power of employers in labour markets.

Techniques of Monetary and Fiscal Management

The devices or tools that states can use in macro-economic management can be classified into two groups: *monetary* and *fiscal*. Techniques of monetary management include manipulation of the value of the domestic currency on international markets, of domestic interest rates, and of the amount of domestic currency in circulation. Techniques of fiscal management include the manipulation of government revenues and of expenditures (Binhammer, 1977).

Fiscal management efforts are the most straightforward, at least in theory. Governments have the ability to raise and lower taxes or increase and decrease their expenditures, and they can do so in a way that will increase and decrease the amount of funds available to market actors for investment in productive activities. The expansion of government expenditures and/or the lessening of taxes paid by market actors serve to increase the funds available to the market for investment and can, at least theoretically, act to spur these actors into expanding their productive activities. The reverse effect is possible through contracting government expenditures and/ or increasing the proportion of incomes and profits that market actors pay to the government in the form of taxes. These actions can serve to reduce the amount of funds available for investment and hence decrease or restrict productive activity within the country. Even if the state wishes to have no effect on the market, it must carefully manage its fiscal resources to ensure that expansions and contractions do not occur accidentally as a result of state expenditure and taxation measures.

Monetary management efforts are more complex and theoretically sophisticated, although they have essentially the same goals as techniques of fiscal management. Monetary management efforts involve the manipulation of the money supply, foreign exchange rates, and domestic interest rates, all aimed at encouraging or discouraging market investment behaviour. The state's primary instrument for modern monetary management is the *central bank*. Through several specific activities, central banking institutions can alter, within limits, interest and exchange rates and the total monetary supply. Central bankers use three specific techniques in their monetary management: manipulation of *reserve requirements* or "*reserve ratios*," manipulation of the *Bank Rate*, and a variety of so-called "*open market transactions*."

To manipulate reserve requirements, the government either increases or decreases the percentage of total deposits that commercial banks must keep "on hand" to guarantee those deposits. Commercial banks operate by accepting deposits from their customers, paying these depositors interest on their accounts and lending the deposited funds out to other customers, who pay the bank a somewhat higher rate of interest, thus generating a profit for the bank on each transaction. When the depositors wish to obtain their original funds, the banks must repay those funds within a short period of time, if not on demand. To meet this eventuality commercial banks have always been required by law to retain a certain percentage of their deposits on hand – the reserve requirement.

One effect of this reserve requirement is to remove certain amounts of cash from circulation. Manipulation of the reserve requirement, then, provides a tool governments can use to inject or withdraw cash from the entire economy. A higher reserve requirement forces commercial banks to withdraw additional cash; lowering the reserve requirement injects new cash into the economy. Changing the total amount of money circulating in the economy, or the money supply, can also change the behaviour of potential borrowers as they find more cash available for investment, or less, as the case may be. When cash is withdrawn, assuming a constant demand, borrowers can be forced to pay more for the scarce funds – as commercial banks adjust interest rates to the new market situation. The borrowers will tend to invest only in projects promising to return profits higher than the new rate, leading to the cancellation of projects expected to be unprofitable at the new rate and a general decrease in productive activity. When reserve requirements are lowered and more money is injected into the system, interest rates fall and previously marginal or submarginal projects become more profitable, leading to a general increase in productive activity.

Manipulation of the Bank Rate by central banks has the same effect. In the modern era banks keep their reserves on deposit with the central bank, which acts as a kind of "banker's bank." The central bank can lend or advance these deposited funds back to the commercial banks whenever the commercial banks require new funds to lend to borrowers or discover a shortfall in the funds required to meet legal reserve requirements. When these advances are made, the central bank charges a commercial bank interest at the "Bank Rate." Like the commercial banks' interest rates, the central bank's bank rate has an impact on market behaviour. A high bank rate discourages commercial banks from borrowing additional funds, and a low rate has the opposite effect. When the banks do borrow funds, this money becomes available to investors desiring to increase their productive activities and has the effect of increasing the money supply and the general level of economic activity in society. The manipulation of the bank rate, therefore, like the manipulation of reserve requirements, can have either a negative or a positive effect on economic activity and market behaviour, as the government-controlled central bank sees fit.

Open-market transactions are of two types. First, to manipulate foreign exchange rates central banks maintain stocks of domestic and foreign currencies and use those funds to intervene in foreign currency markets to increase or reduce the supply of the domestic currency in circulation and thereby regulate its price or value. Central banks purchase foreign currency with domestic funds whenever they wish to increase the amount of the domestic currency in circulation in international markets and hence reduce its price. Similarly, they can purchase domestic currency with foreign funds whenever they wish to decrease the amount of the domestic currency in circulation and hence increase its price or value.

Central banks make these transactions to regulate the amount of money flowing in and out of the country – the balance of payments – and to regulate the amount of goods flowing in and out of the country – the balance of trade. A domestic currency with low value on international markets helps exports by making them cheaper in international markets; this can boost export activity. A cheap domestic currency also makes imports more costly and makes repayment of debts denominated in foreign currencies more expensive. A relatively highly valued domestic currency can have the opposite effect, reducing exports, increasing imports, and easing repayment of foreign debt. Governments usually seek to increase the amount of funds flowing into the country and to reduce their balance-of-payments deficits, if any, and to a certain extent they can manipulate the exchange rate through central bank transactions to accomplish these goals.

The second type of open market transaction is more directly related to the domestic money supply and works in much the same fashion as do manipulations of reserve requirements and bank rates. Commercial bank deposits with central banks are usually not retained as cash but invested in government securities – sometimes long-term bonds, but more often short-term Treasury Bills. The central bank purchases additional securities from commercial banks or sells these securities to them in exchange for cash. When the central bank sells securities to the commercial banks, the banks deposit additional cash with the central bank in payment. This has the effect of withdrawing cash from the economy and reducing the money supply, with all the attendant effects on investor and borrower behaviour. Similarly, the central bank can itself repurchase these securities from the commercial banks, thereby injecting additional cash into the system, increasing the money supply, and encouraging additional productive activity.

Through the use of these macro-level fiscal and monetary management techniques governments are capable of altering the performance of the market. The tools, however, influence only the general decisions made by market actors about whether or not to invest in additional productive capacity at a particular time; they don't determine the actual content of those decisions – which the state can manipulate through micro-level activity. Although the two types of decisions, and corresponding government activities, are clearly linked, they can be usefully disaggregated for analytical purposes.

Whether or not, to what extent, and how successfully a state participates in this type of macro-level activity is a significant question for political-economic analysis. A survey of how these techniques have been used in Canada reveals a great deal about this question and the operation of the Canadian political economy.

The History of Fiscal and Monetary Management

Like everything else in Canada, the state's macro-level activity is influenced by Canada's federal system of government. Under the Constitution Act of 1867, the federal government received exclusive jurisdiction over important areas of monetary policy, such as the issuance of currency and the regulation of banks and interest. In addition, in the field of fiscal policy the federal government received the right to raise funds on the "public credit" and by "any mode or system of taxation" (Sections 91 [3], [4], [14-16], [18-20] of the Constitution Act, 1867). Provincial governments, on the other hand, have no influence over monetary policy. Their fiscal powers are restricted to raising funds on "the sole credit of the province" and raising revenues only through "direct taxation within the province" (LaForest, 1981)[1] and to whatever revenues accrue to them from natural resource and landownership (Sections 92[2], [3], [5] and [109] of the Constitution Act 1867).

This jurisdictional situation makes monetary policy relatively straight-forward, since it is strictly a matter of federal policy-making. Fiscal policy is more complex (Courchene, 1986, pp.49-100), because provincial governments have limited revenue-raising capabilities but at the same time they have jurisdiction over major expenditure areas, such as health, education, and social welfare (Sections 92 [7], [13] and [93] of the Constitution Act 1867). The oft-resulting "fiscal gap" has been addressed by a variety of means:

- first through statutory payments to provincial governments, culminating in the present-day, constitutionally entrenched equalization process;
- later through the extension of conditional federal government financing to provincial programs; and
- more recently, through systems of unconditional grants or block transfers (Maxwell, 1937; Lynn, 1967; Smiley, 1963; Canada, Parliamentary Task Force on Federal-Provincial Fiscal Arrangements, 1981).

Provincial expenditures, tax rates, and debt loads can have a major impact on federal expenditures. Combined, they all influence the country's general fiscal situation. Unlike monetary policy, then, which is highly centralized, fiscal policy is decentralized in Canada. But jurisdictional disputes over monetary and fiscal policy were not a great concern of Canadian governments until the post-World War II period, when major efforts were made to integrate fiscal and monetary policy in a program of macro-economic stabilization fashioned along Keynesian lines. Since that time, federal-provincial collaboration on macro-economic regulation has been essential, though rarely forthcoming. The reasons for this lack of co-operation can be traced to the different structures of the regional and central Canadian economies and the very different impact that stabilization policies have on the regions and on their particular configuration of political and economic interests.

Fiscal and Monetary Policy Before World War I

In 1964, writing for the Royal Commission on Banking and Finance, Grant Reuber (p.34) suggested that the aims of monetary policy were to promote full employment, stable prices, and economic growth. In this sense, Canada has only had a "monetary policy" in recent times – essentially since

World War II. This is not to say, though, that Canada did not have a policy for money and banking before World War II.

Canada has had a private banking system since the early years of the nineteenth century when groups of large merchants joined forces to create the first chartered banks. Before then, barter transactions between local merchants and settlers had prevailed under both the French and the British regimes, with larger merchants in cities extending their own credit to local merchants (Shortt, 1986). These bills of exchange formed the basis of most commerce, and a variety of coinages, including Spanish, Dutch, Portuguese, and those of other countries involved in the West Indian trade, circulated freely in the country. Throughout the eighteenth century the British government restricted itself to establishing correct exchange values for these currencies, using sterling, and to limiting the issuance of paper money by colonial authorities (Shortt, 1986).

Following the creation of the chartered banks, bank notes issued by these institutions became the norm. Those notes remained as valid currency until the Bank of Canada took over the issuance of currency in 1934. Both the British and colonial governments quickly became involved in the regulation of bank activities, including note issue, however, in order to ensure the integrity of the entire banking system against the dual threats of bank failure and monetary inflation. Restrictions were quickly placed on the amount of money the banks had to reserve against note issues, and such restrictions remain to this day in successive bank legislation.

For a brief period in the 1850s the colonial governments experimented with U.S.-style "Free Banking" in which charters were issued to any individuals who deposited appropriate securities with colonial officials. This plan, along with another to establish a uniform system of colonial coinage, was disliked by British officials, who argued that such rights were reserved for the monarchy. Free banking was abandoned after the fall of the Hincks-Morin administration in 1854, and the colonial currency legislation was disallowed by the Imperial government. The colonial governments also attempted to wrest control over note issue from the banks from 1860 onwards, but succeeded only in instituting the issue of Dominion of Canada notes alongside bank notes (Shortt, 1986).

Following Confederation, under the terms of the British North America Act, banking became an area of federal government jurisdiction, and the ties with Britain were cut. The federal government proceeded quickly to pass the Bank Act of 1871, which, with regular revisions every ten years, continues to govern Canadian banking practices. Until World War I, the federal government's monetary strategy had two components.

- First, the government was concerned with maintaining its control over the financial levers of monetary policy – that is, interest rates and bank charters – and virulently defended its jurisdiction against provincial efforts to expand credit for regional development. Numerous provincial government bills were reserved and disallowed by the federal government. The federal government also won several important cases at the Judicial Committee of the Privy Council, which backed its claims (LaForest, 1955; Olmsted, 1954; Howlett, 1986).

- Second, the government continued to press for control over note issue, still encountering resistance from the chartered banks. Along with its own note issues, the government was only able to institute various sorts of insurance schemes designed to protect holders of bank notes from loss in the event of the failure of the issuing bank (Breckenridge, 1910).

Fiscal policy was another matter altogether and was never considered conjointly with monetary policy. Governments in Canada were concerned with balancing their budgets, and given the overinvestment of many provincial governments in railway, canal, and other infrastructural undertakings, the federal government became involved in programs of provincial debt relief. The chief mechanism used for this purpose was the federal statutory subsidy. This involved cash grants to the provincial governments, made for a number of reasons, including maintenance of the provincial legislatures as well as debt relief (Canada, Royal Commission, 1940).

Although provincial revenue-sources in natural resources and direct taxation were expected to be adequate to meet provincial expenditure needs at the time of Confederation, judicial committee decisions restricting federal government powers and expanding those of the provincial governments produced a fiscal imbalance, with the provinces in a deficit position. This led to constant demands by provincial governments for "better terms" and the renegotiation of the statutory subsidies on several occasions. In 1905 the subsidies were permanently linked to increases in provincial populations (Maxwell, 1937).

More significant, however, was the fact that many expenditures associated with continued industrial development fell into provincial jurisdiction and increased the need of the provincial governments for additional revenues. This was true of many matters related to agriculture and immigration and, especially, education, highway transportation, and unemployment relief. The growth of expenditure programs in these areas exacerbated the fiscal deficit position of the provincial governments and resulted in the establishment of a new instrument for federal funding of provincial programs: the conditional grant (Gettys, 1938).

These grants involved federal transfers to the provincial governments, usually on some sort of shared-cost basis, providing that provincial governments used the funds for the intended purposes, which were set out as conditions attached to the grant. The grants began to be used extensively immediately before World War I, and their use accelerated thereafter, although their constitutionality has always been in question. The use of this federal spending power to influence provincial governments in their approach to legislation within their areas of constitutional jurisdiction has always been resented by the provinces (Smiley, 1963), but it has never actually been challenged in the courts.

The hallmark of this period of monetary and fiscal policy in Canada is the division into separate areas of policy. Monetary policy existed as an effort to preserve the integrity of the Canadian currency and banking system from multiple threats: the threat of simple currency inflation caused by printing excess bank notes; the more complex threat resulting from fragmented, provincially led, easy credit legislation; the threat of a loss of confidence caused by bank failures or a loss of trust in the banking system as a whole by depositors. The government fully realized the need to maintain a stable currency to protect domestic savings and investment from inflation as well as to preserve the value of the currency on international exchanges and, thus, the value of Canadian exports in international markets.

Fiscal policy, on the other hand, was oriented almost exclusively towards retaining the solvency and favourable credit position of both levels of Canadian government. Although by the first decades of the twentieth century the federal government had begun to use fiscal transfers as a device for correcting what had come to be perceived as a structural problem of fiscal federalism – that is, a long-term, and growing, provincial fiscal deficit – these transfers and government expenditures in general were not seen as linked in any manner to the general performance of the economy or the relative strength or weakness of the nation's currency. Hence, observers such as R.C. McIvor (1958) could argue, many years afterwards, that Canada had continued to lack a long-term monetary and fiscal policy during the pre-World War I era.

Fiscal and Monetary Policy 1914-45

That all changed during World War I, when the government undertook massive borrowing to fund the war effort. It was forced in 1917 to implement a comprehensive system of personal income taxation to offset war-related expenditures (Perry, 1955). Under the strains of attempting to maintain and equip a large army, the federal government was forced to intervene in the economy not only to develop a massive armaments industry but also to manage both fiscal and monetary policy in an integrated manner.

The Canadian currency was removed from the gold standard in 1914 and its exchange value regulated, while strict controls were placed on prices and supplies of goods, as well as upon banks and the issuance of credit. Savings were attracted through Canadian War Savings Bonds, while government expenditures on non-war-related activities were curtailed (Deutsch, 1940). Nevertheless, these efforts were devoted simply to ensuring that Canadian production would be directed towards the war and the maintenance of the military overseas. Although monetary and fiscal policies were united for the first time, this union took place because of the emergency, without any long-term commitment. After the war monetary and fiscal policies were redivided and most government wartime regulatory arrangements undone. Questions of monetary theory and policy did become a focal point for liberal economic theory after the war: both A.C. Pigou and John Maynard Keynes wrote major works reflecting on the success of British wartime fiscal and monetary arrangements in overcoming the otherwise apparently endemic employment and credit problems of modern capitalist economies. But in Canada permanent changes did not occur until the events of the 1930s brought home the problems of an unregulated laissez-faire approach to government and the economy (Brecher, 1957).

After the war Canada attempted to go back onto the gold standard for international exchange and to return in other ways to prewar arrangements. Throughout the 1920s, however, the major concern of the federal government was with inflation and its control. The control of inflation had always been a key target of Canadian monetary policy, and the severe price inflation that followed the end of World War I caused great consternation and a rethinking of the traditional mechanisms for controlling prices and the value of Canadian currency.

The problem was quickly perceived as involving the failure of traditional banking regulations to control the issuance of credit. By that time most business in the country was carried on through the use of chequing accounts in banks, a system that had replaced specie payments and the exchange of cash or notes. Without proper reserve requirements for those new accounts, banks were able to create huge amounts of credit, which had the effect of driving up prices for goods and services in the marketplace. In 1923 a new Finance Act attempted to give the federal Department of Finance control over the extension of credit by restricting total bank loans to a percentage of the dominion notes held by the bank. The reconversion to the gold standard in 1926 represented an effort in the same direction. But the mere increase in the volume of international trade after the war made the move back to gold impractical. Canada was quickly forced off the standard by the events of the early 1930s and the threat of the flight of large amounts of gold out of the country (Plumptre, 1934; Curtis, 1931, 1932; Knox, 1934). By the early 1930s many people realized that some new mechanism was required to control credit and foreign exchange regulation. In 1934, spurred on by Western provincial governments and federal opposition Progressive members who blamed much of the damage of the post-1929 Depression on "eastern" bankers, the R.B. Bennett government, following a brief and perfunctory Royal Commission investigation into the subject, created the Bank of Canada to perform these functions (Canada, Royal Commission, 1933; Neufeld, 1958; Watts, 1972).

Meanwhile, government fiscal policy in the years immediately after World War I had also given support to those who wished to see monetary and fiscal policy integrated in a way that would moderate swings in the economy. Having created new revenue sources capable of raising large amounts of funds, not surprisingly the government moved quickly to increase taxes so it could pay off the huge war debts it had amassed. This dampened the postwar boom resulting from the increase in domestic demand for goods and services and had some salutary effects on countering inflation.

After most of the wartime debt had been paid off by the mid-1920s, tax rates were reduced, and this reduction, in conjunction with easy credit, caused a major expansionary boom. This boom lasted until 1929 when poor agricultural conditions and an oversupply of manufactured goods resulted in a sudden depression and a massive demand for governments to provide social relief (Brecher, 1957). Faced with these additional demands for funds, the federal government again responded in an orthodox manner by raising taxes, only exacerbating the slide towards worsening economic circumstances.

The degree to which government fiscal arrangements sometimes benefited and sometimes worsened economic upturns and downturns in the 1920s was not lost on the economists and politicians who had become sensitive to the effects of government spending on economic performance after reading the work of Keynes and others in Europe and the United States (Granatstein, 1982). Some of these individuals, both in the federal administration and Parliament, pressed for the adoption of a more coherent and unified monetary and fiscal policy that could control swings in the economy, depressing expansions and expanding depressions. The monetary tools were available through the new central bank, and all that was required was a change in government thinking supportive of the adoption of countercyclical spending and taxation measures. Such a change in fiscal policy involved more than simply a decision to adopt enhanced policy tools; it therefore arrived more slowly than the decision to create the Bank of Canada.

Proposals that the government adopt just such a policy emerged from the 1937 and 1938 Reports of the National Employment Commission and the recommendations of the 1940 Royal Commission on Dominion-Provincial Relations. The National Employment Commission recommended that the federal government maintain a series of programs in such areas as housing and public works and tailor its use of these spending programs to economic conditions – promoting the economy when necessary and demoting it when required. The Rowell-Sirois Commission devoted a large part of its analysis to devising mechanisms by which provincial fiscal deficits could be eliminated and federal and provincial constitutional responsibilities and spending plans could be better harmonized.

Although the government of William Lyon Mackenzie King moved to strengthen the powers of the Bank of Canada and rescued the three prairie provinces from bankruptcy, it did little in the 1930s to follow up on the proposals for a more integrated monetary and fiscal policy. The Liberals faced opposition from the provinces to such a policy, but in any case they only halfheartedly accepted the need for a move that would clearly involve greater government "intervention" in the economy than they were willing to countenance. As a result, little was accomplished in this direction until after World War II (Neatby, 1969).

Fiscal and Monetary Policy 1945-75

Until recently, judging from the utterances of Canadian politicians in the post-World War II era, it was assumed that Canada had consciously adopted a Keynesian monetary and fiscal policy in 1945 and that this policy remained in place until the mid-1970s when it crumbled under the new phenomenon of "stagflation" (the combined and simultaneous presence of high rates of inflation and unemployment) (Samuelson and Scott, 1971; Wolfe, 1984; Perry, 1989). Indeed, Canadian politicians and administrators did espouse Keynesian objectives (Reuber, 1964; Will, 1966; Gordon, 1966). But a close study of the actual performance of the Canadian federal government during this period casts doubt on whether this rhetoric was matched in reality (Campbell, 1987; Gillespie, 1979).

The federal government formally stated its acceptance of Keynesian principles of fiscal and monetary policy in its 1945 *White Paper on Employment and Income* (Canada, Dept. of Reconstruction, 1945; Mackintosh, 1966). In this document the federal government expressed its intention to engage in countercyclical budgeting and to follow a taxation and interest rate policy designed to encourage investment in times of need and discourage it in times of expansion (Perry, 1989).

Virtually from its inception doubts were raised about the efficacy of such a policy. Many economists pointed out that the federal government in the immediate postwar period was faced with paying off a large wartime debt and as a result had to keep interest rates low to minimize repayment costs. These actions were certainly not Keynesian and as often as not exacerbated business cycles rather than offsetting them (Barber, 1957; McIvor and Panabaker, 1954; Brewis, 1968). Commentators also noted that in the Canadian context, with an economy reliant on international trade, trade flows and trade cycles can have an enormous impact on the domestic economy and are largely outside of the government's control. If a government in such a situation attempted to follow a strict Keynesian regime, it would have to constantly react to changes in trade balances with monetary and fiscal measures that would in themselves create a very uncertain climate for business and discourage long-term investment. Therefore, it was argued, Keynesian demand-management techniques were inappropriate for a small, open economy (Brewis, 1968). Although finance ministers continued to pay lip service to Keynesian ideals in their annual budget speeches

(Perry, 1989), the record of fiscal and monetary policy initiatives displays a distinctly non-Keynesian approach (Campbell et al., 1967).

In fact, rather than attempt to regulate the domestic economy by using domestic tools alone, successive Liberal governments attempted to ensure that international conditions would not unduly harm the performance of the Canadian economy. Canadian governments not only wholeheartedly supported the negotiation and implementation of the General Agreement on Tariffs and Trade (GATT) in 1947, but they had also already enthusiastically accepted other U.S.-sponsored proposals to stabilize the international banking and currency markets through the 1944 Bretton Woods agreement. This agreement established major international financial institutions such as the International Bank for Reconstruction and Development (the World Bank) and the International Monetary Fund and finally replaced the gold standard for international exchange with a standard based on fixed convertibility against the U.S. dollar. Canadian officials, and especially Bank of Canada officials, were very active in the negotiation and implementation of this postwar international financial system (Watts, 1973a; Plumptre, 1977, pp.17-60).

Once again, however, Canada was unable to maintain a fixed exchange rate against the U.S. dollar, as U.S. investment poured into the country's resource industries after World War II and drove up the value of the Canadian dollar. To abate the pressure the federal government had to purchase large amounts of foreign exchange to be held in reserves. In 1950, as the cost continued to mount, the government was forced to float the Canadian dollar, allowing its value to rise and fall against the U.S. dollar as economic changes occurred (Watts, 1974). This decision eliminated the possibility of a strictly domestic monetary policy, because any actions of the government in the area of interest rates could now easily be negated by flows of capital in and out of the country (Caves and Reuber, 1969; Mundell, 1964).

In addition, during this period the federal government greatly accelerated its use of conditional grants and especially tax transfers to the provincial governments to provide funding for major program expenditures in areas such as education, health, and welfare (Banting, 1982; Guest, 1980; Taylor, 1987). The net effect of these programs and techniques was to lock the federal government into major long-term expenditure commitments and to reduce even further its ability to use fiscal measures for short-term stabilization purposes (Perry, 1982).

By the time the Progressive Conservative government of John Diefenbaker was elected in 1957, even the lip service paid to Keynesian ideals by federal finance ministers had disappeared, to be replaced by a policy of national economic expansion based on the extraction and processing of Canada's resource wealth (Canada, 1957). Under the Conservatives the federal government abandoned any pretence at countercyclical budgeting and pursued an expansionary program – at least until fears of rising inflation drove it back to a balanced budget orthodoxy (Will, 1966). This more or less ad hoc and reactive approach to fiscal and monetary policy would continue under the successive Liberal minority governments of the 1960s, with monetary policy reacting to international events and circumstances and fiscal policy to domestic needs (Purvis and Smith, 1986).

Throughout the 1960s and early 1970s, the government was faced with rapidly rising real inflation rates. Although unsure of the origins of this inflation, government ministers began to argue that the problem was not cyclical but structural in nature, that the root of the problem lay in monetary and government expenditure increases that had not been matched by increases in productivity (Perry, 1989). To deal with the problem, the government argued in its 1968 white paper *Policies for Price Stability* that new policy tools were required, especially wage controls to combat inflation. In 1969 the government established the Prices and Incomes Commission to review wage and price increases (Haythorne, 1973). Although the imposition of mandatory controls was delayed by the 1972 election of a minority Liberal federal government that required NDP backing to remain in power, a new Liberal majority government after 1974 quickly moved to implement wage and price controls.

Fiscal and Monetary Policy after 1975

By the early 1970s the international situation had deteriorated. The U.S. government had abandoned the Bretton Woods dollar standard and allowed its own currency to float under the inflationary pressures brought about by the expansion of the Vietnam war. The New Economic Policy adopted by President Nixon in 1971 not only altered the nature of the international financial system but also imposed wage and price controls in the United States as well as a global 10 percent surcharge on imports (Plumptre, 1977).

Although Canada was able, eventually, to negotiate an exemption from the import surcharge and avoid major economic disruption, its economy appeared to be more and more vulnerable to international developments – especially given the major changes that followed the increases in oil prices announced by the Organization of Petroleum Exporting Countries (OPEC) in 1973-74. These increases exacerbated inflationary problems in Canada and reinforced the federal government's desire to undertake a major and permanent shift in monetary and fiscal policy to combat inflation (Perry, 1989; Courchene, 1976a,b).

The new policy adopted by the government in 1975 was motivated by the desire to manage macro-economic policy in accordance with the general growth in the national economy. It replaced the little-observed Keynesian doctrine based on the manipulation of monetary and fiscal tools to boost or cool down the economy with fiscal restraint and monetary gradualism (Courchene, 1976b; Sparks, 1986; Howitt, 1986). In both cases the object of policy became the restriction of monetary and expenditure growth to the same rate of growth as GNP in order to avoid government activities in these areas that might fuel inflation.

One part of the government's strategy was to create the Anti-Inflation Board (AIB), an arms-length government regulatory agency with powers to review and overturn wage or price increases if it felt these were inflationary. The AIB operated without the consent of organized labour, which mounted a large-scale campaign against the use of mandatory controls and in favour of retaining the collective bargaining process for establishing wage rates. This protest culminated in a one-day national general strike led by the Canadian Labour Congress in February 1976. The imposition of price controls also upset organized business. The Business Council on National Issues was set up primarily to ensure that the views of the business sector would be taken into consideration by governments in the future.

Although the AIB was eventually disbanded and wage and price controls removed from the private sector, the federal and several provincial governments retained self-imposed controls on public sector expenditures throughout the 1970s and 1980s. Proposals to restrict the growth of government spending to the level of the GNP were made at the 1978 Federal-Provincial Conferences on the Economy (British Columbia, 1978a, 1978b), and controls were put into place by most governments in the early 1980s, although not without considerable opposition from public sector unions and provincial governments opposed to cuts or limits placed on federal transfer payments. The most publicized restraint program was in British Columbia (Magnusson, Doyle, et al., 1984), but other provinces and the federal government acted in similar ways (Perry, 1989).

Although the Progressive Conservative victory of 1984 brought with it a renewed emphasis on fiscal management, and especially on balanced budgeting, the record of federal governments throughout the 1980s was of increased expenditures and deficit financing (Wolfe, 1985). This was largely because of the long-term, committed nature of federal expenditures, which, despite Conservative efforts to find programs to cut, proved intractable (Canada, 1985). The diverse path of political discourse and political activity only changed in 1989 when the federal budget attempted to match expenditures not with program cuts but with tax increases, using a new Goods and Services Tax (GST) for this purpose.

On the monetary side the federal government was also forced to abandon its efforts to target monetary growth and link that growth with growth of the economy as a whole. This failure occurred as the government found itself in the position of having to accept the international rate of inflation, because international inflation kept international interest and exchange rates at levels over which the Bank of Canada had no control (Courchene, 1981, 1982). By early 1981 the inflation rate in Canada was over 10 percent and interest rates stood at close to 20 percent as the Bank of Canada attempted to retain the value of the dollar against high interest rates offered in the United States. The U.S. government was also attempting to control inflation via monetarism and to attract foreign capital at the same time in an effort to spark economic growth. This situation forced the Bank of Canada to formally abandon the policy of monetary gradualism in 1982 and replace it with a strategy of slavishly following U.S. interest rates (Courchene, 1983). This approach did prove successful in combating inflation, although at the cost of plunging the entire economy into a serious recession. Later, interest rates were allowed to fall both in the United States and in Canada in the effort to reinvigorate the economy. Eventually bank officials began to rationalize this new approach, calling it "adaptive monetary control." This strategy accepts that medium-term fluctuations in money supply will occur within a broadly conceived goal of long-term supply (Howitt, 1986).

Constraints on Macro-Economic Management

Some of the reasons for the failure of Canadian governments to establish a unified fiscal and monetary policy with twin goals of low inflation and full employment are international in origin and intimately linked to Canada's role as a small open economy in the international political economy (Katzenstein, 1985; Macdonald Commission, 1985). The Canadian economy is open to investment flows and must retain a "competitive" interest rate if capital is not to flow elsewhere. Raising Canadian rates above international limits may cause additional funds to flow to Canada, but it dampens the domestic demand for money. Lowering Canadian rates below the international standard, on the other hand, might increase the domestic demand for funds, but it makes Canadian investments less attractive to both national and international lenders. In either case, the expected Keynesian result of contraction or expansion may not necessarily result.

Being a small, open economy also makes Canada susceptible to balance-of-payments problems that alter the value of the Canadian dollar and are largely beyond Canada's control, originating as they do in fluctuations in the terms of trade and the changing international demand for Canadian dollars. Again, a very important aspect of monetary supply is subject to fluctuations beyond the government's control, since interventions by the Bank of Canada to sell or purchase Canadian dollars to stabilize international exchange also substantially change the amount of currency in domestic circulation. Thus, regardless of the government's monetary aims, it is forced to alter them in the course of pursuing a stable exchange rate for the Canadian dollar.

Keynesian fiscal mechanisms, on the other hand, tend to be constrained by domestic circumstances, although these are not without their international aspects. In the first place, the amount governments spend is only mildly discretionary; many expenditures have been promised and guaranteed over the long term, and there are powerful constituencies opposed to the removal of benefits. It is difficult to manage these types of expenditures in any meaningful countercyclical manner.

Second, governments are constrained in the amount of revenues they can command. Although the actual crisis point varies by country, at some point additional taxes will inevitably result in electoral difficulties for the government that imposes them, either from taxpayer resistance or from capital flight (Przeworski, 1991). Additionally, governments can only borrow so much from external or internal sources without risking repayment difficulties if interest rates rise or revenue sources disappear. The use of public sector restraint techniques is also politically problematic. Public sector unions, large, well-organized, and resourceful, not only have the ability to resist restraint programs through work actions, but also in many jurisdictions are large enough to create severe electoral problems for a government that institutes such measures (Howlett and Brownsey, 1988; Chorney and Hanson, 1985).

The current Canadian macro-economic policy, then, is a highly reactive, uncoordinated, and non-interventionist strategy that aims at the same two goals – foreign exchange stability and low inflation – that have traditionally characterized Canadian monetary and fiscal policy. After international constraints are taken into account, the only device that remains in government hands for influencing the general direction of the economy is high interest rates. But high interest rates can only deflate an economy and have very serious consequences for government finances. Any increase in interest rates also results in an increase in government domestic debt charges, which can seriously restrict its fiscal manoeuvrability. This is especially important in Canada because a majority of government debt is held in Canada Savings Bonds (CSBs) which are easily converted to cash or other investments if CSB rates are allowed to fall below market norms.

Similarly, domestic constraints greatly limit the use of government spending and other fiscal instruments to influence economic activity in the country. Resistance from taxpayers reduces the possibility of stimulating a depressed economy by raising new revenues and spending them on public works projects. According to current macro-economic thinking, such an economy should be left to correct itself through the traditional market technique of having increased unemployment stimulate reductions in production costs through wage cuts. Resistance from labour, on the other hand, as well as from taxpayers concerned about their entitlements, reduces the possibility of using fiscal restraint to deflate an overheated economy.

State macro-level activity is not a simple technical exercise in economic planning and efficiency, nor is it in any manner a purely automatic process. Rather, macro-level activity thoroughly combines economics and politics. It has significant political dimensions in which key political actors pursue their own interests and in so doing can either seriously constrain state actions or force the state to make tradeoffs between the different interests involved. At the same time, the state must operate within an international economy, which can also serve to constrain its actions or force difficult choices to be made in the policy process. In attempting to formulate macroeconomic policy, Canadian federal governments have thus been constrained by an array of changing international, institutional, and partisan forces.

Note

1 The distinction between direct and indirect taxation is ambiguous. In practice the terms have been interpreted by the courts as referring to whether a tax is paid directly by the consumer or passed on by some middle agent to a final taxpayer – who thus pays it "indirectly." Examples of direct taxes are personal and corporate income taxes. Indirect taxes include most customs and excise taxes.

CHAPTER **11**

The Micro-Political Economy: Industrial Development

Since the last century Canada has been among the most industrialized nations in the world (Laxer, 1989a). Yet some analysts describe it as an "underdeveloped" nation, referring to the natural-resource orientation of its economy, which is not unlike the economies of many Third World nations. Others oppose this description, and the ensuing controversy has generated some of the liveliest debates in Canadian political economy – debates not confined to scholars but involving politicians, bureaucrats, and business and labour leaders. The controversy concerns the state's role in strengthening Canada's manufacturing sector. Some view the state's role as critical in promoting manufacturing industries. Others believe that state intervention is unlikely to enhance Canada's competitiveness in manufacturing or that if it does the gains are likely to be at an excessive cost to the economy as a whole.

Although this theoretical controversy remains unresolved, in practice the Canadian state has intervened extensively in the market to promote industrial development for more than a century. The character and extent of the intervention have varied over the years. The intervention has been carried out in a highly incoherent, even contradictory, fashion, but it has never been inconsequential.

The Instruments and Ends

Industrial policy is another concept that is almost impossible to define comprehensively in a precise or meaningful sense. There is a danger of being either too specific to capture the numerous elements of such a policy or too general to be of much analytical use. We prefer the rather narrow definition proposed by D.G. McFetridge (1985), who says industrial policies are "those government policies which are intended to have a direct effect on a particular industry or firm" (p.1). They represent an effort by the state "to encourage particular types of industrial activity" (p.2). The policies can involve encouraging the use of certain inputs such as plastics instead of steel, the production of certain goods or services such as computers or high-price consumer items, or the adoption of certain organizational forms such as larger firms or Canadian ownership. But government does not necessarily have to take particular actions before it can be described as having an industrial policy. Even the decision not to have an industrial policy is itself a policy – of leaving the course of industrial development in the hands of the market.

The concept of *industrial strategy* is broader than that of industrial policy. Industrial policy describes individual policy measures aimed at altering industrial activity in a country. Industrial strategy, on the other hand, describes a collection of interrelated policies directed at industrial development. It is more than the sum of individual policies, for it requires the various policies to form an integral whole and be complementary to each other. The emphasis is on coherence and co-ordination among policies. A lack of cohesiveness among different industrial policies, no matter how effective they are individually, will make for a poor industrial strategy. Indeed, it can be more harmful than not having any policy at all.

Rationales for Industrial Policy

The rationales behind the need for industrial policy can be classified loosely into two broad categories. The first is the approach of mainstream liberal Keynesian-welfare political economists; using the terms of welfare economics, they see policy as involving the adoption of measures necessary to correct market failures. The second is the approach of social democratic political economists, who are inspired by economic nationalism.

The first group has economic efficiency as a goal and tends to use technical arguments to justify particular policy choices. The second group makes use of a variety of arguments, including many borrowed from the first group, to justify its preferences. Both have a huge corpus of literature to back them, and both enjoy sizable support among scholars and the general populace. There are, of course, analysts who have other ideas; especially those of the neoconservative variety, who do not see any role at all for the government in industrial development.

The most commonly cited rationale for government actions in this area relates to the public goods character of many industrial inputs. It is argued that the nature of scientific and managerial information, technology, or labour inputs is such that their producers cannot restrict their usage to those paying for them. Others – so called "free riders" – can benefit without incurring any costs for their usage – which eliminates the profit incentive for creating them. While society as a whole clearly benefits from the production of those public goods, the work is not undertaken unless the producers are compensated. This is often cited as the main reason why governments should, for example, provide subsidies for industrial research and development and labour training.

Another market-failure rationale relates to infant industries. It is argued that the initial costs, and the corresponding risks, to firms in new industries are sometimes so high that companies are deterred from getting started, even though it is in society's interest to see them established. Similarly, new industries may not be able to compete in the short run with imports. In such circumstances, the government can provide subsidies to facilitate the establishment of socially desirable industries. Just about every country has to various degrees supported industries on these grounds. The protection of infant industries was one of the professed goals of the Canadian National Policy tariffs.

Yet another argument in support of industrial policy is that the government can improve the efficient operation of market forces by easing the economy's adjustment to changing circumstances. This is called *positive adjustment policy*. When an industry is faced with increased competition from imports or a decline in consumption of its products, business and labour in that industry often seek government protection from change. However, the result of increased protection is economic inefficiency and a reduction in the wealth of society as a whole. In such circumstances, it will be to society's benefit for government to compensate the victims of change, encouraging them to leave the industry and to invest or seek employment in more competitive industries.

There are numerous other rationales for industrial policy, but the ones cited here should convey their general thrust – that industrial policies ought to be employed only to correct market failures (Watson, 1983). Neoclassical and neoconservative liberal political economists, while broadly agreeing that there can be instances of market failures that might be corrected through state intervention, remain suspicious about the need or efficacy of such interventions. They insist that before intervention is undertaken, the government must ascertain, first, whether the market has indeed failed and, second, whether the state is genuinely more capable than the market of correcting the failure.

In the case of government support for industrial research and development (R&D), for instance, these neoconservatives argue that it must be demonstrated – and not just assumed – that the existing level of R&D is indeed lower than socially desirable. Next, it must be ascertained whether the lower R&D is caused by lack of demand or lack of supply, because if it is a lack of demand government subsidies for undertaking R&D would not solve the problem. Even after the case for intervention has been established, the government's capacity to intervene effectively must be questioned. How will the government know which R&D activity to target? How will it implement its decisions unhindered by political pressures from industries competing for subsidies? Neoconservatives have similar misgivings about the infant industry rationale. They wonder how an industry that grows up in a protected environment will survive when protection is removed and the industry is exposed to open competition. In fact, such industries might become dependent on protection and be unable to survive without it. Positive adjustment measures, especially those directed at labour adjustment, find more widespread support among liberal political economists of all stripes and colours.

The economic nationalist rationale put forward by social democrats favours a state-led industrial policy to promote the nation's interests, and especially the interests of the working class. Underlying this rationale is the belief that international market forces do not deliver equal benefits to all nations and tend to favour the strong, which necessitates state intervention to correct the imbalances. Manufacturing is of special interest to economic nationalists because of the positive spinoffs it supposedly generates and the national autonomy it promotes. They see a healthy manufacturing industry as essential for national well-being, which is an argument largely rejected by most liberal economists, who subscribe to the notion of comparative advantage. Most social democrats propose that the government, at a minimum, should nurture indigenous manufacturing industries through protection from imports and subsidies of various kinds until these industries become internationally competitive.

Another rationale for supporting domestic industries is to correct the problem of the low level of research and development undertaken in Canada. While this argument is essentially the same as the public goods argument, it is not usually expressed in the same formal language by social democrats. The most commonly cited social democratic argument in favour of industrial policy is that it is needed to offset the adverse affects of extensive foreign, mainly U.S., ownership of Canadian manufacturing. The social democrats argue that foreign-owned subsidiaries do not undertake sufficient R&D; do not make adequate efforts to export; and maintain small plants engaged in small-scale production of a wide variety of products – thus lacking the economies of scale required to be internationally competitive. In addition, in recent years many economic nationalists have been concerned that with the increasing liberalization of trade, and especially with the adoption of the U.S.-Canada Free Trade Agreement, foreign branch plants will be wound down and the Canadian market supplied from offshore plants in low-wage countries or from excess capacity in U.S. facilities. They propose that the government try to increase Canadian ownership in manufacturing and, in addition, pressure foreign-owned firms to serve Canada's interests.

Techniques of Industrial Strategy

The mainstream debate on the direction of Canadian industrial strategy displays three different visions: (1) a strategy of *non-intervention*; (2) a strategy of *positive adjustment*; and (3) a strategy of *targeting*. Neoconservative political economists tend to support the first strategy, welfare-Keynesians the second, and social democrats and post-Keynesians the third. The differences among these relate to the debate over the level of state intervention in the market process, the debate that is endemic to both contemporary liberal and socialist political economy.

Non-intervention is the traditional liberal strategy that postulates that the market is the most efficient means of allocating society's economic resources and must be left alone to work out the course of industrial development based on the principle of comparative advantage. It follows that the state should keep its hands off industrial development and must pursue the strategy of having no strategy. This is, of course, an extreme position, and there are only a few Canadian economists and politicians, such as the hard-core neoconservatives, who propose such a strategy. Most people associated with this school of thought are content with minor state interventions to correct market failures.

The strategy of positive adjustment begins from the same premise, assuming that the market is the most appropriate mechanism for determining the course of industrial development. What distinguishes this strategy from the non-interventionist strategy is that it recognizes the existence of rigidities in the market or society that impede the withdrawal of labour and capital resources from declining industries and their deployment in growth industries. Advocates of this position consider that government activities to remove these rigidities are legitimate as long as the goal of economic efficiency is pursued. In other words, they call for positive adjustment strategies to neutralize or eliminate the sources of resistance to change in order to enhance "the flexibility and resilience of markets in the face of change" (OECD, 1983). Firms and workers faced with the prospect of a decline in their industries are often reluctant to leave and seek employment in growth industries, and this reluctance introduces inefficiencies into the economy. The government can help the adjustment process along by subsidizing the retraining and mobility costs of the workers involved. This mode of reasoning is typical of welfare-Keynesian approaches to industrial policy, which are concerned with government intervention to increase the efficiency of the market.

There is, however, a general scepticism about subsidizing the adjustment costs borne by capital. David Richardson (1985) summarizes the reasons for opposition to subsidies for capital adjustment: "Capital markets are national and international; labour markets are local. Risktaking owners of capital are presumably better informed than workers about prospects for international change, and also about finding more lucrative employment of their resources by moving to other industries. They therefore have more opportunities to diversify than workers" (p.177). The strategy of positive adjustment, especially for workers, has few opponents in Canada, and the Canadian federal government claims to be following this strategy. Those favouring the strategy of targeting argue that the government ought to support winning industries as well as aiding the winding down of declining industries.

The industrial strategy of targeting suggests that the government ought to aid industrial development not generally but in a focused way, aiding only certain industries singled out for their growth potential. As elaborated by social democrats and post-Keynesians, the theory maintains that winning industries will be in the high-growth, high-technology sectors, which are supposed to generate above-average returns and spinoffs to other industries. This strategy is based on the assumption that comparative advantage is not entirely dependent on the existing endowment of natural resources, labour, and capital (which is what the traditional theory of comparative advantage assumes) but can be "engineered" with the assistance of the government.

The theoretical underpinning of this strategy is the familiar argument related to the public goods character of technology that discourages private risk-taking, a problem that can be corrected through government intervention. It is assumed that without government support for high-growth, high-technology industries, the established industries and industries in countries that receive such support will dominate the market. The proponents of this strategy cite Japan and South Korea, and also France and Sweden to some extent, as having engineered comparative advantage through the strategy of targeting. In addition to adjustment policies for workers to help them leave declining industries, the proponents of targeting are not averse to subsidies and protection for declining firms to preserve employment in communities while the firm is undergoing restructuring. This strategy is only distantly related to welfare economics, because it does not justify state intervention necessarily in terms of market failure.

The more orthodox neoclassical and neoconservative liberal political economists disagree with this strategy entirely, on both theoretical and practical grounds. Mainstream welfare-Keynesians, while agreeing that it is theoretically possible to engineer comparative advantage in certain industries, remain unconvinced about the government's capacity to "pick winners." They doubt that the state is better equipped than the market to predict the future and target its efforts accordingly.

The strategy a government chooses to follow in practice is never simply a question of theoretical elegance. Rather, the types of activities a state considers and implements are determined by the nature of the constraints it faces in the national and international political economy. Especially significant is the organization of state and societal actors, a variable that is extremely important in determining whether governments will be able to develop and enunciate a consistent and coherent industrial strategy. In Canada the fragmentation of state and societal actors has prevented the state from articulating any general industrial strategy and has resulted instead in an ad hoc and incremental response to the problems faced by industry.

The History of State Intervention in Industrial Development

Manufacturing in Canada is as old as the earliest European settlements. It accounted for 18 percent of GNP as early as 1851 and grew rapidly in the subsequent decades (Pomfret, 1981, p.122). In fact, by the 1890s the share of the GNP accounted for by manufacturing (21 percent) was not much lower than it is today. However, the scale of production remained small until the turn of the century. In 1870, for example, the average plant size was 4.7 employees and the value added was only $2,414 (Blackbourn and Putnam, 1984). Manufacturing grew rapidly between 1870 and 1929. By 1920 Canadian manufacturing had shed much of its artisan character, and the average size of capital invested in manufacturing firms had increased dramatically. This was reflected in the reduction of the workforce by one-third between 1870 and 1929, even though the value added in Canadian manufacturing had increased eightfold (ibid., p.24). After a period of stagnation due to the Depression, growth resumed with the outbreak of World War II and was rapid immediately after the war.

The comparative advantage arising from the local availability of natural resources and the adverse transportation costs for foreign exporters wishing to sell in Canada were to a large extent responsible for the establishment of an indigenous manufacturing capacity. However, the role of the Canadian state was by no means insignificant. Lord Durham, in his *Report on the Affairs of British North America* in 1839, remarked that whereas in Europe the main role of the state was national defence, in North America it was active engagement in the construction of public works, mostly canals, highways, and railroads (Aitken, 1967). Before Confederation, for example, the government of the Province of Canada was directly involved in the construction of canals on the St. Lawrence River, such as the Welland, Cornwall, Williamsburg, Beauharnois, and Lachine systems.

The support for canals pales in comparison to the government's subsidization of railroad construction. Under the Guarantee Act of 1849, $33 million was disbursed to the Grand Trunk Railway alone (Pomfret, 1981). Similarly, under a contract reached with the Canadian Pacific Railway in 1880, the government provided the company with $25 million in cash, 25 million acres of land, existing rail lines worth $38 million, and many other indirect subsidies (ibid.). The actual value of the subsidy to CPR in 1885 has been estimated at between $121 million and $146 million (ibid). In following decades other private railroad companies, including the Canadian Northern and Grand Trunk Pacific Railways, received similar substantial subsidies for building lines north of CPR lines.

Whether the railway subsidies were a success or failure depends on the criteria used to evaluate them. At a minimum, it can be argued that as a result of the subsidies the railways were built much earlier than would have otherwise been the case. They provided the infrastructure required for the settlement of the Prairies and movement of goods, all of which had a beneficial impact on the growth of Canadian manufacturing. But if the size of the subsidies is compared to the actual returns to government revenues resulting from them, the evaluation must be negative (ibid.). The subsidies were undoubtedly excessive, and more often than not they were used to line the pockets of powerful politicians and railroad barons – often the same people.

Another instrument the government used to assist manufacturing was the tariff on imports imposed under the National Policy of 1879. The Cayley-Galt Tariffs of 1858-59 had been the first Canadian use of tariffs as a means of not only generating revenue but also protecting Canadian manufacturing from imports. This was reflected in the differential level of tariff protection levied on goods depending on their level of processing: the average tariff on primary products was in fact reduced from 2.3 percent to 0.13 percent, that on intermediate goods was increased marginally from 5.24 percent to 7.18 percent, and that on manufactured products was increased by a much larger margin, from 12.81 percent to 19.62 percent (ibid.). A concerted effort to promote manufacturing through differential tariffs began with the National Policy, which represented a substantial increase in most existing tariffs. The spread between tariffs on inputs, now subject to between 10 to 20 percent tariffs, and on finished manufactured goods, subject to a 30 percent duty, was especially increased, clearly indicating the desire on the part of the federal government to encourage domestic production of manufactured goods by discouraging imports (ibid.). The pattern for Canadian industrialization behind high tariff walls was firmly set. It began to be eroded only after World War II, but its legacy can still be felt in Canada's existing industrial structure.

The tariffs succeeded in giving a boost to Canadian manufacturing, though perhaps at a high cost to the economy as a whole. As Richard Pomfret concludes:

Since the protective tariffs remained at high levels for much longer than normal expectations of maturity, it seems probable that the net economic effects were negative. In cases where firms became internationally competitive, they were shielded from competing imports and were able to exploit monopoly positions in the Canadian market. In other cases, inefficient firms could remain in business behind the protective tariff wall. The presumption of net economic costs from the protective tariff is generally accepted by supporters and opponents of the tariff policy alike. (Ibid., p.81)

Many of the manufacturing industries established as a result of tariff protection never really outgrew their "infancy," and, in fact, many continue to need protection to this day. They were generally small and unspecialized firms, producing a wide variety of products in short runs, and hence they were not very efficient. The higher costs of living and the corresponding lower standard of living in Canada caused by this inefficiency played a role in the net emigration to the United States that was a characteristic feature of the period around the turn of the century. The tariffs also had a differential impact on regional economies, favouring Central Canada, where manufacturing has been traditionally located, at the expense of the Maritime and Western provinces.

The emphasis on tariffs as the main instrument for assisting Canadian manufacturing continued until the end of World War II. The only new development was the greater willingness of the state to own firms directly and to provide the necessary economic infrastructure. The establishment of Ontario Hydro in 1906 for this purpose was one of the first examples of public enterprise in the English-speaking world. One of the chief reasons for its existence was to provide cheap electricity to manufacturers in Ontario. During World War I the federal government established several firms for the production of armaments and other related products. In 1919 the government established the Canadian National Railway (CNR) through the merger of most of the privately owned railroads in the country (except for those belonging to the CPR), all of them facing bankruptcy because of overexpansion during the previous decades. Over the course of World War II Ottawa established twenty-eight crown corporations, some new, others through nationalizing privately owned firms. These corporations played a critical role in the economy at the time, employing 12 percent of the total manufacturing workforce in Canada. At the end of the war, most of them were either returned to their original owners or sold to the private sector.

In the decade immediately after the war, indications of a significant change in Canada's industrial policy began to appear. While tariffs remained generally high, the acceptance of the terms of GATT represented a commitment by the Canadian government to their reduction. The period between the end of the war and the late 1950s was marked by efforts at instituting Keynesian demand-management policies, establishing new social programs, and providing strong incentives to attract foreign investments. Although Canadian governments at the provincial level continued to promote industrial expansion through direct grants, subsidies, and the provision of the necessary infrastructure, at the federal level the government shifted its strategy towards ensuring a sizable market for Canadian products. In the 1950s and 1960s this process involved augmenting the purchasing power of Canadian consumers. In the 1960s and 1970s, it involved efforts to expand international markets for Canadian goods.

By the beginning of the 1960s numerous weaknesses had become apparent in the Canadian economy, relating both to Canada's international competitiveness and to the domestic capacity for growth – weaknesses that increased with the passage of time. This led policy-makers to re-evaluate Canada's basic approach to economic and industrial development and rekindled the debate on the need for industrial strategy and the form it should take. The first major concern was the acceleration of the pace of industrial change resulting from the progressive liberalization of international trade and the rapid rate of innovation and diffusion of technology throughout the world in the postwar period. While the growing population and the opening up of export markets enlarged the potential demand for Canadian products, a large proportion of that new demand was filled by increased imports. According to one study of thirteen manufacturing industries during the 1967-81 period, increases in domestic demand and exports contributed 5.6 and 2.7 percent respectively to the total annual average increase in employment in those industries (Robertson and Grey, 1985). But these increases in employment were largely offset by employment losses of 4.1 percent and 3.6 percent resulting from increases in imports and productivity respectively for these industries during the same period. The increases in exports, imports, and productivity all created pressures on Canadian industry to improve its competitiveness, and many in business and government regarded government assistance as indispensable for this initiative.

The second concern related to the slowdown in productivity growth. Between World War II and the early 1970s, productivity growth in manufacturing had been higher in Canada than in most industrialized nations, despite the somewhat higher wages paid in Canada, because of the even higher increase in labour output. The situation deteriorated in the early 1970s when wage increases surpassed the growth in output per hour, leading to higher unit labour costs (Wilkinson, 1980). This situation continued until the early 1980s. As a result, the international competitiveness of Canadian manufacturing suffered.

A third concern arose because, beginning in the early 1960s, Canada came under intense pressure from certain Third World nations in the labour-intensive, standard-technology manufacturing sectors. The Canadian radio and television and rubber footwear industries were all but wiped out by foreign competition, while other sectors such as textiles, clothing, and leather footwear survived only because of the imposition of ad hoc protection from imports. Canadian policy-makers were well aware that the level of protection accorded to many of these vulnerable industries could not be continued forever and that they must either become internationally competitive or be eliminated. Many industrial adjustment programs were devised to modernize or rationalize the industries to equip them to face growing foreign competition.

The fourth cause for concern about Canada's industrial future was the low level of spending on R&D, which is essential for maintaining and increasing competitiveness in the long term. The gross expenditures on R&D as a percentage of the Canadian GNP, after increasing slowly in the 1960s, declined during much of the 1970s (from 1.26 percent in 1969 to 0.98 percent in 1977), and then began to rise again, reaching 1.36 percent of the GNP in 1983 (McFetridge, 1986, p.46). Canadian expenditures were low compared to those of other industrialized nations: while Canada spent 1.25 percent of its GNP on R&D in 1981, the United States spent 2.5 percent, Japan 2.4 percent, and France 2 percent (Macdonald Commission, 1985, Vol.II, p.98). In fact, Canada has one of the lowest rates of spending on R&D in the OECD. Canadian efforts in this area seemed to be seriously lagging, and the government made many efforts to overcome the perceived shortcomings.

Fifth, the lack of economies of scale in manufacturing was also a source of consternation. Compared to the huge internal markets of the United States, Japan, and the EC, Canada's domestic market is small. This problem has been aggravated by the traditionally high Canadian tariffs, which encouraged the establishment of small firms, foreign and Canadian, behind protective barriers. Most of these firms were not large enough to be internationally competitive and were not intended for international trade. There was a pressing need for government assistance towards rationalizing manufacturing and otherwise encouraging large-scale production.

Sixth, regional economic disparities and the highly regionalized nature of the Canadian industrial structure have also occasioned the need for government response. The per capita income in the Atlantic provinces has been almost 30 percent lower than the national average over the last few decades. Similar disparities are seen in unemployment rates; in fact, in some Maritime provinces the level of unemployment has been twice as high as the national average. Manufacturing activity in Canada is also highly regionalized, being heavily concentrated in Ontario and Quebec. The economies of the Western and Eastern provinces continue to be dependent on resource exports, which are highly vulnerable to international price fluctuations and result in continuous "boom and bust" cycles. The decline of many manufacturing industries because of imports from Third World countries has been disproportionately concentrated in Quebec. This has resulted in certain regions paying disproportionately high prices for Canada's efforts to reduce trade barriers and rationalize production accordingly. Many of the industrial policies since the early 1970s have been directed solely at reducing the resulting regional economic disparities.

The final concern arose from the high level of foreign, especially U.S., ownership in Canadian manufacturing, which explains many industrial policy initiatives during the 1970s. From the beginning much Canadian industrial development was financed by foreign capital, most of it at first from Britain and later most of it from the United States. What was especially disturbing was that much of the increase in foreign ownership was financed out of Canadian production. For example, of the total new U.S. investment in 1983, 30 percent was reinvested profits, 65 percent was borrowed from Canadian sources, and only 5 percent came from U.S. sources. The level of foreign investment began to decline gradually in the late 1970s as a result of numerous government measures to increase Canadian ownership in certain sectors as well as the general deterioration in the United States' own international economic position. By 1980 only 45 percent of the assets in mining and 48 percent in manufacturing were foreign-owned (McFetridge, 1986).

Much of the U.S. investment in Canada was of the direct variety, unlike the earlier British investments, which were primarily portfolio investments. *Portfolio investments* are in the form of ownership of bonds and loans and give no direct control to the investor in the day-to-day management of the borrowing firm. *Direct investments*, in contrast, give the foreign investors ownership and control over the day-to-day management of the recipient firms through the election of representatives of major shareholders to the company's board of directors. Any investing firm would certainly put its own interests ahead of those of its subsidiaries. The critics of such investments see the subsidiaries as "truncated" branch plants that do not undertake sufficient R&D or export efforts, leaving these functions to the parent firms, to the disadvantage of the Canadian economy. The "miniature replica effect" resulting from the inefficient scale of production undertaken by foreign subsidiaries is also seen as damaging to the Canadian economy as a whole. Other analysts challenge these criticisms, arguing that the foreign multinationals are the source of complex modern technology required for industrial development (McFetridge, 1986, pp.22-23).

Canadian Industrial Policies After 1960

The concerns about the pattern of Canadian industrial development occasioned numerous government interventions after 1960 – so many that an exhaustive list would be difficult to compile. In the first place it is difficult to distinguish industrial policy instruments from other economic policy instruments. Moreover, the range and nature of the programs available during the period underwent numerous changes.

The primary instruments used to assist industrial development are protection from imports, subsidies (including the subsidy components of loans), and tax benefits. The total cost of protection from imports in the form of tariffs, quotas, and other non-tariff barriers is almost impossible to calculate, but the data available for a few products can provide a rough idea. The aggregate cost to the economy for protecting the dairy industry was $286 million in 1980. For the footwear industry the annual average cost of protection between 1978 and 1983 was $13.9 million, and for the garments industry it was $163 million (Salembier et al., 1987). Similarly, the total cost of the federal and provincial subsidies to Canadian industry (excluding agriculture and services) was $98 million in 1978, $223 million in 1981, and $350 million in 1984 (ibid.). The aggregate value of the tax incentives to the manufacturing sector provides a similar picture: in constant (1971) dollars, it was $294.3 million in 1975 and $539.5 million in 1979 (ibid.). The Canadian government has clearly given generous assistance to industrial development.

International Trade Measures

Tariffs have provided progressively lower protection to Canadian industries since the mid-1960s. After the tariff cuts in 1987, more than two-thirds of imports entered Canada under no tariffs; but for the products that continued to be subject to tariffs, the Canadian rates remained somewhat higher than in other industrialized nations. The phased elimination of tariffs on imports from the United States under the Free Trade Agreement will further reduce the importance of this instrument. The export orientation of the Canadian economy and the need to secure increased access to foreign markets have motivated Canadian governments to reduce tariffs. At the same time, tariffs on certain products have been kept high to protect the industries and the jobs they have provided, which otherwise could not compete against imports. Canada relies to a small extent on quotas on imports; textiles, clothing, and agricultural products, though, are important exceptions to this rule.

Like most other nations Canada has made sustained efforts to promote its exports. Since 1970 the Export Development Corporation – which replaced the Export Credit Insurance Corporation (1944) – has existed to provide loans, loan guarantees, and export insurance to Canadian exporters. Various kinds of government assistance have also been available to Canadian exporters through the Program for Export Market Development and the Trade Commissioner Service.

Measures to Control Foreign Investment

As uneasiness about the level of foreign ownership in the Canadian economy grew in the 1960s, so too did government measures to reduce it and otherwise shape it in accordance with Canadian objectives. In 1966 the government issued the Guidelines of Good Corporate Citizenship to foreign subsidiaries operating in Canada to encourage greater contributions to the Canadian economy. The guidelines were voluntary and had no significant impact on the performance of foreign-owned firms. In 1971 the government established the Canada Development Corporation (CDC) as a holding company to provide venture capital to Canadian-owned firms and to buy back foreign subsidiaries in critical mining and manufacturing industries. By 1981 the renamed Canada Development Investment Corporation (CDIC) provided the largest pool of venture capital in the country and owned several firms in high-technology industries (Morici et al., 1982, p.60). In the early 1990s the CDIC was sold in stages to private investors.

The establishment of the Foreign Investment Review Agency (FIRA) in 1974 embodied Canada's strongest effort ever to control foreign investments. It displayed the government's shift in orientation away from buying back foreign-owned firms and towards exercising greater control over their performance. FIRA's approval was required for all new foreign investments and for the purchase of Canadian companies by foreign firms, including the purchase of existing foreign subsidiaries by other foreign firms involving assets of $250,000 or gross revenues of $3 million. The criterion for evaluating the proposed investment was its potential to bring "significant benefits to Canada." As a condition of approval, the agency could impose certain performance requirements on foreign firms, such as requiring the use of Canadian products or services or the creation of a specified number of domestic jobs. While FIRA approved well over 80 percent of the proposals submitted for review during its existence, the figures reveal neither the extent to which foreign firms avoided investments for fear that approval would be denied nor the number of proposals that had to be modified to reflect Canadian priorities.

Immediately after its election in 1984, the Tory government replaced FIRA with Investment Canada, reflecting a more welcoming attitude on the part of the new government towards foreign investments. The new agency was established to court foreign investments rather than restrict them. The threshold value of the assets acquired that were to be subject to review was raised to $5 million, and the criteria for evaluation were relaxed as well. Later the restrictions on foreign investment were further reduced as a result of the 1989 Free Trade Agreement with the United States.

Perhaps the most dramatic measure towards Canadianization ever undertaken was in the area of energy resources: the establishment of Petro-Canada in 1975 extended Canadian ownership in the industry; the unveiling of the National Energy Program in October 1980 displayed the determination of the government to control critical sectors of the economy. The program's policy objective was to achieve majority Canadian ownership of the oil and gas industry by 1990 regardless of the performance of the foreign firms, which then owned (as they still do) an overwhelming proportion of the industry. The program established a complex tax and subsidy structure to favour domestically owned firms. In addition to enhancing domestic ownership, the program kept Canadian prices of oil below world prices with the purpose of subsidizing Canadian consumers and industrial users located mainly in Central Canada. Needless to say, the foreign oil companies, which together form perhaps the single most powerful private economic group in the world, launched a massive campaign against the program. They were assisted in their efforts by the government of Alberta, which wished to capture windfall oil and gas rents and use these revenues to promote the diversification of the provincial economy. The Conservative government dismantled most of the programs that formed the National Energy Program and began working towards the privatization of Petro-Canada – again displaying its more favourable attitude towards foreign investment and its policy orientation of reduced involvement in the domestic economy.

Crown Corporations

While crown corporations, or public enterprises, enjoy a considerable degree of operating autonomy from the government, they are ultimately responsible to the government and are supposed to operate in a manner that furthers the government's stated objective in establishing and maintaining them. One of the various objectives a government might seek through crown corporations is industrial development. As Peter Morici and his co-authors put it, state investment in a crown corporation can be regarded as "an element of industrial policy only when it is undertaken to establish, maintain or accelerate the growth of a particular industry and/or support the incomes of particular labour-force groups or regions" (1982, p.57). While many crown corporations make profits for the government, this is not always their primary goal, and their operations quite often run deficits, which are borne by the government. The extent of the shortfall in revenues compared to expenditures (covered by the government) is regarded as a subsidy to the corporation.

Canada has a long history of using crown corporations as an instrument of industrial policy. Ontario Hydro is one example. Seven other provinces own similar utility companies to maintain a stable supply of relatively inexpensive electricity. Petro-Canada and CDC were established to further the goals of "Canadianizing" the economy and exploring for new oilfields. Some crown corporations, whose sole purpose seems to be to maintain employment, exist in economically depressed regions, such as Sydney Steel and the Cape Breton Development Corporation (which operates coal mines) in Nova Scotia. In some instances, the objective has been to maintain a presence in high-technology sectors – this was the case with Teleglobe Canada, Canadair, and de Havilland, all of which have been sold to private owners in recent years. Numerous other crown corporations at both the federal and provincial levels exist for a wide variety of reasons, few of them related to industrial policy. In 1980 there were 454 crown corporations in Canada; 242 of them were owned entirely by the federal government (Economic Council, 1986). They were heavily concentrated in the utilities, transportation, and communication sectors (in which they accounted for 59.5 percent of total corporate assets in 1980). They had a relatively small presence in the mining (4 percent) and the manufacturing (5.9 percent) sectors (McFetridge, 1986, p.25). Under the current Canadian governments many highly visible crown corporations began to be fully or partly sold off.

Incentives for Research and Development

While Canada's expenditure on R&D is one of the lowest among industrialized nations, the Canadian government has still spent billions of dollars over the years to encourage industrial R&D undertaken by private firms, universities, and various public and private research institutions. In the late 1970s the R&D undertaken directly by the government formed 29 percent of all such activities in the country, which was a higher rate than in most industrialized nations (Macdonald Commission, 1985, Vol. II, p. 99). In the 1980s the government made attempts to contract out its own R&D, but this did not result in any significant reduction in the government share of the total. The departments responsible for most government R&D are: Agriculture, Environment, Fisheries and Oceans, National Defence, Energy, Mines and Resources, the National Research Council, and Atomic Energy Canada Ltd. The R&D performed at Canadian universities cost $1 billion, funded almost entirely by the federal and provincial governments and forming 20 percent of the total R&D in the country in 1983 (ibid., p.101).

Most R&D in Canada, however, is performed by private firms. Their expenditures formed 55 percent of the total, which was 14 percentage points higher than in the 1960s (ibid., p.102). But the costs were not borne entirely by the firms conducting them; the companies received generous government subsidies and tax benefits. About 13 percent of the private sector's total R&D expenditures were paid for by government grants and subsidies, excluding tax incentives (the government's share would increase even further if tax incentives were included). In 1983-84 federal R&D payments to Canadian industry, mostly in the form of grants and contracts, amounted to $461.5 million, an increase from $187.6 million in 1977-78 (ibid.). A large proportion of the R&D expenditures have been eligible for tax credits, which meant tax savings of $203.4 million to those firms involved in 1982.

Industrial Adjustment Measures

Canadian industry has recently faced tremendous adjustment pressures from imports, shifts in demand, and the obsolescence of many domestically manufactured products. Pressures to adjust to changed circumstances affect both capital and labour. While labour finds adjustment more difficult, and hence needs more government assistance, most adjustment programs have been directed at firms. The underlying rationale for this is that the adjustment of private companies will lead automatically to the adjustment of their employees. Adjustment assistance to firms usually takes the form of loans, loan guarantees, and grants, usually available for the purpose of modernizing and rationalizing plants and undertaking additional marketing efforts. While the firms are attempting to adjust the government has sometimes provided quota protection from imports to provide breathing space.

A firm faced with the need for adjustment has three options:
- to exit, by winding down its operation altogether or entering another line of business;
- to revitalize itself, by modernizing and rationalizing its operation to become competitive; or
- to seek government protection to shield it from adjustment pressures.

Exit by firms is a constant feature of any growing economy, and no government seeks to prevent it altogether, despite the social dislocations that result. The Economic Council has estimated that 40 percent of the firms operating in the average manufacturing industry in 1970 had left the industry by 1979 (Economic Council, 1988a, p.7). Revitalization is the preferred option from society's point of view: it preserves jobs without introducing inefficiencies in the economy; and rejuvenation results in enhanced competitiveness. But revitalization is expensive because it involves modernization of plants and adoption of modern management techniques and additional marketing efforts. The costs of modernization may be too high for firms to bear on their own, and hence the government often assists them, financially and otherwise. However, while revitalization is the most desirable objective from society's point of view, the most rational objective for any firm is to seek protection from adjustment and thereby save itself the hardships of exit or the expenses of modernization.

Many of the industrial adjustment programs in Canada are coupled with regional development or R&D expenditures, making them difficult to catalogue. Some industrial adjustment programs have been generally available to all eligible industries, while others are directed specifically at certain industries recognized as needing special attention. The Industrial and Regional Development Program (IRDP), which consolidated a host of similar existing programs, was the most important industrial adjustment program when it was established in 1983. It provided grants, loans, and loan guarantees to needy firms to help cover the costs of innovation, plant establishment or modernization and expansion, marketing, and restructuring. Each proposal was examined against certain specified criteria to determine the nature and amount of assistance. In 1984-85 the estimated government expenditure under this program was $470 million (Macdonald Commission, Vol.II, p.147).

Industry-specific adjustment programs have included the Pulp and Paper Modernization Program (PPMP), the Shipbuilding Industry Assistance Program (SIAP), and the Canadian Industrial Renewal Program

(CIRP). The PPMP, designed to assist in the modernization of pulp and paper plants, cost the government (both federal and provincial, since it was a joint program) $542 million over the 1979-84 period (Economic Council, 1988a, p.20). The SIAP was directed at subsidizing construction of new vessels and modernization of shipyards. Between 1975 and 1985 the federal government spent $480 million under the program; $426 million was for vessel construction and only a small amount for modernization (Economic Council, 1988a). The program was discontinued, but other kinds of assistance continue to be available to the industry under various programs. The CIRP was available to the textile, clothing, footwear, and tanning industries between 1981 and 1986. Its main thrust, as indicated by its expenditure pattern, was towards plant modernization and industry restructuring, which received $364 million during the life of the program.

Labour Adjustment Measures

Labour, with its more severe problem of adjustment, faces difficulties not only when employing firms become uncompetitive against imports or when demand for products drops, but also when firms increase their competitiveness by adopting capital-intensive (often labour-displacing) production techniques. Even at times when the number of jobs in the economy as a whole or in a particular industry is increasing, there are still industries and firms that are reducing employment. Thus, while the annual average growth in employment in trade-sensitive industries was 0.65 percent during the 1967-81 period, the leather, textiles, knitting, and clothing industries suffered an annual average decline of almost 1 percent (Robertson and Grey, 1985, p.186).

Two broad types of labour adjustment measures are available to Canadian workers: general programs that are available to individuals in need of adjustment assistance (regardless of the region or industrial sector they are located in); and programs directed specifically at individual workers in particular regions or industries faced with an unusual degree of adjustment. The first category covers most of the available programs and includes Unemployment Insurance, Canada Mobility Programs, Canada Manpower Industrial Training Program, Critical Trade Skills Training Program, and placement services provided by local Canada Employment Centres. These are continuing programs that provide various kinds of assistance to individual workers who meet certain eligibility criteria.

The specialized programs are directed at workers who need additional assistance that cannot be met by the regular programs. The categories include older workers, workers in economically depressed communities, and workers employed in industries experiencing decline. The Adjustment Assistance Benefits Program was established in 1971 (subsequently modified in 1982 and renamed the Labour Adjustment Benefits Program) to provide preretirement benefits to older workers in textiles, clothing, footwear, and tanning industries who would be unable to find employment in different communities, industries, or occupations. In 1981 the government announced its Industry and Labour Adjustment Program (ILAP) designed for workers in designated economically depressed communities. While the program had a significant industrial adjustment component, the labour adjustment component provided enriched (that is, more benefits than those available to all workers) training and mobility assistance, wage subsidies to employers, and direct job creation measures. The Canadian Industrial Renewal Program (CIRP), established in 1981, assisted workers in the textiles, clothing, footwear, and tanning industries regardless of where they were located, unlike the ILAP, which was available only in designated communities. Otherwise it paid the same benefits as the ILAP. The ILAP was closed down in 1984 and the CIRP in 1986.

These special programs were extremely expensive to operate. For instance, the Labour Adjustment Benefits Program entailed an expenditure of $60,000 per recipient (Robertson and Grey, 1985, p.191). Similarly, the labour adjustment components of ILAP entailed the expenditure of $97 million between 1981 and 1983, and the CIRP entailed expenditure of $51.3 million between 1981 and 1986. The federal government of the late 1980s-early 1990s discontinued most of the special labour adjustment programs because of their high costs.

Regional Development Measures

In Canada many of the industrial development programs have had an inseparable regional development component. Moreover, there are many regional assistance programs whose main purpose is not to aid regional development but to compensate individuals and provincial governments in the poorer regions for their lower income and high unemployment. Programs administered by the Department of Regional Industrial Expansion (DRIE) prior to 1990 and the Department of Regional Economic Expansion (DREE) before 1982 can be broadly regarded as industrial development measures in the economically disadvantaged regions. The average annual expenditure by DREE during the 1968-73 period was $235.2 million; during 1973-81 it was $486.3 million; and between 1981 and 1983 it was $484.4 million (Lithwick, 1987, p.150). Many of these expenditures were directed at encouraging new firms to locate in depressed regions or at modernizing and expanding existing firms in the regions. Large as the DREE expenditures were, they are insignificant compared to compensatory fiscal transfers to the provinces. DREE expenditures formed only 5.9 percent (1968-73), 4.3 percent (1973-81), and 2.5 percent (1981-85) of the total federal transfers to provinces, municipalities, and individual citizens and families (ibid.). Thus, compensatory fiscal transfer payments rather than economic or industrial development have formed the main thrust of the federal regional development programs.

Provincial Industrial Policies

The division of powers between the federal and provincial governments and the fragmentation of business and labour along provincial lines are reflected once again in the area of industrial policy. Parallel to the federal government's industrial policies, the provincial governments maintain their own industrial policies to promote development within their borders. While not quite as sophisticated or extensive as Ottawa's policies, these provincial efforts are by no means insignificant. The increase in the provinces' financial capacities and administrative resources in the 1960s and 1970s ensured that they would undertake to expand their industrial bases. Quite often their programs were inspired by their desire to resist what they saw as the adverse effects of national economic policies on their provincial economies. As the Macdonald Commission concluded, "The provinces' industrial policies varied with their economic conditions and needs, their available resources, the ideologies of their government, and the pressures that private interests brought to bear on their leaders" (1985, Vol. II, p.143).

The Western provinces' industrial policies were designed to reduce their dependence on exports of unprocessed natural resources and to diversify their economic base. The Central Canadian provinces were more concerned with maintaining the competitiveness of their traditional manufacturing industries and with promoting high-tech industries. Quebec has also sought to enhance the francophone presence in the economy. For the Atlantic provinces, the objective was usually to attract any kind of manufacturing activity. Towards these objectives, the provinces have employed the full panoply of industrial policy instruments, including grants, loans at below-market rates, corporate tax incentives, preferential government procurement from local suppliers, subsidized electricity, and ownership of provincial crown corporations (Jenkin, 1983). While provincial industrial policies have no doubt added to the incoherence of industrial policies in Canada and introduced economic inefficiencies by vying for industries regardless of their competitiveness, it is generally agreed that their effects, beneficial or otherwise, have been local. The federal government has continued to maintain its dominance in the industrial development field, and its policy has the strongest effects. According to one estimate, federal transfers to business for economic development are almost three times as large as those of all ten provinces combined (McFetridge, 1985, p.12).

Canadian Industrial Strategy After 1970

There has been no dearth, then, of industrial policies in Canada. But a collection of policies does not necessarily make an industrial strategy. There is a general consensus among analysts that Canada has no coherent industrial strategy. As one commentator concludes rather bluntly, "No sane individual would or could construct the barrage of industrial policies that presently exist in Canada, with their duplication, overlap, unknown inter-action and unmeasured effect" (McFetridge, 1985, p.2). In fact, in the prewar period, when the phrase "industrial strategy" was yet to be coined, government policies displayed more coherence than they do now.

Tariffs and the construction of transportation infrastructures were the main vehicles of industrial development until World War I. At the time, however, the policy-makers hardly realized that they were engaged in what would later be called an industrial strategy. As Michael Bliss rightly points out:

> One of the most common views of nineteenth century industrial policies is that the major policies . . . coalesced or cohered into or were planned as part of one grand national development strategy, usually called the National Policy. . . . In fact . . . the term "National Policy" was used by politicians who invented it to refer to the policy of tariff protection. . . . Throughout the nineteenth century the term did not refer to the other national development policies. (1982, p.16)

Bliss also notes (p.18) that the

> aggregation of national policies [by economic historians] into one National Policy tends to obscure the piecemeal, ad hoc, and sometimes contradictory way in which policies were developed by real politicians dealing with real problems on a day-to-day basis. As well, by linking all of the national policies with the prosperity generated in the decades just before World War I, the view shades into a whiggish judgement that late-nineteenth century policy making was vindicated by national economic success.

Whether the policy-makers understood the ramifications of their actions or not, the National Policy tariffs had the effect of nurturing the establish-ment of indigenous manufacturing industries behind tariff walls and fostered the immigration of foreign companies to evade them. Later histo-rians have categorized this strategy as one of *import-substitution industrialization*.

While free trade as a major issue died with the 1911 elections, tariff protection of Canadian manufacturing industries continued for many dec-ades to come. There were always some in business and government who supported the lowering of the level of protection while others supported its continuation. During the 1930s, in the midst of depression, there was talk of employing new instruments to boost industrial development, but the debate was not yet conducted in terms of industrial strategy. In the period immediately after World War II, the debate revolved around Keynesian demand-management and the need to attract foreign investments to Can-ada, while the familiar controversies about the wisdom of lowering tariffs, which were slated for reduction under GATT, declined in significance.

The first serious debate on the need for an industrial strategy began in the late 1950s when the effects of the liberalization of international trade and the emergence of Japan as an aggressive exporter began to be visible. However, the main force behind the debate was the growing concern about U.S. ownership of the Canadian economy. The Gordon Commission's Report in 1957 drew attention to the adverse effects of foreign investments on the Canadian economy and the need to control them. Despite a lot of talk and some feeble attempts, however, little was done to implement the report until the mid-1960s.

In 1968 the Watkins Report argued along the same lines as the Gordon Commission. This was followed by the report of the House of Commons Committee on External Affairs and National Defence (the Wahn Report) in 1970, which also sought restrictions on foreign investment and advocated 51 percent Canadian ownership of major foreign subsidiaries. In 1972 the Gray Report (named after Herbert Gray, a long-serving cabinet minister in the Trudeau government) was published, the last of the series of economic policy documents inspired by economic nationalism and concentrating on foreign investment in Canada. It spelled out the dangers of concentrating on staples exports and pointed out that foreign subsidiaries in the manufacturing sector had "less opportunity for innovation and entrepreneurship, fewer export sales, fewer supporting services, less training of Canadian personnel in various skills, and less specialized product development aimed at Canadian needs or tastes." It recommended strict screening processes for all foreign investment and the drawing up of government guidelines to compel foreign firms to operate in a manner conducive to Canada's national interest. The federal Liberal government was not sympathetic to most of its proposals. However, relying upon NDP support in a minority government situation, the Liberals did establish FIRA to screen foreign investment.

The debate on industrial policy during the 1970s was less obsessed with foreign investment and displayed more understanding of the problems of Canadian manufacturing. The 1972 announcement by Jean Luc Pépin, the Minister of Industry, Trade and Commerce, that the federal government would develop a general national industrial strategy marked a high point in Canada's efforts to devise such an initiative. Pépin declared: "My Department and I are committed to try and produce an industrial strategy for Canada. . . . The strategy [will] embrace all sectors of economic activity from resources to services but must emphasize manufacturing and processing" (French, 1980, pp.105-106). As it turned out, this was no more than a pious hope. Pépin was soon out of the cabinet, and his successors favoured not a comprehensive industrial strategy, but rather "a coherent set of industrial policies," particularly "strategies for sectors on an industry-to-industry" basis (ibid., p.107). The move away from the idea of developing a comprehensive strategy covering all sectors reflected the difficulties of devising a policy that met all the divergent needs and interests.

In the mid-1970s the debate was conducted most vigorously between two semi-autonomous government bodies: the Economic Council and the Science Council of Canada. The Economic Council had by this time concluded that there was little hope for any significant change in Canada's industrial position in the near future and recommended bilateral free trade with the United States and a non-interventionist policy (Economic Council, 1975). In contrast, the Science Council blamed foreign investment for Canada's industrial malaise and recommended a highly interventionist government policy in support of Canadian-owned industries, especially in the high-technology sector (Britton and Gilmour, 1978). The two bodies continue to be rivals in the debate on the Canadian industrial strategy.

In 1977 the federal government showed a renewed interest in formulating an industrial strategy. It established twenty-three task forces, each dealing with a different economic sector (twenty-one in manufacturing, the others in construction and tourism) and consisting of business, labour, academic, federal, and provincial representatives. The reports of these task forces formed the basis for a final report by a so-called "Tier II" committee, also consisting of representatives from business, labour, and academia. The final report, published in 1982, was no more than a patchwork of compromises among the self-serving demands of the twenty-three sectors. The government, not surprisingly, made no serious attempt to implement the report.

In 1980-82 two other alternative industrial policy documents appeared to compete for acceptance by the government. One was by Herb Gray, as federal Minister of Industry, Trade and Commerce, and it contained many of the same recommendations on foreign investment as in his earlier report, except that it had an additional emphasis on the need to support research and development activity and high-technology industries in the country. The other proposal was contained in the Ministry of State for Economic Development's "Medium Term Track" position paper put out in 1982. In contrast to the Gray proposal, this paper emphasized the resource sector and recommended a policy that was not particularly interventionist. It argued that Canada had a comparative advantage in extracting and processing resource products and must concentrate only on those products and on the manufacturing industries directly related to them.

The Blair-Carr Committee's Task Force on Major Projects report, *Major Projects for Canada* (1981), also became a serious contender for acceptance. It concentrated on energy and resource-related "megaprojects" and prepared an inventory of projects spread across all regions. The projects were to be completed by the end of the century at a total cost of $440 billion. The report contained numerous other recommendations to maximize the benefits accruing from resource development, to distribute the development equitably among regions, and to ensure Canadian control in the sectors to be developed.

Thus, in 1981, when the government set out to announce its economic development strategy, it had before it a wide variety of recommendations. The strategy that eventually emerged and was presented to Parliament in November 1981 contained three main elements (Canada, 1980).

- It proposed to emphasize the natural-resource sector, with the manufacturing sector being encouraged mainly to "supply machinery, equipment and material needed for resource development and to extend the future processing of resource products beyond the primary state."
- It stated that resource development offered better opportunities for equitable regional development than would be possible through development of manufacturing.
- It recommended that the surplus generated from resource development could be employed to finance the industrial restructuring that would be necessary to make Canadian manufacturing industries internationally competitive.

The government's *Economic Strategy for Canada* statement was a classic compromise among the various contending proposals that had been on the table over the decade. It represented a half-way measure between interventionist and free market approaches, between nationalist and continentalist approaches, and between proposals that emphasized manufacturing and those that emphasized the resource sector. In any case, the onset of economic recession in 1982 (the worst since the Great Depression of the 1930s) and the parallel collapse of international commodity prices made the strategy irrelevant as a policy guide – it had been based on the necessity for continued high prices for Canadian natural resources, and especially oil and gas resources, as a means to finance the major project investments. Little was heard of the strategy in subsequent years.

As a result, more than two decades of effort and billions of dollars in state expenditures on promoting industrial development had little to show for themselves in terms of a coherent and consistent industrial strategy. The Canadian economy remained as dependent as ever on the export of natural resources, and the economically disadvantaged regions remained as dependent as ever on federal transfer payments. The only measure of success was achieved in the area of reducing the level of foreign ownership in the Canadian economy. Even the utility of this achievement, however, appeared dubious as Canada scrambled for investments to boost its economy in the midst of the 1982 recession. Studies by the Economic Council and OECD continued to hammer home the point that the state was incapable of improving upon the performance of the market, and that the best that it could do was to promote "positive adjustment" to market changes. The same Trudeau government that had displayed tremendous confidence in the state's ability to solve social and economic problems in its early years had run out of ideas in its final years in power.

In this context the government established the Macdonald Commission to report on Canada's economic prospects and the government's role in the economy. The Liberal Party lost the 1984 election, and the Conservatives won on a pro-market platform. The Macdonald Commission presented its report in 1985, and the general thrust of its recommendations was in line with the new government's thinking, even though it had apparently arrived at its conclusions independently.

Inspired by the reasoning of liberal political economy, the Macdonald Commission took the promotion of economic efficiency as the primary goal of its recommendations. In the context of industrial development, this meant promoting the domestic and international competitiveness of the Canadian economy. In the commission's words, "Concern for productivity and competitiveness has been a compelling theme . . . and we are convinced that their significant improvement must be the fundamental objective of our future industrial policy" (Macdonald Commission, 1985, Vol. II, p.185). Its recommendations were geared towards allowing market forces to determine the allocation of economic resources, without state intervention. It was especially opposed to pursuing the strategy of "picking winners." It argued:

> In view of the practical difficulties of developing a targeted approach to industrial policy, this Commission does not recommend such an approach for Canada. Rapidly changing international and domestic circumstances demand a highly flexible and adaptive economic system; it is very doubtful whether governments can respond to such situations better than private enterprise can. (Ibid., p.184)

In line with its commitment to economic efficiency, the commission recommended free trade with the United States. It reasoned: "Increased competition from the world in general, and the United States in particular, would work powerfully to induce Canadians to allocate our human, capital and natural resources in ways that would improve the country's productivity" (ibid., p.201).

The Mulroney government, while not explicitly stating that it was following the commission's recommendations, has followed a similar pro-market industrial policy. It has privatized several crown corporations, reduced the level of regulations in certain sectors, does not talk about the need to develop an integrated industrial strategy, and, most importantly, signed the Free Trade Agreement with the United States. Critics of its policies abound, as do supporters. But even this government has not been able to wash its hands of interventions in the industrial development process. It too has had to establish many programs to meet the special needs of the different regions and different sections of the economy. But they have been for the most part ad hoc, and the government has not tried to rationalize them in terms of a general industrial strategy.

Constraints on the Formulation of Industrial Strategies

The persistent failure to formulate a cohesive industrial strategy in Canada is understandable given the country's institutional constraints. The organization of the Canadian state and society, in addition to the structure of the domestic and international political economy, makes the formulation of a strategy for industrial development an enormously difficult task. These institutions condition what can or cannot be done, as well as the degree of coherence that can obtain among the various measures.

The first constraint that the formulation of industrial strategy in Canada faces is the structure of the Canadian economy. An industrial strategy that does not give primacy to the export interests of Canada's natural-resource industries is unthinkable. It is similarly unthinkable to have a strategy that ignores the manufacturing sector, whose weaknesses occasioned the search for an industrial strategy in the first place. But reconciling the interests of the two sectors is not easy, given the contradictory nature of their interests. The regional nature of the Canadian economy imposes similar constraints on the policy-makers, insofar as it is difficult to reconcile the interests of the various regions in a single industrial strategy. Measures to promote industrial development are almost invariably viewed as favouring one region at the expense of others.

The second constraint is rooted in the international political economy. International agreements such as GATT and the FTA limit what the government can do to aid its domestic industries. Opting out of the agreements is not a viable option, because although they restrict Canada's options they also protect its interests. Moreover, the middle-power status that Canada enjoys in the international arena limits its say in shaping the international political economy. The actions of the main actors on the world scene – the United States, the EC, and Japan – are particularly severe for Canada, given its higher degree of trade dependence. Moreover, Canada's position as an exporter of primary products, with their highly fluctuating prices determined on the international market, undermines the state's capacity to make predictions for the future, which is essential for the development of a coherent strategy. The industrial strategy announced in 1981, based as it was on the optimistic forecasts for the resource sector, floundered as commodity prices collapsed in the following year.

The third constraint on policy-makers is the organization of the state. The existence of provinces with their own governments and business and labour interests produces mini-states of sorts, which pursue their own industrial development. While provincial industrial policies have not posed a major problem so far, the federal government's need to balance the interests of the various provinces has added to the incoherence of its broader industrial strategy.

The fourth constraint relates to the organization of labour in Canada. The divisions between industrial and craft-based unions, between U.S. and Canadian-affiliated unions, and between the labour employed in exporting industries and the labour employed in the import-competing industries obviously do not make for a unity of interests within the Canadian labour movement. Each has its own sectional interests, which often override the interests of labour as a whole and prevent it from using its collective strength to pressure the state and business to pursue policies beneficial to labour. The lack of a strong trade union central, the localized nature of union activity, and the existence of large numbers of unorganized workers prevent labour from taking a strong position on many outstanding policy issues or from pursuing the stands it does take in a united and consistent manner.

The fifth constraint shaping the pattern of Canadian industrial policy and its incohesive nature is the organization of capital. The divisions between finance and industrial capital, between staples-exporting and import-competing businesses, and between foreign-owned subsidiaries and indigenously controlled firms make the formulation of policies to meet joint interests difficult to accomplish. Government policies nevertheless often reflect the intention to satisfy all of them, or at least not to antagonize any of them. The lack of a strong national business organization that could aggregate the competing interests of the conflicting capitalist factions does not help the situation.

Although the Canadian state has participated actively in industrial development since the last century, the purpose of the intervention has been to supplement rather than supplant the market. Huge subsidies – in the form of grants, tax incentives, tariffs and quotas on imports, regulation of foreign investments, and so on – have been directed towards the domestic manufacturing industry to artificially boost its international competitiveness. All the money and effort spent on strengthening the manufacturing sector, however, have produced few results. There has been no significant change in the competitiveness of Canadian manufacturing as a result of the government's assistance. By the 1970s it was recognized that the lack of cohesion, that is, the lack of a consistent strategy, was responsible for the ineffectiveness of many individual government measures. But the ensuing efforts to devise a coherent industrial strategy led to naught – largely thanks to the constraints imposed by the structure of the domestic economy, international political economy, and the fragmented internal organization of the state, labour, and capital.

CHAPTER 12

Conclusion: The Political Economy of Canadian Capitalism

We set out in this text to accomplish two goals: first, to describe the functioning of the Canadian political economy and discuss why it operates as it does; second, to use this information to answer questions about the capacity of Canadian governments to deal with an emerging series of new challenges. Defining political economy as the mix of state and market, we have focused on the historical evolution of ideas and institutions related to the development of state and market structures in Canada.

We soon found that the two general theories in political economy – liberal and socialist – both undertheorize the state; that is, they undermine the importance of the state as an independent organization. Both theories construct general models of market-based societies and deductively analyze existing political economies to fulfil their theoretical expectations. The result is often the generation of ill-founded prescriptions for the reorganization of state and market interactions.

Most liberal theorists view the state as an inert institution that is called in to correct the failings of the market. The recent theoretical contributions by the neoconservatives and post-Keynesians bridge this shortcoming to a certain degree, but generate other problems in its place. The neoconservatives regard the democratic state as excessively interventionist, and hence inefficient, and see the solution in restricting the responsiveness of the state to popular pressures. The post-Keynesians diagnose the critical problems in the political economies of the industrialized nations as resting in the organization of both the state and market institutions. They call for concerted action by state, capital, and labour to resolve the problems – although they often fail to realize that this action might not be possible for historical reasons pertaining to the fragmentation of these actors.

The socialist theory, by viewing the state as merely an extension of the dominant classes in the society, commits the same mistake of not recognizing the autonomous role of the state. Even the neo-Marxists, who do recognize the state's relative autonomy from class interests, are not able to overcome the problem entirely because of their fundamental theoretical precepts, which locate the determinants of state activities in the structural imperatives of a capitalist mode of production. Their argument tends to be remarkably circular: in essence they say the state is both autonomous and constantly working towards furthering the long-term interests of capital.

Both the liberal and socialist theories are ideological projects. The chief objective of liberal political economy is to extend the market system and, by implication, to support those who benefit from it the most, the owners of capital. They work to accomplish this by arguing for the superiority of the market and for the restriction of the state's role in it. While the liberal theory has permitted an increasingly larger role for the modern state, that role is still meant to be supplementary to the market. Thus, liberal political economy is a powerful ideological device for researching, imposing, and justifying the strengthening of capitalism. The most important problems encountered by such a prescriptive, deductive approach is the proclivity to mould the observation of realities to match those projected by theory. The analysis is often manipulated to sustain the elegance of theoretical assumptions and fit the rules of formal logic rather than to understand the true nature of the phenomenon under consideration.

Socialist political economy has its own problems, since it too is a deductive and prescriptive theory. Socialist analyses lead to conclusions that seek to further the interests of labour or, at minimum, loosely defined anticapitalist forces. Its ultimate objective is to facilitate the transition from an exploitative capitalist system to a socialist order. As a theory of radical restructuring of the existing order, socialist political economy has had a much larger agenda than liberal political economy, including the critique of existing society, the theorization of its replacement, and the theorization of the transition from the old to the new. This conceptualization has aroused the ire not only of Liberals but also of numerous other theorists who argue that class exploitation is only one form of domination characteristic of capitalist society and that other groups are also oppressed and may in fact be more progressive than the easily co-opted working class – for example, women or members of new social movements concerned with peace, civil rights, or the environment (Cohen, 1982; Roemer, 1986).

Liberal political economy, of course, denies that it furthers the interests of the propertied class. It claims to arrive at universally valid generalizations on the basis of a strictly logical application of immutable principles of human behaviour. Although usually not willing to engage socialist political economy in direct debate, liberal political economy tends to depict socialist political economy as at best well-intentioned and at worst mistaken, ill-informed, cynical, and malicious. In the best-case scenario, socialist political economy is portrayed as retaining laudable moral imperatives for such issues as justice, equality, and fairness that a "pure science" such as liberal political economy cannot engage with (Lindblom, 1977). In this scenario, socialist political economy is usually condemned not for its aims or goals, but for the inadequacy of the means by which it intends to accomplish its stated goals – means such as planning, centralization of decision-making, or a one-party state (Lindblom, 1977; Nove, 1983). In the worst-case scenario, socialist political economy is portrayed as a partial and ill-conceived analysis, which, in replacing the individual with classes as the primary unit of analysis, leads inevitably to the replacement of the general good or public interest by class interests (Flathman, 1966). This replacement of the general interest by class interests inevitably leads to dictatorship, police states, and totalitarianism, which, it is argued, run counter to the entire tradition of Western political, moral, and ethical development (Hayek, 1944). Socialist political economists, on the other hand, insist that the socialist project simply replaces the interests of the capitalist class with that of another class, and they tend to reject the concept of a general will or public interest (Arendt, 1958; Marcuse, 1958; Fehér, 1983).

For the most part staples political economists in Canada have avoided the propensity of socialists and liberals to apply general theories to the examination of the Canadian political economy. While they too underestimated the role of the state in the Canadian economy – by viewing it as a byproduct of the exigencies of international trade – they advanced the discussion of the market found in liberal and socialist analyses by focusing on the specific nature of production found in Canada, particularly the continued dependence of the economy on the export of natural resources. In doing so they highlighted aspects of the Canadian political economy that had been ignored or glossed over by many liberal and socialist analyses.

The staples approach lost its chief strength, its empirical orientation, when it was revived in the early 1970s, especially when it became linked to dependency theory in its post-Innisian version. The objective of analysis shifted to reducing U.S. control of the Canadian economy rather than to monitoring and detailing the operation of the Canadian political economy itself. The state and capital in Canada were simply assumed to be instruments of U.S. interests. This particular staples approach became increasingly untenable as the international economic position of the United States itself began to wane and investment patterns shifted. By the late 1980s, on an annual basis, Canadian investment in the United States began to exceed U.S. investment coming to Canada.

These are difficult times for political economists, in Canada and elsewhere. Socialist theory, and the extended role it prescribes for the state, stands discredited as the East Europeans march with vehemence towards establishing market institutions (Przeworski, 1991). The staples approach has degenerated into a somewhat crude anti-Americanism and resists efforts to resurrect it (Clement and Williams, 1989; Pal, 1989). It has been marginalized by the increasing interpenetration of the Canadian and U.S. economies as a result of trade liberalization under GATT and, since 1989, under the Canada-U.S. Free Trade Agreement.

The contemporary discourse in political economy is perhaps more narrowly confined than ever before. Virtually all alternatives at the centre of the public agenda are grounded in liberal political economy. At the theoretical level, the most lively debate is between the neoconservatives, who unabashedly admire the market and abhor state intervention, and the post-Keynesians, who call for an expanded role for the state in guiding the economy.

Neoconservatism is evident in the publications not only of the Fraser Institute, which is to be expected, but also of respected think-tanks such as the Economic Council of Canada and the C.D. Howe Institute. All of these groups have called for the curtailment of state expenditures and a re-emphasis on markets.

In opposition to the neoconservatives stand the post-Keynesians. This group includes adherents of virtually all of the various competing perspectives on Canadian political economy – Liberal Keynesians, social democrats, New Staples theorists, and even neo-Innisians. The common theme that runs through their works is that the state ought to play a larger role in the functioning of the economy. In a liberal vein, the former federal deputy minister of finance, Ian Stewart, has argued that for practical and ethical reasons there is a need to establish a new social consensus around an expanded role for the state in the provision of public goods and the protection of the citizenry against the adverse effects of globalism and continental integration (Stewart, 1990). Recent publications by prominent social democrats and neo-Innisians such as Daniel Drache (Drache and Gertler, 1991), James Laxer (1984), John Richards (Richards and Cairns, 1991), and Abe Rotstein (1984) are significant because they not only espouse a strong state presence in the economy but also a greater role for domestic and international market forces.

Regardless of what the various theories of political economy prescribe as the state's appropriate role in society, what matters ultimately is its capacity to arrive at decisions and implement them (Hall and Ikenberry, 1989, pp.96-97). That is why we have so closely examined the organization of the state and the societal constraints and opportunities it encounters. Our analysis indicates the weakness and limited policy capacity of the Canadian state. As such, those liberal, socialist, and staples analyses that base their political-economic theory on the assumption of a strong state capable of influencing or controlling the general direction of Canadian society are simply off the mark.

In examining the nature of the Canadian state and its activities from a neoinstitutional perspective and assessing the nature of the constraints placed on government activities by the organization of the domestic and international political economies, we have indicated several areas in which theorists argue that opportunities exist for further state action in the organization of production and distribution. Whether or not these opportunities can be realized depends on the ability of the state to mobilize societal support for its activities or – and this amounts to the same thing – whether or not the state is capable of overcoming societal resistance to the activities it chooses to pursue. The answer to this question depends largely on the extent to which the state is capable of designing and implementing its own policies in the face of opposing societal pressures. This question of state autonomy is a complex one: it is not only a function of the organizational capacity of the state, but it is also directly dependent on the organizational capacity of other major social actors.

In considering the question of the organizational capacity of state and societal actors – focusing on the two major societal actors found in every capitalist economy, business and labour – we have noted that the Canadian state is fragmented along a number of lines. Executive authority in Canada is fragmented because of the operation of the federal system and the difficulties encountered by political executives in controlling and directing large administrative apparatuses. While it is possible to overcome the fragmentations arising from federalism, this can be accomplished only through a complex and time-consuming process of intergovernmental collaboration and consultation. The federal and provincial governments in Canada are capable of organizing autonomous initiatives within their jurisdictions, but they are severely handicapped in dealing with areas affecting the entire country, except in times of crises such as war.

While Canada has a weak state, it is not the case that this state lacks autonomy altogether. This is because labour and capital in Canada are also poorly organized and fragmented. Labour, especially, is for the most part unorganized, and those elements that are organized are divided into numerous small local unions. It must also cope with separate regulatory regimes at the federal and provincial levels and according to the representation of private and public sector workers. And it has a historical legacy of divisions along international-national and skilled-unskilled lines. In addition, the labour movement has only succeeded in unionizing about one-third of the workforce. The small number of unionized workers are affiliated to at least six central organizations, each of them claiming to speak authoritatively on behalf of all labour. Although capable of placing real pressure on governments through job action in certain sectors, labour remains weak as a political actor and incapable of influencing the direction of state policy. In fact, labour is more successful in the negative sense of being capable of thwarting a proposed measure than in participating constructively in the policy process.

Capital in Canada is also fragmented, divided sectorally and in terms of domestic and foreign ownership. The divisions are exacerbated by the existence of a number of business associations claiming to speak for capital. The lack of a strong business organization that cuts across sectors leaves it up to large firms to deal directly with the state. The cumulative result of state measures in response to demands by individual firms is disjointed policies.

The situation in Canada, then, is one of a weak state, weak labour, and weak capital. This allows the state some autonomy in its activities, and much more autonomy when federal-provincial divisions are overcome through intergovernmental co-ordination. But the exercise of this autonomy is not as consistent or cohesive as it could be if weak business and weak labour were to face a strong state.

The Canadian state's role in the areas of industrial development and fiscal and monetary management illustrates the effects of the organizational weaknesses of state, capital, and labour in Canada and the constraints imposed by the organization of the domestic and international political economies. Efforts to develop forward-looking and cohesive industrial strategies have failed because of the inability of the state to overcome resistance from capital or to fashion some sort of coalition among the different factions of the Canadian business community supporting specific industrial policy measures. Similarly, efforts by the state to develop well co-ordinated fiscal and monetary management regimes have failed as a result of divisions between capital and labour over whether the primary aim of such efforts should be the control of inflation or the elimination of unemployment and the preservation of the social wage. They have failed especially because of the inability of Canadian governments to control events occurring in the international political economy. The result has been that Canadian government activities have had an uncoordinated, ad hoc, and incremental effect on markets, except in wartime when the state has overcome its own divisions and been able to impose its plans on reluctantly acquiescent capital and labour.

As a result of this empirical study, it is apparent that the strategies proposed by the currently dominant theoretical analyses of the Canadian political economy are suspect. Any fundamental state-based restructuring of the Canadian political economy – whether this would involve radically augmenting or diminishing the role of the state – is unlikely to occur. Instead, it is much more likely that the Canadian state will respond to societal problems and concerns in much the same way as it has in the past; that is, through a process of ad hoc, incremental, and reactive change.

While this might appear to be an entirely negative situation, some analysts take solace from the fact that despite its record of failed state interventions, the market-driven Canadian political economy has still managed to provide most Canadians with a high quality of life by international standards. In fact, during much of the late 1980s Canada experienced an enviable economic performance among industrialized nations. Analysts also point approvingly to the fact that in the past the state has been able to overcome its own divisions and societal resistance when it counted the most, in times of major political and economic crises.

What concerns many Canadians, though, is that past performance is not necessarily a guarantee of future success. They point to the fact that Canada's wealth has been based on resource production and note that this situation will not last forever, because many resources are finite while others are expensive to renew. They see few signs of the Canadian political economy being able to overcome problems of resource exhaustion and transform itself into some other kind of economy. They have little hope that a process of incremental, reactive policy-making can accomplish this end.

The adverse effects of trade liberalization also cannot be taken lightly. Liberalized international trade is a two-edged sword. It allows the importation of goods if they are produced more cheaply abroad, thus benefiting less well-off consumers. At the same time, import competition from low-wage countries exerts downward pressure on wages, especially in low-technology manufacturing industries, which already pay low wages. This dual process will undoubtedly result in increasing income inequities in Canada, while democratically expressed pressures will be exerted on governments to shield the populace from the adverse effects of trade liberalization. In this, as in the situation of resource depletion – or for that matter in dealing with any of the outstanding legacies of past problems – the response of the Canadian state will be constrained both by its internal fragmentation and by the fragmentation of the key social actors.

Over the first 125 years of Confederation, then, Canada has developed a set of state and market institutions that are highly resistant to change. Although these institutions have performed reasonably well, they have existed within a relatively stable domestic and international political-economic environment, based on more or less open trade in resource commodities. Resource depletion and globalized industrial production and competition are now threatening to undermine the stability of that environment. In this situation there is little doubt that both state and societal actors will become increasingly disenchanted with muddling, reactive, and largely ineffective micro- and macro-economic policy-making.

In the 1990s change is needed – and being demanded. At the same time a polarization of Canadian political-economic discourse is emerging: pro-market neoconservatives on one side and pro-state post-Keynesians on the other. With the present fragmentation of major political actors it is unlikely that either of these agendas can be successfully implemented. Still, if any of the actors can overcome their fragmentation, the situation would be open for major change.

Bibliography

Abella, Irving (1973). *Nationalism, Communism and Canadian Labour*. Toronto: University of Toronto Press.

Acheson, T.W. (1972). "The National Policy and the Industrialization of the Maritimes, 1880-1910." *Acadiensis* 1: 3-28.

Adie, Robert F. and Paul G. Thomas (1987). *Canadian Public Administration: Problematical Perspectives*. Scarborough: Prentice-Hall.

Aglietta, Michel (1979). *A Theory of Capitalist Regulation: The U.S. Experience*. London: New Left Books.

Aitken, H.G.H. (1967). "Defensive Expansionism: The State and Economic Growth in Canada." In *Approaches to Canadian Economic History*, edited by W.T. Easterbrook and M. Watkins. Toronto: McClelland and Stewart.

Aitken, Hugh G.J. (1959). *Conference on the State and Economic Growth*. New York: Social Science Research Council.

Aitken, H.G.J. (1961). *American Capital and Canadian Resources*. Cambridge, Mass.: Harvard University Press.

Aitken, H.G.J. (1964). "Government and Business in Canada: An Interpretation." *Business History Review* 38: 4-21.

Aitken, H.G.J. et al. (1959). *The American Economic Impact on Canada*. Durham, N.C.: Duke University Press.

Alavi, H. (1982). "The State and Class under Peripheral Capitalism." In *Introduction to the Sociology of "Developing Societies,"* edited by H. Alavi and T. Shanin. London: Macmillan.

Albert, Michael and Robin Hahnel (1981). *Marxism and Socialist Theory*. Boston: South End Press.

Albert, Michael and Robin Hahnel (1981). *Socialism Today and Tomorrow*. Boston: South End Press.

Albion, Robert G. (1926). *Forests and Sea-Power: The Timber Problems of the Royal Navy, 1652-1862*. Hamden, Conn.: Archon Books.

Albo, Gregory and Jane Jenson (1989). "A Contested Concept: The Relative Autonomy of the State." In *The New Canadian Political Economy*, edited by W. Clement and G. Williams. Montreal: McGill-Queen's Press.

Alexander, David (1983). *Atlantic Canada and Confederation*. Toronto: University of Toronto Press.

Alford, Robert R. and Roger Friedland (1985). *Powers of Theory: Capitalism, the State, and Democracy*. Cambridge: Cambridge University Press.

Althusser, Louis and Etienne Balibar (1977). *Reading "Capital"*. London: New Left Books.

Amin, Samir (1974). *Accumulation on a World Scale: A Critique of the Theory of Underdevelopment*. New York: Monthly Review Press.

Anderson, F.J. (1985). *Natural Resources in Canada: Economic Theory and Policy*. Toronto: Methuen.

Arblaster, Anthony (1984). *The Rise and Decline of Western Liberalism*. Oxford: Basil Blackwell.

Arendt, Hannah (1958). *The Origins of Totalitarianism*. New York: Meridian Books.

Arrighi, Giovanni (1978). *The Geometry of Imperialism: The Limits of Hobson's Paradigm*. London: New Left Books.

Atkinson, Michael A. and William D. Coleman (1989). *The State, Business, and Industrial Change in Canada*. Toronto: University of Toronto Press.

Audley, Paul (1983). *Canada's Cultural Industries: Broadcasting, Publishing, Records and Film*. Toronto: James Lorimer and Co., in association with the Canadian Institute for Economic Policy.

Avakumovic, Ivan (1975). *The Communist Party in Canada: A History*. Toronto: McClelland and Stewart.

Avakumovic, Ivan (1978). *Socialism in Canada*. Toronto: McClelland and Stewart.

Avineri, Shlomo, ed. (1968). *Karl Marx on Colonialism and Modernization*. New York: Doubleday.

Bagehot, Walter (1920). *The English Constitution*. London: K. Paul, Trench, Trubner and Co.

Baggaley, Carmen (1981). *The Emergence of the Regulatory State in Canada, 1867-1939*. Ottawa: Economic Council of Canada.

Bain, Joe S. (1968). *Industrial Organization*. New York: Wiley.

Banting, Keith G. (1982). *The Welfare State and Canadian Federalism*. Kingston, Ont.: McGill-Queen's University Press.

Baran, Paul A. and Paul M. Sweezy (1966). *Monopoly Capital: An Essay on the American Economic and Social Order*. New York: Monthly Review Press.

Barber, C.L. (1957). "Canada's Post-War Monetary Policy, 1945-54." *Canadian Journal of Economics and Political Science* 23: 349-362.

Basran, G.S. and David A. Hay, eds. (1988). *The Political Economy of Agriculture in Western Canada*. Toronto: Garamond Press.

Bealey, Frank (1988). *Democracy in the Contemporary State*. Oxford: Clarendon Press.

Bell, Daniel (1960). *The End of Ideology: On the Exhaustion of Political Ideas in the Fifties*. Glencoe, Ill.: Free Press.

Berger, Carl (1976). *The Writing of Canadian History: Aspects of English-*

Canadian Historical Writing, 1900-1970. Toronto: Oxford University Press.

Bernstein, Eduard [1899] (1961). *Evolutionary Socialism: A Criticism and Affirmation.* New York: Schocken Books.

Berry, L.Y. (1977). *Planning a Socialist Economy.* Moscow: Progress.

Bertram, G.W. (1964). "Historical Statistics on Growth and Structure of Manufacturing in Canada 1870-1957." In *Canadian Political Science Association: Conference on Statistics, 1962.* Toronto: University of Toronto Press.

Bertram, Gordon W. (1963). "Economic Growth and Canadian Industry, 1870-1915: The Staple Model and the Take-Off Hypothesis." *Canadian Journal of Economics and Political Science* 29: 159-184.

Binhammer, H.H. (1977). *Money, Banking and the Canadian Financial System.* Toronto: Methuen.

Bird, Richard M. (1970). *The Growth of Government Spending.* Toronto: Canadian Tax Foundation.

Black, Don and John Myles (1986). "Dependent Industrialization and the Canadian Class Structure: A Comparative Analysis of Canada, the United States, and Sweden." *Canadian Review of Sociology and Anthropology* 23: 157-181.

Blackbourn, Anthony and Robert G. Putnam (1984). *Industrial Geography of Canada.* London: Croom Helm.

Bladen, Vincent W. [1941] (1956). *An Introduction to Political Economy.* Toronto: University of Toronto Press.

Blais, André (1986). "Industrial Policies in Advanced Capitalist Democracies." In *Industrial Policy,* edited by A. Blais. Toronto: University of Toronto Press.

Blais, André (1986). *Political Sociology of Public Aid to Industry.* Toronto: University of Toronto Press.

Bliss, Michael (1973). "Another Anti-Trust Tradition: Canadian Anti-Combines Policy, 1889-1910." *Business History Review* 47: 177-188.

Bliss, Michael (1982). *The Evolution of Industrial Policies in Canada: An Historical Survey.* Ottawa: Economic Council of Canada.

Block, Walter and Michael Walker (1985). *On Employment Equity: A Critique of the Abella Royal Commission Report.* Vancouver: Fraser Institute.

Bobbio, Norberto (1987). *Which Socialism? Marxism, Socialism, and Democracy.* Cambridge: Polity.

Boggs, Carl and David Plotke (1980). *The Politics of Eurocommunism.* Montreal: Black Rose Books.

Boismenu, G. (1989). *La vraisemblance de la problematique de la regulation pour saisir la realité Canadienne: Etude des indicateurs economique en moyenne periode.* Montreal: Université de Montreal.

Boismenu, G. and D. Drache, eds. (1990). *Politique et Regulation*. Montreal: Editions du Meridien.

Bottomore, Tom (1978). *Austro-Marxism*. Oxford: Clarendon Press.

Bourque, Gilles and Gilles Dostaler (1980). *Socialisme et indépendance.* Montreal: Boréal Express.

Boyer, R., ed. (1986). *Capitalismes fin de siècle*. Paris: PUF.

Bradford, N. and J. Jenson (1989). *The NDP in Fordism and Post-Fordism: The Impacts of Internal and External Pluralism*. Harvard University, Center for European Studies.

Braverman, Harry (1974). *Labor and Monopoly Capital: The Degradation of Work in the Twentieth Century*. New York: Monthly Review Press.

Brecher, I. (1957). *Monetary and Fiscal Thought and Policy in Canada, 1919-1939*. Toronto: University of Toronto Press.

Brecher, Irving (1981). *Canada's Competition Policy Revisited: Some New Thoughts on an Old Story*. Montreal: Institute for Research in Public Policy.

Breckenridge, R.M. (1910). *The History of Banking in Canada*. Washington, D.C.: Government Printing Office.

Brennan, Geoffrey and James M. Buchanan (1980). *The Power to Tax: Analytical Foundations of a Fiscal Constitution*. Cambridge: Cambridge University Press.

Brenner, Robert and Mark Glick (1991). "The Regulation Approach: Theory and Practice." *New Left Review* 188: 45-120.

Brewis, T.N. (1968). *Growth and the Canadian Economy*. Toronto: McClelland and Stewart.

Brewis, T.N. (1965). "Monetary Policy." In *Canadian Economic Policy*, edited by T.N. Brewis, H.E. English, A. Scott, and P. Jewett. Toronto: Macmillan.

British Columbia. Ministry of Economic Development (1978a). *An Economic Strategy for Canada*. Victoria: Crown Publications of Victoria.

British Columbia. Ministry of Economic Development (1978b). *An Economic Strategy for Canada: The Industrial Dimension*. Victoria: Crown Publications of Victoria.

Britton, John and James Gilmour (1978). *The Weakest Link: A Technological Perspective on Canadian Industrial Underdevelopment*. Ottawa: Science Council of Canada.

Brodie, Janine M. and Jane Jenson (1988). *Crisis, Challenge, and Change: Parties and Class in Canada Revisited*. Ottawa: Carleton University Press.

Browne, Gerald P. (1967). *The Judicial Committee and the BNA Act: An Analysis of the Interpretative Scheme for the Distribution of Legislative Powers*. Toronto: University of Toronto Press.

Brus, Wlodzimierz (1973). *The Economics and Politics of Socialism*. London: Routledge and Kegan Paul.

Brus, Wlodzimierz (1985). "Socialism – Feasible and Viable?" *New Left Review* 153: 43-62.

Brym, Robert J., ed. (1985). *The Structure of the Canadian Capitalist Class*. Toronto: Garamond Press.

Buchanan, James M., Gordon Tullock and Robert Tellison (1980). *Towards a Theory of the Rent-Seeking Society*. College Station: Texas A and M Press.

Buchanan, James M. and Richard Wagner (1977). *Democracy in Deficit: The Political Legacy of Lord Keynes*. New York: Academic Press.

Buckley, Kenneth (1958). "The Role of Staple Industries in Canada's Economic Development." *Journal of Economic History* 18: 439-450.

Buckley, K.A.H. and M.C. Urquhart (1965). *Historical Statistics of Canada*. Toronto: Macmillan.

C.D. Howe Institute. *Flexibility as the Best Protection*. Brief No. 604. Submission to the Royal Commission on the Economic Union and Development Prospects for Canada.

Cairns, Alan C. (1975). "Political Science in Canada and the Americanization Issue." *Canadian Journal of Political Science* 8: 191-234.

Cairns, Alan C. (1968). "The Electoral System and the Party System in Canada, 1921-1965." *Canadian Journal of Political Science* 1: 55-80.

Cairns, Alan C. (1971). "The Judicial Committee and Its Critics." *Canadian Journal of Political Science* 4: 301-345.

Cameron, Duncan (1988). *The Free Trade Deal*. Toronto: James Lorimer.

Cameron, D. and F. Houle, eds. (1985). *Canada et la nouvelle division internationale du travail/Canada and the New International Division of Labour*. Ottawa: University of Ottawa Press.

Cameron, D.M. (1986). "The Growth of Government Spending: The Canadian Experience in Comparative Perspective." In *State and Society: Canada in Comparative Perspective*, edited by Keith Banting. Toronto: University of Toronto Press.

Campbell, Robert M. (1987). *Grand Illusions: The Politics of the Keynesian Experience in Canada, 1945-1975*. Peterborough, Ont.: Broadview Press.

Canada (1986). *Constitution Act of 1867*. Ottawa: Minister of Supply and Services.

Canada (1885). *Report Relative to Manufacturing Industries in Existence in Canada*. Ottawa: King's Printer.

Canada (1968). *Eleventh Report of the Standing Committee on Defence and External Affairs Respecting Canada-U.S. Relations*. Ottawa: Minister of Supply and Services.

Canada (1972). *Foreign Direct Investment in Canada*. Ottawa: Information Canada.

Canada (1980). *Statement on Economic Development for Canada in the 1980s*. Ottawa: Minister of Supply and Services.

Canada. Department of Consumer and Corporate Affairs (1968). *Policies for Price Stability.* Ottawa: Minister of Supply and Services.

Canada. Department of External Affairs (1983). *A Review of Canadian Trade Policy: A Background Document to Canadian Trade Policy of the 1980s.* Ottawa: Minister of Supply and Services.

Canada. Department of Finance (1979, 1980). *Government of Canada Tax Expenditure Account, 1979 and 1980.* Ottawa: Minister of Supply and Services.

Canada. Department of Finance (1985). *Account of the Cost of Selective Tax Measures.* Ottawa: Minister of Supply and Services.

Canada. Department of Finance (1988a). *The Canada-U.S. Free Trade Agreement: An Economic Assessment.* Ottawa: Minister of Supply and Services.

Canada. Department of Finance (1988b). *Quarterly Economic Review: Annual Reference Tables.* Ottawa: Minister of Supply and Services, June.

Canada. Department of Justice (1965). Lajoie, P.G. *The Amendment of the Constitution of Canada.* Ottawa: Queen's Printer.

Canada. Department of Justice (1983). *Canada: A Consolidation of the Constitution Acts 1867 to 1982.* Ottawa: Minister of Supply and Services.

Canada. Department of Reconstruction (1945). *Employment and Income with Special Reference to the Initial Period of Reconstruction.* Ottawa: King's Printer.

Canada. Department of Regional Industrial Expansion (1988). *Canada-U.S. Free Trade Agreement and Industry: An Assessment.* Ottawa: Minister of Supply and Services Canada.

Canada. National Employment Commission (1938). *Final Report of the National Employment Commission.* Ottawa: King's Printer.

Canada. Parliamentary Task Force on Federal-Provincial Fiscal Arrangements (1981). *Fiscal Federalism in Canada.* Ottawa: Minister of Supply and Services Canada.

Canada. Royal Commission on Banking and Currency in Canada (1933). *Report of the Royal Commission on Banking and Currency in Canada* Ottawa: King's Printer.

Canada. Royal Commission on Canada's Economic Prospects (1957). *Report of the Royal Commission on Canada's Economic Prospects.* Ottawa: Queen's Printer.

Canada. Royal Commission on Corporate Concentration (1978). *Report of the Royal Commission on Corporate Concentration.* Ottawa: Minister of Supply and Services.

Canada. Royal Commission on Dominion-Provincial Relations (1940). *Report of the Royal Commission on Dominion-Provincial Relations: Book I.* Ottawa: King's Printer.

Canada. Royal Commission on Dominion-Provincial Relations (1940).

Report of the Royal Commission on Dominion-Provincial Relations: Book II. Ottawa: King's Printer.

Canada. Royal Commission on the Economic Union and Development Prospects for Canada (Macdonald Commission, 1985). *Report of the Royal Commission on the Economic Union and Development Prospects for Canada*. 3 vols. Ottawa: Minister of Supply and Services Canada.

Canada. Task Force on Program Review (1985). *Study Team Reports*. Ottawa: Minister of Supply and Services Canada.

Cardoso, F.H. (1972). "Dependent Capitalist Development in Latin America." *New Left Review* 74: 83-95.

Carrillo, Santiago (1978). *Eurocommunism and the State*. London: Verso.

Carroll, William K. (1986). *Corporate Power and Canadian Capitalism*. Vancouver: University of British Columbia Press.

Carroll, William K. (1988). "The Political Economy of Canada." In *Understanding Canadian Society*, edited by J. Curtis and L. Tepperman. Toronto: McGraw-Hill Ryerson.

Castells, Manuel (1980). *The Economic Crisis and American Society*. Princeton: Princeton University Press.

Caves, Richard E. and Grant L. Reuber (1969). *Canadian Economic Policy and the Impact of International Capital Flows*. Toronto: University of Toronto Press.

Chambers, Edward J. and Donald F. Gordon (1966). "Primary Products and Economic Growth: An Empirical Measurement." *Journal of Political Economy* LXXIV: 315-332.

Charlesworth, James (1962). *The Limits of Behavioralism in Political Science*. Philadelphia: American Academy of Political and Social Science.

Chorney, Harold and Philip Hanson (1985). "Neo-Conservatism, Social Democracy and 'Province Building': The Experience of Manitoba." *Canadian Review of Sociology and Anthropology* 22: 1-29.

Christian, William (1977a). "Harold Innis as Political Theorist." *Canadian Journal of Political Science* 10: 21-42.

Christian, William (1977b). "The Inquisition of Nationalism." *Journal of Canadian Studies* 12 (Winter): 62-72.

Christian, William and Colin Campbell (1974). *Political Parties and Ideologies in Canada*. Toronto: McGraw-Hill.

Clark-Jones, Melissa (1987). *A Staple State: Canadian Industrial Resources in Cold War*. Toronto: University of Toronto Press.

Clement, Wallace (1975). *The Canadian Corporate Elite: An Analysis of Economic Power*. Toronto: McClelland and Stewart.

Clement, Wallace (1977). *Continental Corporate Power*. Toronto: McClelland and Stewart.

Clement, Wallace (1981). *Hardrock Mining*. Toronto: McClelland and Stewart.

Clement, Wallace (1986). *The Struggle to Organize: Resistance in Canada's Fishery.* Toronto: McClelland and Stewart.

Clement, Wallace (1988). *The Challenge of Class Analysis.* Ottawa: Carleton University Press.

Clement, Wallace and Glen Williams, eds. (1989). *The New Canadian Political Economy.* Montreal: McGill-Queen's University Press.

Coats, R.H. (1917). "The Labour Movement in Canada." In *Canada and Its Provinces*, edited by Adam Shortt and Arthur G. Doughty. Vol.9. Toronto: Glasgow Brook and Company.

Cohen, Jean (1982). *Class and Civil Society: The Limits of Marxian Critical Theory.* Boston: University of Massachusetts Press.

Colander, David (1984). *Neo-Classical Political Economy.* Cambridge: Ballinger.

Coleman, William D. (1985a). "Analyzing the Associative Action of Business: Policy Advocacy and Policy Participation." *Canadian Public Administration* 28: 413-433.

Coleman, W.D. (1985b). "The Emergence of Business Interest Associations in Canada: An Historical Overview." Paper presented to the Canadian Political Science Association, Montreal.

Coleman, W.D. (1986). "Canadian Business and the State." In *The State and Economic Interests*, edited by Keith Banting. Toronto: University of Toronto Press.

Coleman, William D. (1988). *Business and Politics: A Study of Collective Action.* Montreal: McGill-Queen's University Press.

Cornwall, John and Wendy Maclean (1984). *Economic Recovery for Canada: A Policy Framework*. Toronto: James Lorimer, in association with the Canadian Institute for Economic Policy.

Copithorne, Lawrence (1979). *Natural Resources and Regional Disparities.* Ottawa: Economic Council of Canada.

Courchene, Thomas J. (1976a). *Monetarism and Controls: The Inflation Fighters*. Montreal: C.D. Howe Institute.

Courchene, Thomas J. (1976b). *Money, Inflation and the Bank of Canada: Vol. I: An Analysis of Canadian Monetary Policy from 1970 to Early 1975*. Montreal: C.D. Howe Research Institute.

Courchene, Thomas J. (1981). *Money, Inflation and the Bank of Canada: Vol.II: Analysis of Monetary Gradualism, 1975-80*. Montreal: C.D. Howe Institute.

Courchene, Thomas J. (1982). *Recent Canadian Monetary Policy, 1975-81: Reflections of a Monetary Gradualist*. Montreal: McGill-Queen's University Press.

Courchene, Thomas J. (1983). *No Place to Stand? Abandoning Monetary Targets: An Evaluation*. Montreal: C.D. Howe Institute.

Courchene, Thomas J. (1986). *Economic Management and the Division of Powers.* Toronto: University of Toronto Press.

Crane, David, ed. (1981). *Beyond the Monetarists: Post-Keynesian Alternatives to Rampant Inflation, Low Growth and High Unemployment*. Toronto: James Lorimer.

Creighton, Donald [1937] (1956). *The Empire of the St. Lawrence*. Toronto: Macmillan.

Cross, Michael (1973). "The Shiner's War: Social Violence in the Ottawa Valley in the 1830's." *Canadian Historical Review* 53: 1-26.

Cross, Michael S. (1960). "The Lumber Community in Upper Canada, 1815-1867." *Ontario History* 52: 213-233.

Cuneo, C. (1978). "A Class Perspective on Regionalism." In *Modernization and the Canadian State*, edited by D. Glenday, H. Guindon, and A. Turowetz. Toronto: Macmillan.

Cuneo, Carl (1980). "State Mediation of Class Contradictions in Canadian Unemployment Insurance." *Studies in Political Economy* 3 (1980): 37-65.

Cunningham, Frank (1987). *Democratic Theory and Socialism*. Cambridge: Cambridge University Press.

Curtis, C.A. (1931). "Canada and the Gold Standard." *Queen's Quarterly*: 104-120.

Curtis, C.A. (1932). "The Canadian Monetary System." *Canadian Forum* 12: 207-209.

Dales, John H. (1957). *Hydro Electricity and Industrial Development in Quebec, 1898-1940*. Cambridge, Mass.: Harvard University Press.

Dasgupta, A.K. (1985). *Epochs of Economic Theory*. Oxford: Basil Blackwell.

Davies, R.J. (1986). "The Structure of Collective Bargaining in Canada." In *Canadian Labour Relations*, edited by W.C. Riddell. Toronto: University of Toronto Press.

Dawson, Robert M. (1947). *The Government of Canada*. Toronto: University of Toronto Press.

Deane, Phyllis (1978). *The Evolution of Economic Ideas*. Cambridge: Cambridge University Press.

Deutsch, J.J. (1940). "War Finance and the Canadian Economy." *Canadian Journal of Economics and Political Science* 6: 525-542.

Dicey, A.V. (1908). *Introduction to the Study of the Law of the Constitution*. London: Macmillan.

Dobb, Maurice (1964). *Studies in the Development of Capitalism*. New York: International Publishers.

Dobb, Maurice (1970). *Socialist Planning: Some Problems*. London: Lawrence and Wishart.

Dofny, Jacques (1968). *Structure et pouvoirs de la Confederation des Syndicats Nationaux*. Ottawa: Privy Council Office Task Force on Labour Relations.

Domhoff, G. William (1967). *Who Rules America?* Englewood Cliffs, N.J.: Prentice-Hall.

Drache, Daniel (1969). "Harold Innis: A Canadian Nationalist." *Journal of Canadian Studies* 4: 7-12.

Drache, Daniel (1977). "Staple-ization: A Theory of Canadian Capitalist Development." In *Imperialism, Nationalism, and Canada*, edited by Craig Heron. Toronto: New Hogtown Press and Between the Lines.

Drache, D. (1978). "Re-discovering Canadian Political Economy." In *A Practical Guide to Canadian Political Economy*, edited by W. Clement and D. Drache. Toronto: Lorimer.

Drache, Daniel (1982). "Harold Innis and Canadian Capitalist Development." *Canadian Journal of Political and Social Theory* 6: 35-60.

Drache, Daniel (1983). "The Crisis of Canadian Political Economy: Dependency Theory versus the New Orthodoxy." *Canadian Journal of Political and Social Theory* 7: 25-49.

Drache, D. and W. Clement (1985). "Introduction: Canadian Political Economy Comes of Age." In *The New Practical Guide to Canadian Political Economy*, edited by D. Drache and W. Clement. Toronto: Lorimer.

Drache, Daniel and Meric S. Gertler, eds. (1991). *The New Era of Global Competition: State Policy and Market Power*. Montreal: McGill-Queen's University Press.

Drache, Daniel and Arthur Kroker (1983). "The Labyrinth of Dependency." *Canadian Journal of Political and Social Theory* 7: 5-24.

Drummond, I. (1986). "Economic History and Canadian Economic Performance since the Second World War." In *Postwar Macroeconomic Development*, edited by John Sargent. Toronto: University of Toronto Press.

Duverger, Maurice (1965). *Political Parties*. New York: Wiley.

Dwivedi, O.P. (1982). *Administrative State in Canada: Essays in Honour of J.E. Hodgett*. Toronto: University of Toronto Press.

Easterbrook, W.T. (1959). "Recent Contributions to Economic History: Canada." *Journal of Economic History* 19: 76-102.

Easterbrook, W.T. and Hugh G.J. Aitken (1956). *Canadian Economic History*. Toronto: Macmillan.

Easterbrook, W.T., and M.H. Watkins (1967). *Approaches to Canadian Economic History: A Selection of Essays*. Toronto: McClelland and Stewart.

Easton, David (1965). *A Systems Analysis of Political Life*. New York: Wiley.

Economic Council of Canada (1975). *Looking Outwards: A New Trade Strategy for Canada*. Ottawa: Information Canada.

Economic Council of Canada (1979). *Responsible Regulation: An Interim Report*. Ottawa: Minister of Supply and Services Canada.

Economic Council of Canada (1981). *Reforming Regulation*. Ottawa: Minister of Supply and Services Canada.

Economic Council of Canada (1983). *Submission to the Royal Commission on the Economic Union and Development Prospects for Canada*. Ottawa.

Economic Council of Canada (1986). *Minding the Public Business*. Ottawa.

Economic Council of Canada (1987). *Making Technology Work: Innovation and Jobs in Canada*. Ottawa.

Economic Council of Canada (1988a). *Managing Adjustment: Policies for Trade-Sensitive Industries*. Ottawa.

Economic Council of Canada (1988b). *Venturing Forth: An Assessment of the Canada-U.S. Free Trade Agreement*. Ottawa.

Edwards, Richard (1979). *Contested Terrain*. New York: Basic Books.

Edwards, Richard C., Michael Reich and David M. Gordon (1975). *Labor Market Segmentation*. Lexington, Mass.: D.C. Heath.

Emmanuel, Arghiri (1972). *Unequal Exchange*. New York: Monthly Review Press.

Engels, F. (1972). "Letters on Historical Materialism." In *The Marx Engels Reader*, edited by R.C. Tucker. New York: Norton.

Esping-Andersen, G. (1980). "The Political Limits of Social Democracy: State Policy and Party Decomposition in Denmark and Sweden." In *Classes, Class Conflict and the State: Empirical Studies in Class Analysis*, edited by Maurice Zeitlin. Cambridge, Mass.: Winthrop Publishers.

Esping-Andersen, G. (1981). "From Welfare State to Democratic Socialism: The Politics of Economic Democracy in Denmark and Sweden." *Political Power and Social Theory* 2: 111-140.

Esping-Andersen, Gosta (1985). *Politics Against Markets: The Social Democratic Road to Power*. Princeton: Princeton University Press.

Esping-Andersen, G. and R. Friedland (1982). "Class Coalitions in the Making of West European Economies." *Political Power and Social Theory* 3: 1-52.

Epsing-Andersen, G., R. Friedland and E.O. Wright (1976). "Modes of Class Struggle and the Capitalist State." *Kapitalistate* 4-5:186-220.

Esping-Andersen, G. and W. Korpi (1984). "Social Policy as Class Politics in Post-War Capitalism: Scandinavia, Austria and Germany." In *Order and Conflict in Contemporary Capitalism*, edited by John H. Goldthorpe. Oxford: Oxford University Press.

Fanon, Frantz (1965). *The Wretched of the Earth*. New York: Grove Press.

Fay, C.R. (1934). "The Toronto School of Economic History." *Economic History* 3: 168-171.

Fehér, Ferenc, Agnes Heller and György Markus (1983). *Dictatorship over Needs*. Oxford: Blackwell.

Fisher, A. (1966). *The March of Progress and Security*. New York: A.M. Kelley.

Flathman, Richard (1966). *The Public Interest*. New York: Wiley.

Forsey, Eugene (1974). *The Canadian Labour Movement, 1812-1902*. Ottawa: Canadian Historical Association.

Forster, Jakob (1986). *A Conjunction of Interests: Business, Politics, and Tariffs, 1825-1879*. Toronto: University of Toronto Press.

Fox, A.B. (1977). *The Politics of Attraction: Four Middle Powers and the United States*. New York: Columbia University Press.

Fox, R.W. and H.K. Jacobson (1973). *The Anatomy of Influence: Decision-Making in International Organization*. New Haven, Conn.: Yale University Press.

Fowke, Vernon C. (1946). *Canadian Agricultural Policy: The Historical Pattern*. Toronto: University of Toronto Press.

Fowke, V.C. (1952). "The National Policy – Old and New." *Canadian Journal of Economics and Political Science* 18: 271-286.

Frank, Andre G. (1970). *Latin America: Underdevelopment or Revolution*. New York: Monthly Review Press.

Frank, D. and N. Reilly (1979). "The Emergence of the Socialist Movement in the Maritimes, 1899-1916." In *Underdevelopment and Social Movements in Atlantic Canada*, edited by R.J. Brym and R.J. Sacouman. Toronto: New Hogtown Press.

Fraser Institute (1983). *Submission to the Royal Commission on the Economic Union and Development Prospects for Canada*. Vancouver.

Freeman, John R. (1989). *Democracy and Markets: The Politics of Mixed Economies*. Ithaca, N.Y.: Cornell University Press.

French, Richard (1980). *How Ottawa Decides: Planning and Industrial Policy-Making, 1968-1980*. Toronto: Lorimer.

French, R. (1985). "Governing without Business: The Parti Québécois in Power." In *Theories of Business-Government Relations*, edited by V.V. Murray. Toronto: Trans-Canada Press.

Friedman, Milton (1982). *Capitalism and Freedom*. Chicago: University of Chicago Press.

Furtado, Celso (1964). *Development and Underdevelopment*. Berkeley: University of California Press, 1964.

Galbraith, John Kenneth (1987). *Economics in Perspective: A Critical History*. Boston: Houghton Mifflin.

GATT (1969). *Basic Instruments and Selected Documents*. Geneva, March.

GATT Secretariat (1987a). *Inventory of Article XlX Actions and Other Measures Which Appear to Serve the Same Purpose*. May 12.

GATT Secretariat (1987b). *Drafting History of Article XIX and Its Place in the GATT*. September 16.

GATT Secretariat (1987c). *Grey-Area Measures: Background Note by the Secretariat*. September 16.

Gettys, Cora L. (1938). *The Administration of Canadian Conditional Grants: A Study in Dominion-Provincial Relationships*. Chicago: Public Administration Service.

Gillespie, W.I. (1979). "Postwar Canadian Fiscal Policy Revisited, 1945-1975." *Canadian Tax Journal* 27: 265-276.

Gilpin, Robert (1987). *The Political Economy of International Relations*. Princeton: Princeton University Press.

Goldthorpe, John H., ed. (1984). *Order and Conflict in Contemporary Capitalism*. Oxford: Oxford University Press.

Gonick, Cy (1987). *The Great Economic Debate: Failed Economics and the Future of Canada*. Toronto: James Lorimer.

Gordon, David (1988). "The Global Economy: New Edifice or Crumbling Foundations?" *New Left Review* 168: 24-65.

Gordon, H.S. (1966). "A Twenty Year Perspective: Some Reflections on the Keynesian Revolution in Canada." In *Canadian Economic Policy Since the War*, edited by S.F. Kaliski. Montreal: Canadian Trade Committee.

Gordon, Walter L. (1975). *Storm Signals: New Economic Policies for Canada*. Toronto: McClelland and Stewart.

Gorecki, P.K. and W.T. Stanbury (1979). *Perspectives on the Royal Commission on Corporate Concentration*. Scarborough, Ont.: Institute for Research in Public Policy.

Gorecki, P.K. and W.T. Stanbury (1984). *The Objectives of Canadian Competition Policy, 1888-1983*. Montreal: Institute for Research in Public Policy.

Gough, Ian (1979). *The Political Economy of the Welfare State*. London: Macmillan, 1979.

Gramsci, Antonio (1972). *Selections from the Prison Notebooks*. New York: International Publishers.

Granatstein, Jack (1967). *The Politics of Survival: The Conservative Party of Canada, 1939-1945*. Toronto: University of Toronto Press.

Granatstein, Jack (1982). *The Ottawa Men: The Civil Service Mandarins, 1935-1957*. Toronto: Oxford University Press.

Grant, Wyn and S. Nath (1984). *The Politics of Economic Policy*. Oxford: Basil Blackwell.

Grayson, John P., ed. (1980). *Class, State, Ideology and Change: Marxist Perspectives on Canada*. Toronto: Holt, Rinehart and Winston.

Grubel, Herbert, and Josef Bonnici (1986). *Why Is Canada's Unemployment Rate So High?* Vancouver: Fraser Institute, 1986.

Guest, Dennis (1980). *The Emergence of Social Security in Canada*. Vancouver: University of British Columbia Press.

Hall, John A. and G. John Ikenberry (1989). *The State*. Minneapolis: University of Minnesota Press.

Hall, Peter A. (1986). *Governing the Economy: The Politics of State Intervention in Britain and France*. Cambridge: Polity Press.

Hall, Peter A. (1989). *The Political Power of Economic Ideas: Keynesianism Across Nations*. Princeton: Princeton University Press.

Hamelin, Jean, Paul Larocque and Jacques Rouillard (1970). *Repertoire des Grêves dans la Province de Québec au XIXe siècle*. Montreal: Presses de l'École des Hautes Études Commerciales.

Hammond, Bray (1957). *Banks and Politics in America: From the Revolution to the Civil War*. Princeton: Princeton University Press.

Hayek, Friedrich A. von (1944). *The Road to Serfdom*. Chicago: University of Chicago Press.

Hayek, F.A. (1960). *The Constitution of Liberty*. Chicago: University of Chicago Press.

Hayek, F.A. (1983). "The Muddle of the Middle." In *Philosophical and Economic Foundations of Capitalism*, edited by Svetozar Pejovich. Lexington, Mass.: Lexington Books.

Haythorne, George (1973). "Prices and Incomes Policy: The Canadian Experience, 1969-1972." *International Labour Review*: 485-503.

Heilbroner, Robert (1980). *Marxism: For and Against*. New York: Norton.

Helleiner, G.D. (1985). "Underutilized Potential: Canada's Economic Relations with Developing Countries." In *Canada and the Multinational Trading System*, edited by John Whalley. Toronto: University of Toronto Press.

Heron, Craig (1989). *The Canadian Labour Movement: A Short History*. Toronto: James Lorimer.

Heron, Craig and Robert Storey (1986). *On the Job: Confronting the Labour Process in Canada*. Kingston, Ont.: McGill-Queen's University Press.

Hibbs, Douglas A. (1976). "Industrial Conflict in Advanced Industrial Societies." *American Political Science Review* 70:4: 1033-1058.

Hibbs, D.A. Jr. (1978). "On the Political Economy of Long-Run Trends in Strike Activity." *British Journal of Political Sciences* 8: 153-175.

Hibbs, Douglas A. (1987a). *The American Political Economy: Macroeconomics and Electoral Politics*. Cambridge, Mass.: Harvard University Press.

Hibbs, D.A. (1987b). *The Political Economy of Industrial Democracies*. Cambridge, Mass.: Harvard University Press.

Hilferding, Rudolf (1981). *Finance Capital: A Study of the Latest Phase of Capitalist Development*. London: Routledge and Kegan Paul.

Hill, Michael and Glen Bramley (1986). *Analysing Social Policy*. Oxford: Basil Blackwell.

Hiller, James and Peter Neary, eds. (1980). *Newfoundland in the Nineteenth and Twentieth Centuries*. Toronto: University of Toronto Press.

Himmelstrand, Ulf, G. Ahrne et al. (1981). *Beyond Welfare Capitalism: Issues, Actors and Forces in Societal Change*. London: Heinemann.

Hirschman, Albert O. (1958). *The Strategy of Economic Development*. New Haven, Conn.: Yale University Press.

Hodgetts, John E. (1973). *The Canadian Public Service: A Physiology of Government*. Toronto: University of Toronto Press.

Holden, Barry (1988). *Understanding Liberal Democracy*. Oxford: Phillip Allen.

Horowitz, Gad (1968). *Canadian Labour in Politics*. Toronto: University of Toronto Press.

Horvat, Branko (1982). *The Political Economy of Socialism: A Marxist Social Theory*. Armonk, N.Y.: M.E. Sharpe.

Houle, François (1983). "Economic Strategy and the Restructuring of the Fordist Wage-Labour Relationship in Canada." *Studies in Political Economy* 11: 127-148.

Howitt, Peter (1986). *Monetary Policy in Transition: A Study of Bank of Canada Policy, 1982-1985*. Toronto: C.D. Howe Institute.

Howlett, Michael (1986). "Acts of Commission and Acts of Omission: Legal Historical Research and the Intentions of Government in a Federal State." *Canadian Journal of Political Science* 19: 363-370.

Howlett, Michael and Keith Brownsey (1988). "The Old Reality and the New Reality: Party Politics and Public Policy in British Columbia." *Studies in Political Economy* 25: 141-176.

Hunt, E.K. (1979). *History of Economic Thought: A Critical Perspective*. Belmont, Cal.: Wadsworth Pub. Co.

Hutcheson, John (1978). *Dominance and Dependency*. Toronto: McClelland and Stewart.

Ikenberry, G. John (1988). "Conclusion: An Institutional Approach to American Foreign Policy." *International Organization* 42,1: 219-243.

Innis, Harold A. (1923). *A History of the Canadian Pacific Railway*. London: P.S. King and Sons.

Innis, Harold A. (1937). "Significant Factors in Canadian Economic Development." *Canadian Historical Review* 18,4: 374-384.

Innis, Harold A. (1938). *Settlement and the Mining Frontier*. Toronto: Macmillan.

Innis, Harold A. (1940). *The Cod Fisheries: The History of an International Economy*. New Haven, Conn.: Yale University Press.

Innis, Harold A. (1956). *The Fur Trade in Canada: An Introduction to Canadian Economic History*. Toronto: University of Toronto Press.

Innis, Harold A. (1982). *Essays in Canadian Economic History*. Ed. Mary Q. Innis. Toronto: University of Toronto Press.

Innis, Harold A. et al. (1933). *Problems of Staple Production in Canada*. Toronto: Ryerson.

Jamieson, A.B. (1953). *Chartered Banking in Canada*. Toronto: Ryerson.

Jamieson, Stuart (1968). *Times of Trouble: Labour Unrest and Industrial Conflict in Canada, 1900-66*. Ottawa: Information Canada.

Jay, Martin (1973). *The Dialectical Imagination: A History of the Frankfurt School and the Institution for Social Research 1923-1950*. Boston: Little Brown.

Jenkin, Michael (1983). *The Challenge of Diversity: Industrial Policy in the Canadian Federation*. Ottawa: Science Council of Canada.

Jenkins, Rhys (1981). "Divisions Over the International Division of Labour." *Capital and Class* 22: 28-58.

Jennings, Ivor (1952). *Constitutional Laws of the Commonwealth*. Oxford: Clarendon Press.

Jevons, William Stanley [1871](1965). *The Principles of Economics*. New York: A.M. Kelley.

Johnson, Harry (1963). *The Canadian Quandary: Economic Problems and Policies*. Toronto: McGraw-Hill.

Jones, Gareth S. (1977). *Western Marxism*. New York: Humanities Press.

Kamerman, S.B. and A.J. Kahn, eds. (1989). *Privatization and the Welfare State*. Princeton: Princeton University Press.

Kaminski, B. (1989). "The Anatomy of the Directive Capacity of the Socialist State." *Comparative Political Studies* 22: 66-92.

Katzenstein, Peter (1985). *Small States in World Markets: Industrial Policy in Europe*. Ithaca, N.Y.: Cornell University Press.

Kautsky, Karl (1909). *The Road to Power*. Chicago: S.A. Block.

Kautsky, Karl [1892](1971). *The Class Struggle*. New York: Norton.

Kealey, Greg S. (1973). *Canada Investigates Industrialism*. Toronto: University of Toronto Press, 1973.

Kealey, G.S. (1985). "The Writing of Social History in English Canada, 1970-1984." *Social History* 10: 347-365.

Kealey, G.S. (1981). "Labour and Working Class History in Canada: Prospects for the 1980's" *Labour/Le Travailleur* 7: 67-94.

Kellogg, Paul (1989). "State, Capital and World Economy: Bukharin's Marxism and the 'Dependency/Class' Controversy in Canadian Political Economy." *Canadian Journal of Political Science* 22: 337-362.

Kernaghan, Kenneth (1979). "Power, Parliament and Public Servants in Canada: Ministerial Responsibility Reexamined." *Canadian Public Administration* 3: 383-396.

Kernaghan, K. (1985). "The Public and Public Servant in Canada." In *Public Administration in Canada: Selected Readings*, edited by K. Kernaghan. Toronto: Methuen.

Kernaghan, Kenneth and David Siegal (1987). *Public Administration in Canada: A Text*. Toronto: Methuen.

Keynes, John Maynard (1936). *The General Theory of Employment, Interest and Money*. New York: Harcourt, Brace.

Khemani, R.S. (1980). *Concentration in the Manufacturing Industries of Canada: Analysis of Post-War Changes*. Ottawa: Consumer and Corporate Affairs Canada.

Kirichenko, V.N. (1979). *Socialist Long-Term Planning*. Moscow: Progress, 1979.

Knox, Frank A. (1939). *Dominion Monetary Policy, 1929-1934*. Ottawa: Minister of Supply and Services Canada.

Korpi, Walter (1983). *The Democratic Class Struggle*. London: Routledge and Kegan Paul.

Kumar, P. (1986). "Union Growth in Canada: Retrospect and Prospect." In *Canadian Labour Relations*, edited by W.C. Riddell. Toronto: University of Toronto Press.

Kuznets, Simon (1966). *Modern Economic Growth: Rate, Structure and Spread*. New Haven, Conn.: Yale University Press.

Lacroix, R. (1986). "Strike Activity in Canada." In *Canadian Labour Relations*, edited by W.C. Riddell. Toronto: University of Toronto Press.

LaForest, Gerard V. (1955). *Disallowance and Reservation of Provincial Legislation*. Ottawa: Department of Justice.

LaForest, Gerard V. (1981). *The Allocation of Taxing Power under the Canadian Constitution*. Toronto: Canadian Tax Foundation.

Lambert, Richard and Paul Pross (1967). *Renewing Nature's Wealth*. Toronto: Department of Lands and Forest.

Lamy, Paul (1976). "The Globalization of American Sociology: Excellence or Imperialism?" *American Sociologist* 11, 2: 104-114.

Latham, A.B. (1930). *The Catholic and National Labour Unions of Canada*. Toronto: Macmillan.

Laux, Jeanne K. and Maureen A. Molot (1988). *State Capitalism: Public Enterprise in Canada*. Ithaca, N.Y.: Cornell University Press.

Laxer, Gordon (1989a). *Open for Business: The Roots of Foreign Ownership in Canada*. Don Mills, Ont.: Oxford University Press.

Laxer, Gordon (1989b). "The Schizophrenic Character of Canadian Political Economy." *Canadian Journal of Sociology and Anthropology* 26: 178-192.

Laxer, James (1981). *Canada's Economic Strategy*. Toronto: McClelland and Stewart.

Laxer, James (1984). *Rethinking the Economy*. Toronto: New Canada Publications.

Laxer, Robert, ed. (1973). *(Canada) Ltd.: The Political Economy of Dependency*. Toronto: McClelland and Stewart.

Laycock, David (1990). *Populism and Democratic Thought in the Canadian Prairies, 1910-1945*. Toronto: University of Toronto Press.

Leadbeater, D. (1984). "An Outline of Capitalist Development in Alberta." In *Essays on the Political Economy of Alberta*, edited by David Leadbeater. Toronto: New Hogtown Press.

League for Social Reconstruction (1935). *Social Planning for Canada*. Toronto: T. Nelson and Sons Ltd.

Lecraw, Donald J. and Donald N. Thompson (1978). *Conglomerate Mergers in Canada*. Ottawa: Royal Commission on Corporate Concentration.

Lembcke, Jerry and William Tattam (1984). *One Union in Wood: A Political History of the International Woodworkers of America*. New York: International Publishers.

Lenin, Vladimir I. [1917] (1939a). *The State and Revolution*. New York: International Publishers.

Lenin, Vladimir I. [1916] (1939b). *Imperialism: The Highest Stage of Capitalism: A Popular Outline*. New York: International Publishers.

Lenin, Vladimir I. [1902] (1966). *What Is To Be Done? Burning Questions of Our Movement*. Moscow: Progress Publishers.

Lermer, George (1984). *Probing Leviathan: An Investigation of Government in the Economy*. Vancouver: Fraser Institute.

Levitt, Kari (1970). *Silent Surrender: The Multinational Corporation in Canada*. Toronto: Macmillan.

Lindberg, L.N. (1982). "The Problem of Economic Theory in Explaining Economic Performance." *Annals of the American Academy of Political and Social Sciences* (January): 14-27.

Lindblom, Charles E. (1977). *Politics and Markets: The World's Political Economic Systems*. New York: Basic Books.

Lingard, Charles C. (1946). *Territorial Government in Canada: The Autonomy Question in the Old North-West Territories*. Toronto: University of Toronto Press.

Lipietz, Alain (1982). "Towards Global Fordism?" *New Left Review* 132: 33-48.

Lipietz, Alain (1984). *Accumulation, crises et sorties de crise: Quelques reflexions methodologiques autour de la motion de 'regulation.'* Paris: CEPREMAP.

Lipietz, Alain (1984). "The Globalization of the General Crisis of Fordism, 1967-84." In *Frontyard Backyard: The Americas in the Global Crisis*, edited by John Holmes and Colin Leys. Toronto: Between The Lines, 1987.

Lipset, Seymour M. (1959). *Agrarian Socialism*. Berkeley: University of California Press.

Lipsey, Richard Peter Steiner and Douglas Purvis (1987). *Economics*. New York: Harper and Row.

Lipsey, R. and R. York (1988). *Evaluating the Free Trade Deal: A Guided Tour through the Canada-U.S. Agreement*. Scarborough, Ont.: C.D. Howe Institute.

Lipton, Charles (1967). *The Trade Union Movement of Canada, 1827-1959*. Montreal: Canadian Social Publications.

Lithwick, N.H. (1987). "Regional Development Policies: Context and Consequences." In *Still Living Together: Recent Trends and Future Direc-*

tions in Canadian Regional Development, edited by W.J. Coffey and M. Polese. Montreal: Institute for Research on Public Policy.

Littler, Craig R. (1982). *The Development of the Labour Process in Capitalist Societies*. London: Heinemann Educational.

Logan, Harold A. (1928). *The History of Trade-Union Organization in Canada*. Chicago: University of Chicago Press.

Logan, Harold A. (1948). *Trade Unions in Canada: Their Development and Functioning*. Toronto: Macmillan.

Lovink, J.A.A. (1970). "On Analyzing the Impact of the Electoral System on the Party System in Canada." *Canadian Journal of Political Science* 3: 497-516.

Lower, Arthur R.M. (1936). "Settlement and the Forest Frontier in Eastern North America." In *Settlement and the Forest Frontier in Eastern Canada*, edited by Arthur R.M. Lower and H.A. Innis. Toronto: Macmillan of Canada.

Lower, Arthur R.M. (1938). *The North American Assault on the Canadian Forest*. Toronto: Ryerson Press.

Lower, Arthur R.M. (1967). "The Trade in Square Timber." In *Approaches to Canadian Economic History*, edited by W.T. Easterbrook and M.H. Watkins. Toronto: McClelland and Stewart.

Lower, Arthur R.M. (1973). *Great Britain's Woodyard: British America and the Timber Trade, 1763-1867*. Montreal: McGill-Queen's University Press.

Lower, Arthur R.M. [1946] (1977). *Colony to Nation: A History of Canada*. Toronto: McClelland and Stewart.

Lukacs, György (1977). *History and Class Consciousness: Studies in Marxist Dialectics*. Cambridge, Mass.: MIT Press.

Lumsden, Ian, ed. (1970). *Close the 49th Parallel etc.: The Americanization of Canada*. Toronto: University of Toronto Press.

Luxemberg, Rosa (1964). *The Accumulation of Capital*. New York: Monthly Review Press.

Lynn, James T. (1967). *Federal-Provincial Fiscal Relations*. Ottawa.

Lyon, Peyton V. and Brian W. Tomlin (1979). *Canada as an International Actor*. Toronto: Macmillan.

MacDonald, L.R. (1975). "Merchants against Industry: An Idea and Its Origin." *Canadian Historical Review* 56: 263-282.

Macdonald Commission (1985). See: Canada. Royal Commission on the Economic Union and Development Prospects for Canada.

Mackintosh, William A. (1934). *Prairie Settlement: The Geographical Setting*. In *Canadian Frontiers of Settlement Series*. Toronto: Macmillan.

Mackintosh, William A. (1939). *The Economic Background of Dominion-Provincial Relations*. Ottawa: Printer to the King.

Mackintosh, W.A. (1966). "The White Paper on Employment and Income in Its 1945 Setting." In *Canadian Economic Policy Since the War*, edited by S.F. Kaliski. Montreal: Canadian Trade Committee.

Mackintosh, W.A. (1967). "Economic Factors in Canadian History." In *Approaches to Canadian Economic History*, edited by W.T. Easterbrook and M.H. Watkins. Toronto: McClelland and Stewart.

McLellan, David, ed. (1972). *Karl Marx: English Texts*. Oxford: Basil Blackwell.

McLellan, David (1979). *Marxism after Marx*. New York: Harper and Row.

Macpherson, Crawford Brough (1953). *Democracy in Alberta: Social Credit and the Party System*. Toronto: University of Toronto Press.

Macpherson, C.B. (1962). *The Political Theory of Possessive Individualism: Hobbes to Locke*. Oxford: Clarendon Press.

Macpherson, C.B. (1974). "After Strange Gods: Canadian Political Science, 1973." In *Perspectives on the Social Sciences in Canada*, edited by T.N. Guinsburg and G.L. Reuber. Toronto: University of Toronto Press.

Macpherson, C.B. (1977). *The Life and Times of Liberal Democracy*. Oxford: Oxford University Press.

Macpherson, C.B. (1979). "By Innis out of Marx: The Revival of Canadian Political Economy." *Canadian Journal of Political and Social Theory* 3: 134-138.

Magnusson, Warren, C. Doyle et al. (1984). *The New Reality: The Politics of Restraint in British Columbia*. Vancouver: New Star Books.

Mahon, Rianne (1979). "Regulatory Agencies: Captive Agents or Hegemonic Apparatuses?" *Studies in Political Economy* 1: 163-200.

Mahon, Rianne (1984). *The Politics of Industrial Restructuring: Canadian Textiles*. Toronto: University of Toronto Press.

Mallory, James R. (1971). *The Structure of Canadian Government*. Toronto: Macmillan.

Mandel, Ernest (1986). "In Defense of Socialist Planning." *New Left Review* 159: 5-38.

Mandel, Ernest (1970). *An Introduction to Marxist Economic Theory*. New York: Pathfinder Press.

Mao Tse Tung (1961). "On the People's Democratic Dictatorship." *In Selected Works*. Vol. 4. Peking: Foreign Languages Publishing House.

Marchak, Patricia (1975). *Ideological Perspectives on Canada*. Toronto: McGraw-Hill Ryerson.

Marchak, Patricia (1979). *In Whose Interests: An Essay on Multinational Corporations in a Canadian Context*. Toronto: McClelland and Stewart.

Marchak, Patricia (1983). *Green Gold: The Forestry Industry in British Columbia*. Vancouver: University of British Columbia Press.

Marchak, Patricia (1985). "Canadian Political Economy." *Canadian Review of Sociology and Anthropology* 22: 673-709.

Marchak, P. (1986). *British Columbia and the New Reality*. Kingston, Ont.:

Queen's University Program of Studies in National and International Development.

Marcuse, Herbert (1958). *Soviet Marxism: A Critical Analysis*. New York: Columbia University Press.

Marfels, Christian (1976). *Concentration Levels and Trends in the Canadian Economy, 1965-1973*. Ottawa: Royal Commission on Corporate Concentration.

Marshall, Alfred [1920] (1930). *Principles of Economics: An Introductory Volume*. London: Macmillan.

Marshall, Herbert, Frank Southard and Kenneth W. Taylor (1936). *Canadian American Industry: A Study in International Investment*. Toronto: The Ryerson Press.

Martin, Chester (1920). *The Natural Resources Question: The Historical Basis of Provincial Claims*. Winnipeg: University of Manitoba.

Martin, Chester (1973). *Dominion Lands Policy*. Toronto: McClelland and Stewart.

Marx, Karl [1867] (1962). *Capital: A Critique of Political Economy*. London: J.M. Dent and Sons Ltd.

Marx, Karl [1848] (1968). *The Manifesto of the Communist Party*. New York: International Publishers.

Marx, Karl [1859] (1974a). "Preface to a Contribution to the Critique of Political Economy." In Karl Marx and Frederick Engels, *Selected Works*. New York: International Publishers.

Marx, Karl [1871] (1974b). "The Civil War in France." In Karl Marx and Frederick Engels, *Selected Works*. New York: International Publishers.

Maxwell, Judith (1977). *The Role of the Government: Searching for a Framework*. Montreal: C.D. Howe Research Institute.

Maxwell, James A. (1937). *Federal Subsidies to the Canadian Provincial Governments*. Cambridge, Mass.: Harvard University Press.

McCormick, P. (1989). "Provincial Party Systems, 1945-1986." In *Canadian Parties in Transition*, edited by A. Gagnon and B. Tanguay. Toronto: Nelson.

McFetridge, D.G. (1986). *The Economics of Industrial Policy and Strategy*. Toronto: University of Toronto Press.

McFetridge, D.G. (1986). "The Economics of Industrial Structure." In *Canadian Industry in Transition*, edited by D.G. McFetridge. Toronto: University of Toronto Press.

McIvor, R.C. (1958). *Canadian Monetary, Banking, and Fiscal Development*. Toronto: Macmillan.

McIvor, R.C. and J.H. Panabaker (1954). "Canadian Post-War Monetary Policy, 1946-52." *Canadian Journal of Economics and Political Science* 20: 207-226.

McNally, David (1981). "Staple Theory as Commodity Fetishism: Marx,

Innis and Canadian Political Economy." Special Issue, "Rethinking Canadian Political Economy," *Studies in Political Economy* 6: 35-64.

Menger, Karl [1871] (1950). *Principles of Economics*. Glencoe: Free Press.

Migdal, Joel (1988). *Strong Societies and Weak States: State-Society Relations and State Capabilities in the Third World*. Princeton: Princeton University Press.

Mills, C.W. (1956). *The Power Elite*. New York: Oxford University Press.

Minville, E., ed. (1944). *La forêt*. Montreal: Fides.

Moore, A.M., J.H. Perry and D. Beach (1966). *The Financing of Canadian Federation: The First 100 Years*. Toronto: Canadian Tax Foundation.

Moore, Barrington (1966). *Social Origins of Dictatorship and Democracy*. Boston: Beacon Press.

Moore, Steve and Debi Wells (1975). *Imperialism and the National Question in Canada*. Toronto: Moore.

Morici, Peter et al. (1982). *Canadian Industrial Policy*. Washington, D.C.: National Planning Association.

Moroz, A. (1985). "Some Observations on Non-Tariff Barriers in Canada." In *Canada-United States Free Trade*, edited by J. Whalley. Toronto: University of Toronto Press.

Morris-Suzuki, Tessa (1984). "Robots and Capitalism." *New Left Review* 147: 109-121.

Morton, Arthur S. (1938). *A History of Prairie Settlement*. Toronto: Macmillan.

Morton, Desmond (1974). *NDP: The Dream of Power*. Toronto: Hakkert.

Morton, William C. (1950). *The Progressive Party in Canada*. Toronto: University of Toronto Press.

Moscovitch, Allan and Glenn Drover, eds. (1981). *Inequality: Essays on the Political Economy of Social Welfare*. Toronto: University of Toronto Press.

Mundell, R.A. (1963). "Capital Mobility and Stabilization Policy Under Fixed and Flexible Exchange Rates." *Canadian Journal of Economics* 26: 475-485.

Murphy, Lawrence et al. (1977). *Perspectives on the Canadian Economy*. Ottawa: Conference Board of Canada.

Murray, Fergus (1983). "The De-centralisation of Production – The Decline of the Mass-collective Worker?" *Capital and Class* 19: 74-99.

Myles, John (1989). "Understanding Canada: Comparative Political Economy Perspectives." Special Issue on "Comparative Political Economy," *Canadian Review of Sociology and Anthropology* 26: 1-9.

Myles, J. and D. Forcese (1981). "Voting and Class Politics in Canada and the United States." *Comparative Social Research* 4: 3-31.

National Council on Welfare (1983). *Poverty in Canada: 1981 Preliminary Statistics*. Ottawa: Minister of Supply and Services Canada.

Naylor, R.T. (1972). "The Rise and Fall of the Third Commercial Empire of the St. Lawrence." In *Capitalism and the National Question in Canada*, edited by G. Teeple. Toronto: University of Toronto Press.

Naylor, R.T. (1975a). "Dominion of Capital: Canada and International Investment." In *Domination*, edited by A. Kontos. Toronto: University of Toronto Press.

Naylor, R.T. (1975b). *History of Canadian Business, 1867-1914*. Toronto: Lorimer.

Neatby, H.B. (1969). "The Liberal Way: Fiscal and Monetary Policy in the 1930's." In *The Great Depression: Essays and Memoirs from Canada and the United States*, edited by V. Hoar. Vancouver: Copp Clark.

Nell, Edward (1988). *Prosperity and Public Spending: Transformational Growth and the Role of Government*. Boston: Allen and Unwin.

Nelles, H.V. (1974). *The Politics of Development: Forests, Mines and Hydro-Electric Power in Ontario*. Toronto: Macmillan.

Neufeld, E.P. (1958). *Bank of Canada Operations and Policy*. Toronto: University of Toronto Press.

Nicholaus, M. (1967). "Proletariat and the Middle-Class in Marx: Hegelian Choreography and the Capitalist Dialectic." *Studies on the Left* 7: 22-49.

Nicholson, Norman L. (1964). *The Boundaries of Canada: Its Provinces and Territories*. Ottawa: Queen's Printer.

Niosi, Jorge (1982). *The Economy of Canada: A Study of Ownership and Control*. Montreal: Black Rose Books.

Niosi, Jorge (1985). *Canadian Multinationals*. Toronto: Between the Lines.

Nkrumah, Kwame (1965). *Neo-Colonialism: The Last Stage of Imperialism*. London: Nelson.

Nordlinger, Eric (1981). *On the Autonomy of the Democratic State*. Cambridge, Mass.: Harvard University Press.

North, Douglass C. (1961). *The Economic Growth of the United States, 1790-1860*. Englewood Cliffs, N.J.: Prentice-Hall.

Nove, Alec (1975). *Socialist Economics*. Harmondsworth, Middlesex: Penguin.

Nove, Alec (1983). *The Economics of Feasible Socialism*. London: Allen and Unwin.

Nove, Alec (1986). *The Soviet Economic System*. Boston: Allen and Unwin.

O'Connor, James (1973). *The Fiscal Crisis of the State*. New York: St. Martin's Press.

OECD (1983). *Positive Adjustment Policies*. Paris: Organization for Economic Co-operation and Development.

Olmsted, R.A. (1954). *Decisions of the Judicial Committee of the Privy Council Relating to the British North America Act 1867 and the Canadian Constitution 1867-1954*. Ottawa: Queen's Printer.

Olsen, Dennis (1980). *The State Elite*. Toronto: McClelland and Stewart.

Olson, Mancur (1965). *The Logic of Collective Action: Public Goods and the Theory of Goods*. Cambridge, Mass.: Harvard University Press.

Ornstein, Michael (1989). "The Social Organization of the Canadian Capitalist Class in Comparative Perspective." *Canadian Review of Sociology and Anthropology* 26: 151-177.

Pal, Leslie A. (1989). "Political Economy as a Hegemonic Project." *Canadian Journal of Political Science* 22: 827-839.

Palda, Kristian S. (1979). *The Science Council's Weakest Link: A Critique of the Science Council's Technocratic Industrial Strategy for Canada*. Vancouver: Fraser Institute.

Palda, Kristian S. (1984). *Industrial Innovation*. Vancouver: Fraser Institute.

Palloix, C. (1976). "The Labour Process: From Fordism to Neo-Fordism." *Conference of Socialist Economists*. London.

Palmer, Bryan (1983). *Working Class Experience: The Rise and Reconstitution of Canadian Labour, 1800-1980*. Toronto: Butterworths.

Palmer, Bryan and Gregory S. Kealey (1982). *Dreaming of What Might Be: The Knights of Labour in Ontario, 1880-1900*. New York: Cambridge University Press.

Palmer, Bryan D. (1979-1980). "Working Class Canada: Recent Historical Writing." *Queen's Quarterly* 86: 594-616.

Panitch, Leo, ed. (1977). *The Canadian State: Political Economy and Political Power*. Toronto: University of Toronto Press.

Panitch, Leo (1981). "Dependency and Class in Canadian Political Economy." *Studies in Political Economy* 6: 7-33.

Parenti, Michael (1988). *Democracy for the Few*. New York: St. Martin's Press.

Parker, Ian (1977). "Harold Innis, Karl Marx, and Canadian Political Economy." *Queen's Quarterly* 84: 545-563.

Penner, Norman (1977). *The Canadian Left: A Critical Analysis*. Scarborough, Ont.: Prentice-Hall.

Pentland, Clare (1981). *Labour and Capital in Canada, 1650-1860*. Toronto: Lorimer.

Perry, J.H. (1955). *Taxes, Tariffs and Subsidies: A History of Canadian Fiscal Development*. Toronto: Canadian Tax Foundation.

Perry, J.H. (1982). *Background of Current Fiscal Problems*. Toronto: Canadian Tax Foundation.

Perry, J.H. (1989). *A Fiscal History of Canada: The Postwar Years*. Toronto: Canadian Tax Foundation.

Pigou, A.C. [1919] (1932). *The Economics of Welfare*. London: Macmillan.

Piven, F.F. and R.A. Cloward (1972). *Regulating the Poor: The Functions of Public Welfare*. New York: Pantheon Books.

Plumptre, A.F.W. (1934). "Canadian Monetary Policy." In *The Canadian*

Economy and Its Problems, edited by H.A. Innis and A.F.W. Plumptre. Toronto: Canadian Institute of International Affairs.

Plumptre, A.F.W. (1977). *Three Decades of Decision: Canada and the World Monetary System, 1944-75*. Toronto: McClelland and Stewart.

Polyani, Karl (1957). *The Great Transformation*. Boston: Beacon Press.

Pomfret, Richard (1981). *The Economic Development of Canada*. Toronto: Methuen.

Porter, John (1965). *The Vertical Mosaic: An Analysis of Social Class and Power in Canada*. Toronto: University of Toronto Press.

Poulantzas, Nicos (1980). *State, Power, Socialism*. London: Verso.

Poulantzas, Nicos (1973). "On Social Classes." *New Left Review* 78: 27-55.

Poulantzas, Nicos (1974). "The Internationalisation of Capitalist Relations and the Nation State." *Economy and Society:* 145-179.

Prebisch, Raul (1968). *Towards a Global Strategy of Development*. New York: United Nations.

Price, Richard (1984). "Theories of Labour Process Formation." *Journal of Social History* 18: 91-110.

Prichard, J.R.S. (1983). *Crown Corporations in Canada: The Calculus of Instrument Choice*. Toronto: Butterworth.

Pross, A. Paul (1986). *Group Politics and Public Policy*. Toronto: Oxford University Press.

Przeworski, Adam (1985). *Capitalism and Social Democracy*. London: Cambridge University Press.

Przeworski, Adam (1990). *The State and the Economy under Capitalism*. Chur, Switz.: Harwood Academic Publishers.

Przeworski, Adam (1991). *Democracy and the Market: Political and Economic Reforms in Eastern Europe and Latin America*. Cambridge: Cambridge University Press.

Purvis, D.D. and C. Smith (1986). "Fiscal Policy in Canada: 1963-84." In *Fiscal and Monetary Policy*, edited by J. Sargent. Toronto: University of Toronto Press.

Qualter, Terence (1970). *The Election Process in Canada*. Toronto: McGraw-Hill.

Radebaugh, L.H. (1988). "International Trade in Services: An Overview." In *The Canada-U.S. Free Trade Agreement: The Impact on Service Industries*, edited by E.H. Fry. Provo, Ut.: Brigham Young University Press.

Reich, Robert (1983). *The Next American Frontier*. New York: Time Books.

Resnick, Philip (1987). "Montesquieu Revisited, or the Mixed Constitution and the Separation of Powers in Canada." *Canadian Journal of Political Science* 20: 97-129.

Reuber, G.L. (1964). "The Objectives of Canadian Monetary Policy, 1949-61: Empirical 'Trade Offs' and the Reaction Function of Authorities." *Journal of Political Economy* LXXII: 109-132.

Reuber, Grant L. (1962). *The Objectives of Monetary Policy: Working Paper Prepared for the Royal Commission on Banking and Finance.* Ottawa: Queen's Printer.

Reuber, Grant L. and Frank Roseman (1969). *The Take-Over of Canadian Firms, 1945-1961: An Empirical Analysis.* Ottawa: Queen's Printer.

Rhoads, S.E. (1985). *The Economist's View of the World: Government, Markets, and Public Policy.* Cambridge, Mass.: Cambridge University Press.

Rich, Edward E. (1960). *The Hudson's Bay Company, 1670-1870.* Toronto: McClelland and Stewart.

Richards, John (1985). "The Staple Debate." In *Explorations in Canadian Economic History: Essays in Honour of Irene M. Spry*, edited by Duncan Cameron. Ottawa: University of Ottawa Press.

Richards, John and Larry Pratt (1979). *Prairie Capitalism: Power and Influence in the New West.* Toronto: McClelland and Stewart.

Richards, John, Robert D. Cairns and Larry Pratt, eds. (1991). *Social Democracy Without Illusions: Renewal of the Canadian Left.* Toronto: McClelland and Stewart.

Richardson, D. (1985). "Factor Market Adjustment Policies in Response to Shocks." In *Domestic Policies and the International Economic Environment*, edited by J. Whalley. Vol 12, *Macdonald Commission Studies.* Toronto: University of Toronto Press.

Riddell, W.C. (1986). "Canadian Labour Relations: An Overview." In *Canadian Labour Relations*, edited by W.C. Riddell. Toronto: University of Toronto Press.

Robertson, M. and A. Grey (1986). "Trade-Related Worker Adjustment Policies: The Canadian Experience." In *Canadian Labour Relations*, edited by W.C. Riddell. Toronto: University of Toronto Press.

Robin, Martin (1968). *Radical Politics and Canadian Labour, 1880-1930.* Kingston, Ont.: Queen's University Centre for Industrial Relations.

Robin, Martin (1972). *The Rush for Spoils.* Toronto: McClelland and Stewart.

Robin, Martin (1973). *Pillars of Profit.* Toronto: McClelland and Stewart.

Roemer, John, ed. (1986). *Analytical Marxism.* Cambridge: Cambridge University Press.

Romanow, Roy, John Whyte and Howard Leeson (1984). *Canada...Notwithstanding: The Making of the Constitution, 1976-82.* Toronto: Carswell/Methuen.

Rosenau, James N. (1988). "The State in an Era of Cascading Politics." *Comparative Political Studies* 21: 13-44.

Rosenblum, Simon and Peter Findlay, eds. (1991). *Debating Canada's Future: Views from the Left.* Toronto: James Lorimer.

Rosenbluth, G. (1955). *Business Concentration and Price Policy.* Princeton: Princeton University Press.

Rosenbluth, Gideon (1957). *Concentration in Canadian Manufacturing Industries*. Princeton: Princeton University Press.

Ross, George and Jane Jenson (1986). "Post-war Class Struggle and the Crisis of Left Politics." *Socialist Register* 1985/86: 23-49.

Rotstein, Abraham (1984). *Rebuilding from Within: Remedies for Canada's Ailing Economy*. Toronto: Lorimer.

Rowley, C.K. (1983). "The Political Economy of the Public Sector." In *Perspectives on Political Economy*, edited by R.J.B. Jones. London: Pinter.

Rugman, Alan (1977). "The Regulation of Foreign Investment in Canada." *Journal of World Trade Law* 11: 322-333.

Rugman, Alan M. (1980). *Multinationals in Canada: Theory, Performance and Economic Impact*. Boston: Martinus Nijhoff Pub.

Russell, P. (1977). "The Supreme Court's Interpretation of the Constitution from 1949 to 1960." In *Politics: Canada*, edited by P. Fox. Toronto: McGraw-Hill Ryerson.

Russell, Peter (1982). "The Effect of a Charter of Rights on the Policy-Making Role of the Canadian Courts." *Canadian Public Administration* 25.

Russell, Peter (1983). "The Political Purposes of the Canadian Charter of Rights and Freedoms." *Canadian Bar Review*: 30-54.

Russell, P. (1988). "The Supreme Court Proposals in the Meech Lake Accord." Supplement, *Canadian Public Policy* 14: 93-106.

Ryerson, Stanley Brehaut (1963). *The Founding of Canada*. Toronto: Progress Books.

Ryerson, Stanley Brehaut (1968). *Unequal Union: Confederation and the Roots of Conflict in the Canadas, 1815-1873*. Toronto: Progress Books.

Sabel, Charles F. (1982). *Work and Politics: The Division of Labour in Industry*. Cambridge: Cambridge University Press.

Sacouman, R.J. (1979). "The Differing Origins, Organization, and Impact of Maritime and Prairie Co-operative Movements to 1940." In *Underdevelopment and Social Movements in Atlantic Canada*, edited by R.J. Brym and R.J. Sacouman. Toronto: New Hogtown Press.

Sacouman, R. James (1981). "The 'Peripheral' Maritimes and Canada-Wide Marxist Political Economy." *Studies in Political Economy* 6: 135-150.

Safarian, A.E. (1966). *Foreign Ownership of Canadian Industry*. Toronto: McGraw-Hill.

Sager, Eric (1987). "Dependency, Underdevelopment and the Economic History of the Atlantic Provinces." *Acadiensis*: 117-137.

Salembier, Gerry E., Andrew R. Moore and Frank Stone (1987). *The Canadian Import File: Trade, Protection and Adjustment*. Montreal: Institute for Research on Public Policy.

Samuelson, Paul A. and Anthony Scott (1971). *Economics*. Toronto: McGraw-Hill.

Saunders, Stanley A. (1939). *The Economic History of the Maritime Provinces*. Ottawa: King's Printer.

Savoie, Donald (1986). *Regional Economic Development: Canada's Search for Solutions*. Toronto: University of Toronto Press.

Schmitter, Philippe and Gerhara Lehmbruch, eds. (1979). *Trends Towards Corporatist Intermediation*. Beverly Hills, Cal.: Sage Publications.

Schott, J. and M.G. Smith (1988). "Services and Investment." In *The Canada-United States Free Trade Agreement*, edited by J. Schott. Washington, D.C.: Institute for International Economics.

Schott, Kerry (1984). *Policy, Power and Order: The Persistence of Economic Problems in Capitalist Europe*. New Haven, Conn.: Yale University Press.

Schreiber, E.M. (1980). "Class Awareness and Class Voting in Canada." *Canadian Review of Sociology and Anthropology* 17: 37-54.

Schurmann, Herbert (1968). *Ideology and Organization in Communist China*. Berkeley: University of California Press.

Science Council of Canada (1979). *Forging Links: A Technology Policy for Canada*. Ottawa.

Science Council of Canada (1984). *Canadian Industrial Development: Some Policy Directions*. Ottawa: Supply and Services Canada.

Science Council of Canada (1988). *Gearing Up for Global Markets: From Industry Challenge to Industry Commitment*. Ottawa.

Shalev, M. (1983). "The Social Democratic Model and Beyond: Two 'Generations' of Comparative Research on the Welfare State." *Comparative Social Research* 6: 315-351.

Sheppard, Robert and Michael Valpy (1982). *The National Deal: The Fight for a Canadian Constitution*. Toronto: Fleet Books.

Shields, J. (1989). *British Columbia's New Reality: The Politics of Neo-Conservatism and Defensive Defiance*. Ph.D. thesis, University of British Columbia, Vancouver.

Shortt, A. (1986). *Adam Shortt's History of Canadian Currency and Banking, 1600-1880*. Edited by Canadian Banker's Association. Toronto: CBA.

Skocpol, T. (1985). "Bringing the State Back in: Strategies of Analysis in Current Research." In *Bringing the State Back In*, edited by P.B. Evans. Cambridge: Cambridge University Press.

Skocpol, Theda and Kevin Finegold (1982). "State Capacity and Economic Intervention in the Early New Deal." *Political Science Quarterly* 97.

Smiley, Donald V. (1963). *Conditional Grants and Canadian Federalism: A Study in Constitutional Adaptation*. Toronto: Canadian Tax Foundation.

Smiley, D.V. (1967). "Contributions to Canadian Political Science Since the

Second World War." *Canadian Journal of Economics and Political Science* 33: 569-580.

Smiley, Donald V. (1987). *The Federal Condition in Canada*. Toronto: McGraw-Hill Ryerson.

Smiley, Donald V. and R. Watts (1985). *Intrastate Federalism in Canada*. Toronto: University of Toronto Press.

Smith, Adam [1776] (1987). *The Wealth of Nations*. Books I-III. Harmondsworth: Penguin.

Smith, Tony (1979). "The Underdevelopment of Development Literature: The Case of Dependency Theory." *World Politics* 31: 247-288.

Sparks, G.R. "The Theory and Practice of Monetary Policy in Canada: 1945-83." In *Fiscal and Monetary Policy*, edited by J. Sargent. Toronto: University of Toronto Press, 1986.

Srinivasan, T.N. (1985). "Neoclassical Political Economy: The State and Economic Development." *Asian Development Review* 3: 38-58.

Staniland, Martin (1985). *What Is Political Economy? A Study of Social Theory and Underdevelopment*. New Haven, Conn.: Yale University Press.

Statistics Canada (1983). *National Income and Expenditure Accounts, 1969-1983*. Cat. No.: 13-001. Ottawa: Minister of Supply and Services.

Statistics Canada (1983). *Provincial GDP by Industry*. Cat. No.: 61-202. Ottawa: Minister of Supply and Services Canada.

Statistics Canada (1984). *GDP by Industry, 1984*. Cat. No.: 61-213. Ottawa: Minister of Supply and Services Canada.

Statistics Canada (1985). *Canada Year Book, 1985*. Ottawa: Minister of Supply and Services Canada.

Statistics Canada (1985). *Income Distribution by Size in Canada*. Cat. No.: 15-207. Ottawa: Minister of Supply and Services Canada.

Stewart, Ian A. (1990). "Consensus and Economic Performance." In *Perspective 2000: Proceedings of a Conference Sponsored by the Economic Council of Canada*. Ottawa.

Stewart, J. (1977). *The Canadian House of Commons: Procedure and Reform*. Montreal: McGill-Queen's University Press.

Stone, D. (1988). *Policy Paradox and Political Reason*. Glenview, Ill.: Scott, Foresman.

Stone, Frank (1984). *Canada, the GATT and the International Trade System*. Montreal: Institute for Research on Public Policy.

Sutherland, Sharon and G. Bruce Doern (1985). *Bureaucracy in Canada: Control and Reform*. Toronto: University of Toronto Press.

Swimmer, G. (1987). "Changes to Public Service Labour Relations Legislation: Revitalizing or Destroying Collective Bargaining." In *How Ottawa Spends, 1987-88: Restraining the State*, edited by M.J. Prince. Toronto: Methuen.

Swinton, Katherine (1988). *Competing Constitutional Visions: The Meech Lake Accord*. Toronto: Carswell.

Taylor, Malcolm (1987). *Health Insurance and Canadian Public Policy*. Montreal: McGill-Queen's University Press.

Teeple, Gary, ed. (1972). *Capitalism and the National Question in Canada*. Toronto: University of Toronto Press.

Teeple, G. (1972). "Land, Labour, and Capital in Pre-Confederation Canada." In *Capitalism and the National Question in Canada*, edited by G. Teeple. Toronto: University of Toronto Press.

Therborn, Göran (1977). "The Rule of Capital and the Rise of Democracy." *New Left Review* 103: 3-41.

Therborn, Göran (1978). *What Does the Ruling Class Do When It Rules? State Apparatuses and State Power under Federalism, Capitalism and Socialism*. London: Verso.

Therborn, G. (1983). "The Rule of Capital and the Rise of Democracy." In *States and Societies*, edited by David Held et al. Oxford: Robertson.

Thompson, E.P. (1978). *The Poverty of Theory and Other Essays*. London: Merlin Press.

Thorburn, Hugh (1984). *Planning and the Economy: Building Federal-Provincial Consensus*. Toronto: Lorimer.

Thorburn, Hugh (1985). *Party Politics in Canada*. Scarborough, Ont.: Prentice-Hall.

Traves, Tom (1979). *The State and Enterprise: Canadian Manufacturers and the Federal Government, 1917-1931*. Toronto: University of Toronto Press.

Trebilcock, M.J. et al. (1982). *The Choice of Governing Instrument*. Ottawa: Canadian Government Pub. Centre.

Truman, D.B. (1965). "Disillusion and Regeneration: The Quest for a Discipline." *American Political Science Review* 59, 4: 865-873.

Tucker, R.C., ed. (1972). *The Marx-Engels Reader*. New York: W.W. Norton.

United States Congress (1987). *The GATT Negotiations and U.S. Trade Policy*. Washington, D.C.: U.S. Government Printing Office, June.

Van Loon, Richard and Michael Whittington (1987). *The Canadian Political System: Environment, Structure, and Process*. Toronto: McGraw-Hill.

Veltmeyer, Henry (1978). "Dependency and Underdevelopment: Some Questions and Problems." *Canadian Journal of Political and Social Theory* 2: 55-71.

Veltmeyer, H. (1979). "The Capitalist Underdevelopment of Atlantic Canada." In *Underdevelopment and Social Movements in Atlantic Canada*, edited by R.J. Brym and R.J. Sacouman. Toronto: New Hogtown Press.

Vipond, Robert (1989). "1787 and 1867: The Federal Principle at Canadian

Confederation Re-considered." *Canadian Journal of Political Science* 22, 1: 3-25.

Walker, Michael, ed. (1984). *On Alberta's Industrial and Science Technology Proposal*. Vancouver: Fraser Institute.

Walker, Michael et al., eds. (1976). *The Illusion of Wage and Price Control*. Vancouver: Fraser Institute.

Walras, Leon [1871] (1954). *Elements of Pure Economics: Or, the Theory of Social Wealth*. Homewood: R.D. Irwin.

Warren, Bill (1973). "Imperialism and Capitalist Industrialization." *New Left Review* 81: 3-44.

Watkins, G.C. and M.A. Walker, eds. (1981). *Reaction: The National Energy Program*. Vancouver: Fraser Institute.

Watkins, Mel (1982). "The Innis Tradition in Canadian Political Economy." *Canadian Journal of Political and Social Thought* 6: 12-34.

Watkins, Melville et al. (1968). *Foreign Ownership and the Structure of Canadian Industry*. Ottawa: Privy Council Office.

Watkins, M.H. (1963). "A Staple Theory of Economic Growth." *Canadian Journal of Economics and Political Science* 29: 141-158.

Watkins, M.H., ed. (1970). *For an Independent Socialist Canada*. Winnipeg: Canadian Dimension.

Watkins, M.H. (1977). "The Staple Theory Revisited." *Journal of Canadian Studies* 12: 83-95.

Watson, William (1983). *Primer on the Economics of Industrial Policy*. Toronto: Ontario Economic Council.

Watts, George S. (1972). "The First Phase of the Bank of Canada's Operations." *Bank of Canada Review*, November: 7-21.

Watts, George S. (1973a). "The Bank of Canada during the Period of Postwar Adjustment." *Bank of Canada Review*, November: 3-17.

Watts, George S. (1973b). "The Bank of Canada during the War Years." *Bank of Canada Review*, April: 3-17.

Watts, George S. (1974). "The Bank of Canada from 1948-1952: The Pivotal Years." *Bank of Canada Review*, November: 3-17.

Webb, M.C. and M.W. Zacher (1985). "Canada's Export Trade in a Changing International Environment." In *Canada and the International Political/Economic Environment*, edited by D. Stairs and G.R. Winham. Toronto: University of Toronto Press.

Weber, Max [1904] (1958). *The Protestant Ethic and the Spirit of Capitalism*. New York: Scribner.

Weber, Max [1915] (1978). *Economy and Society: An Outline of Interpretive Sociology*. Berkeley: University of California Press.

Weldon, J.C. (1966). "Consolidations in Canadian Industry, 1900-1948." In *Restrictive Trade Practices in Canada*, edited by L.A. Skeoch. Toronto: McClelland and Stewart.

Whalley, John (1985). *Canadian Trade Policies and the World Economy*. Toronto: University of Toronto Press.

Wheare, K.C. (1964). *Federal Government*. Oxford: Oxford University Press.

Whitaker, Reginald (1977). *The Government Party: Organizing and Financing the Liberal Party of Canada, 1930-1958*. Toronto: University of Toronto Press.

Whitaker, Reginald (1983). "To Have Insight into Much and Power over Nothing: The Political Ideas of Harold Innis." *Queen's Quarterly* 90: 818-831.

Wilkinson, B. (1985). "Canada's Resource Industries." In *Canada's Resource Industries and Water Export Policy*, edited by J. Whalley. Toronto: University of Toronto Press.

Wilkinson, Bruce W. (1980). *Canada in the Changing World Economy*. Montreal: C.D. Howe Institute and the National Planning Association.

Will, Robert M. (1966). *Canadian Fiscal Policy, 1945-63*. Ottawa: Queen's Printer.

Williams, Glen (1986). *Not for Export: Toward a Political Economy of Canada's Arrested Industrialization*. Toronto: McClelland and Stewart.

Wolf Jr., Charles (1988). *Markets or Governments: Choosing between Imperfect Alternatives*. Cambridge, Mass.: MIT Press.

Wolfe, Alan (1977). *The Limits of Legitimacy: Political Contradictions of Contemporary Capitalism*. New York: Free Press.

Wolfe, D.A. (1977). "The State and Economic Policy in Canada, 1968-75." In *The Canadian State: Political Economy and Political Power*, edited by L. Panitch. Toronto: University of Toronto Press.

Wolfe, David A. (1981). "Mercantilism, Liberalism, and Keynesianism: Changing Forms of State Intervention in Capitalist Societies." *Canadian Journal of Political and Social Theory* 5, 1-2: 69-96.

Wolfe, D.A. (1984). "The Rise and Demise of the Keynesian Era in Canada: Economic Policy, 1930-1982." In *Modern Canada, 1930-1980's*, edited by M.S. Cross and G.S Kealey. Toronto: McClelland and Stewart.

Wolfe, D.A. (1985). "The Politics of the Deficit." In *The Politics of Economic Policy*, edited by G.B. Doern. Toronto: University of Toronto Press.

Wolfe, David A. (1989). "The Canadian State in Comparative Perspective." *Canadian Review of Sociology and Anthropology* 26: 95-126.

Wolff, R.D. and S.A. Resnick (1987). *Economics: Marxian versus Neoclassical*. Baltimore: Johns Hopkins University Press.

Wood, Bernard (1988). *The Middle Powers and the General Interest*. Ottawa: North-South Institute.

Wood, Louis A. (1975). *A History of Farmers' Movements in Canada*. Toronto: University of Toronto Press.

Wood, N. and E. Wood (1970). "Canada and the American Science of

Politics." In *Close the 49th Parallel, etc.: The Americanization of Canada*, edited by I. Lumsden. Toronto: University of Toronto Press.

Wood, W.D. and P. Kumar, eds. (1981). *The Current Industrial Relations Scene in Canada*. Kingston, Ont.: Queen's University Industrial Relations Centre.

Woodside, K. "The Political Economy of Policy Instruments: Tax Expenditures and Subsidies in Canada." In *The Politics of Canadian Public Policy*, edited by M. Atkinson and M. Chandler. Toronto: University of Toronto Press.

Wynn, Graeme (1981). *Timber Colony: A Historical Geography of Early Nineteenth Century New Brunswick*. Toronto: University of Toronto Press.

Young, Walter (1969). *The Anatomy of a Party: The National CCF, 1932-1961*. Toronto: University of Toronto Press.

Young, Walter (1969). *Democracy and Discontent: Progressivism, Socialism and Social Credit in the Canadian West*. Toronto: Ryerson.

Zakuta, Leo (1964). *A Protest Movement Becalmed: A Study of Change in the CCF*. Toronto: University of Toronto Press.

Index

aboriginal people; economic system, 177; European occupation of lands, 14; standard of living, 114

absolute surplus value, 64, 74

abstract labour, 63

accumulation of capital, 17, 28, 103. *See also* profit

Act for the Prevention and Suppression of Combinations Formed in Restraint of Trade, 197-8

"adaptive monetary control," 223

Adjustment Benefits Program, 243

adjustment measures; industrial, 241-3; labour, 243-4. *See also* positive adjustment strategy

administrative accountability, 168, 170

Africa and socialism, 70

aggregate demand, 34, 35, 54

Aglietta, Michel, on capitalism, 75, 76

agricultural sector, 192; business associations, 204; and Free Trade Agreement, 148-9; unions, 185. *See also* economy of Canada; wheat

Albo, Gregory, on the state, 106

alienation of workers, 66

American Federation of Labor (AFL), 180, 185

ancien régime, 177

anti-combines acts, 197-8

antidumping and countervailing duties, 137, 151

Antidumping and Countervailing Duty Panel, 151

Anti-Inflation Board (AIB), 222

Anti-Trust (Sherman) Act (U.S.), 197

Appeal Panel, 152

Arblaster, Anthony, on Keynes, 36

aristocratic state government, 176

Asia and socialism, 70

Asia-Pacific trade with Canada, 135

assembly lines, 74

Australia and Canada trade similarities, 141

Auto Pact (Canada-U.S.), 119, 136, 149

automotive products and Free Trade Agreement, 149

average labour, 63

"backward linkage," 104

balance of payments, 211, 212, 223

balance of trade, 119, 120, 211; surplus, 131, 133, 135, 136

Bank Act (1871), 214

bank charters, control of, 214

Bank of Canada, 217, 218, 220, 222-3

Bank Rate, 210, 211

banking, 102, 193, 201, 214, 216, 217; operations, 210-1

barter exchange, 13, 16, 214

"base" in Marx's theory, 60

Bell, Daniel, on politics and economy, 18

Bernstein, Eduard, 70, 77

Bertram, Gordon, on staples industries, 92

bicameral, 173

Binational Arbitration Panel, 152

"black" markets, 15

Bladen, V.W., 94

Blair-Carr Committee's Taskforce on Major Projects, 248

Bliss, Michael, on industrial policies, 246

bourgeoisie, 62, 102

branch-plant manufacturing, 96, 101, 102, 133, 201; and free trade, 229. *See also* foreign investment